Complete
Mandarin Chinese
Elizabeth Scurfield

For UK order enquiries: please contact Bookpoint Ltd, 130 Milton Park, Abingdon, Oxon OX14 4SB. *Telephone*: +44 (0) 1235 827720. *Fax*: +44 (0) 1235 400454. Lines are open 09.00–17.00, Monday to Saturday, with a 24-hour message answering service. Details about our titles and how to order are available at www.teachyourself.com

For USA order enquiries: please contact McGraw-Hill Customer Services, PO Box 545, Blacklick, OH 43004-0545, USA. *Telephone*: 1-800-722-4726. *Fax*: 1-614-755-5645.

For Canada order enquiries: please contact McGraw-Hill Ryerson Ltd, 300 Water St, Whitby, Ontario L1N 9B6, Canada. *Telephone*: 905 430 5000. *Fax*: 905 430 5020.

Long renowned as the authoritative source for self-guided learning – with more than 50 million copies sold worldwide – the **Teach Yourself** series includes over 500 titles in the fields of languages, crafts, hobbies, business, computing and education.

British Library Cataloguing in Publication Data: a catalogue record for this title is available from the British Library.

Library of Congress Catalog Card Number: on file.

First published in UK 1999 as *Teach Yourself Chinese* by Hodder Education, part of Hachette UK, 338 Euston Road, London NW1 3BH.

First published in US 1999 by The McGraw-Hill Companies, Inc.

This edition published 2010.

The **Teach Yourself** name is a registered trade mark of Hodder Headline.

Copyright © 1999, 2003, 2010 by Elizabeth Scurfield.

Typeset by Graphicraft Limited, Hong Kong.

Illustrated by Sally Elford and Barking Dog Art.

Printed in Great Britain for Hodder Education, an Hachette UK Company, 338 Euston Road, London NW1 3BH, by CPI Cox & Wyman, Reading, Berkshire RG1 8EX.

The publisher has used its best endeavours to ensure that the URLs for external websites referred to in this book are correct and active at the time of going to press. However, the publisher and the author have no responsibility for the websites and can make no guarantee that a site will remain live or that the content will remain relevant, decent or appropriate.

Hachette UK's policy is to use papers that are natural, renewable and recyclable products and made from wood grown in sustainable forests. The logging and manufacturing processes are expected to conform to the environmental regulations of the country of origin.

Impression number   10 9 8 7 6 5 4 3
Year   2014 2013 2012 2011

Contents

Dedication

In joyous memory of my sister, Janet Anderson,
whose life continues to bless.

Acknowledgements

My grateful thanks to my partner, Martina Weitsch, for all her support and encouragement. My special thanks to Song Lianyi for his unfailing patience and good humour in the face of all my questions and to my editor Virginia Catmur for all her encouragement and support.

Credits

Meet the author

I've always loved languages – strange since neither of my parents spoke a word in any language other than English. I have always wanted to communicate with other people in their own language and understand more of their culture and compare it with my own. I ended up specializing in languages at secondary school and while I was there the Cultural Revolution in China broke out. I looked at the TV coverage and at the Red Guards waving Mao's little red book and thought to myself 'We have to understand why they are doing this and what they are saying'. So that's how I came to study Chinese – a decision I have never regretted.

The first time I went to China I fell in love with the country and the people. I have learned so much (not only the language, although that was a big part of it) and had such fun. I hope that my long experience of teaching Chinese at all levels successfully will be so infectious that my enthusiasm comes off the pages of this book as you study this fascinating language.

When I started to study Chinese, there was no sense that this might be the language of the future – for business, for culture, for tourism and for sport. After the Beijing Olympics and the growth of the Chinese market for export and import, this has changed and there are now even more good reasons to learn this language. It may be a difficult language, but the rewards of mastering it are immeasurable.

Elizabeth Scurfield

Only got a minute?

Chinese, in one form or another, is spoken by more people around the globe than any other language. For this reason alone, it is worthwhile trying to learn at least a little of the language. It is also the world's oldest language and its cultural history can be traced back over 3500 years. Mandarin is the Chinese language with the most speakers; and even those Chinese for whom Mandarin is not the mother tongue will be proficient in Mandarin, as it is the dominant language of the People's Republic of China. It is also the main language of Taiwan.

While you may have an idea that Mandarin will be a difficult language to learn, this is not necessarily true, at least as far as speaking it is concerned. Its grammar is remarkably simple and regular. For example, there is only ever one form of the verb, unlike in English, where we have 'to be, am, is, are, was, were, will be . . .' In Mandarin one verb form covers all these functions.

Some learners worry that they won't be able to learn the 'tones' of Mandarin: but if you learn the tone every time you learn a new word, you will soon find that you produce the correct tone automatically.

You may want to learn to write in Chinese characters too, and, of course, this is an entirely different proposition – there is no getting away from the fact that all the characters have to be memorized. But a big plus is that speakers of all the Chinese languages write with more or less the same characters, even though their languages sound completely different.

We hope that, with the aid of this book, you should have a decent grounding in both spoken and written Mandarin Chinese and that, by the end of the course, you will have the confidence to give it a go when you go to China, whether that be for business or for pleasure.

5 Only got five minutes?

Now that China is starting to claim a major role for itself in the global economy, it seems like a really good time to get to grips with learning at least some of the language. After all, China is not only the largest country in the world, it is also the most populous (1.3 billion people, at the last census), so it stands to reason that more people speak Chinese worldwide than speak any other language. Further estimates have Mandarin Chinese as being spoken by something in the order of 836 million people as their mother tongue. The 'official' language is spoken in Hong Kong, the New Territories and Taiwan, in addition to China itself and, as is the case with many other widely spoken languages, each of these countries has its own variation. There are also immigrant populations spread across the world, in Australia, the United Kingdom and the United States, to name but three of the largest.

The cultural heritage of China is very old indeed and once you have got even the smallest amount of knowledge under your belt, you will find a world of delight in the literature and art that abound in that culture and until such time as you can manage written Chinese more readily and competently, the transcribed form of Chinese, known as *pinyin*, exists as an aid in all sorts of places: look out for road signs, street names and so on, as these will help you get around on any visits you may make to China and, of course, the big international players in the modern globalized world have an instantly recognizable look, whether their names are written in Chinese or not!

One major difference between learning Chinese and, say, another European language is that you have no indication, when looking at the character, as to what the word might mean. With French, German or Italian, for example, there are often similarities between an English word and the corresponding word in those languages.

In addition, the 'foreign' word might be a loanword in English (e.g. fiancé, delicatessen, kindergarten). By simply looking at the Chinese character, you have no idea at all of what you are looking at – until you know the character itself. This problem is compounded by the fact that you can combine characters to form another word and the meanings of the component characters are retained in the resultant compound word, but confusion can arise because of this – it is only through the context of the word that you can be sure of its meaning.

The Chinese we will be learning on this course is known as 'Mandarin Chinese' and you may well be trying the course for the very reason that you are familiar with this term – this is, obviously, not the term the Chinese themselves use for the language spoken by the majority of Chinese people but, rather, an historical, perhaps somewhat derogatory term that was applied by non-Chinese and was originally used to describe the language because that was what westerners heard spoken at the Chinese court, i.e. by the mandarins who ruled the country at the time. Later the term was used to encompass the majority of the population (the Han). It has since come to be regarded as 'national' Chinese, as more than 70% of Chinese people speak it, in one dialect or another. The Chinese themselves call this language *putonghua*, which means 'common speech'. Although the term 'Mandarin Chinese' is still in common usage, we in the west are starting to use the expression Modern Standard Chinese (MSC) instead, which is possibly more acceptable to our PC ears. Throughout this course, you will be getting quite a broad exposure to it!

This 'national' language, just referred to as *putonghua*, is what is taught in educational institutions across the country and is used in China-wide media of all types, including film. This is particularly useful for you, as a learner, as wherever you happen to find yourself in this large country, you should be able both to understand what is being said to you and also make yourself understood when you respond to what is being said. Of course, there is always the problem of regional variations in dialect and accent, but persevere! In the countries referred to in the opening paragraph, *putonghua* is also spoken (although, naturally, the people refer to it by another name!) and it is definitely the language of choice in Hong Kong now, which may be a decider for you should you be planning a trip to the Far East and China seems, perhaps, a little daunting. Hong Kong is, after all, an international hotspot for culture, nightlife and tourism – as well as being at the forefront of global trading activities.

We have mentioned *pinyin* earlier, too: this is the name given to the method of transcribing the Chinese characters into an acceptable phonetic 'alphabet' for western learners. This system did not come into regular commission until the late 1950s but has now reached the stage of widespread use in the west. It helps with native children in teaching pronunciation and, as a phonetic way of transliterating the characters, it is very effective in transmitting the complexity of the language in a relatively straightforward way. We mentioned street signs with *pinyin* on them in China – in fact, you do not have to stray that far away from home – there are Chinatowns all over the world. Should you find yourself in London for example, take a stroll through its Chinatown. You will see plenty of signs there in Chinese characters with transliteration underneath but unfortunately the transliteration is mostly in Cantonese spelling. Even the telephone boxes have Chinese characters on them! A very useful and practical way in which to practise what you have learned – and interesting, too, for you can see the Chinese community at work and at play in your own country.

The characters that make up Chinese are essentially monosyllabic and there are over 400 basic syllables, there being so comparatively few because of simplification over the 3500 years in which Chinese has been evolving and developing. Although monosyllabic, Chinese is also tonal, so the complexity that arises is due to the combination of these two aspects in conjunction: there are four tones, therefore we end up with four times the number of monosyllables that we started this paragraph with, i.e. we now have about 1400 different sounds (as some sound and tone combinations don't exist). We mentioned character combinations earlier and this also goes towards enriching and enhancing the word stock in Chinese. In actual communication, always in a given context, confusion and ambiguity rarely occur.

This system of forming 'words' will, of course, be gone into in greater depth in the course of this book, but we hope that this short introduction has encouraged you to let yourself go and – have a go!

10 Only got 10 minutes?

The Chinese language

Chinese can now be considered as very much an international language and is one of the six official languages of the United Nations, alongside Arabic, English, French, Russian and Spanish. With over 1.4 billion mother-tongue speakers spread across the globe, Chinese is quite possibly the fastest growing spoken language in the world, in terms of numbers. In addition to its being an official language of the UN (and, obviously, in China itself), Chinese is also the official language in Hong Kong (Cantonese, rather than Mandarin – English is the other official language), Taiwan and Macau (with Portuguese the other official language) and one of the four official languages spoken in Singapore (but it is not the *main* language in this last country). It is recognized as a regional language in Malaysia and, interestingly enough, in the United States of America. The large immigrant population is obviously the reason for this and it can be seen that similar immigrant populations to other parts of the globe are having the same sort of effect.

Spoken Chinese has a high level of internal diversity, although all spoken regional varieties have tonality and monosyllabicity in common. There are generally considered to be in the region of 13 main dialectic/language (even this distinction is controversial) groups, and the language that is spoken by the most people by far is the language we are going to be learning in this course: Mandarin Chinese, which is spoken as a mother tongue by approximately 900 million people. Other groupings include Wu and Cantonese, the latter being spoken by between 60 and 70 million. Furthermore, it is usually thought that these main groupings are mutually unintelligible.

Chinese as it is spoken within China shows huge variations, as we have just seen, from north to south, west to east. It is, therefore, to be expected that there is no one form of Chinese when it is spoken as the main language in another country (see earlier for these other countries) – each of these countries has its own dialect and once more we find that even within these countries, there are marked differences from one region to another, whether this be accent, pronunciation or more marked and profound differences that might render a speaker of one dialect not understood by a speaker of another.

With China's expansion into the global market, the numbers of non-Chinese people, businesspeople and other people who are turning to the learning of Chinese as an essential medium of communication for the future are booming. With so much manufacturing taking place in China nowadays and outsourcing of other industries and with China's own push to leave the third world behind and try to forge entry for itself and its people into the first, it makes enormous sense for westerners to learn at least the basics of Chinese, because protocols are very different from those of the west and, if we wish to avoid antagonizing our friends, business colleagues and other people, these protocols must be learned, too.

Of course, there are so many native speakers of Chinese because of the size of the Chinese population: some 1.4 billion worldwide. Until fairly recently, Chinese government policy included a 'one child' requirement for families, in order to try and keep population growth within bounds. This requirement has now been dropped and the expectation is, therefore, that China's population will swell even more rapidly. Another reason to learn some Chinese, because you will have many more people to practise your language skills with!

So, we can see that globalization, international trade and, now, tourism have all played a huge role in contributing to the continuing and wide spread of Chinese – and, of course, Beijing's staging of the Olympic Games in 2008 has boosted China's image on the worldwide stage, in addition to its possessing some of the most famous tourist attractions in the world (the Great Wall being but one).

Written documentation on the development of Chinese goes back for nearly four centuries, making Chinese the oldest language on the planet. And, as the speakers of the language have developed and changed over this time, so, too, has the language itself, probably the main change would be the apparent simplification of the form of the language, resulting in the 'alphabet' (i.e. character set) consisting of a mere 400 or so 'syllables'. And yet, the language continues to be vibrant and evolving, due to the extensions possible through compounding and tonal additions.

Other languages spoken in China

We have mentioned that, in addition to regional variations and dialects, there are several other actual languages spoken in China – although Mandarin is spoken by the overwhelming majority of the population. The second language, in terms of numbers speaking it, is Wu, which is estimated to be spoken by between 90 and 100 million (e.g. in Shanghai and surrounding regions); Min is spoken by a further 60–70 million (estimated number e.g. in Fujian Province and Taiwan) and, the other language you have undoubtedly heard of, Cantonese, is also spoken by approximately 60–70 million people (e.g. in Hong Kong and Guangdong Province). Then there are two reasonably widespread languages that are spoken in China, namely, Xiang and Hakka, although, as we mentioned briefly earlier, there is some controversy as to whether these constitute languages as such or whether they are really dialects. Xiang (known also as Hunanese, as it spoken predominantly (but not exclusively) in Hunan province) is a language that has been profoundly influenced by Mandarin and is spoken by between 35 and 40 million people in Hunan and also Sichuan province. (It may be of interest to know that Mao Zedong was born in Hunan province and belief has it that, although a native speaker of Xiang, he was not at all fluent in Mandarin!)

Hakka is spoken mainly in the south of China and was originally confined to the Hakka people, but is now also predominant in Taiwan and in Chinese immigrant populations around the world (very approximate numbers of Hakka speakers: 35–40 million).

Grammar: the essentials

The fundamental building block of the Chinese language is the *character*, a single-syllable morpheme whereby each individual character forms one idea. And there are in the region of 400 of these basic monosyllables in Chinese – when these individual 'cells' of the language are combined, they form homophones, in which Chinese abounds. Unfortunately, this is what adds to the complicated nature of the language. This difficulty (for us as learners of Chinese) is ameliorated somewhat by Chinese being a *tonal* language. *Putonghua* has four tones, so our original paltry 400-odd monosyllables become over 1400 different sounds (as some sound plus tone combinations don't exist), in one fell swoop. But also the characters that in Chinese we find combined in this way have similar meanings when used to form the new 'word' – confusion here is avoided since, when used separately, individual characters may take on another meaning; in combination, they can only mean one thing.

Most syllables in Chinese consist of two elements: an *initial* and a *final*, the former being a consonant at the beginning of the syllable and the latter, the rest of the syllable.

Initials

There are some 21 initials in Modern Standard Chinese (MSC), which is what you will be learning on this course. The semi-vowels 'w' and 'y' are considered by some to be initials, too. In addition, there is 'ng', a sound that occurs at the end of a syllable, as the same sound does in English. This sound includes six aspirated initials and six unaspirated initials, all 12 of which are voiceless.

When making an aspirated sound, a feather or a sheet of paper held in front of your mouth will move; when making an unaspirated one, it should not. Lack of vibration in your vocal chords renders the initial voiceless.

There are also some initials that could be referred to as 'difficult'. (See Introduction for a fuller explanation of initials and charts with examples.)

Finals

Chinese has 36 finals, which are composed of a simple or compound vowel or a vowel plus a nasal consonant. Some syllables may lack the initial consonant but none lacks a vowel. (See Introduction for more guidance on this topic.)

Tones

The four tones in Chinese (remember from our earlier discussion that their presence multiplies the number of possible 'words' available to about 1400) are variations in pitch – rising, continuing and falling. Each syllable in the language has its own specific tone, so they are an important component in 'word' formation.

The first tone is high and level, the second high and rising, the third tone is falling and rising and the fourth tone is a falling tone. (Note, however, that you do not have to produce a particular sort of sound in your own speech – all the tones occur naturally within the voice range.)

There is also a *neutral* tone, i.e. the syllable is toneless: all particles are neutral, the second half of a repeated word may be in neutral tone, fill-in syllables are neutral and the second syllable in a compound may be neutral (but on other occasions not, so this neutrality has to be indicated in the text). One example is **xièxie**, 'thank you'.

In the spoken language, you will find that it is rare for tones to be given their full value, but this doesn't let you off the hook! You should still learn them as if they were and, also, be aware that learning the words with their tone takes time, practice, and lots of listening and repetition on your part. So do persevere!

Some additional points

Here are a couple of little extras, to cheer you up as you are about to embark on this course – it's all in the mind, you know:

- One way in which to ask questions in Chinese is to use both positive and negative forms of the verb together. And then the corresponding answer is neither *yes* nor *no* but either the positive or negative form of that verb.
- As you know by now, Chinese does not have a phonetic alphabet and *pinyin* is the nearest we in the west get to a recognizable form of transcribing it. It will be very useful for you in this course, as it provides a relatively accurate guide to correct pronunciation.
- Where names in the west appear in the form title, given name, surname, in Chinese they appear totally the other way around, viz. surname, given name, title. Hence, Mao, to whom we referred earlier on in this section, is the Chinese leader's surname and Zedong is actually his given name.
- Some adjectives function as verbs, a form known as stative verbs, meaning that, in a 'to be' verb, there is no need for the 'to be' bit of it.
- One feature of the language that should please you immensely (especially if you have learned other languages in the past or if English is not your first language and you have had to struggle with this aspect) is that all verbs are invariable – meaning that they remain exactly the same, no matter what else is going on! Another feature of verbs that you will like is that (with one exception – 'to have' *yǒu*) negation comes through use of *bù*, which precedes the verb. While we are taking a quick look at *bù*: it is usually fourth tone, unless followed by another fourth tone (in which case, it changes to second tone).

- Unlike in English, an adverb will always go in front of the verb it is qualifying.

I hope that this short introduction has kindled that spark of interest which led you to pick up this book in the first place. One last piece of good news to finish on: you need not worry about the use of capital letters in written Mandarin, because, of course, there aren't any!

Introduction

The first question you may ask is: 'Why learn Chinese?'
The answers could vary enormously based on your particular
interests, but I offer a few tentative suggestions here. The Chinese
are the largest single ethnic grouping in the world, so a *form* of
Chinese is spoken by more people than any other language.
Chinese is also the world's oldest language, its written records
stretching back about 3500 years. Surely a very good reason for
more people to learn it? Most people imagine Chinese to be a
very difficult language to learn. However, after shedding some of
the possible preconceptions about language that you may have,
you could find that spoken Chinese is not as difficult as you
had first thought – it could even be comparatively easy for you!
The written language is a different kettle of fish entirely, being
made up of individual characters that do have to be memorized,
but I hope Unit 14 will whet your appetite and make you eager
for more.

China's cultural and philosophical heritage is enormous, a rich
storehouse of knowledge and wisdom waiting to be tapped and
although it would be foolish to pretend that by working through
this book you will have access to very much of it in the original,
it will, at the very least, have given you the possibility of seeing a
little into that inscrutable Oriental mind and of making interesting
and valuable comparisons with your own culture and way of
thinking. I have found these reasons stimulating enough to go on
studying Chinese for over 40 years and propose to go on doing so
for at least another 20 or so! The Chinese have a saying:

Xué dào lăo, huó dào lăo, hái yŏu sānfēn xué bu dào.
Study reach old, live reach old, still have three-tenths study not reach.

This is certainly true as far as Chinese is concerned, but the
rewards are great. It will take time, but if you can keep your mind
open you will be surprised at the results.

Zhù nǐ xuéxí yúkuài!
Wish you study happy!

(You will find out what the 'accents' over the words mean in the section on 'tones', later in this introduction.)

The Chinese language

Some of you will have heard the term 'Mandarin' or 'Mandarin Chinese', which was how the west referred to the language spoken by the officials or 'mandarins' at the Imperial Court. It was then broadened to refer to the northern dialect, a version of which is spoken by over 70% of the Chinese or Han people and has become the *lingua franca* for the whole of China. This national language is known in China as *putonghua* 'common speech', which is now sometimes referred to in the west as Modern Standard Chinese, although the term Mandarin still lingers. Beijing (Peking) pronunciation is taken as the standard but there are many regional variations, some not easy to cope with. Try to find someone who claims to have a fairly standard accent to practise with in the first instance and listen hard to the recording that is available with this book. *Putonghua* is taught in schools and used in universities and colleges all over China. The majority of TV and radio programmes as well as films for the cinema are also made in *putonghua*. This means that, with any luck, you will be understood all over China, although you may sometimes have difficulty in understanding non-standard accents. But rest assured, Chinese people themselves have this problem too!

Putonghua is known as *huayu* 'Chinese language' in overseas Chinese communities and as *guoyu* 'national language' in Taiwan, but it is all the same language. There are many different dialects in Chinese, some of which are as different from one another as, say, English is from French, although they all have the same written language. The Cantonese dialect *guangdonghua* is spoken in Canton, Hong Kong and the New Territories and by many Chinese people all around the world. Many more Hong Kong Chinese are now learning *putonghua*, so this is the one to go for!

Romanization

The written language (the characters so typical of Chinese) does not have a phonetic alphabet as such but various systems have been devised for transcribing Chinese sounds into the Latin script. The standard form in use today is known as *pinyin* (literally 'spell sound'), which was adopted as the official system of the People's Republic of China in 1958. It has now been almost universally adopted in the west for transliterating Chinese personal and place names, replacing the Wade–Giles system that had been used previously. A few examples using the two different systems are given below.

Pinyin	*Wade–Giles* (and earlier)
Deng Xiaoping	Teng Hsiao-p'ing
Mao Zedong	Mao Tse-tung
Beijing	Peking
Guangzhou	Kwangchow (Canton)
Tianjin	Tientsin

Pinyin is used as a tool to teach the correct pronunciation of the Chinese language to children starting elementary school and to enable them to write little essays in Chinese before they have mastered enough characters. It is taught for a relatively short time in the north where *putonghua* is widely spoken as a first language but for a longer period in the south where many children speak a different dialect at home. Difficult characters in children's books often have the *pinyin* in brackets next to them as an aid to learning. Many street signs in big cities are written in *pinyin* as well as characters, which can be quite useful when you are trying to find your way around!

Mao Zedong once expressed the aim of eventually turning the Chinese written language into an alphabetic system of writing but this idea seems to have been quietly dropped. Aesthetically and visually pleasing, Chinese characters are too much part of the Chinese national heritage to disappear without a very long struggle, if, indeed, ever.

The Chinese language is essentially still based on the character, which is per se monosyllabic (one character representing one idea) so the single-syllable morpheme is the basic unit in Chinese. As a result, there is still discussion in China as to what units of speech should be written together in *pinyin*. In general, I have tried to keep to the system adopted by the Beijing Language [and Culture] University for its textbooks, using the *Xiandai Hanyu Cidian* (Modern Chinese Dictionary) produced by the Chinese Academy of Social Sciences as a definitive reference. Thus, 'syllables' are written separately except where they are seen as being one idea. I have, however, kept verb objects separate for clarity.

Sounds and tones: general introduction

There are just over 400 basic monosyllables in Chinese, which seems an incredibly small number and must be the result of sound simplification over a few thousand years. It is not surprising, therefore, that the language has so many homophones (words that sound the same), but the difficulty is alleviated somewhat by the fact that Chinese is a tonal language. Tones are obviously one way of coping with this phonetic poverty. There are four tones in *putonghua*, so by multiplying 400 by four we get a total of approximately 1600 different syllables, although not all basic sounds exist in all four tones. In fact, there are about 1400 in total when tones are attached. The other way is by combining two syllables with a similar meaning into one 'word'. For example, *ài* and *qíng* mean 'love' and 'feelings' respectively and could be confused with other 'words' if used separately, but together they can only mean 'love' *àiqíng*. This makes communication considerably easier all round.

What we mean by 'syllable' in Chinese is usually composed of an initial and a final. The initial, if there is one, is a consonant at the beginning of the syllable and the final is the rest of the syllable, e.g. *hang* in which *h* is the initial and *ang* is the final.

Initials

Modern Chinese has 21 initials, 23 if you count 'w' and 'y', which some people regard as semi-vowels. There is also a sound 'ng', which only occurs at the end of a syllable as in English. These include six pairs (i.e. 12 initials of which six are aspirated and six are not). These 12 are all voiceless. (Aspirated means that the air is puffed out strongly when you make these sounds.) If you hold a piece of paper in front of your mouth it should move when you make an aspirated sound, but not when you make an unaspirated one. Voiceless means that the vocal chords do not vibrate. The six pairs are listed in the following table.

Unaspirated	Aspirated	Description (all voiceless)
'b' like **b** in *b*ore	'p' like **p** in *p*oor	labial plosive
'd' like **d** in *d*oor	't' like **t** in *t*ore	alveolar plosive
'g' like **g** in *g*uard	'k' like **c** in *c*ard	velar plosive
'z' like **ds** in ad*ds*	'c' like **ts** in i*ts*	blade-alveolar affricate
'zh' like **j** in *j*elly	'ch' like **ch** in *ch*illy	blade-palatal (or retroflex) affricate
		The tongue must be curled back
'j' like **g** in *g*enius	'q' like **ch** in *ch*ew	front-palatal affricate
		Tongue flat, corners of lips drawn back as far as possible

Other small groups could be:

'm' like **m** in *me*	voiced, labial, nasal
'n' like **n** in *need*	voiced, alveolar, nasal
'ng' like **ng** in *sing*	voiced, velar, nasal

'sh' like **sh** in *shy*	voiceless blade-alveolar fricative
	The tongue must be curled back
'r' like **r** in *ray*	voiced, blade-palatal fricative
	The tongue must be curled back with only slight friction

's' like **s** in *say*	voiceless blade-alveolar fricative
	Tongue flat, corners of lips drawn back
'x' like **sh** in *sheet*	voiceless, palatal fricative
	Tongue flat, corners of lips drawn back as far as possible

'f' like **f** in *fan*	voiceless labio-dental fricative
'h' like **ch** in *loch*	voiceless velar fricative
	Arch the back of the tongue towards the roof of the mouth
'l' like **l** in *lie*	voiced alveolar lateral

'w' like **w** in *way*	voiced labial-velar approximant
'y' like **y** in *yell*	voiced palatal approximant

i 'c', 'q' and 'x' bear little resemblance to western alphabetic values so take particular care with them.

ii Pay attention to the retroflexes 'zh', 'ch', 'sh' and 'r', made with the tongue curled back. Southern Chinese have difficulty with them too!

These examples are only approximate equivalents. Purchase of the accompanying recording is strongly recommended.

Difficult initials

◀) CD 1, tr 2

'z', 'c', 's' *as in* 'zi', 'ci', 'si'   'zh', 'ch' *as in* 'zhu', 'chu'
'j', 'q', 'x' *as in* 'jian', 'qian', 'xian'   'sh', 'r', 'h' *as in* 'she', 're', 'he'

There are additional difficult initials on the audio.

Finals

There are 36 finals in Chinese. A final is a simple or compound vowel or a vowel plus a nasal consonant. A few 'syllables' may have no initial consonant but every one has to have a vowel. The tables that follow should be of some assistance in guiding you, although the recording is essential if you are to attempt more than an approximate pronunciation of the sounds.

'a' like **a** in f**a**ther
'ai' like **i** in b*i*te
'ao' like **ow** in c**ow**
'an' like **an** in m**an**
'ang' like **ang** in b**ang**

'e' like **ur** in f**ur**
'ei' like **ay** in pl**ay**
'en' like **un** in **un**der
'eng' like **ung** in d**ung**

'i' (after z, c, s, zh, ch, sh and r only) like **er** in wond**er**
'i' like **ea** in t**ea**
'ia' like **ja** in German *ja*
'iao' like **eow** in m**eow**
'ie' like **ie** in French P*ie*rre
'iu' like **yo** in *yo*-yo
'ian' like **yen** in *yen*
'in' like **in** in b*in*
'iang' like **yang** in *yang*
'ing' like **ing** in r*ing*
'iong' like **Jung** in *Jung* (the psycho-analyst)
('y' replaces 'i' at the beginning of syllables if there is no initial consonant)

'o' like **ore** in m*ore*
'ou' like **o** in g*o*
'ong' like **ung** in J*ung*

....

'u' like **oo** in m*oo*
'ua' like **ua** in s*ua*ve
'uo' like **war** in *war*
'uai' like **wi** in s*wi*pe
'ui' like **weigh** in *weigh*
'uan' like **wan** in *wan*gle
'un' like **won** in *won*drous
'uang' like **w–ong** in *wrong* without the 'r' (very approximate)
('w' replaces 'u' at the beginning of syllables if there is no initial consonant)

'ü' like **eu** in pn*eu*monia
'üe' like **eu** of pn*eu*matic plus *air* said quickly
'üan' like **eu** of pn*eu*matic plus *end* said quickly
'ün' like **eu** of pn*eu*matic plus p*un* said quickly
(Written as *yu, yue, yuan* and *yun* as complete syllables)

....

'er' as in *err* making the 'r' retroflex

....

i   The '-i' in *zi, ci, si, zhi, chi, shi* and *ri* is quite different from the '-i' with all the other consonants, which is a long '-i'. This 'i' is more or less only there for cosmetic reasons because no syllable can occur without a vowel. Say the consonant and 'sit on it' and you have the sound.

ii 'e' is made by dropping the jaw straight down. Get hold of your jaw, pull it down and make the sound!

iii 'a', 'i', 'o', 'u' and 'ü' – the degree to which the mouth is opened gets narrower and narrower as the lips get rounder and rounder. (Look in a mirror!)

iv 'ang', 'eng', 'ong' are nasalized vowels. The mouth aperture gets narrower, the lips rounder. Hold your nose as you practise these sounds. You should be able to feel the vibration!

v   '-ian' is pronounced as '-ien'.

vi 'ü' occurs only with the consonants 'n', 'l', 'j', 'q' and 'x'. As 'j', 'q' and 'x' cannot occur as j+u, q+u or x+u, the Chinese in their wisdom have seen fit to omit the umlaut (¨) over the 'u' in *ju, qu* and *xu*! N and l, however, occur as both *nu* and *nü, lu* and *lü* so the umlaut has been retained.

vii The '-r' suffix may be added to some words e.g. *bian* → *bianr*, *wan* → *wanr*, *hai* → *hair*, *tian* → *tianr* and is used extensively in the Beijing dialect. Normal 'spelling' practice is to add the '-r' but you can choose whether or not to say it. I have sometimes used it so that you can become familiar with it.

Tones

The tone is the variation of pitch whether it be rising, falling or continuing. In speech, we move smoothly from one tone to another, not in leaps and bounds. Every syllable in Chinese has its own definite tone and so tones are as important as vowels and consonants in forming syllables. *Putonghua* has four distinct tones so almost every basic monosyllable can be rendered in four different ways. These four tones all fall within your natural voice range, so some people speak Chinese at a higher or lower pitch than others because their voices are naturally higher or lower. You don't have to have a particular type of voice to speak Chinese. Now to the four tones themselves.

◄ CD 1, tr 3

The first tone is a high, level tone and is represented as ‾. The tonemark is placed over the vowel (if there is only one vowel) e.g. *zhōng* 'middle' or on the main vowel of a syllable where there are two or three vowels, e.g. *gāo* 'tall', but *tiē* 'to stick'.

The second tone is a high, rising tone and is represented by the tonemark ´, e.g. *guó* 'country'.

The third tone is a falling and rising tone. It descends from below the middle of the voice range to nearly the bottom and then rises to a point somewhere near the top. It is represented by the tonemark ˇ, e.g. *jiǎn* 'to cut'.

The fourth tone is a falling tone. It falls from high to low and is represented by the tonemark `, e.g. *zhù* 'to live'.

The following figure may help to make this clearer.

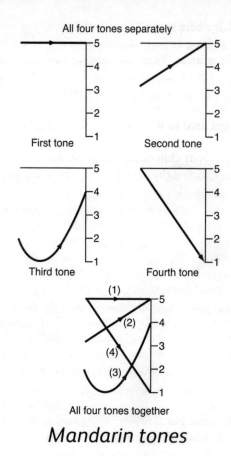

All four tones separately

First tone

Second tone

Third tone

Fourth tone

All four tones together

Mandarin tones

The common problems that occur are:

a pitching the first tone too high
b getting the second and fourth tones confused
c getting down on the third tone but not being able to get up again.

Here are the solutions and how to practise the tones (you may need a mirror).

First tone: Pitch it where *you* feel comfortable. Say 'oo' as in 'zoo' and keep going for as long as you can. You should be able to keep it up for maybe half a minute. When you have got used to that, change to another vowel sound and practise that in the same way and so on.

Second tone: Raise your eyebrows every time you attempt a second tone until you get used to it. This method is infallible!

Third tone: Drop your chin onto your neck and raise it again. Then practise the sound doing the movement at the same time.

Fourth tone: Stamp your foot gently and then accompany this action with the relevant sound.

◀) CD 1, tr 4

Try saying two third tones together. Difficult, isn't it? When this happens, the first one is said as a second tone but it is still marked as a third in the text, otherwise you may think that the syllable in question is always a second tone, which it is not: *Nǐ hǎo* is said as *Ní hǎo* 'How are you?' If *three* third tones occur together, the first two are said as second tones: *Wǒ yě hǎo* is said as *Wó yé hǎo* 'I'm OK too'.

Bù (不) is *fourth* tone but it becomes second before another fourth tone. As this is a straightforward rule I have marked *bu* as second tone when it occurs before a fourth in the text.

Yi (一) is first tone as an ordinary number: *yī* 'one', *shíyī* 'eleven', *yīyuè* 'January' but when it precedes other syllables it is fourth tone before first, second or third tones and becomes second tone before another fourth tone: *Yìxiē* 'some', *yìqǐ* 'together', *yílù* 'all the way'. It has been so indicated in the text. (Many dictionaries always list *bu* and *yi* as fourth tone and first tone respectively.)

Note that in the phrase *yí ge rén* 'one measure word person', the *ge* is said without a tone, although it is actually fourth, but it still carries enough weight to change the *yi* into a second tone.

Neutral tone: Some syllables in Chinese are toneless or occur in the neutral tone.

  i Particles are always in the neutral tone.

  ii The second half of a reduplicated word is often in the neutral tone: *gēge* 'elder brother', *māma* 'mum', *bàba* 'dad', *mèimei* 'younger sister'.

 iii Syllables such as *zi* that only have a 'fill-in' function (i.e. to make the word disyllabic) are toneless: *bēizi* 'cup', *bèizi* 'duvet', *zhuōzi* 'table', *yǐzi* 'chair'.

  iv The second syllable in compound words is sometimes toneless and is so indicated in the text. In another context, it may have a full tone. Some people may pronounce certain words with a tone, some without, as in the word *dōngbiān* 'east side' which may also be pronounced as *dōngbian* particularly when 'r' is added: *dōngbian(r)*.

In actual speech, tones are rarely given their full value but they have to be learnt as if they were. Stress and intonation are also very important but this is best learnt by imitating the speakers on the recording as closely as possible without thinking too much about individual tones, and by listening to any Chinese native speaker. Intonation does not *remove* tones, it only modifies them. Learn the tone that goes with a word and as you listen and speak more you should find that you increasingly pick up the correct tones and intonation.

Just as a final word on tones, it's amazing how much most Chinese understand even if your tones are largely wrong so don't give up just because you think you haven't got the right ear! The Chinese love punning so I expect they enjoy lots of jokes at our expense, but does it really matter? Tones come with practice, listening and imitating – don't try too hard with them.

The following 10 sounds, each written in the four different tones and therefore represented by four different characters, should serve to illustrate some of the points I have been making.

四声 (Four tones)

1. 一
   yī (one)

   姨
   yí (aunt)

   椅
   yǐ (chair)

   亿
   yì (hundred million)

2. 屋
   wū (house)

   无
   wú (none)

   五
   wǔ (five)

   雾
   wù (fog)

3. 烟
   yān (cigarette)

   盐
   yán (salt)

   眼
   yǎn (eye)

   燕
   yàn (swallow)

4. 妈
   mā (mother)

   麻
   má (hemp)

   马
   mǎ (horse)

   骂
   mà (scold)

5. 八
   bā (eight)

   拔
   bá (to pull up)

   把
   bǎ (to hold)

   爸
   bà (father)

6. 靴
   xuē (boot)

   学
   xué (study)

   雪
   xuě (snow)

   血
   xuè (blood)

7. 汤
   tāng (soup)

   糖
   táng (sugar)

   躺
   tǎng (to lie down)

   烫
   tàng (scalding hot)

8. 腰
   yāo (waist)

   摇
   yáo (shake)

   咬
   yǎo (to bite)

   药
   yào (medicines)

9. 枪
   qiāng (gun)

   墙
   qiáng (wall)

   抢
   qiǎng (to rob)

   呛
   qiàng (irritate the throat)

10. 书
    shū (book)

    熟
    shú (ripe)

    鼠
    shǔ (rat)

    树
    shù (tree)

Working through the book

A few sentences introduce the text of each unit. By Unit 9, this introduction is also written in Chinese. All the texts except for that in Unit 11 are dialogues, as this allows scope for good, colloquial Chinese to be used. The continuous passages used in Unit 11 mean that a great deal of useful vocabulary can be introduced in a fairly natural way.

Units 1–6 are in *pinyin* romanization with a literal translation directly underneath to enable you to see how the 'nuts and bolts' of the language work. There is an idiomatic translation on the right.

Unit 7 shows many of the objects to be found in a house and lists the vocabulary for them. This can be used for reference later.

Units 8–11 are in *pinyin* with an English translation either at the side or directly underneath. In Unit 11, the beginning and end of each sentence in Chinese and English is indicated with a '/' to enable you to mentally 'line up' the two more easily.

Unit 12 has the dialogue in *pinyin* with an English translation following. This will give you a real chance to see how much you have learned without referring to the English as soon as you hit a problem!

Unit 13 is a small reference grammar, expanding on a few of the points referred to in the units themselves. Some of them are presented in tabular form for ease of reference.

Unit 14 gives an introduction to Chinese characters, their background and how to write them, with many examples.

The characters used in this book are always in the simplified script. Simplified characters are used in the People's Republic of China, Singapore and increasingly in Chinese communities overseas. They are commonly taught to foreign students learning

Chinese. Full-form characters are used in Taiwan and Hong Kong (although this may change in the future in the case of Hong Kong).

Units 15–19 are in characters with the *pinyin* romanization underneath. The vocabularies show all the new characters used in that unit even if they have appeared in *pinyin* in previous units. In addition, the vocabularies of Units 15 and 16 show the radicals or significs of all the characters introduced in that particular unit. Units 15–19 also contain tables showing the stroke order of some of the difficult Chinese characters.

Unit 20 is in characters with the *pinyin* beside them. Try covering up the *pinyin* and see how much you understand by just looking at the characters and then checking this against the *pinyin*.

Units 21–22 have the character text in a block followed by the *pinyin* also in a block. You can decide to work in *pinyin* or characters or both.

Some of you may not want to get too involved in the learning and writing of characters, so I have made it possible to work through the entire book almost solely in *pinyin*, but do still read the introductory unit on characters (Unit 14) to understand how they work, as this is essential background knowledge as well as good fun. Conversely, those who are particularly interested in characters can go back to Units 1–12 and write out the texts in Chinese characters for extra practice. You will find the character texts for Units 1–6 and 8–12 in a section at the back of the book.

Within each unit, the text appears first followed by the vocabulary in the order in which it appears. In the vocabularies, I have sometimes split up a word by means of a dash to show how the different parts fit together but have kept to the orthodox system in the text, grammar points and exercises. The grammar section deals with the new grammar points, also in the order in which they appear in the text. Any exercise relating to a particular grammar point follows on directly after that grammar point. Each unit also contains at least one item of interest about the Chinese way of life.

It should be noted, however, that China is changing so quickly that some situations and any prices or figures and percentages that occur in the book should not be taken as necessarily accurate.

At the end of each unit, there are exercises of a more general kind. Both these and the information passages often contain useful supplementary vocabulary. Any new words in the exercises that do not appear in the vocabulary proper of a subsequent unit *are* included in the vocabularies at the back of the book, but without a unit number. This is to avoid confusion with new words that occur in the texts. (It was impossible to include *all* supplementary vocabulary for reasons of space.) It is important to note that there are extra practice exercises on the recording that do not appear in the book.

A key to the exercises precedes the Chinese (*pinyin*)–English vocabulary and the English–Chinese (*pinyin*) vocabulary, which give all the vocabulary items (*pinyin* and English) that have occurred in the texts in alphabetical order. Note that in the English–Chinese (*pinyin*) vocabulary, entries beginning with 'be' have been listed under the second item for ease of reference so that 'be willing' for instance will be found under 'willing', 'to be engaged' under 'engaged' and so on. This also applies to similar entries such as 'feel jealous', which are glossed under 'jealous'. Do remember that variations are possible in some of the answers to the exercises so don't assume you're wrong if your answer is not the same. Bear in mind, too, that the exercises are there to help you to learn as well as to practise what you have learned, so not all answers will be immediately obvious.

A final note regarding Chinese grammar. Over 40 years of experience have taught me that I should never be too categorical as far as Chinese grammar is concerned and always to preface remarks with 'nearly', 'always', 'almost invariably', etc. If I have forgotten to do so at any point in this book please regard it as said. *Putonghua* is still developing as a language so that even Chinese linguistics experts may, for example, hold a three-day meeting to discuss '*le*'. It is as exciting to be in on this as it is to be learning a language with its roots 3500 years in the past – with Chinese you have both!

About the author

Elizabeth Scurfield graduated with a First Class Honours degree in Chinese from the School of Oriental and African Studies in London and has taught Chinese for nearly 40 years, 30 of them at university level. She was co-founder of the Chinese Department at the University of Westminster (1974) at the tender age of 23 and brought new ideas and enthusiasm to its creation. Her own university course did not include a year spent in China (neither did any other university courses at that time) so that was one of the things she was determined to change. She and her colleague set up the first undergraduate exchange scheme with the Chinese Ministry of Education in 1977, some years before any other British university did so. They also introduced the writing of undergraduate dissertations in Chinese, which had never been done before.

She has made numerous short and extended visits and study trips to China since her first visit in 1976 as the only female participant on a delegation of younger sinologists. In addition to this book, her current titles in the *Teach Yourself* series include *Get Started in Mandarin Chinese*, *Learn to Write Chinese Script* and *Speak Mandarin Chinese with Confidence*.

List of abbreviations

adj	adjective	N	proper name
adv	adverb	num	numeral
aux v	auxiliary verb	o	object
CDE	compound directional ending	pp	pronoun plural
		ps	pronoun singular
coll	colloquial	PW	place word
conj	conjunction	prep	preposition
DE	directional ending	QW	question word
dem adj	demonstrative adjective	RV	resultative verb
dem p	demonstrative pronoun	RVE	resultative verb ending
interj	interjection	s	subject
MW	measure word	TW	time word
neg	negative	v	verb
n	noun	v-o	verb object

Note: I have chosen what I feel to be the most helpful grammatical descriptions. Other people may well use another term for auxiliary verb, resultative verb and so on.

1

Making friends (i)

In this unit you will learn
- *how to say* hello
- *how to observe basic courtesies*
- *how to say* please *and* thank you
- *the order of names in Chinese*

◀)) **CD 1, tr 5–7**

Mr King (*Wáng xiānsheng*) has come to China to take up a job in a joint venture company (*hézī qǐyè*). Mr Li (*Lǐ xiānsheng*) is a friend and colleague of Mr King's Chinese teacher in Britain. The meeting takes place in Mr Li's office.

Lǐ	**Wáng xiānsheng, nǐ hǎo!**	*How do you do, Mr King?*
	King/first-born/you/good/	
Wáng	**Lǐ xiānsheng, nǐ hǎo!**	*How do you do, Mr Li?*
	Li/first-born/you/good/	
Lǐ	**Qǐng zuò.**	*Please, sit down.*
	Invite/sit/	
Wáng	**Xièxie.**	*Thank you.*
	Thank/	
Lǐ	**Qǐng hē kāfēi.**	*Have some coffee.*
	Invite/drink/coffee/	
Wáng	**Xièxie, wǒ bù hē kāfēi.**	*No, thanks, I don't drink*
	Thank/I/not/drink/coffee/	*coffee.*

Lǐ	Nàme, Zhōngguó chá xíng bu xíng? *So/middle country/tea/ be OK/not/be OK/*	*Would you like some China tea then?*
Wáng	Xíng, xièxie nǐ! Wǒ hěn xǐhuan hē Zhōngguó chá. *Be OK/thank/you/I/very/ like/drink/middle country/tea/*	*Yes, thank you, I'm very fond of China tea.*

xiānsheng *(n)* Mr, gentleman
nǐ *(ps)* you
hǎo *(adj)* good
qǐng *(v)* to invite
zuò *(v)* to sit
hē *(v)* to drink
kāfēi *(n)* coffee
xièxie *(v)* to thank
wǒ *(ps)* I, me
bù *(neg)* not
nàme in that case, so
Zhōngguó *(N)* China
chá *(n)* tea
xíng *(v)* to be all right
hěn *(adv)* very
xǐhuan *(v)* to like

QUICK VOCAB

Grammar

1 Names

In Chinese, names always appear in the following order: surname, given name (Christian name), title (when used), e.g. *Máo Zédōng tóngzhì*, where *Máo* is the surname, *Zédōng* the given name and *tóngzhì* is used in place of a title and means 'comrade'.

2 Nǐ hǎo

Some Chinese adjectives can also function as verbs so *hǎo* means 'to be good' as well as 'good'. (Some people call such adjectives stative verbs.) Thus no separate verb for 'to be' is used. Note word order in *Wáng xiānsheng, **nǐ hǎo***. 'Mr King' comes first in Chinese.

It is very difficult to say two third tones together. When this happens, the first one is said as a second tone, but it is still marked as a third tone in the text, otherwise you might think that the syllable in question is always a second tone, which it is not: *Nǐ hǎo* is therefore said as *Ní hǎo* 'How are you?'

3 *Use of* qǐng

Qǐng means 'to invite or to request somebody to do something'. Do not think of it as 'please' as this will create problems with word order later on. Note also that Chinese verbs are invariable, which means that we use the same form throughout.

4 *Negation with* bù

With one exception (the verb 'to have' *yǒu*), all verbs are negated by putting *bù* in front of them.

5 *Questions* 'xíng bu xíng?'

One common way of asking a question in Chinese is to put the positive and negative forms of the verb together in that order: *Xíng bu xíng?* 'Is it all right (or not)?' The answer is not 'yes' or 'no' but either the positive form of the verb, in this case *xíng* or the negative form, i.e. *bù xíng*. (This construction is often referred to as the choice-type question form.) Note that the second half of the question, i.e. *bù* plus the verb, is sometimes written without tones, as it is normally said unstressed in everyday speech. I have followed this convention at times to familiarize you with it.

6 Position of adverbs

Most adverbs in Chinese precede the verb, e.g. 'I like you very much' is Wǒ **hěn xǐhuan nǐ.**

7 Tone of bù

Bù is normally fourth tone (`) but changes to second tone (´) when followed by another fourth tone, e.g. *bú zuò* not *bù zuò*. Also note that in *Xíng* **bu** *xíng?*, **bu** is toneless.

Exercise 1.1
Make the following sentences negative:

Wǒ hē kāfēi → **Wǒ bù hē kāfēi.**

1 *Wǒ zuò.*
2 *Nǐ hǎo.*
3 *Wǒ hē chá.*
4 *Nǐ xǐhuan Zhōngguó.*
5 *Lǐ xiānsheng xièxie wǒ.*
6 *Wáng xiānsheng qǐng nǐ hē Zhōngguó chá.*

Exercise 1.2
Make the following statements into questions and then answer them first in the positive and then in the negative:

Nǐ hē chá. → **Nǐ hē bu hē chá?** → **Wǒ hē chá.**
Wǒ bù hē chá.

1 *Wǒ xǐhuan hē kāfēi.*
2 *Nǐ xièxie wǒ.*
3 *Wáng xiānsheng qǐng wǒ zuò.*
4 *Lǐ xiānsheng xǐhuan hē shuǐ* (water).
5 *Tā* (he/she) *xǐhuan hē Zhōngguó chá.*

Exercise 1.3
Translate into colloquial English:

1 *Wáng xiānsheng qǐng wǒ hē Zhōngguó chá.*
2 *Lǐ xiānsheng hěn bù xǐhuan Wáng xiānsheng.*
3 *Wáng xiānsheng yě* (also) *bù hěn xǐhuan Lǐ xiānsheng.*
4 *Nǐ bú xièxie wǒ, nàme wǒ yě bú xièxie nǐ.*
5 *Tā qǐng wǒ zuò. Tā yě qǐng wǒ hē kāfēi.*

Insight: learning tip

Go back to the pronunciation guide before you start Unit 2. Listen, repeat, listen again and repeat. Make sure you are really comfortable with Unit 1 before you go onto Unit 2.

On meeting people

On meeting somebody for the first time on a formal occasion, the Chinese will usually shake hands and incline the head a little at the same time in greeting. This will probably be accompanied by such questions as *Nín guìxìng?* 'What is your surname?' (*Lit.* you [polite form] expensive/honourable surname) or *Qǐng wèn dàmíng?* 'May I ask your (big/famous) name?' or *Jiǔyǎng, jiǔyǎng* 'I'm very pleased to meet you' (*Lit.* long time raise head looking up to you).

In less formal situations, an older person may pat a younger one on the shoulder, close friends of the same sex may hug each other and pat each other on the back a few times and say for instance, *Nǐ hái huózhe?* 'You're still alive!' or *Shénme fēng bǎ nǐ chuī lái le?* 'What wind blew you here?' (This phrase is normally used when you meet someone unexpectedly.) Secondary school students still stand up when the teacher comes in and chorus out *Lǎoshī hǎo!* 'How do you do teacher?' (*Lit.* teacher good!) and the teacher will normally answer *Tóngxuémen hǎo!* 'How do you do students?' (*Lit.* fellow students good).

Hopefully this will give you a few guidelines which you can then supplement from your own observations.

TESTING YOURSELF

You've arrived at the end of Unit 1, so now for some quick revision. Please respond to the following questions in Chinese:

1 *What would you say on meeting a Mr Li?*

2 *How would you ask him to sit down?*

3 *How would you ask him if he would like some coffee?*

4 *What would he say if he didn't drink coffee?*

5 *How would you ask if he would like [some]* tea instead?*

6 *What would he say if he didn't drink tea?*

7 *What would he say if he liked Chinese tea?*

8 *How do you say 'Thank you'?*

9 *How do you say 'I like you'?*

10 *How do you say 'I like you very much'?*

* English words in square brackets should *not* be translated into Chinese.

2

Making friends (ii)

In this unit you will learn
* *how to make simple introductions*
* *how to exchange greetings*
* *how to address people correctly*
* *how to make simple apologies*
* *what measure words are*
* *numbers 0–99*

◀) **CD 1, tr 9–11**

Mr King has invited Mr and Mrs Li (*Lǐ tàitai*) to his apartment for a drink.

Lǐ	**Wáng xiānsheng, zhè shì wǒ tàitai, Zhōu Déjīn.** *King/first-born/this/be/I/ wife/Zhou/Dejin/*	*Mr King, this is my wife, Zhou Dejin.*
Wáng	**Lǐ tàitai, nín hǎo!** *Li/Mrs/you/good/*	*How do you do, Mrs Li?*
Lǐ (t)	**Wáng xiānsheng, nín hǎo! Rènshi nín, wǒ zhēn gāoxìng.** *King/first-born/you/good/ Know/you/I/really/happy/*	*How do you do, Mr King? I'm really pleased to meet you.*

Wáng	**Qǐng zuò, qǐng zuò.**	*Please sit down. How*
	Hē yì bēi jiǔ ba.	*about a drink?*
	Invite/sit/invite/sit/	
	Drink/one/cup/alcohol//*	
Lǐ	**Xièxie, wǒ hē yì bēi.**	*Thanks, I'll have one.*
	Thank/I/drink/one/cup/	
Wáng	**Lǐ tàitai ne?**	*What about you,*
	Li/Mrs//	*Mrs Li?*
Lǐ (t)	**Xièxie, wǒ bú huì hē jiǔ.**	*No, thanks. I don't*
	Thank/I/not/know how to/	*drink.*
	drink/alcohol/	
Wáng	**Nàme, júzizhī hǎo ma?**	*What about an orange*
	So/orange juice/good//	*juice then?*
Lǐ (t)	**Hǎo, xièxie nín.**	*Fine, thank you.*
	Good/thank/you/	

[* Extra obliques (//) signify the existence of a Chinese word that has no simple English equivalent.]

zhè *(dem p/adj) this*
shì *(v) to be*
tàitai *(n) Mrs, wife*
nín *(ps) you (polite form)*
rènshi *(v) to know, recognize*
zhēn *(adv; adj) really; true, real*
gāoxìng *(adj) happy*
yī *(num) one*
bēi *(MW) cup(ful)*
jiǔ *(n) alcohol*
ba *particle indicating suggestion*
ne *question particle*
huì *(aux v) to know how to; can; will*
júzi-zhī *(n) orange juice*
ma *question particle*

QUICK VOCAB

Grammar

1 *Use of* shì

The verb 'to be' is used much less in Chinese than in English.
It is mostly to be found in A = B sentences: *Lǐ tàitai shi nǐ péngyou*
'Mrs Li is your friend.' The test of whether *shi* has been used
correctly is to turn the sentence round and if it still makes sense
(albeit clumsily) then the *shi* is correct: *Nǐ péngyou shì Lǐ tàitai*
'Your friend is Mrs Li.' Note that *shi* is unstressed unless the
speaker wishes to emphasize it: *Tā* (she) *shì nǐ tàitai* 'She **is** your
wife.' (Doubt having been cast as to whether or not she was.)

2 Nín

Nín is the polite form of *nǐ* but it is not used frequently. It is used
to indicate respect, e.g. when addressing one's 'elders and betters'.
It is *not* used in the plural. The following table lists the other
personal pronouns.

Personal pronouns			
wǒ	*I, me*	**wǒmen**	*we, us*
nǐ	*you* (sing)	**nǐmen**	*you* (pl)
nín	*you* (polite)		
tā	*he, she, it*	**tāmen**	*they, them*

3 *Topic construction*

The Chinese are very fond of this construction and use it
frequently. It consists of stating what you are going to talk about
first, often in the very broadest sense, and *then* going on to state
your view or reaction to it.

Rènshi nín,   wǒ zhēn gāoxìng.
  topic   *reaction*

4 *Measure words*

In Chinese, something called a measure word has to be used between a number and its noun. Different measure words are used with different categories of noun. For example, *běn* is used for books and magazines, whereas *zhāng* is used for rectangular, flat objects such as tables, beds, maps, but is not a true measure as to length or anything else. Some measure words like *bēi* are actual indicators of quantity. The noun accompanying the number and measure word is often omitted when it is clear from the context what this is. For example, Mr Li says in answer to Mr King's question that he will *hē yì bēi* (*jiǔ* is understood). (For a more comprehensive table of measure words, see Unit 13.)

5 Ba

Ba is placed after a verb or phrase to denote a suggestion or to ask for confirmation of a supposition: *Hǎo ba* 'Is that all right then?'

6 Ne

When the same question is put to two or more people consecutively, *ne* is usually used to replace the question that has been put to the first person. For example, Mr King suggests to Mr Li that he might like a drink and then turns to Mrs Li and asks: *Lǐ tàitai ne?*

7 Huì

One of several auxiliary verbs expressing 'to be able to, can'. *Huì* conveys the idea of 'knowing how to, having learned it'. It is used to express knowledge of a foreign language: *Wǒ huì Yīngwén* 'I know English' and ability to smoke or drink, etc. 'I don't drink (alcohol)' becomes *Wǒ bú huì hē jiǔ* ('I don't know how to drink alcohol') in Chinese. Its other meaning is to express the possibility that something 'will happen in the future': *Tā huì lái* 'He will come.' Both meanings are used in the exercises.

8 Question particle

The addition of *ma* at the end of any statement makes it into a
question. For example: *Júzizhī hǎo* becomes *Júzizhī hǎo ma?*
Compare this with the other way of making questions (the positive
negative way) as shown in grammar point 5 in Unit 1.

9 Numbers 0–99

◀) CD 1, tr 13 (Numbers 1–10)

0	líng	8	bā	16	shíliù
1	yī	9	jiǔ	17	shíqī
2	èr	10	shí	18	shíbā
3	sān	11	shíyī (10 + 1)	19	shíjiǔ
4	sì	12	shí'èr (10 + 2)	20	èrshí (2 × 10)
5	wǔ	13	shísān	30	sānshí
6	liù	14	shísì	65	liùshíwǔ
7	qī	15	shíwǔ	99	jiǔshíjiǔ

An apostrophe (') is used to show where the break comes between
two syllables if there is any possible ambiguity in pronunciation,
so it is *shí'èr* and not *shíèr*.

Insight: learning tip

You'll find it beneficial to practise your numbers in all sorts of
ways. It will help you with your pronunciation and make you
feel much more comfortable with speaking Chinese. Try saying
the following out loud: *yī èr sān, sì wǔ liù, qī bā jiǔ shí;* then
yī sān wǔ, èr sì liù, sān wǔ qī, sì liù bā, wǔ qī jiǔ, liù bā shí.

Exercise 2.1
Translate into colloquial English:

*Wáng xiānsheng qǐng Lǐ xiānsheng hē jiǔ. Lǐ xiānsheng hěn
gāoxìng. Tā hěn huì hē jiǔ. Tā tàitai Zhōu Déjīn ne? Tā tàitai bú
huì hē jiǔ. Tā hē júzizhī. Tā yě hěn bù xǐhuan Lǐ xiānsheng hē jiǔ.*

Female equality

In the People's Republic of China (PRC), *àiren* used to be the most common term used to refer to one's 'husband' or 'wife' but it is now used much less often, although apparently slightly more on formal occasions. In overseas Chinese communities, such as Singapore, Taiwan and Hong Kong, *àiren* can still mean 'lover', so be careful how you use it! The term most commonly used in the PRC for 'wife' now is *tàitai*. *Qīzi* is also used to refer to one's wife but mostly on formal occasions and when the wife is not present. (The most common term for 'husband' is *lǎogōng*, a term that comes from Hong Kong and southern China.) A Chinese woman, married to a Mr Zhang is seldom, if ever, addressed as Mrs Zhang (*Zhāng tàitai*), unless she is an overseas Chinese or is being addressed by a foreigner. She keeps her maiden name and when being introduced, this will be given together with her 'Christian or given name', e.g. *Zhōu Déjīn*. A foreigner married to a Mr King/Wang may be variously addressed as *Wáng tàitai* or *Wáng fūrén*.

Exercise 2.2
Rearrange the words given to produce the meaning in brackets:

Yì bēi hē huì wǒ jiǔ. *[I (can) drink a little alcohol.]*
→ **Wǒ huì hē yì bēi jiǔ.**

1 *Gāoxìng Lǐ tàitai nín rènshi zhēn wǒ.* [I'm really happy to meet you, Mrs Li.]
2 *Ba júzizhī nàme hǎo.* [How about an orange juice, then?]
3 *Hē wǒ xǐhuan hěn jiǔ.* [I adore drinking.]
4 *Bù hē sì huì bēi pútáojiǔ* (grape alcohol) *nín.* [You won't drink four glasses of wine.]
5 *Wǒ tàitai zhè shì Wáng xiānsheng.* [Mr King/Wang, this is my wife.]

TESTING YOURSELF

You've arrived at the end of Unit 2, so now for some quick revision. How do you say in Chinese:

1 *Do you drink?*

....

2 *I'm a teetotaller. What about you? (use* nín)

....

3 *Mr Zhou, this is my wife.*

....

4 *Does she know him?*

....

5 *[When]* my husband smokes (*xī yān v-o*), I'm very cross.*

....

6 *How about [some]* coffee? (use* ba)

....

7 *Mr Zhang (Zhāng) doesn't know English (Yīngyǔ).*

....

8 *You won't drink seven glasses of wine.*

....

* English words in square brackets should *not* be translated into Chinese.

3

Making friends (iii)

In this unit you will learn
- *how to ask someone if they have children*
- *how to ask how old the children are*
- *how to ask if someone is married or has a partner*
- *about question words and their position in the sentence*

◆) CD 1, tr 14–17

Mr King continues his conversation with Mr and Mrs Li.

Wáng	**Lǐ xiānsheng, nǐmen yǒu xiǎoháir ma?** *Li/first-born/you (pl)/have/ children//*	*Do you have any children, Mr Li?*
Lǐ	**Yǒu, wǒmen yǒu liǎng ge – yí ge nánháir, yí ge nǚháir.** *Have/we/have/two/MW/one/MW/ male child/one/MW/female child/*	*Yes, we have two; a boy and a girl.*
Wáng	**Nánháir jǐ suì? Nǚháir jǐ suì?** *Male child/how many/years/ Female child/how many/years/*	*How old are they?*
Lǐ	**Nánháir shísì suì, nǚháir jiǔ suì.** *Male child/14/years/female child/ 9/years/*	*The boy is 14, the girl is 9.*

Lǐ (t)	**Wáng xiānsheng, jié hūn le ma?**	*Are you married,*
	King/first-born/tie marriage///	*Mr King?*
Wáng	**Méi yǒu.**	*No, I'm not.*
	Not/have/	
Lǐ (t)	**Yǒu nǚ péngyou ma?**	*Do you have a*
	Have/female/friend//	*girlfriend?*
Wáng	**Yǒu.**	*Yes, I do.*
	Have/	
Lǐ (t)	**Tā zài nǎr? Tā yě zài**	*Where is she? Is she*
	Zhōngguó ma?	*in China too?*
	She/be at/where/She/also/	
	be at/middle country//	
Wáng	**Tā míngtiān lái Zhōngguó**	*She's coming to*
	xuéxi.	*China tomorrow to*
	She/tomorrow/come/	*study.*
	middle country/study	

yǒu *(v) to have*
xiǎoháir *(n) child (small)*
liǎng *(num) two (of a kind)*
gè *(MW) see 3.1**
nán *(adj) male*
nǚ *(adj) female*
jǐ *(QW) how many (fewer than ten)*
suì *(n) year (of age)*
jié hūn *(v-o) to marry, to get married*
le *modal particle*
méi *(neg) not (only used with* **yǒu***)*
péngyou *(n) friend*
zài *(v; prep) to be at; at*
nǎr *(QW) where*
yě *(adv) also, too*
lái *(v) to come*
míngtiān *(TW) tomorrow*
xué(xí) *(v) to study*

QUICK VOCAB

* i.e. Unit 3, grammar point 1.

32

Grammar

1 *More on measure words:* gè

Gè is by far the most common measure word in Chinese and is used with a whole range of nouns that do not have their own specific measure word. When in doubt as to which measure word to use, use *gè* – not all native Chinese speakers get their measure words right every time either! When said in normal speech, *gè* is usually toneless.

2 *More on numbers* èr *and* liǎng

Liǎng (two of a kind) is used with measure words instead of *èr*, so 'two children' is *liǎng ge xiǎoháir* not *èr ge xiǎoháir*. Some people find it helpful to think of *liǎng* as the bound form 'two of a kind'. *Liǎ* (an abbreviated form for *liǎng gè*) is often used with personal pronouns 'we', 'you' (plural), 'they', instead of *liǎng gè*, thus 'the two of us' may either be *wǒmen liǎ* or *wǒmen liǎng gè*.

3 *Question words and their position*

In Chinese, question words such as *jǐ* 'how many' (generally expecting an answer fewer than ten), which is always used with a measure word, *duōshao* 'how many' (indicating any number), *shénme* 'what', *shénme shíhou* 'when' (*Lit.* what time), *shéi* 'who' (also pronounced *shuí*), *nǎr* 'where', *jǐ diǎn (zhōng)* 'what time' (*Lit.* what o'clock), *zěnmeyàng* 'what about it, how', appear in the sentence in the *same* position as the word that replaces them in the answer. *Tāmen jǐ suì?* 'How old are they?' *Nánháir shísì suì, nǚháir jiǔ suì.* (Note that no verb is necessary when stating age in terms of years.) *Tā zài nǎr? Tā yě zài Zhōngguó.*

The particle *ne* is often to be found at the end of the sentence containing a question word and has a softening effect. It also helps to make the sentence feel more balanced. Try saying such sentences with and without *ne* and hear the difference:

Jǐ diǎn zhōng qù *(go)*? → **Jǐ diǎn zhōng qù ne?**
Tā zài nǎr? → **Tā zài nǎr ne?**

Note that sentences containing question words do **not** take *ma*.

Exercise 3.1
Replace the words in **bold** with an appropriate question word:
Nánháir wǔ suì → **Nánháir jǐ suì?**

1 *Wǒmen hē júzizhī.*
2 *Lǐ xiānsheng hé* (and) *Lǐ tàitai yǒu* **liǎng ge** *xiǎoháir.*
3 *Pútáojiǔ* **hěn hǎo.**
4 *Wáng xiānsheng zài* **Běijīng.**
5 *Tā nǚ péngyou míngtiān xiàwǔ* (afternoon) **liǎng diǎn zhōng** *lái Zhōngguó.*
6 *Nǚháir* **jiǔ** *suì.*

Insight: learning tip

Look back at all the question words you have been given in 3.3 and make up as many simple questions and answers as you can using all the vocabulary you have learnt so far:
e.g. *Xiǎoháir jǐ suì? Xiǎoháir liù suì. Lǐ xiānsheng zài nǎr? Lǐ xiānsheng zài Zhōngguó. Tā hē shénme? Tā hē júzizhī.*

As you learn more constructions, e.g. how to tell the time in the next unit, go back and repeat this exercise, practising what you have just learnt and trying to use the new vocabulary as well.

---

4 *Verbal suffix* -le

Le is the delight of all Chinese grammarians, but only its more straightforward aspects will be dealt with in this book. Here it is put *after* the verb to indicate that the action of the verb has been completed:

Wáng xiānsheng jié hūn **le** *ma?* If he had been married the answer would have been: *Jié hūn le.* The negative form of this construction is *méi yǒu* + *verb* where the *yǒu* may be omitted. The *verb* may be omitted when answering a question with *-le* in the negative but *yǒu* then has to be retained, so Mr King could equally well have replied: *Méi yǒu jié hūn* or *Méi jié hūn* instead of *Méi yǒu*. There is *no* completed action indicated in the negative so there is no *-le*. Note that the negative form of *yǒu* is *méi yǒu*. This is the one exception to the rule that all verbs are negated by *bù*. (See 1.4.)

The question form is made by adding *ma* to the statement or *méi yǒu* after it: *Wáng xiānsheng jié hūn **le ma**?* or *Wáng xiānsheng jié hūn **le méi yǒu**?*

This is identical to the choice-type question form found in 1.5 except that the verb is *not* repeated. (*Yǒu* is never omitted in this type of question form.) Another alternative question form is: *Wáng xiānsheng **jié hūn méi jié hūn**?*, the answers, whether positive or negative, being as before.

··

Chinese straight talking

The Chinese love to know everybody else's business and do not feel at all inhibited about enquiring how much you paid for your house, your car, your CD player, your television, your clothes or anything else. They are always particularly interested in your age, marital status and whether you have children and, if not, why not! Although customs are changing gradually, it is still extremely unusual for a Chinese adult in his or her 30s to be unmarried or childless. Conversely, it is quite in order for you to ask the same sort of questions. Being of a 'curious' disposition myself, I have always felt very much at home in China. Of course, as contact with the outside world increases, many more Chinese are learning that some foreigners regard such questions as impolite and therefore may, on occasions, restrain their natural curiosity (and genuine openness) on such matters.

··

Exercise 3.2

The following sentences are incorrect: they contain common errors (the Chinese call such sentences *bìngjù* 'sick sentences'). Give the correct version. For example: *Tā jié hūn míngtiān → Tā míngtiān jié hūn.*

1 *Wǒ yǒu èr ge xiǎoháir.*
2 *Tā bù yǒu nǚháir.*
3 *Nǐmen yǒu liù péngyou.*
4 *Zhōngguó shi nǎr?*
5 *Jǐ suì tāmen?*
6 *Wǒ xǐhuan hē Zhōngguó chá hěn.*
7 *Lǐ tàitai gāoxìng zhēn rènshi nín.*
8 *Tā zài Zhōngguó yě ma?*
9 *Wǒ bù yǒu nǚ péngyou.*
10 *Xiānsheng Wáng lái Zhōngguó míngtiān.*

TESTING YOURSELF

You've arrived at the end of Unit 3, so now for some more revision. Please respond to the following questions in Chinese:

1 *What do you say if you want to ask somebody whether they have children or not?*

....

2 *How do you ask somebody if they have a daughter?*

....

3 *How do you ask somebody if they have a son?*

....

4 *How do you ask somebody how old their children are?*

....

5 *How do you ask somebody if they are married?*

....

6 *How do you ask somebody if they have a girlfriend?*

....

7 *How do you ask somebody if they have a boyfriend?*

....

8 *How do you ask somebody where their boyfriend is?*

....

9 *How do you ask somebody where their girlfriend is?*

....

10 *How do you ask someone if they are coming tomorrow?*

....

11 *How do you ask someone if he or she is studying in China?*

....

12 *How do you say 'I'm not married'?*

....

4

Two days later

In this unit you will learn
- *how to invite someone to your home*
- *to tell the time*
- *about verb-object constructions*

◆)) **CD 1, tr 18–21**

Mrs Li telephones Mr Wang to invite him and his girlfriend to dinner.

Lǐ (t)	**Wáng xiānsheng nǐ hǎo, wǒ xiǎng qǐng nǐmen qù wǒmen jiā wánr, hǎo ma?** *I/feel like/invite/you (pl)/ go/our/home/play/good//*	*I'd like to invite you both over to our home. What do you say?*
Wáng	**Nà tài hǎo le.** *That/too/good//*	*That would be great.*
Lǐ (t)	**Nǐmen míngtiān wǎnshang yǒu kòng ma?** *You (pl)/tomorrow/ evening/have/space//*	*Are you free tomorrow evening?*
Wáng	**Yǒu kòng.** *Have/space/*	*Yes, we are.*

Lǐ (t)	**Nàme, qǐng nǐmen liǎ míngtiān wǎnshang qù wǒmen jiā chī fàn ba.**	*Then how about you both coming over for a meal tomorrow evening?*
	So/invite/you (pl)/two/ tomorrow/evening/go/ our/home/eat/cooked rice//	
Wáng	**Nà tài xièxie nǐmen le! Jǐ diǎn zhōng qù ne?**	*Thank you very much indeed. What time shall we come?*
	That/too/thank/you (pl)// How many/point/clock/go//	
Lǐ (t)	**Liù diǎn zěnmeyàng?**	*How would 6 o'clock suit you?*
	6/point/how about it/	
Wáng	**Xíng, jiù liù diǎn ba.**	*Fine, 6 o'clock then.*
	Be all right/then/6/point//	

xiǎng *(aux v; v)* to feel like doing something; to think
qù *(v)* to go
jiā *(n, MW)* home; family; measure word for restaurant
wán(r) *(v)* to have fun; to play
nà *(dem p/adj)* that
tài *(adv)* too, extremely
wǎnshang *(TW)* evening
yǒu kòng *(v-o)* to have free time
liǎ *(num + MW)* two
chī fàn *(v-o)* to eat (meal)
diǎn zhōng *(MW + n)* o'clock
zěnmeyàng *(QW)* what about (it)?, how?
jiù *(adv)* then; just, only, merely

Grammar

1 Tài *verb* le

As *le* is Chinese grammar's *bête noire*, any hints on its usage are indispensable. For example, it is almost invariably to be found with the adverb *tài* 'too' as in *tài hǎo le* 'great', *tài xièxie nǐmen le* 'thank you very much indeed'. Don't ask me why!

2 *Adverbial phrases of time (time when)*

As is stated in 1.6, most adverbs in Chinese *precede* the verb. Adverbs of 'time when' are no exception to this rule (for adverbs of 'time how long' see 11.13), so that in *Qǐng nǐmen míngtiān lái* 'Please come tomorrow' *míngtiān* precedes *lái*. This is the reverse of normal English usage. Such adverbs can also precede the subject or topic for emphasis. For example *Wǒ jīntiān lái, míngtiān wǒ bù lái* 'I'll come today, (but) I am **not** coming tomorrow.'

3 *Verb-object constructions*

This construction is a feature of the Chinese language so that whereas an English speaker is quite happy with simply stating that 'He likes eating' or that 'She is going to eat', a Chinese will normally say that he likes 'eating cooked rice' or that she is 'going to eat cooked rice' (*chī fàn*), where *chī* is the verb 'to eat' and *fàn* the object 'cooked rice'. There are numerous examples of this construction; some of the most common are given in the list below, with the literal meanings in brackets.

chī fàn	(eat cooked rice)	'to eat'
shuì jiào	(sleep sleep)	'to sleep'
dú shū	(read books)	'to study'
shuō huà	(speak speech)	'to speak, talk'
huà huàr	(draw drawings, paint paintings)	'to draw, paint'

tán huà	(chat speech)	'to chat'
xī yān	(smoke tobacco/cigarettes)	'to smoke'
jiāo shū	(teach books)	'to teach'
kāi chē	(drive vehicle)	'to drive'
zǒu lù	(walk road)	'to walk'
kàn shū	(read book, look book)	'to read'
zuò chē	(sit vehicle)	'to go by some form of transport'
lù yīn	(record sound)	'to record'
qǐng kè	(invite guest)	'to invite somebody for a meal'

Even *jié hūn* (tie marriage) is strictly speaking a verb-object construction and not a compound verb. The test is whether *le* can be inserted between the two parts or not. If it can (and only finding or hearing examples can sometimes tell you this), then it is a verb-object construction, so we can say *chī le fàn* but we cannot say *xiè le xie* (*xièxie*) or *xǐ le huan* (*xǐhuan*). Classical Chinese is monosyllabic (one syllabled), whereas modern Chinese has become increasingly disyllabic (two syllabled) so the verb-object construction can be seen as conforming to this trend. Of course, if the verb in question already has an object, then these 'fill-in' objects are not used.

Note that there is great confusion as to whether these verb objects should be written as one or two words in *pinyin*. I have kept them separate in the interests of clarity.

4 Telling the time

Question: **Xiànzài** (now) **jǐ diǎn (zhōng)?** (*Lit.* Now/how many/ points/clock)

Answer: **Xiànzài yì diǎn zhōng.** (*Lit.* Now/one/point/clock)

Zhōng is normally omitted except when asking the time or on the hour, where it is optional.

liǎng diǎn (zhōng)

sān diǎn (líng)
wǔ fēn (minute)
líng 'zero' is
optional

sì diǎn shíwǔ fēn
or more commonly
sì diǎn yí kè (one
quarter)

wǔ diǎn sānshí
fēn or more
commonly *wǔ diǎn*
bàn (half)

liù diǎn sìshíwǔ fēn
or more commonly
liù diǎn sān kè
(three quarters) or
chà yí kè qī diǎn
(lack/one/quarter/
7/point)

qī diǎn wǔshí fēn
or more commonly
chà shí fēn bā diǎn
(lack/10/unit/8/
point)

Some people use *líng* 'zero' when telling the time between one and
nine minutes past the hour but some do not, especially when in
speech.

(For more information on time in general see Unit 13.)

Exercise 4.1
What time is it on each of the clocks below?

1

2

3

4

5

6

7

8

Now listen to further examples of telling the time.

Insight: learning tip

Write down times at random. Try to think of all the different ways to say them. Practise during the day when you are at work or at home either by looking at your watch or at a clock or by practising saying in Chinese when your various appointments are.

5 *The adverb* jiù

Jiù is used in many different ways, some of which you will meet in this book. Here it is used to link two clauses together and at the same time show acceptance: *Xíng, jiù liù diǎn ba.* As an adverb, *jiù* can never precede a noun or pronoun. Note that *ba* also expresses agreement or approval here (cf. 2.5).

Beijing's courtesy campaign

As we said in the previous unit, it is normal for the Chinese to ask people they have just met questions of a personal nature. You might be interested to know that in the run-up to the Beijing Olympics, Beijing residents were urged by the Beijing municipal government not to ask foreigners whom they met questions on their salary, sex life, age, health, income, political views, personal experiences or religious beliefs. These were called the 'Eight don't asks'. Beijing residents were also encouraged to learn 1000 English sentences printed in a Chinese daily, in order to make foreigners feel more at home. Apparently, the 984th of these read: 'Tonight I think I'd like Sichuan food. I prefer the taste.'

Exercise 4.2
The following sentences are incorrect: they contain common errors (the Chinese call such sentences *bìngjù* 'sick sentences'). Give the correct version. For example: *Tā qù wǒmen jiā wǎnshang* → *Tā wǎnshang qù wǒmen jiā.*

1 *Wǒmen qù shí diǎn zhōng.*
2 *Zěnmeyàng hē lǜ* (green) *chá?*
3 *Zhōu Déjīn méi yǒu jié hūn le.*
4 *Wáng tàitai bù chī fàn wǎnshang.*
5 *Zhāng xiānsheng xiǎng qǐng wǒmen, jiù wǒmen bù qǐng tā.*

Exercise 4.3
Translate the following passage into colloquial English:

Wǒmen yǒu sì ge xiǎoháir, sān ge nǚháir, yí ge nánháir. Wǒ de péngyou hěn duō (many). *Wǒ qǐng liǎng ge péngyou míngtiān wǎnshang lái wǒmen jiā chī fàn. Wǒ tàitai/àiren hěn bù gāoxìng yīnwèi* (because) *tā bú rènshi tāmen.*

TESTING YOURSELF

You've arrived at the end of Unit 4, so now for some more revision. How do you say the following in Chinese:

1 *The girl is three years old, the boy is two.*

2 *Is he married? No, he isn't.*

3 *Are you (pl) going to his home for a meal tomorrow evening?*

4 *Where is she now (xiànzài TW)? She is in London (Lúndūn).*

5 *Do you have a boyfriend? No, I don't. I am only (use cái) 15!*

6 *The two of us are really fond of coffee.*

7 *What time will you be at home?/How about 7 o'clock?/Fine, 7 it is then. (use jiù)*

8 *My wife is smashing, but (dànshi) she doesn't like talking much (shuō huà).*

9 *Where is your friend? I'd like to invite him for a meal.*

Mini revision

I Correct the following *bìngjù* (refer back to Exercises 3.2 and 4.2):

a) *Wáng tàitai rènshi Lǐ xiānsheng bu rènshi?*
b) *Tā lái míngtiān wǎnshang chī fàn.*
c) *Wǒ yǒu èr ge xiǎoháir.*
d) *Nǐmen bù yǒu jié hūn.*
e) *Lǐ xiānsheng hé* (and) *Lǐ tàitai qù shíyī diǎn zhōng hē kāfēi.*

II Fill in the blanks using the words given above the passage.
Each word may only be used once.

kāfēi zhēn qù fàn péngyou jiā méi Liú jié hūn nǚ

Zhāng xiānsheng hái (still) **méi yǒu** ____. **Tā yǒu hěn duō** ____
dànshi (but) **tā** ____ **yǒu** ____ **péngyou. Tā hěn xǐhuan chī** ____,
hē jiǔ bù chángcháng (often) **zài** ____. **Yǒu yī tiān** (day) **tā** ____
hē ____ **rènshi yí ge** ____ **xiǎojie** (Miss/Ms). **Xiànzài** (now) **Zhāng**
xiānsheng yǒu nǚ péngyou, tā ____ **gāoxìng.**

III A
Write down the Chinese for the following numbers. Try to do the
exercise without looking the words up. If you can't do this, spend
some time revising the numbers (see Unit 2) and then come back
and try the exercise. Do this until you can write down the numbers
almost without thinking:

a) 7   *b)* 9   *c)* 22   *d)* 45   *e)* 68   *f)* 81   *g)* 93   *h)* 74

III B

Now let's practise telling the time in the same way. This time go back to earlier on in this unit and revise telling the time first and then attempt the exercise. Again do this until you can write down the times without thinking too much about them:

a) 8.20 *b)* 12.05 *c)* 2.30 *d)* 5.40 *e)* 9.45 *f)* 11.10 *g)* 6.15 *h)* 4.55

Congratulations!

You have now come to the end of Unit 4. Make sure you feel completely happy with the contents of all four units before continuing. It's much better to go more slowly and build on firm foundations than to race ahead but not be confident about what you have learnt.

5

At the Lis' (i)

In this unit you will learn
- *how to say where you come from and what nationality you are*
- *the Chinese equivalents of foreign names*
- *more about measure words*
- *about how to understand abbreviations*
- *to 'sing' a Chinese song*

◀) **CD 1, tr 23–24**

Mr King and his girlfriend Ms Shaw (*Shǐ xiǎojie*) have arrived at the Lis' for dinner.

Wáng	Wǒ gěi nǐmen jièshào yíxià, zhè wèi shì wǒ de nǚ péngyou, Shǐ Àilǐ. Zhè wèi shì Lǐ xiānsheng, zhè wèi shì Lǐ tàitai. *I/give/you/introduce// this/MW/be/my/female/ friend/Shi Aili/This/MW/ be/Li/first-born/this/MW/ be/Li/Mrs/*	*May I introduce you to my girlfriend, Shi Aili? This is Mr Li and this is Mrs Li.*
Lǐ } Lǐ (t) }	Shǐ xiǎojie, nín hǎo! *Shi/Miss/you/good/*	*How do you do, Ms Shaw?*

Shǐ	Lǐ xiānsheng, Lǐ tàitai, nǐmen hǎo! *Li/first-born/Li/Mrs/you/good/*	*How do you do, Mr and Mrs Li?*
Lǐ	Qǐng suíbiàn zuò ba. *Invite/follow convenience/sit//*	*Please make yourselves comfortable.*
Lǐ (t)	Shǐ xiǎojie, nín yě shì cóng Yīngguó lái de ma? *Shi/Miss/you/also/be/from/hero country/come// //*	*Are you from Britain too, Ms Shaw?*
Shǐ	Shì, wǒ yě shì cóng Yīngguó lái de dàn shì zài Měiguó chūshēng, zhǎngdà de. *Be/I/also/be/from/hero country/come//but/at/beautiful country/out be born/grow big///*	*Yes, I am, but I was born and grew up in America.*
Lǐ	Nín bàba yǐqian zài Měiguó gōngzuò ma? *You/daddad/previously/at/beautiful country/work do///*	*Did your father work in America previously?*
Shǐ	Duì, wǒ bàba yǐqian zài Měiguó gōngzuò. Wǒ māma shì Měiguórén. *Correct/my/dad/previously/at/beautiful country/work do/My mum/is/beautiful country person/*	*Yes, he did. My mother is American.*
Lǐ (t)	Shǐ xiǎojie, nín lái zhèr xuéxí shénme? *Shi/Miss/you/come/here/study/what/*	*What have you come here to study Ms Shaw?*
Shǐ	Wǒ lái zhèr xuéxí Hànyǔ. *I/come/here/study/Chinese language/*	*I have come here to study the Chinese language.*

Lǐ	Nín zài nǎ ge xuéxiào xuéxí Hànyǔ?	Which school are you (studying Chinese language) at?
	You/at/which/MW/school/ study/Chinese language/	
Shǐ	Wǒ zài Běijīng Dàxué xuéxí Hànyǔ.	I am studying (Chinese language) at Beijing University.
	I/at/Beijing/big study/study/ Chinese/	
Lǐ	Xuéxiào lǐ shēnghuó zěnmeyàng?	What's it like there?
	School inside/life/ how/	
Shǐ	Hěn búcuò!	It's great!
	Very/not wrong/	
Lǐ (t)	Nǐmen yídìng hěn è le. Wǒmen chī fàn ba.	You must be ravenous. Let's eat.
	You/definitely/very/hungry//	

gěi *(prep; v)* for; give
jièshào *(v)* to introduce
yíxià see 5.2
wèi *(MW)* for persons (polite)
xiǎojie *(n)* Ms, young lady
suíbiàn do as one pleases
shì . . . de see 5.7
cóng *(prep)* from
Yīngguó *(N)* Britain, England
à *(interj)* ah, oh
dōu *(adv)* both, all
Yīngguórén *(n)* British (person)
dànshi *(conj)* but
Měiguó *(N)* America (USA)
chūshēng *(v)* to be born
zhǎngdà *(v)* to grow up
bàba *(n)* Dad, papa
yǐqián *(adv, conj)* previously, before

QUICK VOCAB

gōngzuò *(v; n) to work; work*
duì *(adj) correct*
māma *(n) Mum, mama*
zhèr *(PW) here*
Hànyǔ *(n) Chinese language*
nǎ *(QW) which?*
xuéxiào *(n) school*
Běijīng Dàxué *(N) Beijing University*
(n+) **li** *inside (+ n)*
shēnghuó *(n, v) life; to live*
búcuò *pretty good*
yídìng *(adv) certainly, definitely*
è *(adj) hungry*
le *new situation*

Grammar

1 *Use of* gěi

Gěi may be used in several ways. Its basic meaning is as a verb meaning 'to give': *Wǒ gěi nǐ júzizhī* 'I'll give you orange juice' or it can stand with a personal noun or pronoun *before* the verb with the meaning of doing the action of the verb *for* that person: *Wǒ gěi nǐ hē* 'I'll drink (it) for you.' 'To introduce A to B' is *gěi B jièshào A* in Chinese.

2 Yíxià

The subtlety of the Chinese language lies in the way it conveys nuances of meaning. In this context *yíxià* softens the abruptness of *Wǒ gěi nǐ jièshào* without having any specific meaning, although in other contexts it can mean 'on one occasion' or 'have a little go at (doing the action of the verb)'.

3 More on measure words

When *zhè* 'this' and *nà* 'that' occur with a noun in the singular or as pronouns (with a singular noun understood) or with a number, then the appropriate measure word must be inserted:

zhè wèi xiǎojie 'this MW (unmarried) young lady'
nà wèi xiānsheng 'that MW gentleman'
zhè wèi 'this MW one (person understood)'
nà liǎng ge rén 'those two MW people'

This rule applies equally well to such question words as *jǐ* 'how many' and *nǎ* 'which' (both of which must be followed by measure words):

Question: **Tā gěi nǐ jǐ bēi jiǔ?**
'How many glasses of alcohol did he give you?'
Answer: **Tā gěi wǒ sān bēi jiǔ.**
'He gave me three.'
Question: **Nǐ zài nǎ ge xuéxiào xuéxí Hànyǔ?**
'Where do you study Chinese?'
Answer: **Wǒ zài Běijīng Dàxué xuéxí Hànyǔ.**
'I study Chinese at Beijing University.'

Note that *wèi* is normally used with more formal nouns such as *xiānsheng*, *xiǎojie*, etc. but not with nouns such as *rén*. The *xiǎo* in *xiǎojie* is pronounced second tone in practice, as *jiě*, though neutral here, still carries enough weight to turn *xiǎo* into a second. Convention has us write it as third tone, however.

Exercise 5.1
Insert the missing measure words in the following sentences:
Nà xuéxiào búcuò → Nà ge xuéxiào búcuò.

1 *Zhè xiǎojie zài Běijīng Dàxué xuéxí Hànyǔ.*
2 *Nǎ xiānsheng shì nǐ lǎogōng* (colloquial word for 'husband')?
3 *Wáng tàitai yǒu jǐ xiǎoháir?*
4 *Nà wǔ rén dōu shì nǐ péngyou ma?*
5 *Tāmen jǐ zhōng lái wǒmen jiā chī fàn?*

4 *Marker* de

A pronoun and a noun may be linked by *de*: *nǐ de jiā* 'your home'; *wǒ de bēizi* 'my cup'; *wǒ de nǔ péngyou* 'my girlfriend'; *tā de kāfēi* 'her/ his coffee'. For obvious reasons, some students tend to regard this *de* as being possessive, but this can be misleading. One way out of this difficulty might be to regard *wǒ de*, *nǐ de*, etc. simply as possessive adjectives meaning 'my', 'your' and not as *wǒ + de*, etc.

In close personal relationships: *tā māma* 'his mum', *nǐ àiren* 'your husband/wife', *wǒ péngyou* 'my friend' the *de* may be omitted. A Chinese newspaper article or official spokesman will also refer to China and to the Chinese government as *Wǒ guó* ('my country' – 'China') and *Wǒ zhèngfǔ* ('my government' – 'the Chinese government').

De is also used with two nouns in the same way, the first being subordinate to the second. Whatever comes **after** *de* is the main idea, i.e. what is being talked about, and what precedes *de* gives additional information about that main idea. Thus, in the phrase *tā māma de jiā*, we are talking about somebody's home which happens to be his mother's, i.e. 'his mother's home'.

5 *Foreign names (I)*

Certain very common and/or very well-known foreign surnames and Christian/given names have set equivalents in Chinese, e.g. Smith: *Shǐmìsī (Shǐ mì sī)*, John: *Yuēhàn (Yuē hàn)*. Thus John Smith would be written *Yuēhàn•Shǐmìsī*, the '•' between the two indicating that the name is foreign. Since the majority of Chinese names consist of three characters or 'syllables', most foreigners who regularly come into contact with Chinese people often adopt a three-syllabled name. Sometimes all three syllables are an approximate transliteration of the foreign surname, otherwise the Chinese practice of generally having one syllable for the surname and two for the given or Christian name is adopted. Thus Ms Shaw has adopted the Chinese surname *Shǐ* 'history' and the given name

Àilĭ (*Ài lĭ*) 'loves principle'. Almost all Chinese given names have a meaning, hence the origin of such names as 'Beautiful Jade' and 'Flowering Plum Blossom', which appear in some English translations of Chinese literature; a good transcription of a foreign name should follow this practice.

6 Adverbial phrases of place

Adverbial phrases of place usually consist of a preposition and a place word and are generally put before the verb as in: *Wŏ zài zhèr xuéxí Hànyŭ* 'I study Chinese here.'

Other prepositions such as *cóng* 'from' and *dào* 'to' also function in this way:

Tā cóng Zhōngguó lái. (*Lit.* He/from/China/comes)
'He comes from China.'
Wŏmen dào Měiguó qù. (*Lit.* We/to/beautiful country/go)
'We go to America.'

When an adverbial phrase of 'time when' (see 4.2) and an adverbial phrase of place both occur before the verb, the rule is time *before* place:

Nĭmen jīntiān zài wŏ jiā chī fàn.
(*Lit.* You/today/at/my/home/eat/cooked rice)
'You are eating at my home today.'

Note that words such as -*lĭ* 'inside', 'on', 'under', etc. occur *after* the noun to which they refer. These will be dealt with in more detail in Unit 18.

7 Shì . . . de

An adverbial phrase of time, manner or place is emphasized by putting *shì* in front of it and *de* after it. This construction can only be used where the action of the verb has been completed, it cannot be used for present or future actions:

Question: **Shǐ xiǎojie, nín yě shì cóng Yīngguó lái de ma?**
Answer: **Shì, wǒ yě shì cóng Yīngguó lái de.**

A negative answer might have been:

Bù, wǒ shì cóng Déguó (Germany) **lái de.**

The stress does not always show in the English translation but the following examples may illustrate the point more clearly:

Question: **Nǐ shì bā diǎn zhōng lái de ma?** *'Did you come at 8?'*
(Was it at 8 that you came?)
Answer: **Bù, wǒ shì qī diǎn bàn lái de.** *'No, at 7.30.'*
(It was at 7.30 that I came.)
Question: **Nǐ shì zuò chē** (sit vehicle) **lái de ma?** *'Did you come by bus/car?'* (Was it by bus/car that you came?)
Answer: **Bù, wo shì zǒu lù lái de.** *'No, I came on foot.'*
(It was on foot that I came.)

8 Abbreviations

You might be forgiven for thinking that, given the nature of the Chinese language, abbreviations would be out of the question, but you would be wrong. The Chinese love abbreviations, the pithiness of which has echoes of their classical past. Hence, *Běijīng Dàxué* 'Beijing University' becomes *Běidà*, *Nánjīng Dàxué* 'Nanjing University' becomes *Nándà* and so on. As you can see the first syllable from each word has been picked out to form the abbreviation but this is not always the case. For example, *Zhōngháng* is the abbreviation for *Zhōngguó Yínháng* 'Bank of China' (*Lit.* China bank) and *Gāo fǎ* is the abbreviation for *Zuì Gāo Rénmín Fǎyuàn* 'the Supreme People's Court'. The most likely targets for abbreviations are institutions and political movements.

9 *The particle* le

When *le* occurs at the end of a sentence it is often referred to as the 'modal particle *le*'. In this text, it is used to indicate that a new state of affairs or situation has appeared:

Nǐmen yídìng hěn è le *'You must be starving'*
(whereas previously you weren't)
Yīngguó rè le *'The UK is getting/will get hot'*
(whereas previously it was rather cool!)

You might find it helpful to think of this as the 'new situation' *le* or the 'change of state' *le*. This has to be accepted in its very broadest sense as the Chinese almost always use it with such questions as:

Xiǎoháir jǐ suì le? *'How old is the child?'*
(*Lit.* Child/how many/years/become)
Xiànzài jǐ diǎn le? *'What time is it?'*
(*Lit.* Now/how many/o'clock/become)

where the concept of a change of state has been stretched to its limits.

....

Interrogation – Chinese style?

Mr and Mrs Li have not previously met Ms Shaw, so they are anxious to find out who she is and what she does where. This is very typical of a first meeting – somewhere, you are being squirrelled away into an imaginary filing system!
....

Exercise 5.2
Answer the following questions on the text:

1 *Wáng xiānsheng de nǔ péngyou shì shéi* (who)?
2 *Shǐ xiǎojie shì bu shi Yīngguórén?*
3 *Shǐ xiǎojie shì zài nǎr chūshēng de?*
4 *Shǐ xiǎojie de bàba yǐqián zài Měiguó gōngzuò ma?*
5 *Shǐ xiǎojie de māma yě shì Yīngguórén ma?*
6 *Shǐ xiǎojie shì zài nǎr zhǎngdà de?*
7 *Shǐ xiǎojie zài Běijīng Dàxué xuéxí ma?*
8 *Zài Běijīng Dàxué shēnghuó hǎo ma?*

Insight: learning tip

In order to practise the measure word 'zhī' which is used
for animals and for one of paired parts of the body, e.g. one
hand/foot/leg, try singing the following 'poem' to the tune
of 'Frère Jacques':

Liǎng zhī lǎohǔ, liǎng zhī lǎohǔ,	*Two tigers (repeated)*
Pǎo de kuài, pǎo de kuài,	*Run quickly (repeated)*
Yì zhī méi yǒu yǎnjing,	*One has no eyes,*
** yì zhī méi yǒu wěiba,**	* one has no tail,*
Zhēn qíguài, zhēn qíguài.	*How strange (repeated)*

TESTING YOURSELF ✳

Translate into Chinese:

1 *Where were you born?*

2 *Are you French? We are both French, too.*

3 *Where did you grow up?*

4 *Did that gentleman come at 2.30? No, he came at 3.*
  (use shì . . . de*)*

5 *Where are you studying Chinese? How are you getting on?*

6 *He came from America. He is working here.*

7 *What's the time? You must be starving!*

8 *I've got no free time today, but I'm not working tomorrow.*
  Would 10 o'clock suit you? (use xíng*)*

6

At the Lis' (ii)

In this unit you will learn
- **to make appropriate remarks and responses during a meal**
- **how to say not to do something**
- **how to express the complement of degree**

◀) **CD 1, tr 26–28**

The conversation continues at the Lis'.

Lǐ (t)	**Jīntiān wǎnshang chī Zhōngguó cài xíng ma?** *Today/evening/eat/China/ dish(es)/be OK//*	*We are going to eat Chinese tonight, if that's all right with you?*
Wáng	**Hǎo jíle!** *Good/extremely/*	*Marvellous!*
Lǐ	**Bié kèqi, zìjǐ lái ba. Nǐmen huì yòng kuàizi ma?** *Don't/be polite/self/come// You/know/use/chopsticks//*	*Make yourselves at home. Do help yourselves. Can you use chopsticks?*
Wáng	**Huì yòng, dànshì yòng de bù hǎo.** *Know/use/but/use/ not/good/*	*Yes, but not very well.*

Lǐ	**Méi guānxi . . . Ñg, nǐmen dōu yòng de búcuò a!** *Not/concern/Hm/you/ both/use/not bad//*	*It doesn't matter . . . Hm, you are both pretty good.*
Lǐ (t)	**Wǒ zuò cài, zuò de bù hǎo. Qǐng yuánliàng.** *I/make/dish/make/not good/invite/forgive/*	*Sorry, I'm not much of a cook.*
Shǐ	**Nín cài zuò de zhēn hǎo.** *You/make/dish/make/ very/good/*	*You cook really well.*
Lǐ (t)	**Shǐ xiǎojie huì zuò cài ma?** *Shi/Ms/know/make/dish//*	*Can you cook, Ms Shaw?*
Shǐ	**Huì yìdiǎnr, dànshi jìshù bù gāo!** *Can/one drop/but/ technique/not/tall/*	*A little, but I am a very plain cook.*
Wáng	**Tā Yīngguó cài zuò de fēicháng hǎo.** *She/hero country/dish/ make/extremely/good/*	*She cooks wonderful English food.*
Lǐ	**Zhōngguó cài zuò de zěnmeyàng?** *Middle country/dish/make/ how/*	*What about Chinese food?*
Shǐ	**Wǒ Zhōngguó cài zuò de bù zěnmeyàng.** *I/middle country/dish/ make/not/how/*	*I'm not much good at making Chinese food.*
Lǐ (t)	**Nǐmen zuìhǎo shǎo shuō huà, duō chī fàn ba, yàobùrán cài dōu liáng le!** *You/most good/less/speak/ speech/more/eat/meal// /otherwise/dish/all/cool//*	*You'd better talk less and concentrate more on your food, otherwise it'll all get cold!*

jīntiān *(TW) today*
cài *(n) dish; vegetable*
jíle *(adj) extremely*
bié *(adv) don't*
kèqi *(adj) polite (Lit. guest air)*
zìjǐ *(p) oneself*
yòng *(v) to use*
kuàizi *(n) chopsticks*
-de *see 6.2*
méi (yǒu) guānxi *it doesn't matter*
ǹg *(interj) hm*
zuò *(v) to do, to make*
yuánliàng *(v) to forgive*
yìdiǎn(r) *(n) a little*
jìshù *(n) technique*
gāo *(adj) tall, high*
fēicháng *(adv) extremely*
bù zěnmeyàng *not up to much*
zuì *(adv) most*
zuìhǎo *(adv; adj) had better; best*
shǎo *(adv; adj) less; few*
shuō *(v) to speak*
shuō huà *(v-o) to speak, talk*
duō *(adj; adv) more; many*
yàobù(rán) *(conj) otherwise*
liáng *(adj) cool*

Grammar

1 *Don't!* bié

The negative imperative is formed by putting *bié* in front of the verb or adjective acting as a verb:

Bié kèqi! *'Don't stand on ceremony!'*
Bié shuō huà! *'Don't speak!'*

If *le* is added after the verb or adjective acting as a verb, the command is softened and sounds much less like an order:

Bié hē jiǔ le! *'Now, now, no drinking!'*

2 De *with the complement of degree*

The Chinese character for this *de* (得) is quite different from the *de* (的) in Unit 5, but they are identical in *pinyin* because they are the same sound and are both toneless. The function of this *de* is to indicate what the Chinese call the complement of degree, i.e. it is used with a word indicating manner or degree as in the following pattern:

yòng de hěn hǎo *'to use something (very) well'*

The following table shows the essential workings of the complement of degree (CD).

a	Positive form:	*S V **de** CD* *Tā **yòng de hěn hǎo**.*	He uses it (very) well.
b	Negative form:	*S V **de bu** CD* *Tā **yòng de bù hǎo**.*	He doesn't use it well.
c	Question form with *ma*:	*S V **de** CD **ma**?* *Tā **yòng de hǎo ma**?*	Does he use it well?
d	Question form without *ma*:	*S V **de** CD **bu** CD?* *Tā **yòng de hǎo bu hǎo**?*	
e	Question form using *zěnmeyàng*:	*S V **de zěnmeyàng**?* *Tā **yòng de zěnmeyàng**?*	How does he use it?
f	With an object:	*S V₁ O V₁ **de** CD* *Tā **yòng kuàizi yòng de hěn hǎo**.*	He uses chopsticks well.
g	With an object omitting the first verb:	*S O V **de** CD* *Tā **kuàizi yòng de hěn hǎo**.*	
h	With object as topic:	*O S V **de** CD* *Kuàizi tā **yòng de hěn hǎo**.*	**i** As for chopsticks, he uses them (very) well. **ii** He uses chopsticks (very) well.

Note that:

1 It is the complement of degree and *not* the verb which has things done to it when we use this construction in the negative or question form (see **b–e** in the table).
2 The complement of degree marker *de* must always directly follow its verb. If there is an object then the construction is as in **f** or **g** above.
3 If we wish to emphasize the *object* this may be put before the subject and the first verb is omitted as in **h**. This has the effect of making the object into a kind of topic which the speaker then goes on to talk about (see 2.3).
4 When adjectives such as *hǎo* act as verbs and are standing alone, they are normally preceded in the affirmative by the adverb *hěn* 'very'. Although in these cases *hěn* does not have the full force of the English word 'very' its function is to indicate that the statement is absolute. Without *hěn* some kind of contrast or comparison is implied:

Tā hǎo. *'He is nice'* (implying that someone else isn't).
Tā hěn hǎo. *'He is (very) nice'* is complete in itself and has no such overtones.

The same rule applies when these adjectives are used as complements of degree in the positive form (see **a**, **f**, **g** and **h** above); but not in the negative or question forms (see **b**, **c**, **d** and **e**).

Exercise 6.1
Answer the following questions on the text:

1 *Tāmen jīntiān wǎnshang chī shénme cài?*
2 *Wáng xiānsheng hé (and) Shǐ xiǎojie kuàizi yòng de hǎo bu hǎo?*
3 *Lǐ tàitai zuò cài zuò de zěnmeyàng?*
4 *Shǐ xiǎojie huì bu huì zuò Yīngguó cài?*
5 *Shǐ xiǎojie Zhōngguó cài zuò de zěnmeyàng?*

Exercise 6.2
Make the following statements into sentences using the
complement of degree given in brackets. Give more than one form
where appropriate:

Tā chī fàn (hěn duō) → Tā chī fàn, chī de hěn duō.
→ Tā fàn chī de hěn duō.
→ Fàn tā chī de hěn duō.

1 *Wǒmen xuéxí (hěn shǎo).*
2 *Nǐmen shuō Hànyǔ (búcuò).*
3 *Tā shēnghuó (bù zěnmeyàng).*
4 *Nà ge rén zuò Zhōngguó cài (hěn hǎo).*
5 *Zhè ge péngyou shuō huà (bù duō).*

Exercise 6.3
Turn the following statements into questions (three forms) and then
answer them in the negative:

Nà ge xiǎoháir zuò de hěn hǎo.
→ Nà ge xiǎoháir zuò de hǎo ma?
→ Nà ge xiǎoháir zuò de hǎo bu hǎo?
→ Nà ge xiǎoháir zuò de zěnmeyàng?
Negative → **Nà ge xiǎoháir zuò de bù hǎo.**

1 *Tā shuō Hànyǔ shuō de hěn hǎo.*
2 *Wǒ yí ge péngyou* (my one MW friend = one of my friends)
  hē jiǔ hē de hěn duō.
3 *Shǐ xiǎojie xuéxí de hěn màn* (slow).
4 *Gōngrén* (worker) *jīntiān lái de hěn shǎo.*
5 *Yīngguórén zuò Yīngguó cài, zuò de hěn hǎo.*
6 *Měiguórén zuò Fǎguó cài, zuò de bù hěn hǎo.*

3 Duō/shǎo + *verb*

Duō or *shǎo* before the verb conveys the idea of doing 'more' or
'less' of the verb: *shǎo shuō huà* 'speak less', *duō chī fàn* 'eat
more'. This construction can only be used with full verbs and not
with adjectives used as verbs. (*Shǎo gāo* does not mean 'to be less
tall'. This phrase would be meaningless.)

Insight: learning tip

Go back and revise all the verb-object constructions you met in 4.3 and then practise saying that you are going to do 'more' or 'less' of each of them in turn:

e.g. **duō** chī fàn   **shǎo** chī fàn
     duō zǒu lù   **shǎo** zǒu lù

Once you have gone through the entire list in this way, go back and say which actions you think would be good to do more or less of and which ones not:

duō shuì jiào hǎo, **shǎo** *shuì jiào bù hǎo*
duō kāi chē bù hǎo, etc.

Modesty

When talking to someone else (a second party), the Chinese have a long cultural tradition of denigrating themselves and their achievements but of praising the other party. They will do this both spontaneously and in response to compliments paid. As food is a major topic of conversation for the Chinese, this cultural tendency is often very pronounced when the quality and quantity of a meal are under discussion. Remarks by the host and the hostess that it is only 'a very simple meal' *yí dùn biàn fàn* (*Lit.* one/MW/simple/cooked rice) and 'there are no dishes worth speaking of' *méi shénme cài*, are almost *de rigueur* even though guests know they have gone to enormous trouble and expense to prepare the meal. Good examples of this modesty are Mrs Li's *Wǒ zuò cài, zuò de bù hǎo, qǐng yuánliàng* and Ms Shaw's very Chinese answer to the question as to her own cooking ability: *Huì yìdiǎnr, dànshi jìshù bù gāo*. Of course, it is common practice for the listener to follow up such remarks with a compliment to the speaker as occurs here. Mrs Li's cooking is delicious *Nǐ zuò cài, zuò de hěn hǎo* and Ms Shaw cooks wonderful English food *Tā Yīngguó cài zuò de fēicháng hǎo!*

Exercise 6.4
Translate the following passages into colloquial English:

1 *Wǒ huì zuò cài dànshi zuò de bù hǎo. Wǒ de nǚ péngyou shuō wǒ de jìshù bù gāo. Wǒmen yǒu hěn duō Zhōngguó péngyou, tāmen zuò Zhōngguó cài zuò de búcuò. Tāmen yòng kuàizi yě yòng de hěn hǎo. Nǐ ne?*

2 *Wǒ yí ge péngyou qù Fǎguó* (France) *gōngzuò. Fǎguó cài hěn hǎo chī – tā chī de hěn duō. Xiànzài tā hěn pàng* (fat) *le. Tā tàitai/àiren shuō: 'Nǐ shǎo chī fàn, duō gōngzuò zěnmeyàng?' Wǒ péngyou shuō: 'Shǎo chī fàn hǎo dànshi duō gōngzuò bù hǎo!'*

TESTING YOURSELF

Translate into Chinese:

1 *I myself (zìjǐ) can't cook but my husband cooks marvellously.*

2 *My mother speaks Chinese very well.*

3 *I was born in America but I was brought up in France.*

4 *A friend of mine smokes [far]* too much.*

5 *I'm not much good at making Chinese food.*

6 *Let's eat French food this (today) evening.*

7 *She's not very good at using chopsticks but she cooks really good Chinese food.*

8 *Please forgive me.*

* English words in square brackets should *not* be translated into Chinese.

7

In the house

In this unit you will learn
- *how to describe the appearance of a house and garden in simple terms*
- *how to describe the furniture and appliances in each room*
- *how to describe the most common items in each room*

Typical modern Chinese apartment block, gōngyù(lóu)

1	roof	*wūdǐng*
2	window	*chuānghu*
3	door	*mén*
4	flowers	*huā [duǒ]*
5	communal garden	*huāyuán*
6	tree	*shù [kē]*
7	ground floor	*yīlóu*
8	first floor	*èrlóu*
9	second floor	*sānlóu*
10	third floor	*sìlóu*
11	balcony	*liángtái*
12	house	*fángzi [suǒ, ge]*
13	apartment block	*gōngyù(lóu) [zhuàng]*

Living room, kètīng

1	sofa	*shāfā*		**15**	table lamp	*táidēng*
2	chair	*yǐzi [bǎ]*		**16**	electric light	*diàndēng*
3	window	*chuānghu*		**17**	ashtray	*yānhuīgāng*
4	curtain	*chuānglián*		**18**	radio	*shōuyīnjī*
5	carpet	*dìtǎn [kuài]*		**19**	CD player	*guāngpán*
6	electric	*diànshàn*				*bōfàngjī*
	fan			**20**	DVD player	*shùzìshìpán*
7	picture	*huàr [zhāng]*				*bōfàngjī*
8	bookcase	*shūjià*		**21**	coffee table	*chájī*
9	vase	*huāpíng*				*[zhāng, ge]*
10	dictionary	*zìdiǎn [běn]*		**22**	table	*zhuōzi*
11	novel	*xiǎoshuō [běn]*				*[zhāng]*
12	book	*shū [běn]*		**23**	radiator	*nuǎnqìpiàn*
13	telephone	*diànhuà(jī) [tái]*			(central heating	*nuǎnqì)*
14	digital	*shùmǎ*		**24**	decoder/	*jiěmǎqì*
	television	*diànshì(jī) [tái]*			digibox	

Kitchen, chúfáng

1	sink	*xǐwǎnchí, chízi*	11	switch	*kāiguān*
2	tap	*lóngtou*	12	pail, bucket	*shuǐtǒng*
3	bottle	*píngzi*	13	washing machine	*xǐyījī [tái]*
4	Thermos flask	*rèshuǐpíng*	14	freezer	*bīngguì*
5	wine bottle	*jiǔpíng*	15	refrigerator	*bīngxiāng*
6	ironing board	*tàngyījià*	16	microwave oven	*wēibōlú*
7	iron	*yùndǒu*	17	hob	*guōjià*
8	plug	*chātóu*	18	oven	*kǎoxiāng*
9	socket	*chāzuò*	19	grill	*kǎojià*
10	electric cable	*diànxiàn [gēn]*	20	dishwasher	*xǐwǎnjī [tái]*

Dining room, fàntīng

1	table	*zhuōzi* [*zhāng*]	**11**	soya sauce	*jiàngyóu*
2	chair	*yǐzi* [*bǎ*]	**12**	vinegar	*cù*
3	knife	*dāozi* [*bǎ*]	**13**	coffee filter machine	*kāfēihú*
4	fork	*chāzi* [*bǎ*]	**14**	teapot	*cháhú*
5	spoon	*sháozi*	**15**	milk	*niúnǎi*
6	chopsticks	*kuàizi*	**16**	sugar	*táng*
7	water glass	*bōlibēi*	**17**	Indian tea	*hóngchá*
8	wineglass	*jiǔbēi*	**18**	Chinese tea	*lǜchá*
9	salt	*yán*	**19**	jasmine tea	*huāchá*
10	pepper	*hújiāo*			

Bedroom, wòshì

1	double bed	*shuāngrén-chuáng* [*zhāng*]
	(single bed	*dānrén-chuáng*)
2	duvet, quilt	*bèizi* [*chuáng*]
3	sheet	*chuángdān*
4	pillow	*zhěntou*
5	pillow case	*zhěntào*
6	wardrobe	*yīguì*
7	mirror	*jìngzi* [*kuài*]
8	alarm clock	*nàozhōng*
9	mattress	*chuángdiàn*
10	blanket	*tǎnzi* [*zhāng*]
11	brush or comb	*shūzi* [*bǎ*]
12	chest of drawers	*wǔdǒuchú/wǔdǒuguì*
13	picture	*huàr* [*zhāng*]
14	table lamp	*táidēng*
15	stairs, staircase	*lóutī*
16	air-conditioning unit	*kōngtiáo*

Study, shūfáng

1	window	*chuānghu*
2	blind	*bǎiyèchuāng*
3	desk	*shūzhuō*
4	chair	*bàngōngyǐ*
5	PC (computer)	*diànnǎo*
6	printer	*dǎyìnjī [tái]*
7	laptop	*bǐjìběn diànnǎo*
8	newspaper	*bàozhǐ [zhāng]*
9	magazine	*zázhì [běn]*
10	mobile phone / BlackBerry	*shǒujī/zhǎng shàng diànnǎo*
11	land-line telephone	*diànhuà(jī) [tái]*
12	dictionary	*zìdiǎn [běn]*
13	novels	*xiǎoshuō [běn]*
14	poetry books	*shīgē*

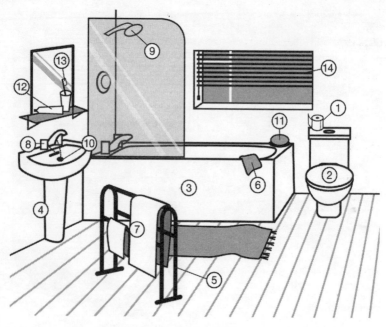

Bathroom, xǐzǎojiān *or* yùshì

1	toilet paper	*wèishēngzhǐ* [*juǎn*]
2	toilet	*cèsuǒ*
3	bath	*xǐzǎopén/yùpén*
4	washbasin	*xǐliǎnpén*
5	towel rail	*máojīnjià*
6	face flannel	*miànjīn/máojīn* [*kuài*]
7	bath towel	*yùjīn/dà máojīn* [*kuài*]
8	tap	*lóngtou*
9	shower	*línyù*
10	plug	*sāizi*
11	toilet soap	*xiāngzào* [*kuài*]
12	toothpaste	*yágāo* [*tǒng*]
13	toothbrush	*yáshuā* [*bǎ*]
14	blind	*bǎiyèchuāng*

TESTING YOURSELF

In which room(s) (in this unit) are these objects to be found? Use the Chinese word for the room in each case and also the measure for the object if you know it, e.g. *xiāngzào* (toilet soap) → *xǐzǎojiān* (bathroom); MW *kuài*.

1 *chuáng*

2 *dìtǎn*

3 *wēibōlú*

4 *diànnǎo*

5 *cèsuǒ*

6 *shāfā*

7 *bīngxiāng*

8 *línyù*

9 *chájī*

10 *jìngzi*

11 *guāngpán bōfàngjī*

12 *wèishēngzhǐ*

13 *bǐjìběn diànnǎo*

14 *zhěntou*

15 *xǐyījī*

16 *yùjīn*

17 *shùmǎ diànshì(jī)*	**24** *bèizi*
18 *yīguì*	**25** *bīngguì*
19 *chuānglián*	**26** *nuǎnqìpiàn*
20 *yáshuā*	**27** *kōngtiáo*
21 *guōjià*	**28** *shūjià*
22 *nàozhōng*	**29** *chuānghu*
23 *shǒujī*	**30** *bǎiyèchuāng*

8

At the Lis' (iii)

In this unit you will learn
- *how to describe the rooms in an apartment/house*
- *how to thank your hosts for their hospitality and to understand their responses*
- *how to ask questions in the form of alternatives*
- *how to express direction towards or away from the speaker*
- *about auxiliary verbs*

◆) **CD 1, tr 32–34**

Mr King and Ms Shaw are just finishing their meal at the Lis'.

Lǐ	Bié kèqi, zài duō chī yìdiǎn(r).	*Don't stand on ceremony, go on, eat a bit more.*
Wáng	Chī bǎo le, cài dōu hěn hǎochī.	*I've had enough, it was delicious.*
Lǐ (t)	Nǐmen xiǎng hē kāfēi háishi hē chá?	*Would you like tea or coffee?*
Wáng	Wǒ suíbiàn.	*I'm easy.*
Shǐ	Hē chá ba.	*Let's have tea.*
[Hē wán le chá.]		[*After having tea.*]
Lǐ (t)	Shǐ xiǎojie, kànyikàn wǒmen de xiǎo fángzi ba?	*Would you like to have a look round our little house, Ms Shaw?*

Shǐ	Hǎo, xièxie nín. Yǒngshòu, nǐ péi Lǐ xiānsheng tán huà ba.	*Yes, please. Yongshou, you chat to Mr Li.*
Lǐ (t)	Zhè shì chúfáng, dìfang hěn xiǎo, suǒyǐ bīngxiāng、xǐyījī yě dōu bú dà.	*This is the kitchen, it's very small so the fridge and the washing machine are not very big either.*
	Wǒmen zhǐ yǒu sì ge fángjiān, wǒ hé lǎo Lǐ yì jiān, érzi yì jiān, nǚ'ér yì jiān, hái yǒu kètīng.	*We only have four rooms, one for myself and old Li, one for our son, one for our daughter and then there's the living room.*
Shǐ	Háizimen yǒu zìjǐ de fángjiān bú cuò, dú shū hěn ānjìng. Nǐmen de kètīng bùzhì de hěn piàoliang. Píngmiàn diànshì yě hěn hǎo kàn. Shì shùmǎ de ma?	*It's great if children have their own room, it's quiet for studying. Your living-room is beautifully furnished. The flat screen TV is also very nice. Is it digital?*
Lǐ (t)	Duì, shì shùmǎ de. Shùmǎ de bǐjiào qīngchu.	*Yes, it is digital. Digital images are clearer.*
Shǐ	À, shíjiān bù zǎo le, wǒmen (yīng)gāi huí qu le.	*Ah, it's getting late, we ought to be getting back.*
Wáng	Shíjiān guò de zhēn kuài. Lǐ xiānsheng, Lǐ taitai, wǒmen děi zǒu le, xièxie nǐmen de rèqíng zhāodài.	*The time's flown. Mr and Mrs Li, we must be on our way, thank you for your marvellous hospitality.*
	Wǒmen wánr de fēicháng gāoxìng, gěi nǐmen tiān le bù shǎo máfan.	*We've had a wonderful time and caused you no end of trouble.*
Lǐ	Méi shénme, huānyíng nǐmen zài lái wánr.	*Not at all, feel free to come again.*

Wáng	Yídìng lái. Xièxie nǐmen.	*Thank you, we*
Wáng/	Zàijiàn.	*certainly will.*
Shǐ		*Goodbye.*
Lǐ	Màn zǒu, màn zǒu.	*Mind how you go.*

From Unit 8 onwards, the appropriate measure word (MW) is placed in square brackets after its noun unless it is *ge*, in which case it is omitted. Some nouns have two measure words, *ge* and a more formal one. Where this is so, both have been indicated.

zài *(adv) again*
chī-bǎo *(RV) to eat one's fill*
hǎochī *(adj) tasty, delicious*
háishi *or (used in questions)*
-wán *(RVE) to finish verb-ing*
kàn *(v) to look; to see; to watch; to read*
xiǎo *(adj) small*
fángzi *(n)* **[suǒ, ge]** *house*
péi *(v) to accompany*
tán huà *(v-o, n) to chat; conversation*
chúfáng *(n)* **[jiān, ge]** *kitchen*
dìfang *(n) place*
suǒyǐ *(conj) therefore*
bīngxiāng *(n) refrigerator*
xǐyījī *(n)* **[tái]** *washing machine*
zhǐ *(adv) only*
fángjiān *(n) room*
hé *(conj) and*
lǎo *(adj) old*
jiān *(MW) for room*
érzi *(n) son*
nǚ'ér *(n) daughter*
hái *(adv) still, in addition*
kètīng *(n) living room, lounge*
háizi *(n) child*
kěyǐ *(aux v) can, may*

QUICK VOCAB

dú shū *(v-o)* to study
ānjìng *(adj)* quiet
bùzhì *(v)* to decorate
piàoliang *(adj)* beautiful
píngmiàn *(n)* flat screen
diànshì (jī) *(n)* **[tái]** television
shùmǎ *(adj)* digital
bǐjiào *(adv)* relatively
qīngchu *(adj; RVE)* clear; clearly
shíjiān *(n)* time
bù . . . le not . . . any more
zǎo *(adj)* early
(yīng)gāi *(aux v)* ought, should
huí *(v)* to return
guò *(v)* to pass, to cross
kuài *(adj)* quick, fast
děi *(aux v)* must, need
zǒu *(v)* to leave, to walk, to go
rèqíng *(adj)* warm hearted, enthusiastic
zhāodài *(n, v)* hospitality, to entertain
tiān *(v)* to add, increase
máfan *(n/v, adj)* trouble, troublesome
méi (yǒu) shénme it's nothing
huānyíng *(v)* to welcome
zàijiàn goodbye
màn *(adj)* slow

Grammar

1 *Resultative verbs (I)*

Not all compound (two syllable) verbs are resultative, e.g. *rènshi*, *jièshào* and *xuéxí* are not. At this stage the easiest way to recognize resultative verbs is by their endings. We have three examples of common resultative verb endings (or complements of result) in this unit, viz. *-bǎo*, *-wán* and *-qù*. *Chī bǎo* means to 'eat one's fill' where *chī* is the verb and *bǎo* is the resultative verb ending expressing satisfaction of appetite. *Bǎo* can only be used with *chī* in this way but it can stand on its own, meaning 'to be full'.

Wǒ bǎo le 'I'm full' (change of state *le*). *Hē wán* means 'to finish drinking' where *hē* is the verb and *wán* is the resultative verb ending expressing completion. Unlike -*bǎo*, -*wán* may be found with many different verbs, e.g. *kàn, zuò, shuō, chī*.

Resultative verbs (II): Simple directional endings

. . .-*qù* is a directional ending indicating direction *away* from the speaker or point of reference and is used with verbs of motion and transference of something or somebody from one place to another. Thus *huí qu* means to go back: *Wǒmen gāi huí qu le* 'We ought to be going back' (change of state *le*), i.e. previously we didn't have to go back, now we do

. . .-*lái* is used in exactly the same way but to indicate direction *towards* the speaker or point of reference. *Huí lai* would mean 'to come back', the point of reference being where the speaker is when using it. For other common resultative verb endings of both types, see the relevant sections in Unit 13. Note that *lái* and *qù* are normally toneless when used as simple directional endings.

Exercise 8.1
Insert *lái* or *qù* in the following sentences depending on the position of 'the speaker', which is given in brackets:
Zhào xiānsheng huí dàxué ____ le. *(We all stayed in town.)*
→ **Zhào xiānsheng huí dàxué qù le.**

1 *Dèng xiǎojie yào huí Zhōngguó ____.* (point of reference is where she is now, i.e. *Yīngguó*)
2 *Érzi jìn* (enter) *kètīng ____ le.* (everybody is in the lounge)
3 *Tā jìn wòshì ____ le.* (everybody is in the lounge)
4 *Nǐmen yīnggāi huí jiā ____.* (parents to children on the phone)
5 *Wǒ xiǎng huí Yīngguó ____.* (speaker is in China)

2 Háishi *in questions*

Háishi 'or' is placed between two statements thereby making them alternatives from which the listener must choose *one*: *Nǐmen xiǎng hē kāfēi **háishi** hē chá?* 'Would you like tea or coffee?'

If the subject or object in both halves is the same it need not be repeated (this holds true for any two clauses, not just ones using *háishi*, and is a feature of Chinese), but there must be a *verb* in both halves even if it is the same verb: *Nǐ mǎi* (buy) *bīngxiāng **háishi** tā mǎi?* 'Are you buying the fridge or is he?'

Note in another example from the text, *Diànshì shì shùmǎ de **háishi** lǎoshì* ('old fashioned' i.e. analogue) *de?*, the *shì* in *háishi* is allowed to stand for the verb *shì* in the second half – this is the only exception to the rule. Try saying *háishi shì* and you'll understand why.

Exercise 8.2
Make the two statements into one question using *háishi*:
Nǐmen kàn diànshì. Nǐmen kàn shū (v-o 'read'). → **Nǐmen kàn diànshì háishi kàn shū?**

1 *Tāmen xǐhuan chī fàn.*
   Tāmen xǐhuan shuō huà.
2 *Dèng tàitai yào mǎi* (buy) *bīngxiāng.*
   Dèng tàitai yào mǎi xǐyījī.
3 *Zhōu xiānsheng qù Fǎguó.*
   Lǐ xiānsheng qù Fǎguó.
4 *Zhāng xiānsheng huí Měiguó.*
   Shǐ xiǎojie huí Měiguó.
5 *Shíjiān guò de kuài.*
   Shíjiān guò de màn.
6 *Wǒ péngyou de fángzi méi yǒu chúfáng.*
   Wǒ péngyou de fángzi méi yǒu yùshì.
7 *Nǐ xuéxí Hànyǔ.*
   Nǐ xuéxí dìlǐ (geography).
8 *Tāmen jiā yǒu sì ge wòshì.*
   Tāmen jiā yǒu sān ge wòshì.

3 Reduplication of verbs

In much the same way as *yíxià* in 5.2, repeating the verb has
the effect of softening the suggestion, question or statement.
Monosyllabic verbs often have *yi* inserted between the two parts
when they are repeated, e.g. *kànyikàn* or *tányitán*. Disyllabic
verbs cannot be treated in this way, so *jièshàoyijièshào* would be
incorrect. Again, like *yíxià*, repeating the verb can also convey the
meaning of 'having a little go' at doing the action of the verb in
both the sense of a trial and in doing something fairly quickly.
It can also indicate repetition of the action with verbs such as
fùxí 'to revise'.

4 Pluralizer suffix -men

We have already met *-men* used after pronouns in the singular
to make them plural, *wǒ* becomes *wǒmen*, etc. Where it is
deemed necessary to avoid ambiguity, it can also be used
after nouns indicating people to show that these are plural,
although it is used quite sparingly and often only under certain
conditions.

The suffix *-men* is commonly used when addressing people in
a speech: *Péngyoumen!* 'Friends', *Tóngzhìmen!* 'Comrades' (This
could be thought of as the 'Friends, Romans, Countrymen' use of
-men!) or when making a statement about people in general as in
the text: *Háizimen yǒu zìjǐ de fángjiān . . .*, but is not used when
the people are specified in any way: *Chúfáng lǐ de háizi* 'The
children in the kitchen' (and not *Chúfang lǐ de háizimen*). It is
probably best avoided unless you are sure of your ground.

5 Adjectives

Monosyllabic adjectives generally occur directly before the noun
they refer to but as soon as they are modified by *hěn*, *fēicháng*, etc.,
the marker *de* (see 5.4) must be inserted between the adjective and
its noun: *Hǎo rén* 'Good person/people' but **Hěn** *hǎo* **de** *rén* 'Very
good person/people'.

6 Hé

Hé 'and' cannot be used nearly as frequently as 'and' in English. It can only be used to join two noun constructions or pronouns, but *not* to join two verbs or two verbal clauses: *Wǒ hé Lǐ xiānsheng* 'Mr Li and I' (in Chinese *wǒ* normally comes first); *Zhōngguórén hé Fǎguórén dōu xǐhuan chī fàn* 'The Chinese and the French both enjoy eating.'

7 Lǎo *and* xiǎo

Instead of using the Chinese equivalent of Christian or given names when addressing colleagues or people in your peer group on an informal basis, *lǎo* or *xiǎo* is often put before the surname depending on whether the person in question is older or younger than you. Thus, an older colleague with the surname *Zhāng* would become *lǎo Zhāng*, whereas a younger colleague called *Dīng* would be *xiǎo Dīng*. There is no hard and fast rule about this, however, and some people in the same peer group who become *xiǎo* or *lǎo* will still be *xiǎo* or *lǎo* even in their 50s, 60s and beyond within that peer group. The choice of which one to use largely depends on your own judgement, but normal practice is to follow the form of address used by your colleagues who have been there longer. It also conveys a feeling of intimacy: note that *Lǐ tàitai* refers to her husband as *lǎo Lǐ*. It is not generally used when addressing foreigners.

8 *The nominalizer* de

a Following on from 5.4 we see that *de* placed after a pronoun or adjective makes it into a noun:

Diànshì shì shùmǎ de háishi lǎoshì de? *'Is it (a) digital (TV) or (an) old-fashioned (one)?'*
Nán de sì suì. *'The boy (Lit. the male one) is 4.'*
Xiǎoháir shi tā de. *'The child is his/hers.'*

Thus *wǒ de* on its own means 'mine', *nǐ de* 'yours', etc.

b Where an adjective and a noun form one idea, *de* is omitted:

rèqíng zhāodài *'kind hospitality'*
Fǎwén zázhì *'French magazines'*

9 Bù *verb* le

The negated form of the change of state *le* (see 5.9) is *bù*
verb . . . *le*, which conveys the meaning that the subject (if there is
one) no longer does the action of the verb or that the situation as
stated by the verb is no longer the case: *Shíjiān bù zǎo le* (*Lit.* time
not early any more) 'It's getting late.' *Wǒ bù hē jiǔ le* (*Lit.* I not
drink wine any more) 'I've given up drinking.'

This is the only case in which *bù* can occur with *le*. Note that if the
verb is *yǒu* then *méi* has to be used instead of *bù*: *Wǒ méi yǒu
diànshì le* 'I no longer have a TV.'

10 Auxiliary verbs

There are several examples of auxiliary verbs in the text, viz.
yuànyì, kěyǐ, yào, gāi and *děi*. (We have already met *xǐhuan* and
xiǎng in previous units.) These occur *before* action verbs or verbal
expressions and cannot take verbal endings or verbal suffixes.
Compare these six examples:

Wǒ xiǎng hē kāfēi *'I'd like some coffee'* (now or in the near future).
Wǒ xǐhuan hē kāfēi *'I like (drinking) coffee'* (permanent state of
    mind).
Wǒ yào hē kāfēi *'I want some coffee'* (now or in the near future,
    expressing a stronger desire than xiAng).
Wǒ (yīng)gāi hē kāfēi *'I ought to drink coffee'* (it is less fattening,
    etc.).
Wǒ děi hē kāfēi *'I must drink coffee'* (necessity).
Wǒ kěyǐ hē kāfēi *'I can drink coffee'* (capability or permission).

For further information on auxiliary verbs, see the relevant sections
in Unit 13.

Insight: learning tip

In order to practise these auxiliary verbs, try putting them
into as many sentences as you can, using as much of the
vocabulary as you can remember from Units 1–8. Try
and change the pronoun/subject at the beginning of the
sentence too:

Nǐ děi xuéxí Hànyǔ.
Tāmen xiǎng hē chá.
Wǒmen xǐhuan chī Zhōngguó cài.

11 Duō *and* shǎo + *noun*

Duō and *shǎo* are exceptions to the rule that monosyllabic
adjectives directly precede their nouns or that when modified
they must take *de*. They cannot stand on their own before the
noun but occur with *hěn* and without *de*. In these two cases, the
hěn tends to be very weak: *Hěn duō rén* 'many people'.

Shǎo is more likely to occur with *bù* with the meaning of 'quite a
lot of' or 'quite a few': *Bù shǎo máfan* 'quite a lot of trouble'.

It is important to note, however, that Chinese usage differs from
the English in that a sentence such as 'many people go/want' is
much more likely to be expressed as *qù de rén hěn duō* rather than
hěn duō rén qù, although both are grammatically correct.

12 *Punctuation*

In a list, even if it only consists of two items, e.g. *bīngxiāng、
xǐyījī*, the Chinese use a form of pause mark or *dùnhào* (、)
between the items and not a comma. A comma is reserved for
longer pauses.

Polite talk

The Chinese have a whole series of expressions for almost every social occasion ranging from *Chī bǎo le ma?* 'Have you eaten your fill?' or *Chī fàn le ma?* 'Have you eaten?' to *Huí lai le ma?* 'Have you come back?' You might only have gone out to pump up your bicycle tyres but are still asked if you are back when you return five minutes later! Such expressions serve as a means of phatic communion between individuals, giving a feeling of community at very little cost to the individuals themselves. Mr King's little speech as he and Ms Shaw are about to leave contains several typical examples of this 'polite talk', which we would consider as clichés but which appear very natural to the Chinese. *Gěi nǐmen tiān le bù shǎo máfan* is a wonderful example of this. *Màn* 'slow' features quite widely in polite talk with such exhortations as *Nǐmen mànmānr chī* 'Take your time (over eating)' if somebody has finished eating and he or the host does not wish the others to feel they have to follow suit. *Nǐmen mànmānr zuò ba* 'Sit slowly' you are told when the person you have come to see is nowhere to be seen and you are in for a long wait! When taking leave of somebody, the standard parting remark is 'go slowly' (usually repeated) *Màn zǒu, màn zǒu*. (If you are on your bicycle [or horse] it becomes *Màn qí, màn qí* 'Ride (astride) slowly'!)

Exercise 8.3

Fill in the blanks with the number(s) supplied in the brackets:

Zhāng xiānsheng yǒu _____ ge nǚháir (3) → **Zhāng xiānsheng yǒu sān ge nǚháir.**

1 *Shǐ xiǎojie yǒu* _____ *ge gēge* (older brother) *hé* _____ *ge mèimei* (younger sister). (2, 1)
2 *Wǒ dìdi* (younger brother) _____ *suì.* (27)
3 *Lǎo xiānsheng* _____ *suì, shēntǐ* (health) *hěn hǎo.* (80)
4 _____ *ge péngyou zài Zhōngguó gōngzuò.* (99)
5 *Nà ge yīshēng* (doctor) *hē* _____ *bēi jiǔ hé* _____ *bēi kāfēi.* (6, 2)

Exercise 8.4

Correct the word order in the following sentences: *Nǐ kàn diànshì zài zhèr → Nǐ zài zhèr kàn diànshì.*

1 *Dìfang xiǎo, bīngxiāng、xǐyījī dōu yě bù dà.*
2 *Xiǎoháir hē niúnǎi (milk) zài chúfáng xiànzài.*
3 *Tā yǒu zìjǐ de fángjiān, hěn ānjìng dú shū.*
4 *Wǒ tiān le hěn duō máfan gěi nǐmen.*
5 *Lǐ lǎoshī (teacher) huí qu dàxué le.*
6 *Rén de kètīng lǐ dōu shì nánde.*

Exercise 8.5

Translate into colloquial English:

Jīntiān wǎnshang xiǎoháir qù wǒ māma nàr (my mum's place). Dìfang hěn dà, bīngxiāng、xǐyījī tā dōu yǒu. Háizi xǐhuan wánr, wǒ māma yě xǐhuan dài (to take) tāmen qù kàn diànyǐng (film) dànshi tā yòu méi yǒu* qián (money) yòu* méi yǒu shíjiān; suǒyǐ ràng (let) tāmen zài dà huāyuán (garden) lǐ wánr. Wánr wán le tāmen kěyǐ zuò zài chúfáng lǐ tán huà、chī fàn. Chī wán fàn tāmen kěyǐ kàn diànshì.

***yòu . . . yòu . . .** (both . . . and . . .)

TESTING YOURSELF

Translate into Chinese:

1 *My friend and I (8.6) would like to go to America.*

2 *Where is he watching TV? In the bedroom or in the sitting room? (leave out lǐ)*

3 *Father (Fùqīn) says he doesn't recognize you any more.*

4 *(When) he got old, (he) (jiù) gave up drinking. (use jiù in the second clause and change of state le in both clauses)*

5 *Would you like to drink tea or coffee?*

6 *Time has flown; we ought to be going home.*

7 *Your living room is decorated beautifully.*

8 *Thank you for your wonderful hospitality. I'll certainly come again.*

9

Eating out

In this unit you will learn
* *how to say if you have ever done something*
* *how to say where places and things are*
* *how to talk about food and restaurants*
* *about the conjunctions* before, when *and* after
* *how to compare and contrast*
* *how to talk about your family*

◄ CD 1, tr 35–37

A Chinese couple (Zhāng Dàmíng and Chén Yīng), both only children (**dúshēngzǐnǚ**), are sitting in a well-known Beijing roast duck (**kǎoyā**) restaurant waiting for the two foreigners, Mr King (Wáng Yǒngshòu) and his girlfriend (Shǐ Àilǐ), whom they have invited for dinner. Zhang Daming's parents are looking after their two grandchildren for the evening. Mr King and Ms Shaw walk into the restaurant (**zǒu jìn fàndiàn lái**) and look around for them (**zhǎo**).

Yí duì Zhōngguó fūfù, Zhāng Dàmíng hé Chén Yīng, dōu shì dúshēngzǐnǚ. Tāmen zuò zài yì jiā zhùmíng de Běijīng kǎoyā diàn děngzhe tāmen qǐng lái chī fàn de (liǎng ge wàiguórén) Wáng Yǒngshòu hé tā de nǚ péngyou Shǐ Àilǐ. Jīntiān wǎnshang, Zhāng Dàmíng de fùmǔ (zài jiā) kānzhe tāmen de sūnzi hé sūnnǚ. (Zhè shí), Wáng xiānsheng hé Shǐ xiǎojie zǒu jìn fàndiàn zhǎo tāmen lái.

Wáng	Nǐmen yǐjing lái le. Wǒ yǐqián méi chī-guo kǎoyā, wǒ zǎo jiù xiǎng chī le.	*Oh, there you are. I've not eaten roast duck before. I am really looking forward to it.*
Shǐ	Wǒ yě yíyàng.	*I am too.*
Zhāng	Běijīng yǒu bù shǎo kǎoyā diàn, měi ge dōu yǒu tāmen de tèsè. Zhèi jiā yǒu diǎnr guì, kěshì měi ge rén dōu shuō zhèr de kǎoyā zuì hǎochī.	*There are quite a few roast duck restaurants in Beijing and each one has its good points and bad points. This one is a bit expensive but everyone says its roast duck is the best.*
Chén	Shì a. Wǒ lái zhè jiā (kǎoyā) diàn yǐqián, cháng qù zài Wángfǔjǐng de nà/nèi jiā, xiànzài wǒ zǒng lái zhèi jiā.	*That's right. Before I came to this restaurant I used to go to the one on Wangfujing but now I always come here.*
Zhāng	Wǒ fùmǔ yě dōu xǐhuān lái zhèi jiā chī kǎoyā. Tāmen tuìxiū yǐhòu, juédìng yào hǎohǎo xiǎngshòu xiǎngshòu shēnghuó.	*My parents always come here, too. After they both retired, they decided they should really enjoy themselves.*
Chén	Zhè shì bu shì yě bāokuò gěi wǒmen kān háizi?	*Does that include babysitting for us?!*
Shǐ	Nǐmen de háizi duō dà le? Wáng Yǒngshòu shuō nǐmen yǒu liǎng ge háizi.	*Oh, how old are your children? Wang Yongshou tells me you have two.*
Zhāng	Shì a. (Wǒmen de) érzi bǐ tā mèimei dà liǎng suì bàn, kěshi nǚ'ér bǐ tā gēge gāo duō le. Wǒmen yě bù zhīdào zhè shì zěnme yì huí shì. Tāmen dōu hěn cōngming, kěshi wǒ juéde nǚ'ér bǐ érzi gèng cōngming.	*That's right. Our son is two and a half years older than his sister but our daughter is already much taller than he is – we don't know why. They are both clever children but I think she is even cleverer than he is.*

Shǐ	Xīwàng (yǒu yì tiān) néng jiànjian tāmen.	*I hope I can meet them one day.*
[Kǎoyā lái le.]		*[The roast duck arrives.]*
	Wà, wǒ zuì xǐhuan chī yǒu Zhōngguó tèsè de fàncài, xiàng kǎoyā、shuǐjiǎo hé bāozi, děngdeng, fēicháng hǎochī, yě bǐ Màidāngláo, Kěndéjī piányi duō le, wèishénme yào chī nà zhǒng kuàicān ne?	*Oh, I do love eating Chinese specialities such as roast duck, (boiled) dumplings and steamed buns – they're so tasty and they're much cheaper than McDonald's or Kentucky Fried Chicken. Why would anyone want to eat fast food like that?*
Chén	Rénmen juéde chī Màidāngláo、Kěndéjī nà zhǒng kuàicān shímáo, kěshi nàxiē kuàicān yòu guì yòu méi yǒu shénme yíngyǎng.	*People think it's 'with it' to eat the sort of food you get at McDonald's or Kentucky Fried Chicken but their food is both expensive and not very nutritious.*
Wáng	Mmm, zhèi kǎoyā zhēn hǎochī. Xièxie nǐmen qǐng wǒmen lái zhèr chī fàn. Yǐhòu wǒmen qǐng nǐmen chī yǒu Yīngguó tèsè de fàncài.	*Mmmm, this roast duck is really delicious. Thank you so much for inviting us here. Another time (later on) we'll invite you to eat some British/English specialities.*
Shǐ	Xīwàng nǐmen huì xǐhuān.	*We hope you will like them.*

94

yǐjīng *(adv) already*
-guo *verbal suffix (see 9.1)*
kǎoyā *(n) roast duck*
zǎo jiù . . . le *for a long time now*
yíyàng *alike, the same*
kǎoyā diàn *(n) roast duck restaurant*
měi *(p/adj) each, every*
tèsè *(n) characteristic, special feature*
guì *(adj) expensive*
kěshì *(conj) but*
cháng (cháng) *(adv) often*
xiànzài *(TW) now, at present*
zǒng(shi) *(adv) always*
fùmǔ *(n) parents*
tuìxiū *(v) to retire*
yǐhòu *(conj; adv) after; afterwards*
juédìng *(v) to decide*
xiǎngshòu *(v; n) to enjoy rights, etc.; treat*
bāokuò *(v) to include*
kān háizi *(v-o) to babysit*
dà *(adj) big, old, grown up (of age)*
bǐ *(prep) compared with*
mèimei *(n) younger sister*
bàn *(num) half*
gēge *(n) elder brother*
zhīdao *(v) to know (a fact)*
zhè shì zěnme yì huí shì *why this happens, how it comes about*
cōngming *(adj) clever, intelligent*
juéde *(v) to feel*
gèng *(adv) even more, still more*
xīwàng *(v; n) to hope; hope*
néng *(aux v) to be able to, can*
jiàn *(v) to see; to meet*
wà *(interj) wow (exclamation)*
fàncài *(n) food*
xiàng *(v) to resemble; like; such as*
shuǐjiǎo *(n) boiled dumpling*

QUICK VOCAB

bāozi (n) steamed bun
děng (děng) (n) and so on, etc.
Màidānglāo (N) McDonald's
Kěndéjī (N) Kentucky Fried Chicken
piányi (adj) cheap
wèi shénme (conj) why
zhǒng (MW) sort, kind
kuàicān (n) fast food
shímáo (adj) fashionable
nà xiē those
yòu . . . yòu both . . . and . . . (see 9.15)
yǒu yíngyǎng (v-o) to be nutritious

Grammar

1 *Verbal suffix -zhe*

The verbal suffix *-zhe* is placed **after** the verb to show that the action of the verb goes on for some time. It may sometimes be thought of as indicating a continuous state: *Chuānghu guānzhe.* 'The window is shut'. *Mén kāi*zhe.* 'The door is open'. *-zhe* often appears with verbs such as *zuò* 'to sit', *zhàn* 'to stand' and *děng* 'to wait' (as in the dialogue) which are often prolonged. In such cases the verb *zhe* is often translated by a continuous tense in English, 'to be -ing':

Tā zuòzhe. 'He is/was sitting'.

The negative is made by putting *méi (yǒu)* in front of the verb with *-zhe*: *Mén méi kāi*zhe.* 'The door isn't/wasn't open (has not remained open)'.

The question form is made by adding *ma* to the statement or by adding *méi yǒu* after it, the implication being that the speaker wishes the state of affairs indicated in his question to continue:

Nuǎnqì kāi*zhe ma? 'Is the central heating on?'
Diànshì kāi*zhe méi you? 'Is the television on?'

* *kāi* 'to open' (of doors, windows); 'to turn on' (of lights, radio, TV and so on)

Note that:

1 An adverbial phrase of manner is often formed with a verb *zhe* (object) which then precedes the main verb: *Tā xiàozhe shuō* (Lit. he/laughing/say) 'He says/said with a smile/laugh'. *Tā qízhe zìxíngchē qù gōngyuán wán(r)* (*Lit.* She/riding astride/ self-propelling machine/go/park/have fun) 'She's going/gone on her bicycle to the part to enjoy herself'.

2 The continuation of an action generally implies that the action is also in progress so that *-zhe* is often to be found together with *zhèngzài, zhèng, zài* or *ne* (see 10.2). *Xiàozhǎng lái de shíhou, wǒ zhèng dǎzhe diànhuà ne* (*Lit.* School head/come/ when/I/in the middle of/hitting/electric speech/) 'I was on the phone when the headmaster/mistress came'.

2 Verbal suffix -guo

In Unit 8, we met *guò* as a verb meaning 'to pass' or 'to cross'. Put *after* the verb it indicates that something happened in the indefinite past, i.e. it emphasizes a past experience and not completion as with verb + *le* (see 3.4):

Wǒ chīguo Yìndù fàn 'I've eaten Indian food' (at some time or other). The negative is formed by putting *méi* before the verb but the *-guo* is retained as there is no idea of completion or non-completion as with the verbal suffix *-le*:

Wǒ méi qùguo hěn duō guójiā. 'I haven't visited many countries' (general statement about past experience).

Wǒ méi qù hěn duō guójiā. 'I didn't visit many countries' (on one specific occasion, e.g. last year). Adverbs such as *yǐqián, cónglái* 'hitherto' often appear before the negated verb to emphasize the idea of having never done the action of the verb:

Wǒ *cónglái méi* ch*ī*guo Yìdàlì *fàn* 'I've never eaten Italian food.' The question form is made by adding *ma* to the statement or by adding *méi you* after it:

Nín yǐqián jiànguo Zhōngwén* càidān (menu) **ma?**
Nín yǐqián jiànguo Zhōngwén càidān méi you?
'*Have you ever seen a Chinese menu before?*' (Note the *pinyin* convention always shows *guo* attached to the verb.)

[* *Zhōngwén* refers to the Chinese language (usually written form).]

3 *X* yǒu *Y*

Besides meaning 'to have' *yǒu* also means 'there is, there are'. The construction is normally word or phrase indicating position + *yǒu* + noun or nominal phrase, i.e. (*zài*) X *yǒu* Y 'there is/are Y at X':

Lúndūn yǒu bù shǎo gōngyuán. (*Lit.* London has not few public enclosures) '*There are quite a few parks in London.*'

Similarly from the text:

Běijīng yǒu bù shǎo kǎoyā diàn. (*Lit.* Beijing has not a few roast duck restaurants) '*There are quite a few roast duck restaurants in Beijing.*'

Zài 'at, in' is often omitted when the adverbial word or phrase of place occurs at the beginning of a clause or sentence. Of course, the sentence above could also be translated as 'London has quite a few parks', the omission of *zài* making such an interpretation possible but it is important to understand how such sentences function grammatically otherwise it is easy to come unstuck when more precision is required as in the following example:

Wòshì lǐ yǒu yì zhāng shuāngrénchuáng hé yí ge yīguì.
(*Lit.* Bedroom inside/have/1/MW/pair people bed/and/1/MW/
wardrobe . . .). In this case, *yǒu* has to be translated by 'there is'
and not by 'have'.

4 Měi . . . (dōu)

One of the ways of expressing 'each, every' in Chinese is by using
the pronoun *měi*. There is usually a measure word between *měi*
and its noun but this may be omitted when the noun is *rén*. *Tiān*
'day' and *nián* 'year' act as measure words as well as nouns and
therefore directly follow *měi*. The sentence with *měi* is often
reinforced by the adverb *dōu* before the verb. In such cases,
dōu refers **back** to *měi* + noun, which may or may not be the
subject of the sentence:

měi zhāng zhuōzi *'every table'*
měi ge rén or **měi rén** *'everybody'*
měi tiān *'every day'*
měi bǎ yǐzi dōu hěn shūfu. *'Every chair/all the chairs is/are very
comfortable'*
Tā měi tiān wǎnshang dōu qù. *'He goes every evening.'*

5 Yǒu yìdiǎn(r) + *adjective*

'A little + adjective'. When the adjective used conveys a negative
or derogatory sense, even if this is only subjective on the part of the
speaker, then *yǒu yìdiǎn(r)* is put in front of the adjective. If no
such sense is implied then the order is adjective + *yìdiǎn(r)*:

Rè yìdiǎn(r) hǎo. *'A bit hotter would be better.'*
Yǒu yìdiǎn(r) rè. *'It's a bit on the hot side.'*

6 Yǐhòu, yǐqián, de shíhou

Yǐhòu 'after', *yǐqián* 'before' and *de shíhou* 'when' occur at the
end of the clause to which they refer, i.e. the reverse of English
word order:

xiūxi *(to rest)* **yǐhòu** *'after having a rest'*
shuì jiào *(to sleep v-o)* **yǐqián** *'before going to sleep'*
chī Kěndéjī de shíhou *'when eating Kentucky Fried Chicken'*

It is common practice for the subject not to appear until the following clause although there is no fixed rule about this: *Shàng cèsuǒ de shíhou wǒmen bù yīnggāi chī fàn.* (*Lit.* get on/toilet/when/we/not/ ought to) 'We ought not to be eating when we go to the toilet.'

Note that *yǐqián* and *yǐhòu* can also act as adverbs with the meanings 'previously' and afterwards', respectively, and as such they precede the verb:

Wǒ xiànzài qù, tā yǐhòu qù. *'I'm going now, she's going later.'*

There is a good example of this usage in the dialogue in this unit:

Wǒ yǐqián méi chī-guo kǎoyā. *'I've not eaten roast duck before.'*

....

Insight: learning tip

You can use grammar points 2 and 5 in this unit to practise saying out loud longer sentences using the vocabulary you have learnt. Let's start with grammar point 5 as it is just above:

Shuì jiào yǐqián, wǒ xǐhuān hē shuǐ. *'I like drinking (some) water before I go to sleep.'*

Then try substituting *shuǐ* with all the drinks you have met so far: *júzi-zhī*, *chá* (as many kinds as you can remember), *jiǔ*, etc. and repeat the sentence, using them one at a time, of course, so the next sentence could be:

Shuì jiào yǐqián, wǒ xǐhuān hē júzi-zhī and so on.

Then move on to *yǐhòu*:

Xiūxi yǐhòu, wǒ xǐhuān chī fàn. *'Before I have a rest, I like to eat (something).'*
Xiūxi yǐhòu, wǒ xǐhuān kāi chē and so on.

Then do the same thing with *de shíhou*.

Now let's go back to grammar point 2. Refer back to Unit 7 and go through each room in the house and say out loud what objects/furniture you can find in each of them. Start off with short sentences and try and make them longer and longer as you go on. Start with the bedroom for example:

Wòshì lǐ yǒu bèizi、 chuángdān hé zhěntou . . . and so on.

Then go onto the living room:

Kètīng lǐ yǒu shāfā hé dìtǎn and continue in the same way, adding items until you are saying out loud quite long sentences. It feels good doesn't it?

7 Order of adverbs

Where more than one adverb precedes the same verb a definite word order has to be observed (see 5.6). Generally speaking, it is the monosyllabic adverb (*yě*, *dōu*, *jiù*, etc.) which directly precedes the verb, but if it occurs with *bù* or *méi* the order is (adverb +) monosyllabic adverb + *bù/méi* + verb:

Wǒmen yě dōu bú qù. *'None of us is going either.'*
Tāmen jiù méi lái. *'So they didn't come.'*

If there is an adverb of time such as *jīntiān*, it also precedes *yě* and *jiù*:

Nǐmen jīntiān yě bú qù ma? *'You're not going tonight either?'*

Another example is with *tóngshí* (at the same time). It also precedes *yě* in:

Kètīng tóngshí yě dāng (to serve as; be) **fàntīng.**
'The living room also serves as the dining room.'

8 *Adverbs* + de

Certain adjectives can be used both *before* verbs as adverbs
(adverbial adjuncts) and *after* verbs as complements of degree.
Such adverbs indicate the manner or state of an action and are used
with the particle *de* before the verb:

Tā kuàikuái de shuō, 'Bié zháojí'. *'He quickly said, "Don't worry".'*

**Wǒ dàshēng de shuō 'Kěshi kuàicān méi yǒu yíngyǎng, hái huì
ràng tāmen zhǎng pàng!'** *'I said loudly, "But fast food is not
nutritious and it will also make them fat".'* (See Unit 10.)

The Chinese character for this *de* (地) is again quite different from
the *de* (的) we met in Unit 5 and the *de* (得) we met in Unit 6, but it
is identical in *pinyin*. When an adverb is used to modify a general
action rather than a specific one *de* may be omitted:

Tā nǔlì xuéxí Hànyǔ *'She studies Chinese hard.'*

And an example from the text: *Tāmen tuìxiū yǐhòu, juédìng yào
hǎohǎo xiǎngshòu xiǎngshòu shēnghuó.* 'After they both retired,
they decided they should really enjoy themselves.'

9 Dà *and* xiǎo

With the basic meaning 'big' and 'small', respectively, *dà* and *xiǎo*
are used here to express age, usually in the comparative sense, even
if this is not explicit. When asking a child her/his age the question
form *Nǐ jǐ suì le?* is used but for adults it is:

Nǐ niánjì duō dà le? *(Lit. You/year record/how/big)* or
Nǐ duō dà niánjì le? *(Lit. You/how/big/year record)*

The modal particle *le* is used here to convey the idea that the
record of years has become big. *Duō* is used in a similar way with
other adjectives such as *cháng* 'long', *kuān* 'wide' to ask the degree

of length, width, etc. and is translated as 'how' in such cases as above: *Duō cháng?* 'How long?' Other compounds with *dà* and *xiǎo* are: *dàren* (big person) 'adult'; *dàxué* (big study) 'university'; *xiǎoxué* (small study) 'primary school'; *dàjiā* (big home) 'everybody'. NB *xiǎorén* (*Lit.* small person) 'a mean person'! As a verb, *dà* conveys the idea of growing up:

Háizi dà le. *'The child(ren) has/have grown up'* (*Lit.* got big).

When stating that an adult is old or young in absolute terms then the adjectives *lǎo* (old) and *niánqīng* (years light) are used **not** *dà* and *xiǎo*.

10 *The comparative with* bǐ

The simplest form of comparative is *A* *bǐ* B + appropriate adjective:

Gēge bǐ jiějie xiǎo.   (*Lit.* Elder brother/compared with/elder sister/ small)
                'Elder brother is younger than elder sister.'
Gēge bǐ wǒ dà.   (*Lit.* Elder brother/compared with/me/big)
                'Elder brother is older than me.'

The amount by which B is older or younger than A comes after *dà* or *xiǎo*:

Gēge bǐ jiějie xiǎo liǎng suì. *'Elder brother is two years younger than elder sister.'*
Gēge bǐ wǒ dà yí suì bàn. *'Elder brother is one and a half years older than I am.'*

Exercise 9.1
Make each of the two statements below into one comparative sentence using *bǐ*:

Wǒ sānshí suì. Wǒ péngyou èrshíliù suì.
→ **Wǒ bǐ wǒ péngyou dà sì suì.**

1 *Érzi shísì suì. Nǚ'ér jiǔ suì.*
2 *Jiějie sānshíwǔ suì. Mèimei èrshíjiǔ suì.*
3 *Shǐ Àilǐ èrshíyī suì. Wáng Yǒngshòu èrshísān suì.*
4 *Lǐ tàitai sìshíqī suì. Lǐ xiānsheng wǔshí suì.*
5 *Zhōngguó chá hǎohē. Zhōngguó jiǔ bù hǎohē.*
6 *Zhōngguó cài hǎochī. Yīngguó cài bù hǎochī.*
7 *Tā de shēntǐ* (body, health) *hǎo. Nǐ de shēntǐ bù hǎo.*
8 *Wǒ nán péngyou gāoxìng. Wǒ bù gāoxìng.*

11 More on the comparative

When we wish to extend the simple comparative to denote 'much more' or 'even more' the constructions are: A *bǐ* B + appropriate adjective *de duō* (complement of degree *de*, see 6.2) or A *bǐ* B + appropriate adjective *duō le*.

e.g. **A bǐ B hǎo de duō** or **hǎo duō le** means *'A is much better than B.'*

The first example of this in the text is:

Nǚ'ér bǐ tā gēge gāo duō le. (*Lit.* daughter/compared with/her/ elder brother/tall/much) *'[My] daughter is much taller than her elder brother.'*

When we wish to say that A is 'even more' or 'still more' the quality of the adjective than B, the construction is: A *bǐ* B *hái* (or *gèng*) + adjective.

e.g. **A bǐ B hái hǎo** means *'A is even better than B.'*

The adverb *hái* has the basic meaning of 'still, in addition'. In this context, it has the same meaning as the adverb *gèng* 'still more, even more'. The example we have from the dialogue is:

Wǒ juéde nǚ'ér bǐ érzi gèng cōngming. (*Lit.* I/feel/daughter/ compared with/son/even more/clever) *'I feel [my] daughter is even cleverer than [my] son.'*

Note that *hěn* 'very' may *never* be used in the comparative.

12 Foreign names (II)

Foreign names can be expressed in Chinese in two principal ways, viz. by rendering the sounds with disregard to the meaning or by translating the meaning. *Mòsīkē* (莫斯科) 'Moscow' falls into the former of these categories as 'no then science' does not appear to have a great deal of significance.

Niújīn (牛津) 'Oxford', by way of contrast, falls into the latter category as *niú* ('ox') and *jīn* ('ford') precisely express the meaning of the English Ox-ford. Of course, there are further refinements in that when rendering the sounds, care can be taken to find characters with a 'good' meaning (if that is the intention of course!). Thus Hyde Park is translated as *Hǎi* (海) *dé* (德) *gōngyuán* (公园) 'sea virtue public enclosure' (park), but it could have been translated as *Hài* (害) *dé* (德) *gōngyuán* 'Harm(s) virtue park'.

Mozambique was originally translated into Chinese as *Mò* (莫) *sān* (三) *bí* (鼻) *jǐ* (给) 'No three nose(s) provide' but was later changed to *Mò* (莫) *sāng* (桑) *bǐ* (比) *kè* (克) 'No mulberry tree compare overcome', which is obviously an improvement as *sāng* has poetic overtones that I won't go into here and *kè* is suitably strong.

Kennedy fared much worse. In Chinese *xiàngshēng* ('cross talk'), his name was translated as *kěn* (啃) *ní* (泥) *de* (的) 'gnaw mud person' but officialdom saw fit to change it to *Kěn* (肯) *ní* (尼) *dí* (迪) 'willing Buddhist nun enlighten'!

Exercise 9.2
Translate the following Chinese renderings of foreign words back into English by **a** looking at the pronunciation and/or **b** finding out the meaning in a Chinese–English dictionary.

e.g. 罗马尼亚 *Luómǎníyà* → Romania

1 热狗包 *règǒubāo*
2 麦当劳 *Màidāngláo*

3 汉堡牛肉包 *hànbǎoniúròubāo*
4 可口可乐 *kěkǒukělè*
5 肯德基 *Kěndéjī*
6 星巴克 *Xīngbākè* (well-known chain of coffee shops!)
7 雅马哈 *Yǎ* __ __ (Have a guess at this one. See page 13)
8 尼康 *Níkāng*
9 佳能 *Jiānéng*
10 贝多芬 *Bèiduōfēn*
11 莫扎特 *Mòzhātè*
12 加拿大 *Jiānádà*
13 古巴 *Gǔbā*
14 剑桥 *Jiànqiáo*
15 华沙 *Huáshā*
16 华盛顿 *Huáshèngdùn*
17 奥巴马 *Àobāmǎ zǒngtǒng* (president)

13 Tiān *and* nián

As we mentioned in 9.4, **tiān** and **nián** act as measure words
as well as nouns so that they directly follow numbers and
demonstrative adjectives such as *zhè* 'this', *nà* 'that', *nǎ*
'which?' and *měi* 'every':

nà tiān *'that day'*
yì nián *'one year'*
liǎng tiān *'two days'*

14 (Yì)xiē, zhè xiē, nǎ xiē

Yìxiē acts as a plural measure word meaning '**some, a few**':
yìxiē fādá guójiā 'some developed countries'. The *yì* is sometimes
omitted, particularly after the verb *yǒu*:

yǒu xiē rén 'there are some people . . .' When used with *zhè*,
nà or *nǎ*, the *yì* is dropped and we have *zhè xiē*, *nà xiē* or *nǎ xiē*,
which mean 'these', 'those' or 'which (ones)', respectively.
As *xiē* is in itself a measure word, they are used directly before
a noun:

Nà xiē kuàicān 'those fast food meals'
Zhè xiē Lúndūnrén 'these Londoners'
Nà xiē Niǔyuērén 'those New Yorkers'
Nǎ xiē Rìběnrén? 'which Japanese?'

NB *Zhè*, *nà* and *nǎ* are also read as *zhèi*, *nèi* and *něi*, respectively.

(yì)xiē (the *yì* may be omitted) can also occur after an adjective with the meaning 'somewhat'. It usually appears in comparative sentences when used in this way: *Chī kǎoyā bǐ chī miàntiáo* (noodles) *guì (yì)xiē* 'Eating roast duck is somewhat more expensive than eating noodles.'

15 Yòu . . . yòu . . .

Yòu . . . yòu . . . is used with two verbs or with two adjectives acting as verbs to express the meaning 'both . . . and . . .'

Tā yòu gāo yòu hǎokàn. 'He's both tall and good looking' (good look/see).

There is also a good example of this in the text:

. . . kěshi nàxiē kuàicān yòu guì yòu méi yǒu shénme yíngyǎng *'but those fast food meals are both expensive and not at all nutritious.'*

16 Huì . . . de

The principal meaning of *huì* is 'to know how to (do), can' (Unit 2), but it can also express the possibility or probability that something will happen and is translated as 'will': *Huì xià yǔ* (*Lit.* will/descend/rain) 'It will rain' or 'It's going to rain.' The addition of the modal particle *de* to such sentences introduces a note of affirmation or confirmation as well as slightly shifting the balance and rhythm of the sentence as a whole. Used in this way, it is generally to be found with such verbs as *huì*, *yào*, *shì*, etc. *Tā huì lái de.* 'He will come.' It is important to stress that *de* is not essential to the sentence but, that said, it is used widely.

One-child policy

The one-child policy in China has been controversial, both in China and internationally, since it was first introduced in the early 1980s. It is claimed that some 300 million births may have been denied as a result. Citizens living in rural areas and minorities living in China, although encouraged to have only one child, are not strictly subject to the one-child policy. Millions of couples from minority nationalities and rural areas have more than one child.

While the policy has been implemented quite harshly in general, there are many conditions in which a couple may have a second child legally, such as, if the couple are both only children themselves, if their first child is seriously disabled, if one of the couple is a seriously disabled former military service person, if a couple have adopted a child, but later get pregnant, etc. There are many regional differences, too.

While it is a social problem everywhere in China with 'little emperors' (spoiled children) enjoying the attention of two parents and four grandparents, many of them are also 'products' of parental and social engineering with resources poured into them.

Exercise 9.3
Answer the following questions based on the text:

1 *Wáng Yǒngshòu yǐqián chī-guo kǎoyā méi yǒu?*
2 *Zhāng Dàmíng hé Chén Yīng yǒu jǐ ge háizi?*
3 *Shéi dà ?* (use *bǐ*)
4 *Shéi gāo?* (use *bǐ*)
5 *Zhōngguó cài guì háishi kuàicān guì?* (use *bǐ*)
6 *Wèi shénme hěn duō rén xiǎng chī kuàicān?*

Exercise 9.4
True or false?

1 *Wáng Yǒngshòu méi chī-guo kǎoyā.*
2 *Zhèi jiā kǎoyādiàn zài Wángfǔjǐng.*
3 *Zhāng Dàmíng de fùmǔ dōu xǐhuān lái zhèi jiā chī kǎoyā.*
4 *Zhāng Dàmíng hé Chén Yīng de érzi bǐ tā mèimei gāo.*
5 *Zhāng Dàmíng hé Chén Yīng de nǚ'ér bǐ tā gēge cōngming.*
6 *Màidāngláo hé Kěndéjī de fàncài bǐ Zhōngguó fàncài piányi duō le.*
7 *Màidāngláo hé Kěndéjī de fàncài hěn yǒu yíngyǎng.*
8 *Shǐ xiǎojie zuì xǐhuān chī Zhōngguó fàncài.*
9 *Shǐ Àilǐ hé Wáng Yǒngshòu xiǎng qǐng Zhāng Dàmíng hé Chén Yīng chī fàn.*

Exercise 9.5
Can you correct the following *bìngjù*?

Sì diǎn zhōng bú jiù xíng → Sì diǎn zhōng jiù bù xíng.

1 *Fángzū* (rent) *de Lúndūn dōu hěn guì.*
2 *Zhōngguórén hǎo, Yīngguórén dōu yě hěn hǎo.*
3 *Tā měi ge nián mǎi duō yīfu* (clothes).
4 *Yǐqián shuì jiào, yīnggāi shuā yá* (brush one's teeth).
5 *Tā nà ge tiān xiūxi* (to rest) *le.*
6 *Tā měi nián qù guo Fǎguó.*
7 *Wǒmen cónglái bù chī guo Rìběn* (Japan/Japanese) *fàn.*
8 *Yìxiē ge Rìběnrén gōngzī* (wages) *hěn gāo.*
9 *Sūgélán* (Scotland) *bǐ Měiguó ānjìng de hěn duō.*
10 *De shíhou tiānqì* (weather) *hǎo, kěyǐ qù kàn diànyǐng* (film).
11 *Wǒde nǚ'ér yòu shi gāo yòu shi shòu* (slim).

TESTING YOURSELF

Translate the following into Chinese:

1 *There are a table and six chairs in the dining room.*

2 *Although it's generally very quiet in a study, many people do not possess one.*

3 *When the weather is cold, everybody likes the central heating on.*

4 *I have been longing to eat Beijing roast duck for ages (use* zǎo jiù . . . le).*

5 *My younger sister is even smarter than I am!*

6 *It is not every sofa (that) is comfortable to sit on (*hǎo zuò).*

7 *My daughter is three and a half years younger than my son.*

8 *The parents didn't go yesterday (*zuótiān), *my eldest sister and I are not going today, either.*

9 *(A) single bed* (dānrénchuáng) *is even cheaper than a double one. (Check vocab. in Unit 7.)*

10 *We don't know what it is all about, either.*

11 *Thank you for inviting us here to eat.*

12 *Although all (the) windows, doors* (mén), *etc. are very clean* (gānjìng), *(the) tables (and) chairs are all filthy* (zāng).

10

....

Teething troubles

In this unit you will learn
* *more about resultative verbs*
* *how to say that something is happening*
* *compound directional endings*
* *the days of the week*
* *how to express the passive*

◄» **CD 1, tr 41–43**

Zhang and Chen have arrived back home after having had dinner
with Wang Yongshou and his girlfriend. Zhang's parents greet
them with a relieved smile.

**Zhāng Dàmíng hé Chén Yīng gēn Wáng Yǒngshòu hé tā de nǚ
péngyou chī wán fàn huí dào jiā. Zhāng de fùmǔ sōng le kǒu qì,
xiàozhe yíng shàng qù.**

Zhāng Mǔ	Āiyā. Nǐmen kuài guòlái ba. Zhēn zāogāo. Zhēn Zhēn shuì bu liǎo jiào. Wǒ gěi le tā yí ge píngguǒ, bù zhīdào shì zěnme (yì) huí shì, tā de yì kē yá diào le. Tā yìzhí zài kū, wǒ xiǎng xiànzài tā hái méi yǒu tíng ne. Tā shuō yáchǐ diào le, tā huì hěn nánkàn.	Oh dear. Please come over here quickly. What a mess! Zhenzhen can't get to sleep. I gave her an apple, and I don't know what happened but a tooth came out. I don't think she's stopped crying yet. She says not having her tooth makes her look ugly.
Chén	Bié zháojí. Zhēn Zhēn de yáchǐ shì rǔyá, tā huì zhǎngchū xīn yá de. Tā zài nǎr?	Don't worry. Zhenzhen's tooth is only a milk tooth, she will grow another one eventually. Where is she?
Zhāng Fù	Tā zài tā de fángjiān li. Wǒmen gēn tā shuō tā kěyi wánr diànnǎoyóuxì jiù bú huì lǎo xiǎngzhe yá de shì'r le.	She's in her bedroom. We told her she could play computer games to take her mind off her tooth.
Zhāng	Hǎo zhǔyi. Wǒ qù gēn tā tántan, xiàng tā jiěshì yíxià yá de shìqing.	Good idea. I'll go and talk to her and explain about her tooth.
Chén	Érzi ne? Tā shuì le ma?	Where's our little boy [son]? Is he asleep?
Zhāng Mǔ	Zǎo jiù shuì zháo le. Tā jīntiān gēn xiǎo péngyoumen qí zìxíngchē dàochù wánr, suǒyi huílái de shíhou yòu lèi yòu è. Tā shuō tā míngtiān hái yào qí. Tā hěn xǐhuan tā de xīn chē.	He's been asleep for ages. He's been riding his bicycle everywhere with his friends today so when he came back he was tired and hungry. He says that he's going to ride [his bike] again tomorrow. He really loves his new bike.

Chén	Nà tài hǎole. Nà liàng zìxíngchē yǒu yìdiǎnr guì, dànshi yòu jiēshi yòu hǎokàn.	That's great. That bike was a bit on the expensive side but it's both sturdy and nice looking.
[Guò le yìhuǐr, Zhāng Dàmíng zǒu jìn kètīng lai.]		[After quite a while, Zhang Daming comes into the living room.]
Zhāng Mǔ	Zhēn Zhēn zěnmeyàng le?	How is Zhenzhen?
Zhāng	Tā shuì zháo le. Wǒ gěi tā jiǎng le yí ge hěn cháng de gùshi, hái méi jiǎng wán, tā jiù shuì zháo le.	She's asleep now. I told her a long story and she fell asleep before I got to the end.
Chén	Míngtiān (shì) xīngqītiān, tāmen bú yòng zǎo qǐ.	It's Sunday tomorrow so they don't have to get up early.
[Duì Zhāng Mǔ.]		[Turning to her mother in law.]
	Shuì jiào qián tāmen xǐ shǒu、xǐ liǎn, shuā yá le ma?	Did they both wash their hands and faces and clean their teeth before they went to bed?
Zhāng Mǔ	Zhèxiē dāngrán dōu zuò le. Nǐ juéde . . .	Of course they did. Do you think . . .
Zhāng	[kuàikuài de] Tāmen wǎnfàn chī de shì shénme?	[Hurriedly] What did they have for supper?
Zhāng Mǔ	Ò, wǒmen qù chī le Màidāngláo. Nǐmen zhīdāo tāmen duō xǐhuan chī Màidāngláo.	Oh, we went to McDonald's. You know how much they like eating (at) McDonald's.
Chén	[dàshēng de] Kěshi kuàicān méi yǒu yǐngyǎng, hái huì ràng tāmen zhǎng pàng!	[Wails] But fast food is so unnutritious and it makes them fat.

| Zhāng Fù | Ō, Chén Yīng, nǐ zhēn (ràng rén) sǎoxìng. Ràng háizimen kuàile kuàile yǒu shénme bù hǎo!? | *Oh, Chen Ying, you're just such a spoilsport. What's wrong with the children enjoying themselves?!* |

QUICK VOCAB

āiyā *(interj)* oh dear (exclamation)
jìn *(v)* to enter
zāogāo what a mess
shuì(jiào) *(v[-o])* to sleep, go to bed
píngguǒ *(n)* apple
yá(chǐ) *(n)* [kē] tooth
diào *(v)* to come out/off
yìzhí *(adv)* to keep on doing something
zài . . . to be in the middle of . . . ing
kū *(v)* to cry, weep
tíng(zhǐ) *(v)* to stop
nán *(adj)* difficult
-nánkàn *(adj)* ugly
zháojí *(adj)* to worry, to be anxious
rǔyá *(n)* [ke] milk tooth
zhǎngchū *(v)* to grow (as of teeth)
xīn *(adj)* new
gēn *(prep; conj)* with; and
lǎo *(adj)* always
diànnǎoyóuxì *(n)* computer game
shì'r/shì(qing) *(n)* [jiàn] matter, thing
xiàng X jiěshi to explain (something) to X
zhǔyì *(n)* idea
-zháo *(RVE)* to succeed in doing the action of the verb
qí *(v)* to ride (as of bicycle, horse)
zìxíngchē *(n)* [liàng] bicycle (self-propelling machine)
dàochù *(PW)* everywhere
. . . de shíhou when . . .
lèi *(adj)* tired
yào *(aux v, v)* want to, must, to want

jiēshi *(adj) strong, sturdy*
hǎokàn *(adj) nice looking*
yíhuìr *(TW) a short while, (after) a moment*
-dào *(RVE) to manage to do the action of the verb, up to*
jiǎng *(v) to tell (a story); to speak; to explain*
cháng *(adj) long*
gùshi *(n) story*
xīngqī *(n) week*
xīngqītiān/xīngqīrì *(n) Sunday*
bú yòng *(v) need not*
qǐ *(v) to get up, rise*
xǐ shǒu *(v-o) to wash one's hands*
xǐ liǎn *(v-o) to wash one's face*
shuā yá *(v-o) to brush one's teeth*
dāngrán *(adv) of course, naturally*
kuàikuài de *(adv) hurriedly*
dàshēng(de) *(adv) loudly*
ràng *(v) to let, allow*
pàng *(adj; v) fat; to be fat*
zhǎngpàng *(v) to get fat*
sǎo xìng *(v-o) to deflate somebody's feelings*
kuàilè *(adj) happy, joyful*
yǒu shénme bù hǎo? *what's wrong with that?*

Grammar

1 *Potential resultative verbs*

(For resultative verbs see 8.1.) A potential result is indicated by the insertion of *de* for the positive form ('can') and *bu* for the negative form ('cannot') between the verb of action and its resultative ending:

Guò qu 'to pass' (as of one's days), *guò **de** qù* 'able to pass', *guò **bu** qù* 'unable to pass'; *kànjiàn* 'to see'; *kàn **de** jiàn* 'can see', *kàn **bu** jiàn* 'can't see'.

The question form can either be made by adding *ma* to the positive form of the statement or by putting the positive and negative forms together as in 1.5:

Tā zhǎo de dào zhǎo bu dào nán/nǚ péngyou? *Can he/she find a boy/girl friend?*
Tā zhǎo de dào nán/nǚ péngyou ma?

(Note that the tone comes back onto simple directional endings and onto the first 'half' of compound directional endings when they form part of a potential resultative verb.)

2 The progressive aspect – to be in the middle of doing something

to show that an action is in progress, one of the adverbs *zhèngzài*, *zhèng* or *zài* is placed before the verb or *ne* is placed at the end of the sentence. However, *zhèngzài*, *zhèng* or *zài* often occur **together** with *ne* to indicate the progressive aspect:

Tā zài kū. *'He/she is crying.'*
Shòuhuòyuán (shop assistant) **zhèngzài liáo tiān(r) (ne).**
'The shop assistant is/was (in the middle of) chatting.'
Tā zài dǎ tàijíquán (ne). *'He is/was (in the middle of) doing taijiquan.'*
Gōngchǎng zhèng shēngchǎn . . . (ne). *'The factory is/was (in the middle of) manufacturing . . .'*
Tāmen zhào xiàng ne. *'They are/were (in the middle of) taking photos.'*

The negative is made by putting *méi (yǒu)* before the verb but if the verb is omitted then *yǒu* **must** be used:

Nǐmen zài shài tàiyáng (v-o to sunbathe) **ma?** *'Are you sunbathing?'*
Wǒmen méi (yǒu) shài tàiyáng, wǒmen kàn diànshì ne. *'We're not sunbathing, we're watching TV.'*
Méi yǒu, wǒmen kàn diànshì ne. *'No, we're watching TV.'*
Méi yǒu. *'No.'*

What the Chinese call 'aspect' is different from 'time' (past, present or future). An action in progress may take place in the past, present or future and it is the use of time words (plus context) that tells us when the action actually takes place. (This is why it is also dangerous to think of the verb + *le* as indicating the past tense.) The following examples will illustrate this point:

Present – *Question*:   **Nǐ xiànzài zuò shénme ne?** *'What are you doing now?'*

        Answer: **Wǒ zài huá bīng ne** (*Lit.* I//slide/ice). *'I'm skating.'*

Past – **Zuótiān** (yesterday) **tā lái de shíhou, wǒ zhèng shuì jiào ne.** *'I was asleep when he came yesterday.'* (Note the clause sequence: the 'when' clause comes first.)

Future – **Míngtiān xiàwǔ** (afternoon) **xià bān** (v-o to finish work) **yǐhòu qù gēn xiǎoháir tán, tā yídìng zài qí zìxíngchē ne.** *'(If) you go and chat with the child tomorrow afternoon after work, she'll certainly be riding her bike.'*

3 *Compound directional endings*

In 8.1, we met the (simple) directional markers *lái* and *qù*, which indicate direction towards or away from the speaker or point of reference. Compound directional endings show even greater precision and are formed by combining verbs such as *jìn* 'to enter', *chū* 'to come or go out' with *lái* or *qù* and attaching them to verbs of motion. Thus, where in English we would say 'he came running in', the Chinese for this would be *Tā pǎo jìnlai le* (*Lit.* He/run/ enter/come), 'we came running out' *wǒmen pǎo chūlai le*, 'they went running in' *tāmen pǎo jìnqu le*, etc.

Note that verbs with a compound directional ending (CDE) are often written as one word, e.g. *pǎochulai*, and as such *both* parts of the CDE are usually indicated as toneless. For the sake of clarity, I have split the verb and its CDE as above and indicated the tone on the first half of the CDE.

Where there is an object involved, this may go between the two parts of the compound directional ending or follow it:

Wǒ ná chū yīfu (clothes) **lai** or **Wǒ ná chūlai yīfu** *'I take out clothes'* (*ná* 'to take' [with the hand]).

Where there is a place word involved, this may *only* go between the two parts of the compound directional ending:

... dà zhuōzi hé yǐzi dōu bān (move) **jìn kètīng lai.** *'The big table and chairs are all moved into the living-room.'*
Tāmen pǎo chū huāyuán qu. *'They run/ran out of the garden.'*

A good example from the dialogue in this unit is:

Zhāng Dàmíng zǒu jìn kètīng lai. *'Zhang Daming comes into the living room.'*

(For further examples of this construction, see Unit 13.)

Exercise 10.1
Make a sentence from the following groups of words using the compound directional ending indicated in brackets.

Yīshēng (doctor) **zǒu fàndiàn** (hospital) **(jìnqu) → Yīshēng zǒu jìn fàndiàn qu.**

1 *Fùmǔ zǒu kètīng (jìnlai).*
2 *Tāmen bān* (to move) *shūzhuō (chūqu).*
3 *Xiōngdì* (brothers) *bān shuāngrénchuáng (jìnqu).*
4 *Xiǎoháir pǎo cèsuǒ (chūlai).*
5 *Jiàoyuán* (teacher) *ná liǎng běn shū* (books) *(xiàlai 'down', direction towards speaker).*

4 Hái méi yǒu ... ne

Méi yǒu (*Lit.* not have) precedes the verb to indicate that the action of the verb has **not** taken place. *Yǒu* may be omitted:

Tā méi (yǒu) jié hūn. *'He/she isn't/hasn't married.'*

The addition of *hái* before *méi* and *ne* at the end of the clause convey the idea that the situation is ongoing, thus in:

Wǒ jiějie . . . hái méi yǒu zhǎo dào nán péngyou ne

the expectation appears to be that she will or that at least she's still in with a chance!

5 Days of the week

◄» CD 1, tr 44

Xīngqī (*Lit.* 'star period'), the Chinese word for 'week' precedes the numerals 1–6 to give the days of the week from Monday to Saturday. 'Sunday' is not *xīngqīqī*, however, but *xīngqītiān* or *xīngqīrì*. 'What day is it today?' is *Jīntiān xīngqījǐ?* (Note that no verb is necessary.)

QUICK VOCAB

xīngqīyī *Monday*
xīngqī'èr *Tuesday*
xīngqīsān *Wednesday*
xīngqīsì *Thursday*
xīngqīwǔ *Friday*
xīngqīliù *Saturday*
xīngqītiān/xīngqīrì *Sunday*

Other useful vocabulary items are *běn xīngqī* or *zhè ge xīngqī* 'this week', *shàng (ge) xīngqī* 'last week' and *xià (ge) xīngqī* 'next week'. The same system applies to *yuè* 'month': *běn yuè* or *zhè ge yuè* 'this month', *shàng (ge) yuè* 'last month' and *xià (ge) yuè* 'next month'. An alternative word for 'week' is *lǐbài*. The days of the week work in exactly the same way as for *xīngqī*.
For example, 'Wednesday' would be *lǐbàisān* and 'Sunday' would either be *lǐbàitiān* or *lǐbàirì*. *Lǐbài* is often used by overseas Chinese rather than *xīngqī* and has religious connotations. *Zuò lǐbài* (v-o) means 'to go to church'.

Exercise 10.2

Fill in the blanks with the appropriate time word or phrase:
Jīntiān xīngqījǐ? → Jīntiān xīngqī'èr.

1 *Jīntiān xīngqīsān. Míngtiān ____.*
2 *Zuótiān* (yesterday) *xīngqītiān. Jīntiān ____? Jīntiān ____.*
3 *Shàng ge yuè wǔyuè. Xià ge yuè jǐ yuè? Xià ge yuè ____.*
4 *Yì nián yǒu jǐ ge yuè? Yì nián yǒu ____.*
5 *Yí ge xīngqī yǒu jǐ tiān? Yí ge xīngqī yǒu ____.*
6 *Jiǔyuè yǒu duōshao tiān? Jiǔyuè yǒu ____.*
7 *Èryuè ne? Èryuè yǒu ____ huòzhě ____.*
8 *Yì nián yǒu duōshao tiān? Yì nián yǒu ____ huòzhě* (or) ____
   (*bǎi* 'hundred').

....

Fast food and coffee

Since China opened up to the outside world in the early
1980s, nearly everything western has flooded into China.
Fast food is no exception, indeed, it has achieved quite a
successful invasion, in fact. With thousands of McDonald's,
KFCs and Pizza Huts all over China, young people in
particular grow up with fast food all around them. While
millions in China are still in poverty, there are other millions
of obese people who have caused serious social concern.
People in China now realize that it is unfair to blame the
western fast food chains for the growing obesity problem in
China. It is the so-called 'modern lifestyle' that should be
examined and perhaps modified.

An interesting case was when Starbucks opened a shop in the
Imperial Palace – it made many people uncomfortable:
western 'cultural' invasion going too far, many shouted. In
the end, Starbucks withdrew from the site, but continued to
expand elsewhere in China at a fast rate.

....

Chinese advertisement for Coca-Cola
(kěkǒu kělè)

6 Zǎo qǐ, wǎn lái?

In 6.3, we saw how putting *duō* or *shǎo* before the verb conveyed the idea of doing 'more' or 'less' of the verb. We also saw that this construction must only be used with full verbs and not with adjectives used as verbs. *Zǎo* 'early' and *wǎn* 'late' are used in a similar way, so *zǎo qǐ* means 'get up early' and *wǎn lái* means 'come late'.

7 Chī de shì shénme?

The whole sentence spoken by Zhāng Dàmíng was: *Tāmen wǎnfàn chī de shì shénme?* Let's refer back to 2.3 where we looked at something called the topic construction. We meet it again here. The sentence literally says: As for them (*Tāmen*) and their evening meal (*wǎnfàn*), **what** (they) ate (*chī de*) was what? (*shì shénme?*) 'What did they have/eat for supper?' The *de* after the verb (and this is the same *de* we met in 5.4, so it would be worth going back to reread that) makes the phrase nominal or a noun phrase so if: '*Wǒmen chī* *de'* means 'what we eat/ate' then *'Tāmen chàng de'* means 'what they sang' and *'Nǐmen hē de'* means 'what you drink/drank' and so on.

8 Duō + verb (take two!)

we met *duō* and *shǎo* before the verb in Unit 6 (6.3) where it conveyed the idea of doing 'more' or 'less' of the verb, e.g. *shǎo shuō huà* 'speak less', *duō chī fàn* 'eat more'. **Duō** before certain types of verb has an additional meaning of 'how (much)' e.g. Wǒ *duō ài nǐ* 'How much I love you' and the example from the dialogue:

Nǐmen zhīdāo tāmen duō xihuan chī Màidāngláo. *'You know how much they like eating (at) McDonald's.'*

You can see from these examples that the verbs used have to be transitive, i.e. ones able to take a direct object.

9 Ràng *and the passive*

Verbs in Chinese are neither active nor passive in themselves – it is their context that makes them one or the other. However some verbs of motion *appear* to be passive, even in Chinese, without changing their form or having anything added to them:

Bào mǎi lái le *'the newspaper has been bought'* (by you, me, etc.).

However, the passive is usually expressed by using the following construction:

Subject + *ràng* (让) + *agent* + verb (+ other elements)
OR　　　 + *jiào* (叫) . . .
OR　　　 + *bèi* (被) . . .

Tā ràng gǒu (dog) **yǎo** (to bite) **le.** *'He was bitten by the dog.'*
Dàngāo (cake) **jiào háizi chī le.** *'The cake was eaten by the children.'*
Wǒ bèi tā dǎ le. *'I was hit by him/her.'*

If it is not clear who (or what) the agent is, an indefinite *rén* (人) may be used instead:

Dīng xiānsheng ràng	rén qǐng qù hē chá le.
jiào	
bèi	

'Mr Ding was invited (by somebody) to have tea.' *Ràng, bèi* and *jiào* can be used interchangeably, but *ràng* and *jiào* are used more in the spoken language, while *bèi* is used more in the formal written language.

Note that when no agent is marked in the sentence, only *bèi* may be used: *Wǒ **bèi** jǐnggào le* 'I was warned.'

The negative adverb and/or auxiliary verb go before *ràng, jiào, bèi*, etc. Other adverbs such as *zuótiān* (昨天) 'yesterday' and *yǐjīng* (已经) normally precede *bèi* (*ràng, jiào*) too.

Insight: learning tip

◄) CD 1, tr 45

Saying long sentences in Chinese can be daunting at the beginning. One way of increasing your Chinese memory banks is by practising what we call 'back-chaining'. You practise long sentences like those that follow by reading them phrase by phrase (the whole gradually increasing in length), starting with the end of the sentence first. Examples 2 and 3 feature on the audio.

1

shuì zháo le

tā jiù shuì zháo le

hái méi jiǎng wán, tā jiù shuì zháo le

hěn cháng de gùshi, hái méi jiǎng wán, tā jiù shuì zháo le

yí ge hěn cháng de gùshi, hái méi jiǎng wán, tā jiù shuì zháo le

tā jiǎng le yí ge hěn cháng de gùshi, hái méi jiǎng wán, tā jiù shuì zháo le

Wǒ gěi tā jiǎng le yí ge hěn cháng de gùshi, hái méi jiǎng wán, tā jiù shuì zháo le.

2

yòu gāoxìng
yòu lèi yòu gāoxìng
huílái de shíhou yòu lèi yòu gāoxìng
suǒyi huílái de shíhou yòu lèi yòu gāoxìng
dàochù wánr, suǒyi huílái de shíhou yòu lèi yòu gāoxìng
qí zìxíngchē dàochù wánr, suǒyi huílái de shíhou yòu lèi
yòu gāoxìng
gēn xiǎo péngyoumen qí zìxíngchē dàochù wánr, suǒyi
huílái de shíhou yòu lèi yòu gāoxìng
Tā jīntiān gēn xiǎo péngyoumen qí zìxíngchē dàochù
wánr, suǒyi huílái de shíhou yòu lèi yòu gāoxìng.

3

yá de shì'r le
xiǎng zhe yá de shì'r le
lǎo xiǎng zhe yá de shì'r le
bú huì lǎo xiǎng zhe yá de shì'r le
jiù bú huì lǎo xiǎng zhe yá de shì'r le
wánr diànnǎo yóuxì, jiù bú huì lǎo xiǎng zhe yá de shì'r le
tā kěyi wánr diànnǎo yóuxì, jiù bú huì lǎo xiǎng zhe yá
de shì'r le
tā shuō tā kěyi wánr diànnǎo yóuxì, jiù bú huì lǎo xiǎng
zhe yá de shì'r le
Wǒmen gēn tā shuō tā kěyi wánr diànnǎo yóuxì, jiù bú
huì lǎo xiǎng zhe yá de shì'r le.

You can pick out long(er) sentences in any of the texts you
have studied so far and practise them in this way. And,
of course, try to remember to do the same thing with all
the new units from now on.

Exercise 10.3
Select *jiào*, *ràng* or *bèi* to fill the blank spaces in the following sentences. Where there is more than one alternative, give all of them:

1 *Zhōngguó yǒu (yì) xiē xuésheng zài 1989 nián liùyuè sān, sì hào ____ zhèngfǔ* (government) *hài* (to harm, persecute) *le.*
2 *Tā ____ lǎoshī* (teacher) *biǎoyáng* (to praise) *le.*
3 *Yīnwèi wǒ gàosu* (tell) *tā bié zhèyàng zuò, suǒyǐ ____ tā mà* (swear at, curse) *le yídùn.*
4 *Wǒ gēge ____ tā péngyou piàn* (to deceive) *le.*
5 *Tā ____ mìmì jǐngchá* (secret police) *dàibǔ* (arrest) *le.*

Exercise 10.4

Answer the following questions based on the text:

1 *Zhēn Zhēn chī le píngguǒ yǐhòu zěnmeyàng le?*
2 *Zhāng Dàmíng hé Chén Yīng zháojí bu zháojí?*
3 *Shéi yào qù gēn Zhēn Zhēn tántan?*
4 *Érzi shuì zháo le méi you?*
5 *Tā jīntiān zuò le shénme?*
6 *Tā de zìxíngchē mǎi de shíhou guì bu guì?*
7 *Míngtiān shì xīngqījǐ?*
8 *Zhēn Zhēn hé tā gēge wǎnfàn shì zài nǎr chī de?*
9 *Chén Yīng wèishénme bù xǐhuān Màidāngláo de kuàicān?*
10 *Háizimen xǐhuan bu xǐhuan chī Màidāngláo?*

TESTING YOURSELF

Translate the following into Chinese:

1 *This bicycle is strong and nice looking.*

2 *The little boy was tired but he couldn't get to sleep.*

3 *I explained to her why she had to wash her hands and face and brush her teeth.*

4 *Fast food can make us fat.*

5 *What's wrong with you? Are you very worried?*

6 *My younger sister kept on crying – I don't know what on earth the matter was.*

11

Weather, dates and seasons

In this unit you will learn
- *about the weather and seasons in Beijing*
- *what Chinese people do when the weather is fine*
- *more about the comparative*
- *the months of the year*
- *how to express the duration of something*

This will be the first time the text is not in the form of a dialogue, so it has been divided into two sections, each followed by its own vocabulary list. For ease of reference within each section, two or three sentences in *pinyin* are followed immediately by their English translation. Again for ease of reference, in each 'block' a sentence ends with a slash (/), except where it is the last sentence in that block.

Wáng Yǒngshòu tán le tā duì Běijīng de qìhòu de kànfǎ (view/opinion). **Tā hái tán le shǒudū de yúlè xiāoqián shēnghuó de qíngkuàng.**

Wang Yongshou gives his views on Beijing's climate. He also describes recreational activities in the capital.

Section 1

Jīnnián Běijīng de tiānqì hěn bú zhèngcháng./Dōngtiān bù lěng, xiàtiān yě bú rè./Yīnggāi xià xuě de shíhou bìng méi yǒu xià, yīnggāi xià yǔ de shíhou yě méi yǒu xià – zhēn qíguài!/Shì bu shi zhěnggè shìjiè de qìhòu zhèngzài biàn ne?

The weather in Beijing has been very odd this year./The winter has not been cold neither has the summer been hot./When it should have snowed it didn't and when it should have rained it hasn't – it's really strange!/Is it because the climate of the entire world is in the process of changing?

Qìhòu biànhuà yuè lái yuè míngxiǎn./Ōuzhōu píngcháng méi yǒu Běijīng nàme lěng dànshi jīnnián fǎn'ér yǒude shíhou bǐ Běijīng hái lěng./Chūntiān、qiūtiān shì Běijīng zuì hǎo de jìjié, kěxī tài duǎn le.

Climate change is becoming more and more obvious./Europe is usually not as cold as Beijing, but this year, on the contrary, it has sometimes been even colder than Beijing./The best seasons in Beijing are spring and autumn but it's a pity they're so short.

Yàoshi zài Zhōngguó lǚxíng de huà, wǔyuè hé jiǔyuè tiānqì zuì hǎo, qíngtiān duō, yīntiān shǎo./Tiānqì yī hǎo, gōngyuán lǐ de rén jiù hěn duō./Lǎorén xià qí de xià qí, dǎ pái de dǎ pái, liáo tiān(r) de liáo tiān(r), zǎoshang dǎ tàijíquán de yǒudeshì.

If you're travelling around in China, May and September have the best weather with many fine days and few cloudy ones./As soon as the weather brightens up, there are many people in the parks./There are some old people playing chess, others playing cards and some chatting to each other. And there are plenty of them doing taijichuan (a form of exercise) in the mornings.

Suīrán shí nián yǐqián, dàbùfen rén qí zìxíngchē shàng bān, xiànzài rénmen huòzhě zuò gōnggòng qìchē huòzhě kāi chē, suǒyǐ zài dà chéngshì zìxíngchē yuè lái yuè shǎo./Lìng yī fāngmiàn, qìchē yuè lái

yuè duō, wūrǎn yě yuè lái yuè yánzhòng./Zài kāi Àolínpīkè yùndòng huì de shíhou, zhèngfǔ cǎiqǔ le xǔduō cuòshī duìfu wūrǎn wèntí.

Although 10 years ago, most people went to work by bike now they either go by bus or by car so that there are fewer and fewer bikes in the big cities now./By way of contrast, there are more and more cars and pollution levels are getting higher and higher/worse and worse./At the time of the Olympic Games, the government had to adopt a great number of measures to deal with it.

A Roman Catholic cathedral in Beijing

QUICK VOCAB

jīnnián *(TW) this year*
tiānqì *(n) weather*
zhèngcháng *(adj) normal, regular*
dōngtiān *(n) winter*
lěng *(adj) cold*
xiàtiān *(n) summer*
rè *(adj) hot*
xià xuě *(v-o) to snow*
bìng *(adv) + **bù/méi** see 11.1*
xià yǔ *(v-o) to rain*
qíguài *(adj) strange*
zhěnggè *(adj) whole, entire*
shìjiè *(n) world*

qìhòu *(n) climate*
zhèngzài . . . ne *in the middle of -ing (refer back to 10.2)*
biàn *(v) to change*
biànhuà *(n) change*
yuè lái yuè *more and more*
míngxiǎn *(adj) obvious*
Ōuzhōu *(N) Europe*
píngcháng *(adv; adj) usually; ordinary, commonplace*
fǎn'ér *(conj) on the contrary*
yǒu (de) shíhou *(TW) sometimes*
chūntiān *(n) spring*
qiūtiān *(n) autumn*
jìjié *(n) season*
kěxī *it's a pity that*
duǎn *(adj) short (in length)*
yào (shi) . . . (de huà), (jiù) . . . *if . . . then . . . (see 11.14)*
lǚxíng *(v) to travel*
yuè *(n) month*
qíng *(adj) (of weather) fine, clear, bright*
yīn *(adj) cloudy, overcast*
yī . . . jiù . . . *no sooner . . . than . . .; as soon as*
gōngyuán *(n) park*
lǎorén *(n) old people*
xià qí *(v-o) to play chess*
dǎ pái *(v-o) to play cards or mahjong*
liáo tiān(r) *(v-o) to chat*
dǎ tàijíquán *(v-o) to do taijiquan*
yǒudeshì *to have plenty of, there's no lack of*
suírán *(conj) although*
bùfen *(n) part, section*
dàbùfen *most*
shàng bān *(v-o) to go to work*
huò(zhě) *(conj; adv) or; perhaps*
zuò chē *(v-o) go by transport*
gōnggòng *(adj) public*
gōnggòngqìchē *(n) [liàng] bus (Lit. public together steam vehicle)*
kāi *(v) to start; to open; to drive*

kāi chē *(v-o) to drive a car*
chéngshì *(n) city, town*
lìng(wài) *(adj; adv) another; separately*
fāngmiàn *(n) aspect, respect*
wūrǎn *(n) pollution*
yánzhòng *(adj) serious*
Ào(línpīkè) yùn(dòng) huì *(N) Olympic Games*
zhèngfǔ *(n) government*
cǎiqǔ *(v) to adopt (e.g. measures)*
xǔduō *(adj) many*
cuòshī *(n) measure*
duìfu *(v) to deal with*
wèntí *(n) question, problem*

Section 2

◀️ CD 1, tr 47

Zhōngguórén yìbān yí ge xīngqī gōngzuò wǔ tiān, xiàng dà bùfen Ōuzhōu guójiā xīngqīliù、xīngqītiān yě xiūxi./Zhōumò yìbān jīguān de gōngzuò rényuán bú shàng bān, xuéxiào de lǎoshī hé xuéshēng bú shàng kè./Kěshì, yínháng、yóujú、shāngdiàn hé qítā fúwù hángyè, yí ge xīngqī qī tiān dōu yíngyè.

The Chinese generally work a five-day week, as does the greater part of Europe where Saturday is also a rest day./People who work in offices generally don't work on Saturdays and Sundays, neither do teachers and students /B(b)ut banks, post offices, shops and other services are open 7/7.

Xīngqītiān, tiānqì tèbié hǎo de shíhou, dàjiā dōu chū qu wánr./ Gōngyuán lǐ sàn bù de sàn bù, zhào xiàng de zhào xiàng. Hěn duō rén xǐhuan guàng dà jiē, suǒyǐ shāngdiàn lǐ zōngshi hěn jǐ, zhěnggè Běijīng rènào jíle./

On Sundays when the weather is especially nice everybody goes out to enjoy themselves./Some people stroll in the parks or take photographs./Many people like to go window shopping, so the shops are always very crowded – the whole of Beijing is a hive of activity.

Chúle zhèixiē huódòng yǐwài, wǎngbā lǐ zǒngshi yǒu hěn duō rén, chàbùduō dōu shì niánqīngrén./Tāmen dàbùfen rén zài wánr diànnǎo yóuxì, yòng Gǔgē gēn Bǎidù* cházhǎo xìnxī, yòng Skype gēn péngyoumen liáotiānr, dōu gēn Ōuzhōu guójiā yíyàng./ Skype hěn liúxíng yīnwei yòng Skype tōng huà shì miǎnfèi de.

Apart from these activities, the internet cafés are always crowded, mostly with young people./They are mainly playing computer games or checking out things on Google or Baidu or using Skype to chat with friends, just (the same) as in European countries./Skype is very popular because it's free if you talk to somebody else using Skype.

Gēn zhèixiē xiàndàihuà de shēnghuó fāngshì xiāngduì de shì, zuò lǐbài de rén yě yuè lái yuè duō./ Shì bu shì yīnwei xiàndàihuà shēnghuó fāngshì hé sīxiǎng méi yǒu mǎnzú yìxiē Zhōngguórén de jīngshén yāoqiú ne?/ Nǐ shuō ne?

In contrast to these modern ways of life, there are also more and more people going to church./Is it because all these modern ways of life and thinking have not satisfied Chinese people's spiritual needs?/Do you think this is the case?

* Bǎidù is the most widely used Chinese search engine in China.

yìbān *(adv; adj) generally; general*
guójiā *(n) country*
xiūxi *(v) to rest*
zhōumò *(n) weekend*
jīguān *(n) offices, organization*
rényuán *(n) personnel, staff*
lǎoshī *(n) teacher*
xuéshēng *(n) student*
shàng kè *(n) to attend class*
yínháng *(n) bank*
yóujú *(n) post office*
qítā *(pr) other*

QUICK VOCAB

fúwù *(n; v)* service; to serve
hángyè *(n)* trade, profession
yíngyè *(v)* to do business
tèbié *(adv; adj)* specially, special
dàjiā *(pr)* everybody
chū *(v)* to come or to go out
sàn bù *(v-o)* to take a walk, to stroll
zhào xiàng *(v-o)* to take a picture; to have one's picture/photo taken
guàng dà jiē *(v-o)* to go window shopping
shāngdiàn *(n)* shop
jǐ *(adv; v)* crowded; to squeeze
rènào *(adj)* bustling; exciting
chúle *(. . . yǐwài)* except, apart from
wǎngbā *(n)* internet café
chàbùduō *(adv; v)* almost, nearly; to be almost the same
niánqīngrén *(n)* young person/people
Gǔgē *(N)* Google
cházhǎo xìnxī *(v-o)* to look up information (on the internet)
liúxíng *(adj)* popular, fashionable
tōng huà *(v-o)* to chat (usually by using the phone, internet etc.)
miǎnfèi *(v; adj)* to be free of charge; free
xiàndài (huà) *(adj; n)* modern; modernization
shēnghuó fāngshì *(n)* way of life, lifestyle
gēn X xiāngduì de in contrast to/with, contrary to
zuò lǐbài *(v-o)* to go to church
sīxiǎng *(n)* thinking, ideology
mǎnzú *(v)* to satisfy
jīngshén *(adj; n)* spiritual; spirit, mind
yāoqiú *(n; v)* demand; to demand, request

Grammar

1 Bìng

Bìng before *bù* or *méi* (*yǒu*) emphasizes the negation and conveys the idea that it is not what might have been expected: *Yīnggāi xià*

xuě de shíhou **bìng** *méi yǒu xià* (*Lit.* ought to/descend/snow/when//
not/have/descend).

2 Shì bu shi

Shì bu shi is used to make the question form when you wish to
indicate to the listener that you are seeking confirmation of
something you believe to be the case. It can be put at the beginning
or end of the sentence or after the subject with the following slight
shifts in emphasis:

Shì bu shi nǐ míngtiān qù yóuyǒng (swimming)?
Nǐ shì bu shi míngtiān qù yóuyǒng?

In both of these sentences you are confident that I am going
swimming tomorrow, but using *shì bu shi* softens the tone and
indicates a wish on your part to discuss the matter with me. It in
no way implies an order:

Nǐ míngtiān qù yóuyǒng shì bu shi?

At the **end** of the sentence, *shì bu shi* seeks a more direct
confirmation and conveys the idea of 'Am I right?' 'Is it true?'

All three sentences can probably be roughly translated as: 'You are
going swimming tomorrow aren't you?'

. . . *shì ma?* or . . . *duì ma?* have the same meaning as *shì bu shi*
used at the end of the sentence and they too may only appear at the
end of the sentence: *Sìchuān rén xǐhuan chī là de* (hot/spicy[food]),
shì ma? 'People from Sichuan like spicy food, don't they?' The
answer to all three forms is *Shì(a)* or *Duì* if the listener agrees and
Bù if he or she does not.

3 Huò(zhě)

Huò(zhě) 'or' is used to link statements or pronouns and nouns
whereas *háishi* 'or' (see 8.2) is used to link questions:

... xiànzài rénmen **huòzhě** zuò gōnggòng qìchē **huòzhě** kāi chē. (*Lit.* now/people/or/sit/public together/steam vehicle/or/drive/ vehicle) 'Now people either go by bus or (they) drive.'

Wǒ xǐhuan kàn bào huòzhě kàn xiǎoshuō. (*Lit.* I/like/read/ newspaper/or/read/small talk) '*I like reading the newspaper or novels.*' *Huòzhě* is used more in spoken Chinese whereas *huò* is more formal.

4 Yuè lái yuè + *adjective*

This construction is relatively easy to use if you remember the basic formula to express 'more and more of the adjective' is:

(i) *yuè lái yuè* + adjective:

> **Shēngyì yuè lái yuè hǎo ... suǒyǐ zài dà chéngshì zìxíngchē yuè lái yuè shǎo.** '*Business gets better and better, so there are fewer and fewer bikes in (the) big cities.*'
> **Lìng yī fāngmiàn, qìchē yuè lái yuè duō, wūrǎn yě yuè lái yuè yánzhòng.**
> '*By way of contrast, there are more and more cars and pollution is also getting more and more serious.*'
> **Zuò lǐbài de rén yuè lái yuè duō.**
> '*There are more and more people going to church.*'
> **Qìhòu biànhuà yuè lái yuè míngxiǎn.**
> '*Climate change is becoming more and more evident.*'

If you wish to convey ideas such as 'the quicker the better' then the construction is:

(ii) *yuè* adjective/verb *yuè* adjective/verb:

> **yuè kuài yuè hǎo** '*the quicker the better*'
> **Wǒ yuè chī yuè pàng (le).** '*The more I eat the fatter I get.*'
> But **Wǒ yuè lái yuè pàng (le).** '*I'm getting fatter and fatter.*'

5 More on the comparative

When we wish to say that 'A is up to B's standard of whatever the
adjective is' then the construction is:

A yǒu B (nàme/zhème) adjective *'A is as adjective as B'.*

Yǒu de shíhou chūntiān yǒu xiàtiān nàme rè. *'Sometimes spring is
as hot as summer.'*

The negative form, which is used more frequently, depicts an
inferior degree, i.e. that A is not up to B's standard of tallness,
goodness, etc. See the example from the text:

Ōuzhōu píngcháng méi yǒu Běijīng nàme lěng. (*Lit.* Europe/
normally/not/have/Beijing/so/cold) *'Europe is usually not as cold
as Beijing.'*

Yǒu may be omitted in the negative form.

6 Kěxī

A whole range of adjectives are made up of *kě* + verb to give the
literal meaning of 'being worth -ing', 'able to be -ed'. Some of the
more common ones are as follows:

kě'ài *'lovable, lovely'*
kělián *'pitiable, pitiful'*
kěxī *'it's a pity'*

kěkào *'reliable'*
kěpà *'terrifying (able to be feared)'*
kěxiào *'laughable, ridiculous'*

7 Months of the year

◄◐ CD 2, tr 1

yīyuè *January*
èryuè *February*
sānyuè *March*
sìyuè *April*
wǔyuè *May*
liùyuè *June*
qīyuè *July*
bāyuè *August*
jiǔyuè *September*
shíyuè *October*
shíyīyuè *November*
shí'èryuè *December*

It's a good idea to memorize these.

Note that whereas *yī* + *yuè* means 'January' (some people say *yíyuè*), *yí ge yuè* means 'one month', *èryuè* means February, but *liǎng ge yuè* 'two months' and so on. If *-chū* 'at the beginning of' or *-dǐ* 'at the end of' is added to a specific month, April for instance, we get *sìyuèchū*, '(in) early April' and *sìyuèdǐ*, 'at the end of April'. This also works with *yuè* on its own so that *yuèchū* means 'at the beginning of the month' and *yuèdǐ* 'at the end of the month'. Similarly with *nián*, 'year', *niánchū* meaning 'at the beginning of the year' and *niándǐ*, 'at the end of the year'.

8 Omission of hěn implies comparison

This point has already been touched on in 6.2 but the example from the text illustrates it beautifully as well as providing another example of the balance that is such a feature of Chinese:

qíngtiān duō, yīntiān shǎo.

9 Yī... jiù...

Yī... jiù... are used to connect two actions which follow on closely from one another:

Wǒ yī huá xuě (*Lit.* slide snow, 'ski') **jiù gāoxìng le.** *'As soon as I get skiing, I'm happy.'*
Tiānqì yī hǎo, gōngyuán lǐ de rén jiù hěn duō. . . .

It may help you to remember this construction if you think of it as *yī* verb₁, *jiù* verb₂, 'as soon as verb₁ happens, then verb₂ happens'.

10 V₁-O de V₁-O

When we wish to convey the idea that in a specified group of people, some are engaged in one activity, others in another and so on, each group and its activity is expressed by the construction V₁-O *de* V₁-O. This is repeated as many times as there are activities, with the verb object changing each time of course: *Lǎo(nián) rén* **xià qí de xià qí, dǎ pái de dǎ pái, liáo tiān(r) de liáo tiān(r)**. In other words, of the old people in the park, some are doing A (playing chess), some are doing B (playing cards) and some are doing C (chatting).

Gōngyuán lǐ sàn bù de sàn bù, zhào xiàng de zhào xiàng.
'Some people in the park are taking a stroll, others are taking photographs.'

11 Dǎ + *object*

In addition to the two examples from the text, *dǎ pái* and *dǎ tàijíquán*, *dǎ* (*Lit.* 'to hit' or 'to strike') can appear with a whole series of different objects, some of which are given below:

dǎ diànbào	打电报*	*'to send a telegram'* (*Lit.* hit electric newspaper)
dǎ diànhuà	打电话	*'to make a telephone call'* (*Lit.* hit electric speech)

dǎ gē(r)	打嗝儿	'to belch'
dǎ gǔ	打鼓	'to beat a drum'
dǎ hān	打鼾	'to snore'
dǎ hāqian	打哈欠	'to yawn'
dǎ hū(lu)	打呼噜	'to snore (coll)'
dǎ pìgu	打屁股	'to spank' (*Lit.* hit buttocks)
dǎ qì	打气	'to pump, inflate'
dǎ qiú	打球	'to play ball'
dǎ zhēn	打针	'to give or have an injection' (*Lit.* hit needle)
dǎ zì	打字	'to type' (*Lit.* hit characters)

* We've given you the Chinese characters here and in the grammar point below because they will serve as a useful reference for those wishing to learn Chinese characters later in the book.

12 *To sit, to drive, to sit astride*

The Chinese language is much more precise than is English when it comes to expressing how or by what form of transport one goes somewhere. One sits (*zuò*) in a car, bus, train, plane or boat:

zuò (坐) qìchē (汽车)	'by car' (*Lit.* steam vehicle)
zuò gōnggòngqìchē (公共汽车)	'by bus' (*Lit.* public together steam vehicle)
zuò fēijī (飞机)	'by plane' (*Lit.* fly machine)
zuò chuán (船)	'by boat'

but 'sits astride' a bicycle, a horse or a motorbike:

qí (骑) zìxíngchē (自行车)	'by bicycle' (*Lit.* self-propelling machine)
qí mǎ (马)	'on horseback'
qí mótuōchē (摩托车)	'on a motorbike'.

Note the horse radical (马) employed in the character for *qí* (you will learn all about radicals in Unit 14). *Qí* (骑) is used to provide the phonetic element for the character as a whole. We have met the verb *kāi* (开) meaning 'to open' (as of doors) or 'to turn on' (as of lights, radios, etc.) in the first grammar point of Unit 9. The same verb also means 'to drive' as of cars, trains, planes and buses.

Exercise 11.1

Choose the correct verb from *zuò*, *qí* and *kāi* to fill the blank in each sentence. Come back to this exercise when you have got to the end of the book and then write out the whole sentence in characters. It will be good practice for you.

Nǐ huì bu huì ____ mǎ? → qí → 你会不会骑马?

1 ____ *huǒchē bǐ* ____ *gōnggòngqìchē kuài duō le.*
2 ____ *fēijī de rén gōngzī hěn gāo.*
3 *Zài Zhōngguó* ____ *zìxíngchē de rén fēicháng duō.*
4 *Yǒude rén xǐhuan* ____ *mótuōchē yīnwei hěn zìyóu* (free/freedom).
5 *Yīngguórén shíqī suì cái kěyǐ* ____ *chē.*

13 Adverbial phrases of time ('time how long')

As we saw in 4.2, adverbs of 'time when' precede the verb, but adverbs of 'time how long' follow the verb: *Zhōngguórén yìbān gōngzuò **wǔ tiān** 'The Chinese generally work five days.'* (Remember that ***tiān*** does not require a measure word, see 9.13.) *Dà bùfen Ōuzhōurén měi tiān gōngzuò **bā ge xiǎoshí** (hour) 'Most Europeans work an eight-hour day'.* (Note that *měi tiān*, 'time when', precedes the verb.)

Where there is a direct object, the construction is:

1	S	V₁	O,	V₁	'time how long'
	Wǒ	**chàng**	**gēr,**	**chàng**	**liǎng ge xiǎoshí**
(*Lit.*	*I*	*sing*	*songs,*	*sing*	*two hours*)

'I sing for two hours.' or

2	S	V	'time how long'	*de* O
	Wǒ	**chàng**	**liǎng ge zhōngtóu**	**de gēr**
(*Lit.*	*I*	*sing*	*two hours' (worth of)*	*songs*

'I sing for two hours.'

De is sometimes omitted but it is helpful to beginners to think of it as always being there. (*Zhōngtóu* 'hour' is interchangeable with *xiǎoshí*.)

Exercise 11.2

This exercise uses a number of verb-object constructions, so it may be helpful to refer back to 4.3 to refresh your memory before beginning the exercise.

Change the following pattern (i) sentences into pattern (ii) sentences:

Tā kàn diànshì, kàn liǎng ge xiǎoshí. →
Tā kàn liǎng ge xiǎoshí de diànshì.

1 *Tā xī yān, xī shí fēn zhōng.*
2 *Lǎoshī* (teacher) *jiāo shū, jiāo yí ge xiǎoshí.*
3 *Gēge lù yīn* (v-o to record)*, lù bàn ge zhōngtóu.*
4 *Wǒ tàitai huà huàr, huà sān kè zhōng.*
5 *Chǎngzhǎng* (head of a factory) *kāi chē, kāi sān ge bàn* (three and a half) *xiǎoshí.*

Change the following pattern (ii) sentences into pattern (i) sentences:

Tāmen xiě yí kè zhōng de zì. → Tāmen xiě zì*, xiě yí kè zhōng.
(*xiě zì 'to write [Chinese] characters')

6 *Dìdi kàn bàn ge xiǎoshí de shū.*
7 *Laǒrén shuì yí ge bàn* (one-and-a-half) *xiǎoshí de jiào.*
8 *Wǒ yí ge péngyou zǒu qī ge zhōngtóu de lù.*
9 *Nà wèi xiānsheng shuō hěn cháng shíjiān de huà le.*
10 *Nǎ wèi xiǎojie néng dǎ jiǔ ge xiǎoshí de zì?*

Insight: learning tip

One way of revising sentences with 'time during which' phrases in them, is to think of all the verb-object phrases you can (make a list or add to those in 4.3 and assign lengths of time to each verb-object phrase) and then practise saying each one until you are fluent. Then change the length of time assigned to each verb-object phrase/action and do it all again. You will feel quite confident about this construction after you have gone through your list several times in this way.

14 *Position of conjunctions*

We have met *suīrán* 'although' in this unit and it is important to note that it is often (but not always) followed by *dànshi* 'but' at the beginning of the second half of the sentence: *Suīrán wǒ hěn lèi dànshi shuì bu liǎo jiào.* 'Although I am very tired, I can't get to sleep.'

Many conjunctions in Chinese occur in pairs as in *suīrán . . . dànshi . . .* Note that *kěshì* and *dànshi* 'but' are interchangeable.

Another example of a pair of conjunctions is *yàoshi . . . (jiù) . . .* 'if . . . then . . .'.

Yàoshi bú duìfu wūrǎn wèntí, qìhòu biànhuà jiù yuè lái yuè yánzhòng. *'If we don't deal with the problem of pollution, climate change will become more and more serious.'*

Yàoshi may sometimes be omitted and, in such cases, it is the *jiù* (and the context) that convey the conditional flavour. It is important to be aware of the existence of these 'hidden if' sentences as they can influence the meaning a great deal.

Yàoshi can be replaced by *rúguǒ* and both are often followed by *de huà*, as in the following example: ***Rúguǒ** tā bù lái (**de huà**), wǒ **jiù** bú qù.* 'If she doesn't come, I won't go.' ... *de huà* conveys the flavour of 'assuming that X is the case' (*tā bù lái*), then Y (*wǒ bú qù*).

We shall meet many more of these conjunctions as we progress through the book. Sometimes one of the pair, often the first, is omitted, although this is not the case in the two examples from the text.

Two other common pairs of conjunctions are *yīnwèi* ... *suǒyǐ* ..., 'because ... (so) ...' and *búdàn* ... *érqiě* ... 'not only ... but also ...'.

Chinese togetherness

The Chinese have developed various ways of handling their enforced 'togetherness' and, in general, they cope with crowd situations in a great deal more good-humouredly way than their western counterparts. In spite of the fact that living accommodation is generally cramped, at least in the cities, most Chinese actually find it unthinkable or even undesirable to spend much time on their own and are often surprised by some westerners' need for privacy.

Exercise 11.3
Mark the following sentences with (+) for the correct ones and (–) for the incorrect ones:

1 *Wǒ zhèng dǎ diànhuà, tā jīntiān lái de shíhou.*
2 *Nǐ míngtiān qù huá xuě* (to ski) *shì bu shì?*
3 *Mèimei shuì jiào, shuì sān ge zhōngtóu.*
4 *Dìdi shuì jiào sì ge xiǎoshí.*
5 *Xià bān yǐqián, tā zhèngzài shài tàiyáng* (v-o to sunbathe) *ne.*
6 *Zǒnglǐ* (premier) *xiǎng bāyuèdǐ qù Yàzhōu* (Asia).
7 *Wǒ péngyou zhēn qíguài, yī huí jiā, jiù tā dǎ tàijíquán.*

8 *Diànshì kāizhe méi ma?*

9 *Zǒngtǒng* (president) *xià ge yuè qù Fēizhōu* (Africa), *qù èr ge yuè.*

10 *Xiàtiān rúguǒ xià dà yǔ, qù lǚxíng jiù bù hǎo bàn le!*

Exercise 11.4

Translate the following passage into colloquial English:

Yǒu rén xiǎng Yīngguó tiānqì bù zěnmeyàng dànshi fǎnguòlái (conversely) *yě yǒu yìxiē rén juéde Yīngguó tiānqì hěn búcuò, bù lěng yě bú rè, dōngtiān yě bù yídìng xià xuě, dànshi yǒu yì diǎn bùdé bù* (cannot but, have to) *chéngrèn* (admit), *Yīngguó bùguǎn* (no matter) *nǐ zài nǎr dōu jīngcháng* (regularly, frequently) *xià yǔ. Zhōngguó yìbān qíngtiān duō, yīntiān shǎo dànshi Yīngguó xiāngfǎn* (opposite), *yīntiān dūo, qíngtiān shǎo. Yǒu rén shuō zhè ge gēn Yīngguórén de guài* (strange) *píqi* (temperament) *yǒu guānxi, yě yǒu rén shuō zhè ge gēn Yīngguórén kě'ài de píqi yǒu guānxi. Nǎ zhǒng shuōfǎ* (way of saying things) *duì ne? Qǐng nǐ shuōshuo!*

TESTING YOURSELF

Translate the following into Chinese:

1 *I was in the middle of watching TV when my friend came on Sunday.*

2 *I'd like to go with you to (use gēn nǐ yìqǐ [together] qù) the internet café.*

3 *As soon as she starts (kāishǐ) snoring, I leave!*

4 *The windows were open but the door was closed.*

5 *There was a lot of activity (use rènào) going on in the park – some people were doing taijiquan, others were taking photographs and some people were playing cards.*

6 *When the weather's fine, I sit outside and read a book (use -zhe).*

7 *We sing for half an hour every evening.*

8 *Because she didn't phone at all on Tuesday I don't know whether I'm going or not (use* bìng*).*

....

9 *If I'm at my parents' home, I frequently go to the park nearby (*fùjìn*) to play tennis (*wăngqiú*) (use* dào . . . qù*).*

....

10 *She said with a smile (*xiào*) that she was already married.*

....

11 *Are you listening to the radio? No, we're listening to a tape (use* lù yīn*).*

....

12 *You're going to see a play (*kàn xì*) tomorrow, aren't you? What a pity I can't go with you.*

....

12

In the restaurant

In this unit you will learn
• *how to express approximate numbers*
• *how to say* first, second, third, *etc.*
• *more about the use of* **le**
• *the difference between* **cái** *and* **jiù**

◄) CD 2, tr 2–6

Yì tiān, Wáng xiānsheng hé Shǐ xiǎojie zài chī wǔfàn. Tāmen yù dào (meet by chance) **le yí wèi hěn yǒuhǎo de fúwùyuán, Liú Hónggāng.**
Mr King and Ms Shaw are at lunch one day when they encounter a friendly waiter, Liú Hónggāng. As you may experience yourself, waiters in China often like to try out their English on you.

Liú	Have you ordered? Nǐmen cài dìng hǎo le méi you?
Shǐ	Dìng hǎo le, xièxie nǐ. Píjiǔ lái le – à, bú shi Běijīng píjiǔ ér shi Qīngdǎo píjiǔ.
Liú	Méi guānxi, Qīngdǎo píjiǔ gèng hǎo hē. Nín pǔtōnghuà shuō de zhēn hǎo.
Shǐ	Guòjiǎng, guòjiǎng, shuō de bù hǎo.
Liú	Shuō de hěn hǎo. Nín shi nǎ guó rén?
Shǐ	Nǐ cāicai ba.
Liú	Bú shi Měiguórén jiù shi Yīngguórén.

Shǐ	Wǒ shi Yīngguórén dànshi wǒ māmā shi Měiguórén. Nǐ zěnme zhīdao ne?
Liú	Yīnwèi gāngcái nín shi gēn nín péngyou shuō Yīngyǔ! Nín péngyou yě huì shuō Hànyǔ ma?
Shǐ	Yě huì shuō.
Wáng	Shuō de méi tā hǎo.
Liú	À, nǐmen liǎ de Hànyǔ zhēn bàng, xué le jǐ nián le?
Shǐ	Xué le liǎng nián le.
Liú	Nín ne?
	[Zhǐ de shì Wáng Yǒngshòu].
Wáng	Xué le sì nián le.
Liú	Nǐmen zài Zhōngguó dāi le hěn cháng shíjiān le ba?
Wáng	Bù cháng, lái le sān ge duō yuè le.
Liú	Zhè shi nǐmen dì yí cì lái Zhōngguó ma?
Wáng	Bù, tā shi dì yí cì, wǒ shi dì èr cì.
Liú	Nǐmen zhēn xíng, fāyīn hěn qīngchu, méi shénme yángwèi(r), hěn biāozhǔn de pǔtōnghuà. Zhōngwén bú shi hěn nán xué ma?
Wáng	Nán shi nán, kěshì yě yǒu tā róngyì de dìfang, bǐfang shuō Zhōngwén fāyīn、yǔfǎ dōu bìng bù nán, nán de shi shēngdiào. Duì wǒmen xīfāngrén lái shuō, Zhōngwén de sìshēng háishi xiāngdāng kùnnan de.
Liú	Xiě Hànzì ne?
Shǐ	Xiě Hànzì hěn bù róngyì, yīnwèi wǒmen wàiguórén yìbān shi chéngniánrén cái kāishǐ xué Zhōngwén, bú xiàng nǐmen liù、qī suì jiù kāishǐ le. Dāngrán hái yǒu yì diǎn, Zhōngwén jiùshì nǐmen de mǔyǔ.
Liú	Nà dàoshì. Xiàng nǐmen zhè yàng de shuǐpíng, bǎozhǐ kàn de dǒng ma?
Shǐ	Kàn de dǒng.
Liú	Xiǎoshuō ne?
Shǐ	Yě xíng, dànshi bú rènshi de zì hái yào chá zìdiǎn. À, cài lái le, zhēn piàoliang a! Kàn qǐlai yídìng hěn hǎo chī.
Liú	Nàme, nǐmen mànmānr chī ba, bú zài dǎrǎo nǐmen le. Yǒu shénme shì, suíshí kěyǐ jiào wǒ.
Wáng	Hǎo de, xièxie nǐ, yǒu shénme shì yídìng zhǎo nǐ. Gēn nǐ liáo tiān(r) hěn yǒu yìsi.

Liu	Have you ordered?
Shi	Yes, we have, thank you. Here comes the beer – oh, it's Qingdao beer not Beijing beer.
Liu	It doesn't matter, Qingdao beer is even better. You (pol) speak really good Chinese.
Shi	You're too kind, I don't speak it well at all.
Liu	Yes, you do. Where are you from?
Shi	Have a guess.
Liu	You're either American or British.
Shi	I'm British but my mother is American. How did you know?
Liu	Because you (pol) were speaking English with your friend just now! Can your (pol) friend also speak Chinese?
Shi	Yes, he can.
Wang	I'm not as good as she is.
Liu	Oh, both of you have got brilliant Chinese. How many years have you been studying it?
Shi	Two years (so far).
Liu	How about you? (He is referring to Wang Yongshou.)
Wang	I've been studying for four.
Liu	I suppose you've been in China for a very long time?
Wang	No, we haven't, we've only been here a little over three months.
Liu	Is this your first time in China?
Wang	No, it's her first but my second.
Liu	You're really great! Your pronunciation is very clear with no foreign overtones. It's good standard Chinese. Isn't Chinese awfully hard to learn?
Wang	Yes, it is, but there are some easy things about it, too – for example, neither Chinese pronunciation nor grammar is at all difficult. What is difficult are the tones. As far as we westerners are concerned, the four tones in Chinese are still pretty difficult.
Liu	How about writing Chinese characters?
Shi	Writing Chinese characters is very difficult because we foreigners generally do not start learning Chinese until we are adults, not like you people who start at six or seven. Of course, the other thing is that Chinese happens to be your mother tongue.

Liu	Yes, indeed. With Chinese at a level like yours, can you read newspapers?
Shi	Yes.
Liu	How about novels?
Shi	They're OK, too, but we still have to look up characters we don't know in the dictionary. Oh, the food's here, it looks great. It certainly looks appetizing.
Liu	I'll leave you to get on with your meal in peace. Call me if you need anything.
Wang	Fine, thank you. If we need anything we'll certainly ask for you. It's been really interesting chatting with you.

yǒuhǎo *(adj) friendly*
dìng *(v) to order (in advance); to book, reserve; to subscribe to*
-hǎo *(RVE) to do the action of the verb satisfactorily*
píjiǔ *(n) beer*
bú shì ... ér shì ... *not ... but ...*
Qīngdǎo *(N) Qingdao*
pǔtōnghuà *(n) common spoken language (Modern Standard Chinese; Mandarin)*
guòjiǎng *you flatter me*
cāi *(v) to guess*
bú shì A jiù shi B *if it's not A then it's B*
zěnme *(QW) how*
yīnwèi *(conj) because (also read yīnwei)*
gāngcái *(TW) just now*
Yīngyǔ *(n) English language*
bàng *(adj) excellent (coll)*
dāi *(v) to stay*
zhǐ *(v) to refer to; to point at/to*
cháng *(adj) long*
duō *(num) used to express an approximate number*
dì *ordinal prefix*
cì *(MW) time, occasion*
fāyīn *(n) pronunciation*

QUICK VOCAB

biāozhǔn *(adj; n) accurate; standard, criterion*
yángwèi(r) *(n) foreign flavour*
A shi A dànshi . . . *it's A all right but* . . .
róngyì *(adj) easy*
bǐfang shuō *for example*
yǔfǎ *(n) grammar*
shēngdiào *(n) tone*
duì X lái shuō *as far as X is concerned*
xīfāngrén *(n) westerner*
sì shēng *(n) the four tones*
háishi *(adv) after all, still (emphatic)*
xiāngdāng *(adv) quite (a bit)*
kùnnan *(adj; n) difficult; difficulty*
xiě (zì) *(v(-o)) to write (characters)*
Hànzì *(n) Chinese character(s)*
Zhōngwén *(n) Chinese language (usually written form)*
chéngniánrén *(n) adult*
cái *(adv) not . . . until . . .; only*
kāishǐ *(v) to begin*
diǎn *(n) point, aspect*
jiùshì *(be) precisely*
mǔyǔ *(n) mother tongue*
dào(shì) *(adv) indeed, as it happens (indicates something contrary to the general train of thought)*
zhè yàng *(dem adj; n) this kind of, such a*
shuǐpíng *(n) level, standard*
bào(zhǐ) *(n) [zhāng or fèn] newspaper*
-dǒng *(RVE; v) -ing with understanding; to understand*
xiǎoshuō *(n) [běn] novel*
chá *(v) to check*
zìdiǎn *(n) [běn] dictionary*
chá zìdiǎn *(v-o) to consult a dictionary*
-qǐlai *(RVE) see 12.13*
dǎrǎo *(v) to disturb*
yǒu yìsi *(v-o) to be interesting*

Grammar

1 Bú shi . . . ér shi . . .

If we wish to convey the idea that 'it is not A but B' we use the construction *bú shi A ér shi B*, where *shi* is the verb 'to be' and *ér* is a conjunction which has come into modern Chinese from the classical language meaning, among other things, 'and', 'but':

Bú shi Běijīng píjiǔ ér shi Qīngdǎo píjiǔ.
Bú shi zhūròu ér shi niúròu. (*Lit.* Not/be/pig meat/but/be/cattle meat) *'It's not pork but beef.'*

2 Bú shi . . . jiù shi . . .

'If it is not A then it is B', *bú shi A jiù shi B*. This construction is easily confused with the one above but by remembering that *jiù* means 'then' you should be able to distinguish them correctly:

Bú shi Měiguórén jiù shi Yīngguórén.
Bú shi niúròu jiù shi yángròu. (*Lit.* Not/be/cattle/meat/then/be/ sheep meat) *'If it's not beef then it's mutton.'*

Of course, *bú shi . . . jiù shi . . .* could be translated as 'either . . . or . . .' but in doing so it somehow loses its flavour.

3 Zěnme *and* zěnmeyàng

Zěnme and *zěnmeyàng* can both be used adverbially before a verb to ask how something is done, although *zěnme* is used much more frequently in this way: *Nǐ zěnme zhīdao ne? Nǐ zěnmeyàng zhīdao?*

Zěnme can also be used to ask the reason why something happens but *zěnmeyàng* cannot be used in this way: *Tā zěnme méi gěi nǐ dǎ diànhuà ne?* (*Lit.* She/why/not (have)/for/you/hit/electric speech) *'How come she hasn't phoned you?'*

Zěnme feels a little less formal than *wèi shénme*, 'why?', hence its translation as 'how come' in the previous example. Note that question words such as *zěnme*, *zěnmeyàng* and *wèi shénme* often take *ne* at the end of the sentence containing them (see 3.3). Only *zěnmeyàng* can be used after the complement of degree marker *de* (see 6.2) or to ask something about the subject of a sentence:

Tā de pǔtōnghuà zěnmeyàng? *'What's his (spoken) Chinese like?'*

4 More on le

i We know that *le* used at the end of a sentence can indicate a change of state (see 5.9). In this position it can also indicate that a certain state of affairs has already taken place:

   a **Píjiǔ lái le.**
   b **Nǐmen liù, qī suì jiù kāishǐ le.**
   c **Wǒ zuótiān xiě zì le.** (*Lit.* I/yesterday/write/characters)
     'I did some writing yesterday.'
   d **Tā jīntiān zhōngwǔ zuò huǒchē le.** (*Lit.* He/today/noon/ sit/fire vehicle) *'He took the train at noon today.'*

In c and d the object is simple and unmodified. As soon as the object is modified in any way we have to use the verbal suffix *le* (see 3.4) and the sentence *le* is dropped: *Wǒ zuótiān xiě le hěn duō zì* 'I did a lot of writing yesterday.' By doing this, we focus our attention on what has been done rather than on what has simply taken place.

ii If the object is quantified, then the use of the verbal suffix *le* and the sentence final particle *le* generally indicates the continuation of some action or state of affairs. Of course, this also involves 'time how long' (see 11.13) so the construction is as follows:

Wǒ xué Zhōngwén, xué le wǔ nián le. or
Wǒ xué le wǔ nián (de) Zhōngwén le.
'I have been studying Chinese for five years (and still am).'

Compare this with:

Wǒ xué le wǔ nián (de) Zhōngwén. *'I studied Chinese for five years (and am no longer doing so, i.e. it's over and done with).'*

Another example may help to highlight this difference:

Tā zài Zhōngguó zhù le bàn nián le. *'She has been living in China for six months (and still is).'*
Tā zài Zhōngguó zhù le bàn nián. *'She lived in China for six months (and is no longer doing so).'*

iii A sentence consisting of a verb *le* followed by a simple object is regarded as being incomplete, something else is expected to follow. Thus *Wǒ chī le fàn* is not a complete sentence in Chinese and must be followed by another clause:

Wǒ chī le fàn jiù zǒu le. *'I left after having eaten.'*
Wǒ chī le fàn jiù zǒu. *'I'll leave after eating.'*

(In the second example, *le* shows completed action in the future, further illustrating the point that *le* should not be thought of as a past tense marker.) Where the object is a simple one, the addition of the final particle *le* makes the sentence complete: *Wǒ chī le fàn le* 'I've eaten.'

iv When a past action is a habitual one or there is no need to emphasize its completion, no *le* is used after the verb: *Qùnián tā chángcháng lái* 'He often used to come last year.' *Qùnián xiàtiān tā zài Běijīng Yǔyán Dàxué gōngzuò* 'Last summer he worked at the Beijing Language [and Culture] University.'

5 Approximate numbers

There are several ways of indicating approximate numbers in Chinese:

i When *duō* is placed after a whole number plus its measure word or after a whole number plus a noun acting as a measure word (*nián*, *tiān*), it represents a fraction of one unit: *sān ge duō xiǎoshí* 'three and a bit hours, over three hours', *yì tiān duō* 'one and a bit days'.

ii When *duō* is placed after the whole number but before the measure word or noun acting as a measure word, it represents a whole number in itself: *sānshí duō nián* 'over 30 years' (anything from 31 to 39), *yì bǎi duō yè* 'one hundred-odd pages' (could be 110, 125, etc.).

iii *Jǐ* can be used to indicate an indefinite number under ten: *Zhǐ shàng xiězhe jǐ ge Hànzì* 'There were several Chinese characters written on the paper.' *Lǎoshī yǒu shí jǐ běn zìdiǎn* 'The teacher has a dozen or so dictionaries' (any number from 11 to 19). *Xuésheng yǐjīng xué le jǐ bǎi ge shēngcí le* 'The students have already learnt several hundred new words (so far).'

iv Two consecutive numbers may be put together: *Wǒ zhǐ* (only) *qùguo liǎng、 sān cì Měiguó* 'I've only been to the States two or three times.' NB The pause mark (*dùnhào*), and not a comma, is used between 'two' and 'three'. *Xuéxiào yǒu bā、 jiǔshí ge háizi* 'There are 80 or 90 children in the school.' *Nǐmen liù、 qī suì jiù kāishǐ le.* If the object is a pronoun, it precedes *yí cì*, etc. *Wǒ kànguo tā yì、 liǎng cì* 'I've seen him/her once or twice.'

v *Zuǒyòu* (*Lit.* left right) may be put after a number to indicate 'around' or 'about': *yì bǎi ge rén zuǒyòu* 'about 100 people', *liǎng diǎn bàn zuǒyòu* 'around 2.30'.

6 Dì + number

Ordinal numbers (first, second, third) are made by putting *dì* in front of the number: *dì yī* 'first', *dì'èr* 'second' and *dì sān* 'third'. Thus, *dì yí cì* means 'the first time'. In competitions of any sort, the Chinese are encouraged to remember *Yǒuyì dì yī, bǐsài dì'èr* 'Friendship first, competition second.' Make sure you distinguish between *èryuè* 'February', *dì'èr ge yuè* 'the second month' and *liǎng ge yuè* 'two months'.

7 Bú shi . . . ma?

Bú shi . . . ma? asks a question which expects the answer 'yes'.

The word order is:
(Topic) subject *bú shi* (adverb) verb (other elements) *ma?*
Tā bú shi hĕn lèi ma? *'Isn't she very tired?' (Yes, she is.)*
Xué Zhōngwén bú shi hĕn nán xué ma? *(Yes, it is.)*

8 *A shi A dànshi/kĕshì . . .*

'It's A all right but . . .'. The main clause (A *shi* A) contains a positive
or negative statement with some sort of a concession being made after
dànshi/kĕshì: **Guì shi guì, dànshi zhìliàng fēicháng hăo** 'It's expensive
all right, but the quality is excellent.' *Tā hăo shi hăo, kĕshì píqi hĕn
huài* 'She is nice, but she's got a terrible temper' (*Lit.* temperament
very bad). *Nán shi nán, kĕshì yĕ yŏu tā róngyì de dìfang.* 'Yes, it is
difficult, but there are some easy things about it too!'

Exercise 12.1
Answer these questions using the A *shi* A construction followed by
a suitable 'but' clause of your own devising:

1 *Tā de fāyīn bú shi hĕn qīngchu ma?*
2 *Wáng xiānsheng de Hànyŭ shuĭpíng gāo ma?*
3 *Zhè bĕn xiăoshuō yŏu méi you yìsi?*
4 *Duì wàiguórén lái shuō, Zhōngwén de sìshēng shì bu shi hĕn
   nán?*
5 *Qīngdăo píjiŭ hăo hē ma?*

9 Cái *and* jiù

Both *cái* and *jiù* are adverbs indicating something about time. *Cái*
indicates that something takes place later or with more difficulty
than had been expected. It translates into English as 'not . . . until . . .',
'then and only then': *Tā sān diăn zhōng cái lái* 'He didn't come
until 3' (but I had asked him to come at 2.30).

It is a common mistake for students to try to translate the 'not' in English with a *bù* or *méi* in Chinese. Remember that 'not' is already contained in *cái*.

Jiù, by the same token, indicates that something takes place earlier or more promptly than expected: *Tā sān diǎn zhōng jiù lái le* 'He came at 3/He was there by 3' (but I had asked him to come at 3.30).

Both *cái* and *jiù* must come *immediately before* the verb regardless of what other elements there are in the sentence. *Jiù* usually takes *le*, whereas *cái* does not, perhaps because the verb with *cái* does not convey any real sense of completion. The following examples should help to make the distinction between the two clearer:

a **Wǒ qǐng tā shàngwǔ bā diǎn bàn lái dànshi tā bā diǎn jiù lái le** '*I asked him to come at 8.30 am but he was there by 8*' (i.e. too early).
b **Wǒ qǐng tā shàngwǔ bā diǎn bàn lái dànshi tā jiǔ diǎn bàn cái lái** '*I asked him to come at 8.30 am but he didn't come until 9.30*' (i.e. too late).

a **Gēn nǐ liáo tiān(r) jiù zhīdao nǐ zhè ge rén hěn yǒu yìsi** '*As soon as I chatted to you I realized what a fascinating person you are.*'
b **Gēn nǐ liáo tiān(r) cái zhīdao nǐ zhè ge rén hěn yǒu yìsi** '*It was not until I'd had a chat with you that I realized what a fascinating person you are.*'

Cái and *jiù* can also be translated as 'only' in sentences such as:

Tā cái sān suì
Tā jiù sān suì   '*She's only 3 years old.*'

Exercise 12.2
Fill in the blanks with the adverbs *jiù* or *cái*:

1 Wǒ dào le Zhōngguó yǐhòu ____ zhīdao Qīngdǎo píjiǔ hěn hǎo hē.

2 *Wǒ dào Zhōngguó qù yǐqián ____ zhīdao Qīngdǎo píjiǔ hěn hǎo hē.*

3 *Nà fēng (MW) xìn (letter) xiě hǎo le méi you? Xiě hǎo le, zuótiān ____ xiě hǎo le.*

4 *Nà fēng xìn yǐjīng xiě hǎo le ma? Hái méi xiě hǎo ne, míngtiān ____ xiě.*

5 *Tā kāishǐ xué Hànyǔ yǐhòu ____ fāxiàn (discover) Hànyǔ yǔfǎ bìng bù nán.*

6 *Diànyǐng qī diǎn bàn kāishǐ, tā bā diǎn ____ lái.*

7 *Qù Měiguó yǐqián ____ tīngshuō (be told/heard it said) Měiguórén hěn kāilǎng (open).*

8 *Yīnwèi shìqing hěn zhòngyào (important) wǒ ____ dǎrǎo nǐmen.*

10 Jiùshì

Jiùshì 'to be precisely (something or somebody)', 'to be nothing else but' is used in the following way:

Question: **Wǒ zhǎo Yuán lǎoshī. Nǐ rènshi tā ma?** *'I'm looking for Teacher Yuan. Do you know him?'*

Answer: **Wǒ jiùshì tā.** *'I am he (and no other).'*

11 Zhè zhǒng *but* zhè yàng de

Unlike *zhǒng* which is a true measure word and can therefore directly precede its noun, *yàng* acts as a noun with *zhè* and *nà* and must therefore take *de* before any noun which follows it: *zhè zhǒng qíngkuàng* 'this sort of situation' but *zhè yàng de shuǐpíng* 'this kind of level'. *Zhèyàng* and *nàyàng* can operate independently as adverbs to mean 'in this way' or 'in that way' ('like this' or 'like that'). *Zhèyàng zuò bù hǎo* 'It's no good doing it like this.' *Zhèyàng lěng, duì shēntǐ bù hǎo* 'Weather as cold as this is bad for the health.' *Tā xiě de zhèyàng kuài, zhēn méi xiǎng dào* 'I never expected him to write so quickly.'

12 More on resultative verbs

Resultative verbs were first introduced in 8.1, potential resultative verbs in 10.1. In this unit, we meet three more resultative verb endings:

-*hǎo* meaning 'to do the action of the verb satisfactorily' (and therefore also expressing the idea of completion).

-*dǒng* meaning 'to do the action of the verb with understanding'.

-*hǎo* can be found with many different verbs such as *zuò*, *shuō*, *zhǔnbèi* ('to prepare') and *xiě* but -*dǒng* is limited to *tīng* ('to listen') and *kàn* ('to read'):

Nǐmen cài dìng hǎo le méi you?
Bàozhǐ kàn de dǒng ma?

-*qīngchu* can also act as a resultative verb ending meaning 'to do (the action of the verb) clearly'.

13 More on directional endings

we met simple directional endings in 8.1 and compound directional endings in 10.3. Apart from their more literal meaning, a certain number of directional endings have extended or figurative meanings: verb + *qǐlai* (*Lit.* 'up': *ná qǐlai* 'to pick up', *zhàn qǐlai* 'to stand up'):

i 'To start to do' the action of the verb (and continue doing it) or for a state of affairs to start (and continue): *tán qǐlai* 'start to chat'. *Tiānqì nuǎnhuo qǐlai le* 'The weather's starting to get warm.'

ii To express a view or convey an impression: *kàn qǐlai* 'from the look of things'. *Kàn qǐlai yào xià yǔ* 'It looks like rain.' *Tīng qǐlai hěn yǒu dàolǐ* (*Lit.* Listen up/very/have/reason). 'It sounds very reasonable.' *Shuō qǐlai róngyì, zuò qǐlai nán* 'It's easier said than done.'

iii *Xiǎng qǐlai* is widely used to mean 'to remember', 'to recall':

A, wǒ xiǎng qǐlai le, tā xìng Chén. *'I've got it, she was called Chen.'*

Another very useful directional ending used in a figurative way is -*xiàqu* (*Lit.* '(go) down') which is used to mean 'to carry on' doing the action of the verb: *zuò **xiàqu*** 'to carry on doing' (in a different context it could mean 'to sit down'!). *Tīng **xiàqu*** 'to carry on listening'.

Exercise 12.3
Fill in the blanks with the most appropriate resultative verb ending (two sets of brackets indicate a compound directional ending). You may need to refer back to 8.1, 10.1 and 10.3 to refresh your memory:

1 *Zhè kè kèwén* (text) *wǒ kàn bu* ( ), *néng bu neng* (be capable of/can) *bāngzhù* (help) *wǒ yíxià?*
2 *Zhuōzi tài dà le, bān bu* ( ) ( ).
3 *Wǒ zài wàimiàn děngzhe nǐ. Qǐng nǐ zǒu* ( ) ( ), *hǎo bu hao?*
4 *Liànxí* (exercise) *wǒ hái méi zuò* ( ) *ne, jīntiān shìqing tài duō le.*
5 *Nǐ zěnme bù chī cài ne? Shì bu shi yǐjīng chī* ( ) *le?*
6 *Wǒ tài bèn* (stupid) *le, gēn bu* ( ) *nǐmen liǎng wèi.*
7 *Jīntiān de bàozhǐ wǒ méi kàn* ( ), *bù zhīdao zài nǎr.*
8 *Zuìjìn* (recently) *hǎishuǐ* (seawater) *rè* ( ) ( ) *le, míngtiān kěyǐ qù yóuyǒng* (swim).
9 *Nà ge shāfā tài xiǎo le, zuò bu* ( ) *sān ge rén.*
10 *Zhè ge zì xiě* ( ) *yìdiǎnr, yàobùrán wǒ zěnme kàn de* ( )?
11 *Nǚ péngyou shénme shíhou* (when?) *zhǎo de* ( ) *shì hěn nán shuō de.*
12 *Zhè běn xiǎoshuō suīrán méi yǒu yìsi, dànshi hái yào kàn* ( ) ( ).

Zhōngwén, Hànyǔ and pǔtōnghuà

Zhōngwén and Hànyǔ can both be translated as 'the Chinese language'. Zhōngwén is used more in connection with the written language, whereas Hànyǔ (the language of the Han people, China's largest nationality) is used more for the spoken language. The Chinese language has eight major dialects but of the Chinese-speaking population, about 70% speak the northern dialect, which is why it has been made the basis of pǔtōnghuà, 'the common spoken language', the *lingua franca* for the whole of China.

Chinese classlessness

One of the delights of Chinese society is that on some levels (as we have seen in the text for instance), people appear unaffected by apparent differences in social status, and natural curiosity and real friendliness win the day. In general it is much easier for foreigners, with or without the right 'credentials' or connections (*guānxi*) to meet relatively well-known public figures, particularly those in the arts, than it would be for them in the west. If you are one of those people who 'succeeds' in this direction, beware of a false sense of your own importance – it may be that your Chinese contacts are just being polite! That many famous people seem to remain relatively untouched by their own success is a measure of how civilized, in real terms, the Chinese are.

Exercise 12.4
Make up your own sentences using the following constructions:

1	yī . . . jiù . . .	5	yuè lái yuè . . .
2	yòu . . . yòu . . .	6	yàoshi . . . jiù . . .
3	bú shi . . . jiù shi . . .	7	suīrán . . . dànshi . . .
4	bú shi . . . ér shi . . .	8	bú shi . . . ma?

Exercise 12.5
Translate the following passage into colloquial English:

Liú Hónggāng shi ge fúwùyuán (waiter). *Tā hěn xǐhuan tā de gōngzuò, yīnwèi tā yǒu jīhuì* (opportunity) *gēn hěn duō bù tóng* (not same, different) *de rén jiēchù* (come into contact with). *Bú shi Měiguórén jiù shi Yīngguórén, bú shi Zhōngguórén jiù shi Rìběnrén. Yǒude wàiguórén huì shuō hěn liúlì* (fluent) *de pǔtōnghuà, dànshi yángwèi(r) hěn zhòng* (heavy), *fāyīn、yǔfǎ dōu bú dà duì, kěshì hái tīng de dǒng. Yǒude wàiguórén yī shuō qǐ Hànyǔ lai jiù hěn hǎoxiào* (funny), *yīnwèi méi yǒu shénme shēngdiào. Yě yǒu yìxiē wàiguórén Hànyǔ shuǐpíng hěn gāo, zài Zhōngguó dāi* (stay) *le hěn cháng shíjiān le, Zhōngwén bàozhǐ, xiǎoshuō dōu kàn de dǒng, Hànzì yě huì xiě yìxiē. Chéngniánrén xué qǐ Hànyǔ lai bìng bù róngyì, zhíde* (be worth) *pèifú* (admire) *tāmen. Yǒude rén lián* (even) *tāmen zìjǐ de mǔyǔ yě shuō bu hǎo, gèng bú bì* (not have to) *shuō yì mén* (MW) *wàiyǔ le!*

NB *lián . . . yě . . .* go together in the same way as *yàoshi . . . jiù . . .* (see 11.14).

TESTING YOURSELF

Translate the following into Chinese:

1 *I guess that if she's not American, she must be English.*

2 *His tones are really excellent but his pronunciation is hopeless.*

3 *I've already been to (1)/China(3)/six times(2)/but (I)* still *can't understand what people are saying.*

4 *As far as my best friend is concerned, writing is even more interesting than reading.*

5 *His hair (tóufa) is really long. How come he hasn't got it cut (jiǎn) yet?*

6 *She mastered (use* xué hǎo*) Modern Standard Chinese after only two years.*

7 *He's been learning Chinese for three years so his standard is pretty good now.*

8 *I didn't know until yesterday that he does not know how to use a Chinese dictionary.*

9 *Everyone likes chatting (use* tán tiān/liáo tiān) *to interesting people but there aren't many of them around (use* zhè yàng).

_____

10 *I'll only disturb you if it's something important (*zhòngyào).

_____

11 *I liked him very much after only talking with him once or twice.*

_____

12 *He is terribly lazy (*lǎn*). It took him until today to read one page.*

_____

*Announcement (*jìnggào*) – come back to this later and see how many radicals you can identify in the 'title' and the first three lines in Chinese characters.*

Halfway review

Exercise 12A

Do you remember what these words mean? For the moment, ignore the characters – you can come back to them later.

Nouns: Find the correct Chinese word in the right-hand column for each of the words in English and put the number of the English word next to the letter of the Chinese word. To make it more interesting, we have added an extra word in Chinese.

1	*dictionary*	___ a	yìsi	意思
2	*level/standard*	___ b	jìjié	季节
3	*season*	___ c	zìdiǎn	字典
4	*activity*	___ d	fāyīn	发音
5	*pronunciation*	___ e	huódòng	活动
		___ f	shuǐpíng	水平

Verbs: Find the correct English word in the right-hand column for each of the words in Chinese and put the number of the Chinese word next to the letter of the English word. This time we have added an extra verb in English.

1	dǎrǎo	打扰	___ a	*to search (on the internet)*
2	cházhǎo	查找	___ b	*to deal with; tackle*
3	duìfu	对付	___ c	*explain*
4	shuā yá	刷牙	___ d	*disturb*
5	jiěshì	解释	___ e	*brush teeth*
			___ f	*play chess*

Adjectives: Find the correct English word in the right-hand column for each of the words in Chinese and put the number of the Chinese word next to the letter of the English word. (Again we have added an extra adjective in English).

1	yǒu yíngyǒng	有营养	___ a	*difficult*
2	yǒu yìsi	有意思	___ b	*serious*
3	yánzhòng	严重	___ c	*clear*
4	cōngming	聪明	___ d	*nutritious*
5	qīngchu	清楚	___ e	*clever*
		有营养	___ f	*interesting*

Exercise 12B

Complete each of these phrases with the correct Chinese word to give the meaning of the English phrase in brackets.

....

1	yì _____ *(a little bit)*		**6**	liǎng _____ *(day)*
2	yì _____ *(straight)*		**7**	sān _____ *(year)*
3	yí _____ *(a little while)*		**8**	sì _____ *(tones)*
4	yì _____ *(usually)*		**9**	wǔ _____ *(years old)*
5	yí _____ *(certainly)*		**10**	liù _____ *(times)*

....

Exercise 12C

How do you say the following phrases in Chinese?

1 to enjoy life
2 chat with someone/people
3 fashionable fast food
4 (of food) both tasty and pleasant to look at
5 a long story
6 increasingly obvious
7 cycle to work
8 most European countries
9 apart from these
10 socialism (*shèhuì zhǔyì*) with Chinese characteristics

Exercise 12D

This next exercise is quite difficult, so you might want to wait rather than try it now and then come back and have another go at it when you have finished the book.

Translate these sentences into Chinese. (The words in bold are ones you have met with recently.)

1 Don't wait till you are retired to start to **enjoy life**.
2 I don't have time to **chat with people** online (*zài wǎng shàng*).
3 In this city, are McDonald's and KFC **fashionable fast food**?
4 The food she cooks is **both tasty and pleasant to look at**.
5 I told him **a long story**, but he said it was not long enough.
6 Is global warming (*quán qiú biàn nuǎn*) **increasingly obvious**?
7 If the weather is good, I will **cycle to work**.
8 **Most European countries** are developed (*fādá*) countries.
9 **Apart from these** characters, I can't write any other ones.
10 Can you explain to us what '**socialism with Chinese characteristics**' means?

Congratulations!

You have now come to the end of Unit 12, which also marks the end of all the major grammatical points, except for *bǎ* in Unit 19. All these grammatical points will, of course, be reinforced in the following units, but it would be a good idea to go back over any points you are still not sure about. You might also like to spend some time on Unit 13, as this is both a revision and an extension of all the grammar points you have met so far.

Unit 14 is an introduction to Chinese characters that I hope all of you will read, even if you don't intend to spend much time actually learning and practising to write them. Chinese characters are an integral part of Chinese culture and even a superficial understanding of them will help you to appreciate their beauty and long history.

13

Grammar review

In this unit you will learn
- *about common measure words*
- *about denominations of money*
- *about time words and expressions*
- *about resultative verbs*
- *about directional endings*
- *about auxiliary verbs and conjunctions*
- *some useful vocabulary that is found nowhere else in this course*

As this unit is for reference, characters have been included where they may be helpful.

Common measure words

Pinyin	Character	Classification	Examples
bǎ	把	*Objects with a handle, chairs*	*knife, umbrella, toothbrush, chair*
bāo	包	*packet (e.g. 20)*	*cigarettes*
bēi	杯	*cup*	*tea, coffee*
běn	本	*volume*	*books, magazines*

Pinyin	Character	Classification	Examples
bù	部		film
dǐng	顶		hats
fèn	份		newspaper
fēng	封		letter
fù	副		sunglasses
gè	个	used if you have forgotten the correct one!	person
jià or tái	架、台	machines	television, radio, computer
jiān	间		room
jiàn	件	piece, article	clothes, luggage
jù	句	phrase	remarks
juǎn	卷	reel, spool	toilet paper, camera film
kē	棵		tree
kè	课		text, lesson
kǒu	口	family members	
kuài	块	piece	soap, land
liàng	辆	wheeled vehicles	car, bicycle
píng	瓶	bottles	
qún	群	crowd, group, flock	sheep, bees
shǒu	首		poem
tào	套	set	suite of furniture, set of stamps
tiáo	条	long and winding, carton (e.g. 200)	towel, fish, street, river, cigarettes
wèi	位	person (polite)	teacher, Mrs
zhāng	张	flat, rectangular objects	map, bed, table
zhī	枝、支	long and thin objects	pencil, cigarette (one)
zhī	只	animals, one of paired body parts	butterfly, cat, hand, foot, leg
zuò	座	large, solid thing	mountain, bridge, building

Denominations of money and time used like measure words

Pinyin	Character	Meaning
fēn	分	1/10 of a **máo**
máo	毛	1/10 of a **kuài**
kuài	块	basic unit of Chinese currency
fēn	分	minute
kè	刻	quarter
tiān	天	day
nián	年	year

Time words and expressions

1 *Time words*

Time words have two functions:

a As adverbs, they stand before a verb or another adverb to form a time background for the verb: *Wǒ **jīntiān** bú qù* 'I'm not going today.' ***Shàng ge xīngqī** tā méi qù gōngzuò* 'She didn't go to work last week.'

b As nouns, they may function as the subject or object of a verb or modify another noun (with *de* 的): ***Jīntiān** shì **xīngqīsì*** 'Today is Thursday.' ***Zuótiān** de bào, nǐ kàn le mei you?* 'Did you see yesterday's paper?'

2 Types of 'time when' expression (standing before the verb)

a Time words and phrases such as:

*cóngqián	formerly
jīntiān	today
yè lǐ	in the night
nà tiān	that day
zhè jǐ ge yuè	these last few months
zuótiān wǎnshang	yesterday evening
tiāntiān zhōngwǔ	every day at noon
qīyuè sì hào	July 4th
dì'èr tiān	the second or next day
měi (ge) xīngqītiān	every Sunday

b Time clauses such as:

xiǎo de shíhou	when one is young
xuéxí Zhōngwén de shíhou	when one is learning Chinese
cóng xīngqīyī dào xīngqīwǔ	from Monday till Friday

c Lapse of time *before* negated verbs:

Wǒ sān tiān méi chī dōngxi.	I didn't eat a thing for three days.
Sān tiān bù chī fàn bù xíng.	It won't do not to eat for three days. (Note the double negative.)
Wǒ hěn jiǔ méi yǒu hē jiǔ le.	I haven't touched alcohol for ages.
Wǒ nà sì nián méi kànjiàn tāmen.	I didn't see them during those four years.

* NB Don't confuse *cóngqián* with *yǐqián*, which can be used as a conjunction at the end of a phrase as well as an adverb. *Cóngqián* cannot be used in this way.

3 *Types of 'time during which' expression (standing after the verb)*

a Num + MW + (*de* 的) and num + MW + noun + (*de* 的) such as: *liù tiān* 'six days', *liǎng ge xīngqī* 'two weeks', *shí nián de Zhōngwén* 'ten years of Chinese', *yí ge bàn yuè de Rìwén* 'a month and a half of Japanese'.

b Indefinite quantities of time
    i **Tāmen zǒu le hěn jiǔ** (a long time) **le.**
      They've been gone for a long time.
    ii **Wǒ zhǔnbèi kèwén, zhǔnbèi hěn jiǔ le.**
      I spent a lot of time on preparing the text.

[NB In sentence **b i** there are two *le*s – action still going on; in **ii** one *le* – action happened in the past.]

Resultative verbs (an introduction)

A resultative verb consists of a stem (an action verb) with a complement expressing the result of the action of the stem, e.g. *Tā kàn cuò le zhè ge zì.* 'S/he read this character wrongly', *Nǐ de huà, wǒ tīng qīngchu le.* 'I heard clearly what you said.' As can be seen from this, the ending or complement may be followed directly by an object.

A resultative ending is regularly followed by the perfective suffix *-le* and is negated by *méi (you)* 没(有), e.g. *Nǐ de huà wǒ méi tīng qīngchu.* 'I didn't hear clearly what you said.' If the result has not yet been achieved then, of course, the sentence is negated by *bù*: *Zhōngwén xiǎoshuō wo hái bù néng kàn dǒng.* 'I can't read Chinese novels (i.e. novels written in Chinese) yet.'

When the sentence refers to future time or is in the imperative form, the suffix *-le*, is not normally used: *Wǒmen yídìng yào xué hǎo Zhōngwén.* 'We certainly must/want to master Chinese', *Niàn shú kèwén.* 'Read the text aloud until you're familiar with it.' (As a resultative verb ending, *shú* only occurs with verbs such as *kàn* and *niàn*.) Apart from common resultative endings such as -*hǎo* and -*wán*, there are also directional endings that can function as resultative endings: *Yào kàn zhè bù diànyǐng de rén fēicháng duō, wǒ hái méi kàn shàng ne.* 'Masses of people want to see this film; I (still) haven't managed to see it (yet).' *Nǐ mǎi dào zhè běn shū méi you?* 'Did you manage to buy this book?'

Resultative verb endings: common functional endings

Ending		Type of result	Used with (examples)	Limitations
wán	完	completion	zuò 作、做、 shuō 说、xiě 写、kàn 看	
hǎo	好	satisfaction, completion	as above + bàn 办、 zhǔnbèi 准备	
huì	会	learning, mastery	xué 学	
zháo	着	attainment	zhǎo 找、mǎi 买、 shuì 睡	
liǎo	了	possibility	zuò 作、ná 拿、chī 吃、 mǎi 买、mài 卖、 shuì 睡	potential form only; actual form: -le 了
cuò	错	error	shuō 说、xiě 写、zuò 作、 tīng 听	
dào	到	arrival, attainment	xiǎng 想、bān 搬、sòng 送、 pǎo 跑、zǒu 走、xué 学、 tán 谈	
qǐ	起	i afford to	mǎi 买、chī 吃	potential only

Ending		Type of result	Used with (examples)	Limitations
		ii *respect for, self-respect*	zhù 住、 duì 对	*potential only*
bǎo	饱	*satisfaction of appetite*	chī 吃	
dǒng	懂	*understanding, comprehension*	tīng 听、 kàn 看	
jiàn	见	*perception (sensory)*	kàn 看、 tīng 听	
kāi	开	*separation, leaving room for movement*	kāi 开、lí 离、 zǒu 走	
dòng	动	*movement*	ná 拿、 bān 搬	*potential only*
gānjìng	干净	*cleanness*	xǐ 洗、shuā 刷	

[NB The example verbs listed under 'used with' are far from an exhaustive list. Some endings such as *-bǎo* 饱, *-dǒng* 懂 and *-jiàn* 见 are limited by their essential meaning.]

Directional endings or complements

Both intransitive action verbs of motion and transitive action verbs indicating the handling of objects commonly take directional endings or complements: *Tāmen cóng wàibian zǒu jìnlai le* 'They walked in from outside', *Wǒ jīntiān ná lai le hěn duō zhàopiàn* 'I've brought a lot of photos today.'

Directional endings are either: (1) simple or (2) compound. In (2), the second element is either *lái* 来 or *qù* 去. Only a small group of simple directional endings form compound directional endings with *lái* 来 or *qù* 去 as the second element. These are *shàng* 上, *xià* 下, *jìn* 进, *chū* 出, *qǐ* 起, *huí* 回, *guò* 过 and *kāi* 开.

If the object is a **place word** it must come **before** *lái* 来 or *qù* 去.
If not, it may come either before *lái* 来 or *qù* 去 or after the verb,
which may have a simple or compound ending:

> **Wǒ yào qù túshūguǎn** (library) **ná wǒ de bàozhǐ lai**. *'I want
> to/must go to the library to fetch my newspaper.'*

> **Tā cóng zhuōzi shang ná qǐ tā de bào lai, zuò xiàlai kàn.**
> *'S/he picked up his/her newspaper from (on) the table and sat
> down and/to read it.'*

> **Tā cóng zhuōzi shang ná qǐlai tā de bào.** *'S/he picked up his/her
> newspaper from (on) the table.'*

Other directional endings are *dǎo* 倒, *zǒu* 走 and *diào* 掉, but these
and other similar directional endings cannot form compound
endings with *lái* 来 or *qù* 去.

Auxiliary verbs

An auxiliary verb (also known as a model verb) is a member
of a limited class of verbs which occur before action verbs or
verbal expressions, adding a semantic value of modality (can,
will, must) to the expression as a whole. They cannot take
verbal complements or verbal suffixes and are not used as
modifiers before nominals. They usually express the modality
of action verbs.

Auxiliary verbs expressing capability

e.g. *néng* 能, *huì* 会, *kěyǐ* 可以:

i   **Néng lái, jiù qǐng lái.** *'Please come if you can.'*
ii **Tā huì shuō Hànyǔ.** *'S/he can speak Chinese.'*
iii **Nà ge gōngchǎng** (factory) **kěyǐ zhìzào** (produce) **hěn duō dà
    jīqì** (machine). *'That factory can produce a lot of heavy machinery.'*

Huì 会 usually expresses an acquired capability, although *néng* 能 and *kěyǐ* 可以 can have a similar meaning:

  i **Nǐ huì huá xuě, wǒ bú huì.** *'You know how to ski, but I don't.'*
  ii **Tā néng kàn Zhōngwén xiǎoshuō.** *'S/he is able to read Chinese novels.'*

Auxiliary verbs expressing permission or prohibition

These are verbs such as *néng* 能 and *kěyǐ* 可以:

  i **Zhèr kěyǐ** (or *néng*) **xī yān.** *'Smoking is permitted here.'*

NB When *néng* 能 and *kěyǐ* 可以 express capability, the negated verb can only be *bù néng* 不能. When expressing prohibition, both *bù néng* 不能 and *bù kěyǐ* 不可以 can be used.

Auxiliary verbs expressing possibility

Verbs such as *huì* 会 (usually in relation to some future occurrence):

  i **Bú huì xià yǔ, nǐ qù ba.** *'Off you go, it can't (possibly) rain/won't rain.'*
  ii **Tā huì lái bāngzhù** (help) **nǐ.** *'S/he may come to help you.'*
  iii **Wǒ xiǎng zhènme jiǎngjiù** (elegant) **de lǚguǎn** (hotel) **bú huì tài piányi (de).** (*Lit.* I think such an elegant hotel can't be too inexpensive.) *'I shouldn't think such an elegant hotel can be very cheap.'*

Yào 要 *as an auxiliary verb*

There are three meanings to *yào* 要 when it is an auxiliary verb:

  1 expressing will, wish or 'wanting to'
  2 expressing necessity 'must'
  3 expressing the future likelihood of something happening.

*Wǒ **yào** qù túshūguǎn* 'I want to go to the library.' This sentence could also mean 'I'll be going to the library' or even 'I must go to the library.' Such ambiguities are removed if the sentence is negated. The negative counterpart of (1) is ***bù xiǎng*** 不想 and of (2) ***bú yòng*** 不用. *Yào* 要 is also used with '*le* 了' to indicate (3), e.g. *yào xià yǔ le* 'It's going to rain.' ***Bú yào (bié)*** 不要(别) is used for negative imperatives, e.g. *Nǐ **bú yào/bié** lái!* 'Don't (you) come!' and not 'You don't want to come.'

Auxiliary verbs expressing desire, inclination or preference

Verbs such as *xiǎng* 想 or *xǐhuan* 喜欢:

i **Wǒ bù xiǎng qù kàn tā, wǒ xiǎng zài jiā lǐ kàn diànshì.**
   'I don't fancy going to see him, I fancy staying at home and watching TV.' Note the overlap with *yào* 要 (1) in the negative.
ii **Háizi xǐhuan wánr.** *'Children like to play.'* (habit)

[NB Both these verbs can function as transitive verbs (as can *yào* 要).]

Auxiliary verbs expressing willingness

Verbs such as *yuànyì* 愿意 and *kěn* 肯:

i **Tā yuànyì cānjiā** (take part in) **pīngpāngqiú** (table tennis) **bǐsài.** *'S/he's willing to/wishes to take part in the table-tennis competition.'*
ii **Tā bú shi bù néng lái, ér shi bù kěn lái.** *'It isn't that s/he can't come, but that s/he's unwilling to.'*

Auxiliary verbs expressing 'ought to', 'should'

Verbs such as *yīnggāi* 应该, *gāi* 该, *yīngdāng* 应当:

i **Nǐ bù yīnggāi nàme shuō.** *'You shouldn't talk like that.'*
ii **Wǒ xiànzài gāi zǒu le.** *'I ought to go now.'*

Auxiliary verbs expressing necessity (other than yào 要)

Verbs such as *děi* 得, *bìděi* 必得, *bìxū* 必须:

i **Wǒ děi zǒu le.** *'I must go.'*
ii **Wǒ jīntiān bìděi kàn wán nà běn shū.** *'I must finish reading that book today.'*

Their negative counterparts are *bú yòng* 不用, *bú bì* 不必 and *bù xūyào* 不需要.

Other modal verbs

Verbs such as *gǎn* 敢 'to dare to', *pà* 怕 'to be afraid of' (*pà* 怕 can take a noun as its object), *hǎo yìsi* 好意思 'have the nerve to':

i **Wǒ bù gǎn** (dare) **gēn tā shuō huà.** *'I don't dare talk to him.'*
ii **Zhè ge háizi hěn pà jiàn shēngrén** (stranger). *'This child is very much afraid of meeting strangers.'*

NB Some grammarians maintain that *pà* 怕 is not a real auxiliary verb because it can take *hěn* 很, *gèng* 更, etc.

iii **Zuò le zhè zhǒng shì, kuī tā hái hǎo yìsi shuō ne!** *'Fancy his doing that sort of thing and then having the nerve to talk about it!'* (This is really hard stuff!)

Remember that auxiliary verbs:

- *cannot* take aspect markers, e.g. *le* 了, *-guo* 过, *-zhe* 着
- *cannot* be modified by intensifiers such as *hěn* 很, *gèng* 更
- *cannot* be nominalized
- *cannot* occur before the subject
- *cannot* take a direct object.

Auxiliary verbs *must* co-occur with a verb (or an 'understood' verb).

búdàn . . . érqiě (or **yě/hái**) . . . **不但 . . . 而且** (or **也/还**)	*not only . . . but also*
rúguǒ (**de huà**) . . . **jiù** . . . **如果** (**的话**) **. . . 就** **yàoshi . . . jiù . . .** **要是 . . . 就**	*if . . . then*
yào bù . . . jiù **要不 . . . 就**	*if not . . . then*
yào bú shì . . . jiù . . . **要不是 . . . 就**	*if not that . . . then*
jiǎrú . . . yě . . . **假如 . . . 也** **jiǎshǐ . . . yě . . .** **假使 . . . 也**	*supposing, in the event that . . . still*
jíshǐ . . . yě (**hái**) . . . **即使 . . . 也**(**还**) **jiùshì . . . yě** (**hái**) . . . **就是 . . . 也**(**还**)	*even if . . . still*
jìrán . . . jiù . . . **既然 . . . 就**	*since . . . then*
bùguǎn . . . **不管 . . .** **búlùn . . .** **yě** (**hái**) . . . **不论 . . .** **也**(**还**) **wúlùn. . .** **无论 . . .**	*no matter whether . . . still*
suīrán . . . dànshi/kěshì . . . **虽然 . . . 但是/可是**	*although . . . but*
yīnwèi . . . suǒyǐ . . . **因为 . . . 所以**	*because . . . therefore*
yóuyú . . . (**jiù**) **由于 . . . 就**	*because, owing to, due to . . . then*
chúfēi . . . cái . . . **除非 . . . 才**	*unless . . .*

Common pairs of conjunctions

zhǐyào . . . yě/jiù . . . 只要…也/就	*if only, as long as . . . then*
zhǐyǒu . . . cái 只有…才	*only if . . . then*
búshi . . . érshi . . . 不是…而是	*it's not . . . but*
búshi . . . jiùshi . . . 不是…就是	*if it's not . . . then it's*
fánshì . . . dōu . . . 凡是…都	*all . . .*
chúle . . . yǐwài . . . 除了…以外	*besides . . .*
lián . . . yě/dōu . . . 连…也/都	*even . . .*
fēi + *verb* **. . . bùkě** 非 + *verb* …不可	*must (do the action of the verb)*

Adverbs as conjunctions

One common type of conjunction has the same element in both the first and the second clause.

yòu . . . 又	**yòu . . .** 又	*both . . . and*
yě . . . 也	**yě . . .** 也	*not only . . . but also*
yuè . . . 越	**yuè . . .** 越	*the more . . . the more . . .*
(yù) . . . 愈	**(yù) . . .** 愈	*(more formal than yuè)*
yìbiān + V_1, **yìbiān** + V_2 一边 + V_1, 一边 + V_2		*doing V_1 at the same time as V_2*

A second type has an element in the second clause that is different from that in the first.

....

yī V_1,	**jiù** V_2	*as soon as V_1 happens, then V_2 begins*
— V_1,	就 V_2	

....

Useful vocabulary

Colours

hóngsè *(de) red*
huángsè *(de) yellow*
lánsè *(de) blue*
lǜsè *(de) green*
bái *(de) white*
hēi *(de) black*

Parts of the body

tóu *head*
bózi *neck*
gēbo *arm*
shǒu *hand*
zhǐ *finger*
yāo *waist*
tuǐ *leg*
jiǎo *foot*

This notice actually means 'Beware slippery path – pay attention to your feet.' It even rhymes:

Xiǎo xīn lù huá
Liú shén zú xià

When you have read and digested Unit 14 and spent more time on Chinese characters, come back and see if you can spot the radical for each of the characters used.

Daily meals

zǎofàn *or* **zǎocān** *(more formal)*
breakfast
wǔfàn *or* **wǔcān** *(more formal)*
lunch
wǎnfàn *or* **wǎncān** *(more formal)*
dinner

QUICK VOCAB

14

An introduction to Chinese characters

In this unit you will learn
- *what the earliest characters looked like*
- *about the evolution of characters over the years*
- *how characters are composed*
- *about radicals or significs*
- *how Chinese children learn to write characters*
- *some basic rules for writing characters*
- *how to recognize some useful public notices and signs*

What are Chinese characters? These are the symbols that the Chinese language is written with. You will surely have seen some written over Chinese restaurants or on the takeaway menus. What on earth have they to do with 'China Garden' or 'Jade Cottage', you may well have asked yourself? Well, here's your chance to find out!

Written Chinese is understood by more people in the world than any other language and its earliest written records date back over 3500 years. These were the markings scratched onto tortoise shells and animal bones that were used to predict future events. These 'oracle bones' were used in divination rites during the Shang dynasty (c. 1500 BC). Even at that time, the Chinese had already developed rather a sophisticated language with quite an extensive vocabulary. From these ancient writings we can see that many of the earliest characters were pictures or what we call *pictographs*.

Take a look at the following examples, which show the evolution of such characters into their modern day form. You should move from left to right, don't forget: the character now in use being the one on the extreme right!

⊙	⊖	⊟	日	**rì**	*sun*
☽	☽		月	**yuè**	*moon*
		几	人	**rén**	*person*
			木	**mù**	*tree*

Abstract concepts could also be represented by symbols:

⌣	⊥		上	**shàng**	*up*
⌢	⊤		下	**xià**	*down*

As time went on and people needed to express more complex ideas or concepts, pictographs were extended or combined to form *ideographs*. A sun and a moon together mean 'bright', a woman under a roof means 'peace', a woman with a child beside her means 'good', a sun rising behind a tree means 'east'. A tree doubled forms the character for 'forest' and if tripled it means a 'dense forest':

日 *sun*   + 月 *moon* = 明 *bright*
女 *woman* + 宀 *roof*   = 安 *peace*
女   + 子 *child* = 好 *good*
日   + 木 *tree*   = 東 *east*
木   + 木   = 林 *forest*
林   + 木   = 森 *dense forest*

(Extensions of meaning were sometimes inherent in the character itself and required no further addition, thus 日 'sun' also means 'day', 月 'moon' also means 'month'.)

What a wonderful way of creating language this was, but, of course, only a limited number of ideas could be expressed in this way. Characters of this type that possess no phonetic element are relatively few and account for maybe 10% of all Chinese characters but many of them are still in common use today.

Most characters contain a phonetic element. Such characters are known as *phonograms* or *radical-phonetic* characters. They are made up of two components, one called the *radical* (the Chinese call these 'significs' or 'common heads'), which indicates the classification of the character, and the other the *phonetic*, which should give a clue to its pronunciation. Thus 青 *qīng* 'blue', 'green', 'black' is a character in its own right but it is the phonetic for such characters as 情 *qíng* 'emotion', 'feelings', 清 *qīng* 'pure', 'clear' and 请 *qǐng* 'ask', 'request' whereas the radical for these is 'heart' 忄, 'water' 氵 and 'speech' 讠 (言), respectively:

青　　　　　　　 = 　*blue, green, black*
忄 *heart*　 + 青 = 情 *emotion, feelings*
氵 *water*　 + 青 = 清 *pure, clear*
讠 *speech* + 青 = 请 *ask, request*

Before you get too carried away with the neatness of this one, I should say that as a result of the gradual development of the language and the many changes that have occurred in pronunciation, many phonetics now only indicate the approximate sound: 工 *gōng* 'work' becomes 空 *kōng* 'empty' (穴 is a cave), silk + *gōng* becomes *hóng* 红 'red' and insect + *gōng* also becomes *hóng* 虹 'rainbow':

工　　　　　　 = 　**gōng**
穴 *cave*　 + 工 = 空 **kōng**
纟 *silk*　　 + 工 = 红 **hóng**
虫 *insect* + 工 = 虹 **hóng**

Others are of even less assistance, but learning to recognize phonetics and radicals is of great help in learning characters. Fortunately, there are not too many radicals to be learnt. Older dictionaries list 214, modern ones have reduced this to 189. If the forms in combination and/or 'full' characters are listed separately, this can increase the number to around 250. A good many of these are very little used, so I have listed 80 or so of the more common ones in this unit, in the hope that they will serve as a useful reference point in your recognition and learning of characters.

Now look at the first column of the radical table: this shows what each radical looks like on its own (not all of them appear as characters in their own right in modern Chinese). The characters in brackets in the first column are known as 'full' characters. The second column shows what they look like when they are combined with a phonetic if there is any change (otherwise this column is left blank). The third gives the romanization and the last column the meaning.

Radicals/significs

In isolation	In combination	Romanization	Meaning
人	人 亻	rén	person
刀	刀 刂	dāo	knife
口	口	kǒu	mouth
土	土 扌	tǔ	earth
女	女	nǚ	woman
宀		–	roof
山	屮 屮	shān	mountain
心	心 忄	xīn	heart
手	手 扌	shǒu	hand
日		rì	sun
木		mù	tree
水	水 氵	shuǐ	water
火	火 灬	huǒ	fire
疒		–	disease/sickness
目		mù	eye
禾		hé	grain
竹	𥫗	zhú	bamboo
纟 (糸/系)		sī	silk

In isolation	In combination	Romanization	Meaning
肉	月*	ròu	flesh
月	*	yuè	moon
艹 (草)	艹 艹	cǎo	grass
言	讠	yán	speech
车 (車)	车	chē	cart/carriage
辶		–	walking
金	钅	jīn	metal (gold)
食	饣	shí	food
马 (馬)		mǎ	horse
鱼 (魚)		yú	fish
鸟 (鳥)		niǎo	bird (long tailed)
亠		–	above
冰	冫	bīng	ice
厂		–	cliff
八	八, ⸌	bā	eight
儿		ér	child, son
又		yòu	also, again
力		lì	strength
口		–	an enclosure
大		dà	big, noble
子	子, 孑	zǐ	child, son
寸		cùn	inch
尸		shì	corpse
巾		jīn	napkin, towel, handkerchief
广		–	covering, roof
彳		chì	to step (with left foot)
攵		–	to tap, rap
阝 on left		–	abundant, mound
邑 on right	阝	yì	region
门 (門)		mén	door
小	小, 丷	xiǎo	small
犬	犬, 犭	quǎn	dog
示	礻	shì	an omen; express

* Characters with the 'moon' and 'flesh' radical are no longer differentiated and appear under the same 'radical', viz. 月.

In isolation	In combination	Romanization	Meaning
玉		yù	jade
戈		gē	spear, lance
贝 (貝)		bèi	shell/object of value
丶		diǎn	dot
一		héng	horizontal
丨		shù	vertical
见 (見)		jiàn	to see
爪	爫	zhuǎ	claw
穴		xué	cave, hole
立		lì	to stand
衣	衣, 衤	yī	clothing
石		shí	stone, mineral
田		tián	field
矢		shǐ	arrow
羊	䒑, 𦍌, 羊	yáng	sheep
米		mǐ	rice
耳		ěr	ear
页 (頁)		yè	page/leaf
虫		chóng	insect
舟		zhōu	boat
走		zǒu	walk/travel
酉		yǒu	(i) 10th of Twelve Earthly Branches (ii) spirit made from ripe millet
足	⻊	zú	foot/enough, satisfied
身	身	shēn	body
角 / 角		jiǎo	horn, angle
青		qīng	blue/green/black
雨	⻗	yǔ	rain
隹		zhuī	bird (short tailed)
革		gé	hide/leather/ remove
骨 / 骨		gǔ	bone
黑		hēi	black/dark
羽 (羽)		yǔ	feather/wing

Many of these radicals were originally pictographs but some of them have been simplified so much that the original picture has almost been lost. Any radicals that appear in brackets in the first column are so-called 'full' characters and these are still in use in Hong Kong, Singapore, Taiwan and other overseas Chinese communities. The Chinese, needless to say, have their own way of describing individual characters (and radicals) as you will see in Unit 17, in which Mr King explains to the assistant in the travel agency how his name is written. If you really 'get into' characters, you will go into this aspect in greater depth. For the moment, however, if we say that the water radical (氵) is described as being *sān diǎn shuǐ* 'three drops water', that characters with the speech radical (讠) on the left-hand side are described as having *yán zì páng(r)* 'yan character side', (i.e. the character *yán* at the side) and that characters with grass *cǎo* (艹) on top are described as *cǎo zì tóu*, having 'a grass character head', you will have some idea of how this works.

Since the founding of the People's Republic of China in 1949, the Chinese have simplified a number of their characters (well over 2000) in an attempt to improve the literacy of the ordinary population. Until then, characters had remained essentially unchanged for about 2000 years. There is now a permanent committee responsible for language policy. The majority of books, magazines and newspapers printed in the People's Republic are now written in simplified characters, as is this book. The main principles used in simplification are: (a) changing one part of a character, (b) striking out one or two parts of a character, (c) substituting a 'simple' character for a 'difficult' one and (d) reconstructing the whole character. The following examples are divided into these four categories. When you have done some more work on characters come back and see if you can work out what has happened in each case!

a *Changing one part of a character*

1	劉 刘	liú
2	禮 礼	lǐ
3	難 难	nán
4	環 环	huán
5	漢 汉	hàn

b *Striking out one or two parts of a Character*

6	務 务	wù
7	處(處) 处	chù
8	開 开	kāi
9	標 标	biāo
10	醫 医	yī
11	習 习	xí
12	滅 灭	miè
13	號 号	hào

14	麗 丽	lì
15	婦 妇	fù
16	鄉 乡	xiāng
17	豐 丰	fēng
18	蟲 虫	chóng

c *Substituting a 'simple' character for a 'difficult' one*

19	鬱 郁	yù
20	穀 谷	gǔ
21	醜 丑	chǒu

d *Reconstructing the whole character*

22	頭 头	tóu
23	靈 灵	líng
24	龜 龟	guī
25	體 体	tǐ

How do the Chinese learn to write characters?

Illiteracy in China is reckoned to be between 20–25%, but in reality it is likely to be higher. Literacy in the towns is far higher than it is in the countryside, for obvious reasons. Primary school education is free in China but university education is now very expensive so there is less incentive for rural children to study. In any case, many rural parents see little use in their children gaining a higher education. They are much keener that their children should work and bring in money.

How do Chinese children master such a complicated system of writing anyway? The answer is that they start *very* young and spend a lot of time on it, both at home and in school, far more than we have to do in learning how to write English. At this point, I shall introduce you to one or two learning aids that are widely used in China and which may serve as an inspiration to you in your learning of characters. There are numerous little books entitled 看图识字, *kàn tú shí zì* 'Look at the picture and recognize the

tóu
头

yǎn jing
眼睛

bí zi
鼻子

zuǐ ba
嘴巴

ěr duo
耳朵

yá chǐ
牙齿

shǒu
手

jiǎo
脚

guō
锅

wǎn
碗

hú
壶

pán
盘

kuài
筷

sǎn
伞

bēi
杯

lán
篮

character' or 你认识吗? *Nǐ rènshi ma?* 'Do you know (it)? (i.e. the character)' and these contain drawings of everyday objects, parts of the body, fruit, vegetables, different types of weather, common actions like singing, washing – you name it and it's there somewhere. The following drawings are extracts from one such little book.

Another system is to have a small card with a drawing of the object on one side and the *pinyin* and characters for it on the other. You will see Chinese children from the age of three upwards shuffling these cards around. Most Chinese couples are only allowed one child and they usually encourage him/her to start learning to read and write as early as possible.

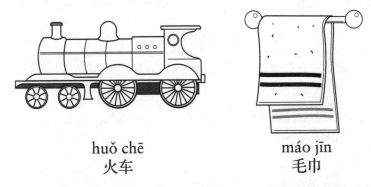

huǒ chē
火车

máo jīn
毛巾

Literal meanings: 'fire vehicle' (train) and 'hair cloth' (towel).

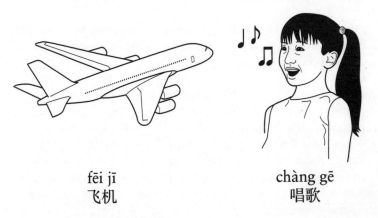

fēi jī
飞机

chàng gē
唱歌

Literal meanings: 'fly machine' (aeroplane) and 'sing song' (to sing).

You can make your own 'flashcards' as you work your way through the book from Unit 15 onwards and you may decide to go back and make them for Units 1–12 also, as these contain a lot of basic vocabulary. The characters for all the vocabulary items in the texts appear in the Chinese (*pinyin*)–English vocabulary at the back of the book. Your flashcards will normally consist of the character or characters on one side and the *pinyin* and the English on the other. Work through them looking at the character side first, seeing how many of the characters you recognize. Check your answers with the *pinyin* and English on the back. Put the ones you get right on one side and then work your way through the ones you got wrong, again putting to one side the ones you get right this time. Carry on until you have mastered them all.

As your vocabulary (and pile of flashcards) increases, you may have to put the ones you are unfamiliar with the first time through on one side and tackle them again on another occasion. This exercise should be repeated constantly! Make your cards a handy size for taking around with you on buses, trains and the underground. Having worked through your flashcards 'recognizing' the characters, do it the other way around. Look at the *pinyin* and English side and try writing out the Chinese character for it. This is much more difficult. Check your answer with the character on the other side. Adopt the same system as before, discarding the ones you get right and 'keeping' the ones you get wrong.

You do realize that, by deciding to learn Chinese, you have made a decision that means you will never again be able to complain that you have nothing to do, don't you?

Chinese children also trace the characters in copybooks, which may or may not contain material that we would regard as propaganda. Here is the first page from a copybook printed in 1970 (Cultural Revolution time) which contains Mao's famous speech on 'Serve the People' *Wèi Rénmín Fúwù* delivered by him at a memorial meeting for Zhang Side. When you have worked through a few of the units in characters come back and see if you can spot the date.

为	人	民	服	务	(一九四四年九月八日)
	我	们	的	共	产	党	和	共
产	党	所	领	导	的	八	路	军、	新
四	军,	是	革	命	的	队	伍。	我	们
这	个	队	伍	完	全	是	为	着	解
放	人	民	的,	是	彻	底	地	为	人

Page from 1970s copybook

This extract illustrates the point that each individual Chinese character occupies the same amount of space, i.e. a square of the same proportions, whether it be in the mind or actually indicated as here (so as to help children keep their characters all the same size). Characters which go together and form a 'word' such as *àiqíng* 爱情 'love' are not written any closer together than the two characters for 'I love' *wǒ ài* 我爱 although 'love' is one word and 'I love' is two words. (At least this avoids the headache we have with *pinyin* of deciding what should be joined and what should be split.) Because each character occupies the same amount of space, I always encourage beginners to start practising characters on squared paper, as this forces you to observe this practice.

Basic rules for writing characters

As you can imagine, in order to be able to write characters, there are some basic rules that you need to master. This is important if you are to remember them, because in order to store them away so that it can reproduce them when you require it to, the brain needs to operate a kind of orderly filing system. To do this, it needs all the help it can get. Most characters are made up of two or more basic structural parts called 'character components' although, of course, some character components such as 日 *rì* 'sun' can stand by themselves as we have mentioned earlier. Although the total number of characters is quite large (I won't put you off by telling you precisely *how* large), the number of character components is limited. These components are written with a number of basic strokes, illustrated now:

Stroke	Name		
、	点	**diǎn**	*dot*
一	横	**héng**	*horizontal*
丨	竖	**shù**	*vertical*
丿	撇	**piě**	*left falling*
㇏	捺	**nà**	*right falling*
㇀	提	**tí**	*rising*
亅乚乙	钩	**gōu**	*hook*
㇕㇖	折	**zhé**	*turning*

These strokes are basically straight lines and were traditionally written in ink with a hair brush. The main directions are from top to bottom and from left to right. The arrows on the following set of basic strokes show how the characters are written by showing the direction each stroke takes:

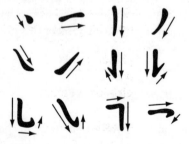

The rules of stroke order in writing Chinese characters and character components are as follows:

Example	Stroke order						Rule
十	一	十					First horizontal, then vertical
人	丿	人					First left falling, then right falling
三	一	二	三				From top to bottom
州	丶	丿	丷	州	州	州	From left to right
月	丿	刀	月	月			First outside, then inside
四	丨	冂	叨	四	四		Finish inside, then close
小	亅	小	小				Middle, then the two sides

There is a table of the stroke order of Chinese characters in Units 15–18 to help you practise writing characters correctly. When looking at a character decide whether it can be split into an upper and lower part or perhaps a left and a right. Has it got some sort of a roof? Or a base? Is it symmetrical? Asking yourself these sorts of questions should give you a better chance of getting the stroke order right. Perhaps you may like to try to copy or trace the following public notices and signs. Numbers 14–18 may be seen in and around Beijing.

Some useful public notices and signs

	Chinese characters	Pinyin transliteration and literal meaning	English translation
1	银行	**yínháng** silver business	bank
2	汽车站	**qìchēzhàn** steam carriage stop	bus stop
3	男厕所	**nán cèsuǒ** male lavatory place	men's lavatory
4	女厕所	**nǚ cèsuǒ** female lavatory place	women's lavatory

	Chinese characters	Pinyin transliteration and literal meaning	English translation
5	派出所	**pàichūsuǒ** *assign/send place*	*police station (local)*
6	邮局	**yóujú** *post office*	*post office*
7	饭馆	**fànguǎn** *rice establishment*	*restaurant*
8	入口	**rùkǒu** *enter mouth/opening*	*entrance*
9	出口	**chūkǒu** *come/go out mouth/opening*	*exit*
10	危险	**wēixiǎn**	*danger*
11	谢绝参观	**xièjué cānguān** *refuse/decline visit*	*no admission*
12	禁止吸烟	**jìnzhǐ xī yān** *prohibit/forbid inhale tobacco*	*no smoking*
13	禁止照相	**jìnzhǐ zhào xiàng** *prohibit reflect appearance*	*photography forbidden*
14	天安门	**Tiān'ānmén** *heaven peace gate*	*Tiananmen/ The Gate of Heavenly Peace*
15	长安街	**Cháng'ān jiē** *long peace street*	*Changan Street*
16	北京饭店	**Běijīng Fàndiàn** *north capital rice shop*	*Beijing Hotel*
17	王府井	**Wángfǔjǐng** *king residence well*	*Wangfujing (Street)*
18	鸟巢国家体育场	**Niǎocháo Guójiā Tǐyùchǎng** *bird nest country physical culture open ground*	*Bird's Nest National Stadium*

Even today, the art of calligraphy (the writing of Chinese characters as an art form) is highly regarded in China and many educated Chinese will hang scrolls of characters, beautifully mounted, on their walls, just as we might hang a print of a picture by, say, Turner or Picasso. Calligraphers all have their own individual styles and, of course, their admirers and critics, just as painters do. (As calligraphy is an art with its roots in the ancient past, these scrolls are always written in the traditional way from top to bottom and usually in their full form which is visually more pleasing.)

Using a Chinese–English dictionary

Most of the dictionaries you will have access to use *pinyin* to list the characters in alphabetical order according to their pronunciation. This is only of use if you know how a particular character is pronounced; if you don't, you will have to look it up using the radical. (There are other systems but this is the most straightforward at this stage.) Having identified the radical (not always an easy task in itself!) and counted up the number of strokes it has, you look for it in the radical index at the front of the dictionary. Radicals are arranged according to the number of strokes they have – all the radicals with 'one stroke' 一画 *yī huà* come first, all the radicals with 'two strokes' 二画 *èr huà* next and so on. Each radical has a number assigned to it and this may vary slightly from dictionary to dictionary – don't automatically assume it is always going to be the same. Having found which number radical it is (the number may be to the left or to the right of the radical itself), then look it up in the character index proper, which follows and, further, which lists each radical in order. Under each radical are listed all the characters that have that radical in common. These are listed in turn according to the number of strokes they have when the radical has been taken away.

Thus 情 *qíng* 'emotions' is listed under the heart radical 忄 as having eight strokes 八画, but it will come after 恨 *hèn* 'hate', which has six. 吗 *ma* (question particle) will come under the mouth radical and be listed as having three strokes 三画 and will precede 哭 *kū* 'weep, cry', which has seven. I hope you have got the idea! Having found the character you are looking for in the index, you will either find a page number next to it or the *pinyin* and tonemark, either of which will enable you to look it up in the dictionary proper. It sounds hard work but it's not as bad as it looks once you get the hang of it and it can actually be quite a satisfying process. It is reckoned that there are around 4000 characters in daily use, of which approximately 2000 are needed to read a newspaper. The radical index from a popular Chinese–English dictionary (汉英词典) is reproduced over the page and may prove useful to you as a reference. The number to the left of the radical indicates the order in which it appears.

When tackling the character exercises, don't expect to get them all right all at once. They are there for you to learn from as you go along and to go back to time and time again. Perhaps you will only recognize a few characters to start with (and be able to write even fewer), but you will gradually recognize more and more (and be able to write more). Be patient, stay with it – believe me, it can be a rewarding experience.

However way you look at them, Chinese characters are fascinating, representing as they do the continuity of Chinese culture. Even if you decide not to spend too much time on them, appreciate their beauty and their long history. If you do decide you want to pursue this side of your Chinese studies, there are many interesting books to read and enjoy. This unit has only scratched the surface of what characters are all about but if it has kept your interest or better still, fired your imagination, it has served its purpose.

A beautiful example of Chinese calligraphy

部 首 检 字
Radical index
（一）部首目录
部首左边的号码表示部首的次序

	一 画	35	又	70	ヨ(彐彑)	105	中	140	业	175	缶	209	金
1	丶	36	廴	71	弓	106	贝	141	目	176	耒	210	鱼
2	一	37	厶	72	己(巳)	107	见	142	田	177	舌		九 画
3	丨	38	凵	73	女	108	父	143	由	178	竹(⺮)	211	音
4	丿	39	匕	74	子(孑)	109	气	144	申	179	臼	212	革
5	一		三 画	75	马	110	牛(牜)	145	㗊	180	自	213	是
6	亅	40	氵	76	幺	111	手	146	皿	181	血	214	骨
7	乙(乛乚)	41	忄	77	纟(糸)	112	毛	147	钅	182	舟	215	香
	二 画	42	扌(⺕)	78	巛	113	攵	148	矢	183	羽	216	鬼
8	冫	43	亡	79	小(⺌)	114	片	149	禾	184	艮(艮)	217	食
9	亠	44	广		四 画	115	斤	150	白		七 画		十 画
10	讠	45	宀	80	灬	116	爪(爫)	151	瓜	185	言	218	高
11	二	46	门	81	心	117	尺	152	鸟	186	辛	219	鬲
12	十	47	辶	82	斗	118	月	153	皮	187	辰	220	髟
13	厂	48	工	83	火	119	殳	154	癶	188	麦		十一画
14	ナ	49	土(士)	84	文	120	欠	155	矛	189	走	221	麻
15	匚	50	艹	85	方	121	风	156	疋	190	赤	222	鹿
16	卜(⺊)	51	廾	86	户	122	氏		六 画	191	豆		十二画
17	刂	52	大	87	礻	123	比	157	羊(⺶⺷)	192	束	223	黑
18	冖	53	尢	88	王	124	聿	158	关	193	酉		十三画
19	冂	54	寸	89	主	125	水	159	米	194	豕	224	鼓
20	亼	55	扌	90	天(夭)		五 画	160	齐	195	里	225	鼠
21	亻	56	弋	91	韦	126	立	161	衣	196	足		十四画
22	厂	57	巾	92	尹	127	疒	162	亦(赤)	197	采	226	鼻
23	人(入)	58	口	93	廿(卄)	128	穴	163	耳	198	豸		
24	八(丷)	59	囗	94	木	129	衤	164	臣	199	谷	227	余类
25	乂	60	山	95	不	130	夹	165	戋	200	身		
26	勹	61	屮	96	犬	131	玉	166	西(覀)	201	角		
27	刀(⺈)	62	彳	97	歹	132	示	167	束		八 画		
28	力	63	彡	98	瓦	133	去	168	亚	202	青		
29	儿	64	夕	99	牙	134	⺷	169	而	203	卓		
30	几(凡)	65	夂	100	车	135	甘	170	页	204	雨		
31	マ	66	丸	101	戈	136	石	171	至	205	非		
32	卩	67	尸	102	止	137	龙	172	光	206	齿		
33	阝(在左)	68	忄	103	日	138	戊	173	虍	207	黾		
34	阝(在右)	69	犭	104	曰	139	业	174	虫	208	隹		

15

买东西 mǎi dōngxi
Shopping

In this unit you will learn
- *how to ask for things in shops*
- *how to ask the price*
- *about Chinese money*
- *the stroke order of useful Chinese characters and their radicals*

◀) **CD 2, tr 8**

Pattern one: 'Specific item' 多少 (*duōshao*) 钱? (*qián?*) How much is this/that item?

Question	那本杂志多少钱?	Nà běn zázhì duōshao qián?
Answer	那本杂志两块六。	Nà běn zázhì liǎng kuài liù.
Question	这张地图多少钱?	Zhè zhāng dìtú duōshao qián?
Answer	这张地图一块四毛九。	Zhè zhāng dìtú yí kuài sì máo jiǔ.
Question	那件衣服多少钱?	Nà jiàn yīfu duōshao qián?
Answer	那件衣服七十三块。	Nà jiàn yīfu qīshí sān kuài.
Question	这件衬衫多少钱?	Zhè jiàn chènshān duōshao qián?

Answer	这件衬衫二十八块钱。	Zhè jiàn chènshān èrshí bā kuài qián.
Question	那件毛衣多少钱?	Nà jiàn máoyī duōshao qián?
Answer	那件毛衣九十一块。	Nà jiàn máoyī jiǔshíyī kuài.

买 [大] **mǎi** *(v) to buy*
东 [一] 西 [西] **dōngxi** *(n) thing(s)*
买东西 *(v-o) to go shopping*
多 [夕] 少 [小] **duōshao** *(QW) how many?*
钱 [钅] **qián** *(n) money*
那 [阝] **nà/nèi** *(dem adj/p) that*
本 [木] **běn** *(MW) for books, magazines*
杂 [木] 志 [心] **zázhì** *(n) magazine*
两 [一] **liǎng** *(num) two (of a kind)*
块 [土] **kuài** *(MW) lump (for money, soap, etc.)*
六 [八] **liù** *six*
这 [辶] **zhè/zhèi** *(dem adj/p) this*
张 [弓] **zhāng** *(MW) for flat, rectangular objects*
地 [土] 图 [囗] **dìtú** *(n) map*
一 [一] **yī** *one*
四 [囗] **sì** *four*
毛 [毛] **máo** *(MW; n) for money; wool*
九 [丿] **jiǔ** *nine*
件 [亻] **jiàn** *(MW) piece, article, item*
衣 [衣] 服 [月] **yīfu** *(n) clothes*
七 [一] **qī** *seven*
十 [十] **shí** *ten*
三 [一] **sān** *three*
衬 [衤] 衫 [衤] **chènshān** *(n) shirt, blouse*
二 [二] **èr** *two*
八 [八] **bā** *eight*
毛衣 **máoyī** *(n) sweater, woolly*

Stroke order of Chinese characters (i)

买	ㄱ 乛 乛 三 买 买
东	一 亡 东 东 东
西	一 丆 襾 襾 西 西
多	丿 勹 夕 夕 多 多
少	丨 丿 小 少
钱	钅(丿 ㅡ ㅌ 钅 钅) 戋(一 二 戋 戋 戋)
杂	九(丿 九) 朩(一 十 才 朩)
志	士(一 十 士) 心(丶 心 心 心)
两	一 丆 兩 兩 丙 两 两
七	一 七
毛	一 二 三 毛
六	丶 亠 六 六
那	那(刀 刁 刁 那) 阝(卩 阝)
张	弓(乛 ㄱ 弓) 长(丿 ㄥ 长 长)
地	土(一 十 土) 也(乛 也 也)
图	口 冬 丨 冂 冂 冈 图 图 图 图
四	丨 冂 四 四 四
九	丿 九

件	亻(ノ 亻) 牛(ノ 二 牛)
衣	丶 亠 产 右 衣 衣
服	月 (ノ 刀 月 月) 艮 (⁊ 尸 艮 艮)
十	一 十
块	圡 夬 (⁊ ⊐ 夬 夬)
二	一 二
衬	衤 (丶 ⁊ ⼺ 衤 衤) 寸 (一 十 寸)
衫	衤 彡 (⁀ ⁀ 彡)
八	ノ 八

◀) **CD 2, tr 10**

Pattern two: Item 多少钱一 MW? How much per unit is item?

Question	报多少钱一份儿？	Bào duōshao qián yí fènr? (*the* 儿 *ér on* 份 fèn *is optional but is often there*)
Answer	报九毛钱一份儿。	Bào jiǔ máo qián yí fènr.
Question	香烟多少钱一包？	Xiāngyān duōshao qián yì bāo?
Answer	中国烟七、八块钱一包。	Zhōngguó yān qī、bā kuài qián yì bāo.
Answer	外国烟十五块五一包。	Wàiguó yān shíwǔ kuài wǔ yì bāo.

Question	香皂多少钱一块?	Xiāngzào duōshao qián yí kuài?
Answer	香皂三、四块钱一块。	Xiāngzào sān、sì kuài qián yí kuài.
Question	苹果多少钱一斤?	Píngguǒ duōshao qián yì jīn?
Answer	苹果两块二一斤。	Píngguǒ liǎng kuài èr yì jīn.
Question	邮票多少钱一套?	Yóupiào duōshao qián yí tào?
Answer	邮票十八块钱一套。	Yóupiào shíbā kuài qián yí tào.

报 [扌] **bào** *(n) newspaper*
份 [亻] **fèn** *(MW) a copy; portion*
香 [禾] 烟 [火] **(xiāng)yān** *(n) cigarette*
包 [勹] **bāo** *(MW) (n) packet (of), package*
中 [丨] 国 [囗] **Zhōngguó** *(N) China*
外 [夕] 国 **wàiguó** *(adj) foreign*
五 [一] **wǔ** *five*
香皂 [白] **xiāngzào** *(n) toilet soap*
苹 [艹] 果 [木] **píngguǒ** *(n) apple*
斤 [斤] **jīn** *(MW) catty (½ kilogram)*
邮 [阝] 票 [示] **yóupiào** *(n) stamp*
套 [大] **tào** *(MW) set*

Stroke order of Chinese characters (ii)

报	扌(一 十 扌)艮
份	亻(丿 亻)分(丿 八 分 分)
香	禾(一 二 千 禾 禾)日(丨 冂 日 日)
烟	火(丶 丿 火 火) 口 木 丨 冂 日 冈 冈 因
包	勹(丿 勹)巳(フ コ 巳)
中	丨 口(丨 冂 口)
国	囗 玉 丨 冂 冂 冋 囯 国 国 国
外	夕(丿 勹 夕)卜(丨 卜)
五	一 丁 五 五
皂	白(丿 丨 白 白 白) 匕
苹	艹(一 艹 艹) 平(一 丷 㔾 平 平)
果	日 木 丨 冂 日 日 旦 甲 果 果
斤	一 厂 斤 斤
邮	由(丨 冂 日 由 由)阝
票	覀 示(一 二 于 示 示)
套	大 县(一 厂 厂 尸 县 县 县)

Pattern three: 我要这 (*Wǒ yào zhè*) MW 'I would like this one.'

售货员	您要买什么？
Shòuhuòyuán	Nín yào mǎi shénme?
史爱理	我要买丝绸，多少钱一米？
Shǐ Àilǐ	Wǒ yào mǎi sīchóu, duōshao qián yì mǐ?
售货员	三十二块五。您要几米？
Shòuhuòyuán	Sānshí èr kuài wǔ. Nín yào jǐ mǐ?
史爱理	两米半。
Shǐ Àilǐ	Liǎng mǐ bàn.
售货员	一共八十一块二毛五。这是八十五块，找您三块七毛五。
Shòuhuòyuán	Yígòng bāshíyī kuài èr máo wǔ. Zhè shì bāshíwǔ kuài, zhǎo nín sān kuài qī máo wǔ.
史爱理	好，谢谢。
Shǐ Àilǐ	Hǎo, xièxie.
售货员	没什么，再见。
Shòuhuòyuán	Méi shénme, zàijiàn.
史爱理	再见。
Shǐ Àilǐ	Zàijiàn.

售 [口] 货 [贝] 员 [口] **shòuhuòyuán** (n) shop assistant
您 [心] **nín** (ps) you (polite)
要 [女] **yào** (v) want
什 [亻] 么 [丿] **shénme** (QW) what?
我 [戈] **wǒ** (ps) I, me
丝 [一] 绸 [纟] **sīchóu** (n) silk
米 [米] **mǐ** (MW) metre
几 [几] **jǐ** (QW/adj) how many?; several
半 [丶丿] **bàn** (num) half
一共 [一] **yígòng** (adv) altogether
是 [是] **shì** (v) to be
找 [扌] **zhǎo** (v) to give back (as of change)
好 [女] **hǎo** (adj) good
谢谢 [讠] **xièxie** (v) to thank; thank you
没 [氵] **méi** (neg) not
再 [一] 见 [见] **zàijiàn** goodbye

Stroke order of Chinese characters (iii)

售	隹 (丿 亻 亻 亽 亽 佇 隹 隹) 口		
货	亻	七	贝 (丨 冂 贝 贝)
员	口	贝	
您	亻	尔 (丿 尒 尒 尔 尔) 心	
要	覀	女 (乚 女 女)	
什	亻	十	
么	丿	厶 (乚 厶)	
我	一 二 千 手 我 我 我		

<u>丝</u>	㇄　幺　纩　纩　丝
绸	纟（㇄　幺　纟）
	周（丿　刀　月　冂　冃　冑　周　周）
米	丶　丷　丷　半　半　米
几	丿　几
半	丶　丷　丷　兰　半
共	一　十　卄　甘　共　共
是	日　定（丅　下　乐　定）
找	扌　戈（一　七　戈　戈）
好	女　子（㇇　了　子）
谢	讠（丶　讠）身（丿　𠂉　𠂊　𠂊　身　身）寸
没	氵（丶　丶　氵）殳（丿　几　𠂤　殳）
再	一　厂　冂　冉　再　再
见	丨　冂　贝　见

Grammar

1 *MONEY*

The Chinese currency is known as 'the people's currency', *rénmínbì* (RMB) 人民币. ('Foreign currency' is *wàibì* 外币.) The largest single unit is the *yuán* 元 (represented by ¥ in many transactions). There are ten *jiǎo* 角 in one *yuán* and ten *fēn* 分 in one *jiǎo*. These are the characters used in the written language and printed on banknotes, tickets, etc. In spoken Chinese, *kuài* 块 'piece/lump' is used for *yuán* and *máo* 毛 for *jiǎo* but *fēn* remains unchanged. When two or more different units of currency are used together, the last one is usually omitted, so it is *sān kuài wǔ* and not *sān kuài wǔ máo*, *sì máo liù* and not *sì máo liù fēn*. If a sum of money involves *kuài* and *fēn* but no *máo*, the absence of the latter is marked by a *líng* 零, 'zero':

27.05 元 *èrshíqī kuài líng wǔ fēn*.

Note that under these circumstances *fēn* cannot be omitted.

The word for 'money' *qián* is sometimes put after amounts expressed entirely in *kuài*, *máo* or *fēn*:

jiǔ kuài qián	9.00 元
qī máo qián	0.7 元
bā fēn qián	0.08 元

Liǎng is often used with *kuài* and *máo* (**liǎng kuài**, **liǎng máo**) but only with *fēn* when there are no *kuài* or *máo*:

liǎng kuài liǎng máo èr   2.22 元

but

liǎng fēn qián   0.02 元

When the last number in a series is 'two' then *èr* is always used:

liǎng kuài èr   2.2 元

RMB (rénmínbì)	Spoken	Written
0.01 yuán	yì fēn (qián)	yì fēn
0.1 yuán	yì máo (qián)	yì jiǎo
1.00 yuán	yí kuài (qián)	yì yuán
3.5 yuán	sān kuài bàn sān kuài wǔ	sān yuán wǔ jiǎo
7.68 yuán	qī kuài liù máo bā	qī yuán liù jiǎo bā fēn
12.09 yuán	shí'èr kuài líng jiǔ fēn	shí'èr yuán líng jiǔ fēn
20.00 yuán	èrshí kuài (qián)	èrshí yuán
99.99 yuán	jiǔshíjiǔ kuài jiǔ máo jiǔ	jiǔshíjiǔ yuán jiǔ jiǎo jiǔ fēn

Chinese banknotes

Exercise 15.1
Supply the missing MW (in *pinyin* and in characters):

Wǒ mǎi zhè _____ zázhì → Wǒ mǎi zhè běn/本 zázhì.

1 *Tā mǎi le sān _____ dìtú.*
2 *Wǒ zuótiān mǎi le yí _____ xīn (new) yīfu.*
3 *Liǎng _____ máoyī shì jiù (old) de.*
4 *Tā měi tiān xī (smoke) sì _____ yān.*
5 *Wǒmen yí ge xīngqī yòng yí _____ xiāngzào.*
6 *Zuò zhè _____ chènshān yào mǎi liǎng _____ bù (cloth).*

Exercise 15.2
Write out in characters the sum of money in each sentence:

Nà jiàn máoyī qīshí kuài qián. → 七十块钱

1 *Zhè jiàn yīfu bāshí wǔ kuài.*
2 *Yì mǐ bù èrshí sì kuài bā.*
3 *Sān jīn píngguǒ shí sān kuài jiǔ.*
4 *Yóupiào èrshí liù kuài qī yí tào.*
5 *Bào jiǔ máo èr yí fèn.*
6 *Zhōngguó yān bā kuài sì yì bāo.*

Exercise 15.3
Learn the following radicals, their romanization and their meaning:

1	大	*dà*	'big'
2	一	*héng*	'horizontal (line)'
3	小	*xiǎo*	'small'
4	钅(金)	*jīn*	'metal'
5	辶	–	'walking radical' (always written last no matter what its position).
6	木	*mù*	'tree'
7	心	*xīn*	'heart'
8	口	*kǒu*	'mouth'
9	囗	–	'enclosure'
10	月	*yuè* or *ròu*	'moon' or 'flesh' (see Unit 14).
11	土	*tǔ*	'earth'

12	衤(衣)	*yī*	'clothing'
13	扌(手)	*shǒu*	'hand'
14	禾	*hé*	'grain'
15	日	*rì*	'sun'

Exercise 15.4
Write out each of the following characters in *pinyin* and say what the radical is: e.g. 国 → *guó* 'enclosure'. (Use Unit 14 if you have any difficulties.)

1 苹 **2** 衬 **3** 没 **4** 谢 **5** 块 **6** 本 **7** 是 **8** 烟 **9** 志 **10** 买

Exercise 15.5
For each of the following characters take out the radical and then count up the number of strokes remaining. Indicate what the radical is: e.g. 钱 → 5 (钅).

1 东 **2** 件 **3** 图 **4** 好 **5** 我 **6** 报 **7** 邮 **8** 套 **9** 您 **10** 找

Made in China

It's difficult not to notice that, in the west, many commodities, from toys to microwaves, from clothes to mobile phones, have the label 'Made in China' stamped on them somewhere. Just a few decades ago, people in China needed allocated coupons to buy daily essentials such as grain products, cooking oil, meat, cloth, etc. In a short period of time (less than two decades from 1979), China has turned into a materialist society where a surplus of commodities and production capability present a serious problem.

TESCO 乐购

Walmart ⁎
中国

Carrefour

Commodities 'Made in China', which flood western countries, are generally viewed by many as being cheap and of poor quality. At the same time, China is now the second largest consumer country in the world for 'foreign-made' luxury products.

Of course, major western retailers will not want to miss out on a slice of this huge cake.

Exercise 15.6
Write the following sentences in Chinese characters and then translate them into English:

1 *Shòuhuòyuán shì Zhōngguórén* (人).
2 *Dìtú liǎng kuài sì yì zhāng.*
3 *Nà běn zázhì yí kuài jiǔ máo wǔ.*
4 *Nín méi mǎi dōngxi.*
5 *Píngguǒ sān kuài bā yì jīn.*

TESTING YOURSELF

Translate into Chinese characters:

1 *I want to buy three magazines and a newspaper.*

....

2 *Yesterday (昨天) I bought (le 了) two shirts.*

....

3 *He (他) wants to go shopping.*

....

4 *How many metres of silk do you want?*

....

5 *Thank you. Goodbye.*

....

16

去影剧院买票
qù yǐngjùyuàn mǎi piào
Buying tickets (i)

In this unit you will learn
- *how to buy tickets for entertainments*
- *how to give the date*
- *more about the stroke order of characters*
- *about China's main dynasties*

🔊 **CD 2, tr 13–15**

史爱理	**十二月十三号的音乐会还有票吗?**
Shǐ Àilǐ	Shí'èryuè shísān hào de yīnyuèhuì hái yǒu piào ma?
售票员	**还有。你要几张?**
Shòupiàoyuán	Hái yǒu. Nǐ yào jǐ zhāng?
史爱理	**要四张。楼下的还有吗?**
Shǐ Àilǐ	Yào sì zhāng. Lóuxià de hái yǒu ma?
售票员	**有。你看，第九排怎么样?**
Shòupiàoyuán	Yǒu. Nǐ kàn, dì jiǔ pái zěnmeyàng?
史爱理	**很好。多少钱一张?**
Shǐ Àilǐ	Hěn hǎo. Duōshao qián yì zhāng?
售票员	**四十块。四张一百六十块。**
Shòupiàoyuán	Sìshí kuài. Sì zhāng yìbǎi liùshí kuài.

史爱理	给你两百块。
Shǐ Àilǐ	Gěi nǐ liǎng bǎi kuài.
售票员	找你四十块，这是你的票。
Shòupiàoyuán	Zhǎo nǐ sìshí kuài, zhè shi nǐde piào.
史爱理	谢谢你。请问，《日出》这部电影怎么样，有意思吗？
Shǐ Àilǐ	Xièxie nǐ. Qǐng wèn, «Rìchū» zhè bù diànyǐng zěnmeyàng, yǒu yìsi ma?
售票员	挺好的。大家都说很有意思。你下个星期来看吧。
Shòupiàoyuán	Tǐng hǎo de. Dàjiā dōu shuō hěn yǒu yìsi. Nǐ xià ge xīngqī lái kàn ba.

QUICK VOCAB

去 [土] qù (v) to go
影 [彡] 剧 [刂] 院 [阝] yǐngjùyuàn (n) cinema and theatre
票 [示] piào (n) ticket
张 [弓] zhāng (MW)
售票员 shòupiàoyuán (n) box office clerk
月 [月] yuè (n) month
号 [口] hào (n) number; date
的 [白] de see 5.4
音 [音] 乐 [木] 会 [𠆣] yīnyuèhuì (n) concert
还 [辶] hái (adv) still
有 [月] yǒu (v) to have; there is/are
吗 [口] ma question particle
你 [亻] nǐ (ps) you
楼 [木] 下 [一] lóuxià (n) downstairs
看 [目] kàn (v) to look, see
第 [竹] dì ordinal prefix
排 [扌] pái (n) row, line
怎 [心] 么样 [木] zěnmeyàng (QW) what about it?
很 [彳] hěn (adv) very
百 [一] bǎi (one) hundred

给 [纟] gěi (v) to give; for
请 [讠] qǐng (v) to invite
问 [口] wèn (v) to ask
日 [日] 出 [丨] Rìchū (N) Sunrise (film version of a play by Cao Yu)
部 [阝] bù (MW) for films
电 [田] 影 diànyǐng (n) film
意 [心] 思 [心] yìsi (n) meaning
有意思 yǒu yìsi (v-o) to be interesting
挺 [扌] tǐng (adj) very, rather
大 [大] 家 [宀] dàjiā (p) everybody
都 [阝] dōu (adv) all, both
说 [讠] shuō (v) to speak, say
下 [一] xià (adj) next
个 [人] gè (MW) see 3.1
星 [日] 期 [月] xīngqī (n) week
来 [一] lái (v) to come
吧 [口] ba particle indicating suggestion

Stroke order of Chinese characters (iv)

去	土	厶
影	日	京 (⎡ 一 广 户 亩 亨 亨 京) 彡
剧	尸 (⎤ ⎡ 尸) 古 (一 十 古 古 古)	
	刂 (丨 刂)	
院	阝	宀 (丶 丷 宀) 元 (一 二 元 元)
号	口	丂 (一 丂)
的	白 (丿 白 白 白 白) 勺 (丿 勹 勺)	

音	立 (丶 一 亠 立 立) 日
乐	一 厂 乐 牙 乐
会	人 (丿 人) 云 (一 二 云 云)
还	不 (一 ア 不 不) 辶* (丶 辶 辶) *this component is always written last
有	ナ (一 ナ) 月
吗	口 | 马 (乛 马 马)
楼	木 | 米 | 女
下	一 丁 下
看	手 (一 二 三 手) 目 (| 冂 冃 月 目)
第	竹 (丿 ⺮ ⺮ ⺮ 竹 竹)
	弟 (一 丷 弓 弔 弟)
排	扌 | 非 (| 丨 丨 丰 丮 非 非 非)
怎	乍 (丿 ⺊ 乍 乍 乍) 心
样	木 | 羊 (丶 丷 丷 兰 羊 羊)
很	彳 (丿 彳 彳) 艮 (乛 彐 彐 艮 艮 艮)
百	一 丆 丆 百 百 百
给	纟 | 合 (丿 人 合 合 合 合)
请	讠 | 青 (一 二 圭 圭 青 青 青)
问	门 (丶 冂 门) 口

出	凵 凵 屮 出 出			
部	立	口	阝	
电	田 (丨 冂 日 日 电) 乚			
意	立	日	心	
思	田	心		
挺	扌	壬 (ノ 二 千 壬) 廴 (乛 廴)		
都	者 (一 十 土 耂 耂 者 者 者) 阝			
说	讠	兑 (丶 丷 丷 丷 丷 兑 兑)		
个	人	丨		
星	日	生 (ノ ト 二 牛 生)		
期	其 (一 十 艹 艹 艹 其 其 其) 月			
来	一 一 一 厄 平 来 来			
吧	口	巴 (乛 ⴼ ⴼ 巴)		

Grammar

1 *Dates*

We have already covered months of the year and days of the week in 11.7 and 10.5 but we still do not know how to tackle dates. The order for a date is the reverse of that used in English: year, month, day, hour.

The year is read as single numbers followed by the word *nián* (年) 'year': 1949 *yījiǔsìjiǔ nián* (*yī jiǔ sì jiǔ nián*), 1976 *yījiǔqīliù nián*, 1988 *yījiǔbābā nián*.

When asking what the date is the Chinese use *jǐ yuè jǐ hào?* (*Lit.* how many months how many numbers):

Question	*Jīntiān (shì) jǐ yuè jǐ hào?*
Answer	*Jīntiān wǔyuè èrshí'èr hào.* (22 May)
Question	*Xīngqītiān jǐ hào?*
Answer	*Xīngqītiān sānshíyī hào.* (31st)

Equipped with this information we can now tackle such phrases as 9 am (use *shàngwǔ* morning) on Monday, 11 July 1936 and so on: *Yījiǔsānliùnián qīyuè shíyī hào (rì*) xīngqīyī shàngwǔ jiǔ diǎn.*

Note that in Chinese, you move from the general to the particular. As we are on dates, the following chart should be of interest!

* *Rì* (日) is used more frequently in formal, written Chinese whereas *hào* is commonly used in the spoken language.

China's main dynasties

夏	**Xià**	*c. 21st–16th century* BC
商	**Shāng**	*c. 16th–11th century* BC
周	**Zhōu**	*c. 11th century–256* BC
秦	**Qín**	*211–206* BC
汉	**Hàn**	*206* BC*–*AD *220*
三国	**Sānguó** Three Kingdoms	*220–280*
晋	**Jìn**	*265–420*
南北朝	**Nán-Běi Cháo** *North/South Dynasties (see 18.1)*	*420–589*
隋	**Suí**	*581–618*
唐	**Táng**	*618–907*
五代	**Wǔdài** *Five Dynasties*	*907–960*
宋	**Sòng**	*960–1279*
辽	**Liáo**	*970–1125*
金	**Jīn**	*1115–1234*
元	**Yuán**	*1279–1368*
明	**Míng**	*1368–1644*
清	**Qīng**	*1644–1911*
中华民国	**Zhōnghuá Mínguó** *Republic of China*	*1912–1949*
中华人民共和国	**Zhōnghuá Rénmín Gònghéguó** *People's Republic of China*	*1949–*

公元前 **gōngyuán qián** *BC*
公元 **gōngyuán** *AD*
世纪 **shìjì** *century*
二十一世纪 **èrshíyī shìjì** *21st century*

QUICK VOCAB

2 Titles

As capital letters cannot exist in the Chinese script, except artificially in romanization, the titles of books, films, plays, etc. are distinguished by placing them between 《 》 marks: 《*Rìchū*》 《日出》 'Sunrise'.

Exercise 16.1
Learn the following radicals, their romanization and their meaning:

1	刂 (刀)	*dāo*	'knife'
2	示 (礻)	*shì*	'omen'
3	𠆢	*rén*	'person' (we used to call it 'the man' radical!)
4	人		
5	目	*mù*	'eye'
6	⺮ (竹)	*zhú*	'bamboo'
7	纟	*sī*	'silk'
8	讠 (言)	*yán*	'speech'
9	丨	*shù*	'vertical (line)'
10	田	*tián*	'field'

Exercise 16.2
Write out each of the following characters in *pinyin* and put the common component contained in the characters of each group in the brackets:

e.g. 谢 *xiè*、说 *shuō*、请 *qǐng* (讠).

1 意 ___、志 ___、怎 ___ ( ).

2 报 ___、挺 ___、排 ___ ( ).

3 号 ___、员 ___、问 ___ ( ).

4 都 ___、部 ___、邮 ___ ( ).

5 来 ___、十 ___、下 ___ ( ).

Exercise 16.3
Write out the characters you have met containing each of the
following components. (In each case, find the number of characters
indicated by the dashes.)

e.g. 口： __吧__ 、 __吗__ 。

1 土： ___ 、 ___ 、 ___ 。
2 女： ___ 、 ___ 。
3 丨： ___ 、 ___ 。
4 木： ___ 、 ___ 、 ___ 、 ___ 、 ___ 。
5 月： ___ 、 ___ 、 ___ 。
6 囗： ___ 、 ___ 、 ___ 。
7 彡： ___ 。
8 亼： ___ 、 ___ 。
9 亻： ___ 、 ___ 、 ___ 、 ___ 。
10 辶： ___ 、 ___ 。

Exercise 16.4
Write the following *pinyin* sentences in Chinese characters and then
translate them into English:

1 *Kàn diànyǐng zěnmeyàng?*
2 *Lóuxià yǒu rén ma?*
3 《*Rìchū*》 *zhè bù diànyǐng yǒu méi you yìsi?*
4 *Shàng* (上 last) *ge xīngqī nǐ méi lái.*
5 *Yīnyuèhuì jǐ yuè jǐ hào?*

Why don't you check out the website on the noticeboard? It is actually sponsored by a shoe company in Fujian Province. How many radicals can you spot?

TESTING YOURSELF

Translate into Chinese characters:

1 *Today* (今天) *is 3 November.*

2 *Excuse me, what is the date today?*

3 *There is nobody upstairs* (楼上 lóushàng).

4 *Everybody says that shopping is very interesting.*

5 *Have you still got any money?/How much do you want?*

6 *I was in* (在 zài) *China in 1968.*

17

打电话买票 dǎ diànhuà mǎi piào
Buying tickets (ii)

In this unit you will learn
- *about telephone numbers*
- *how to describe the characters in your Chinese name*
- *how to describe imminent action*
- *more about radicals*

🔊 CD 2, tr 16–18

(王永寿：拨八么么六，零九七五，过了一会儿才有人接)
(Wáng Yǒngshòu: Bō bā yāo yāo liù, líng jiǔ qī wǔ, guò le yíhuìr cái yǒu rén jiē)

售票员	喂，天安旅行社。您好！
Shòupiàoyuán	Wèi, Tiān'ān lǚxíngshè. Nín hǎo!
王	我想给我女朋友订一张三月十二号去西安的飞机票。
	Wǒ xiǎng gěi wǒ nǚ péngyou dìng yì zhāng sān yuè shí'èr hào qù Xī'ān de fēijī piào.
售票员	可以。回程日期是几月几号？
	Kěyǐ. Huíchéng rìqī shì jǐ yuè jǐ hào?

228

王	回程日期是三月二十九号。
	Huíchéng rìqī shì sān yuè èrshíjiǔ hào.
售票员	嗯，七百人民币。您女朋友来取还是您自己来取？我们也可以给您送去。
	Ng, qī bǎi rénmínbì. Nín nǚ péngyou lái qǔ háishi nín zìjǐ lái qǔ? Wǒmén yě kěyǐ gěi nín sòng qù.
王	我自己来取。我今天下午四点半来取。
	Wǒ zìjǐ lái qǔ. Wǒ jīntiān xiàwǔ sìdiǎn bàn lái qǔ.
售票员	行，可是今天下午一定来取，因为票快卖完了，不好留。
	Xíng, kěshì jīntiān xiàwǔ yídìng lái qǔ, yīnwei piào kuài mài wán le, bù hǎo liú.
王	您放心吧，我一定会去。
	Nín fàng xīn ba, wǒ yídìng huì qù.
售票员	您贵姓？
	Nín guìxìng?
王	我姓王，名字叫王永寿。
	Wǒ xìng Wáng, míngzi jiào Wáng Yǒngshòu.
	王是三横一竖的王，'永'是'永远'的'永'，'寿'是'长寿'的'寿'。
	'Wáng' shì sān héng yí shù de 'Wáng', 'yǒng' shì 'yǒngyuǎn' de 'yǒng', 'shòu' shì 'chángshòu' de 'shòu'.
售票员	好了，我记下来了。
	Hǎo le, wǒ jì xiàlai le.
王	太谢谢您了，下午见。
	Tài xièxie nín le, xiàwǔ jiàn.
售票员	再见。
	Zàijiàn.

From now on, where a vocabulary item has appeared in previous units but without characters, we have given the (new) character and the *pinyin* but not the English translation. This way you can see how much vocabulary you have mastered.

打电话 **dǎ diànhuà** *(v-o) to telephone*
拨 **bō** *(v) to dial*
么 **yāo** *(num) one (used orally only)*
零 **líng** *(num) zero*
过 **guò**
了 **le** *modal particle*
一会儿 **yíhuìr**
才 **cái**
人 **rén** *(n) person*
接 **jiē** *(v) take hold of, receive; to meet*
喂 **wèi** *hello (on telephone)*
天安 **Tiān'ān** *(N) Heavenly Peace*
旅行社 **lǚxíngshè** *(n) travel agency*
订 **dìng**
西安 **Xī'ān** *name of city in NW China*
飞机 [架] **fēijī** *(n)* [jià] *aeroplane*
票 **piào**
回程 **huíchéng** *(n) return journey*
日期 **rìqī** *(n) date*
人民币 **rénmínbì** *(n) RMB (Chinese currency)*
取 **qǔ** *(v) to get, fetch; withdraw (money)*
自己 **zìjǐ** *(p)*
送 **sòng** *(v) send; give as a present; see somebody off*
今天 **jīntiān**
下午 **xiàwǔ** *(TW) afternoon*
半 **bàn**
行 **xíng**
可是 **kěshì**
一定 **yídìng**
因为 **yīnwei** *or* **yīnwèi**
快......了 **kuài ... le** *see 17.3*
卖 **mài** *(v) to sell*
–完 **-wán**
留 **liú** *(v) to reserve for someone; remain; let grow*
放心 **fàng xīn** *(v-o) to set one's mind at rest*
会 **huì**
您贵姓? **Nín guìxìng?** *(Lit. your expensive surname) May I ask your name?*

名字 **míngzi** *(n) (given) name*
叫 **jiào** *(v) to be called; to call*
横 **héng** *(adj) horizontal*
竖 **shù** *(adj) vertical*
永远 **yǒngyuǎn** *(adj) forever*
长寿 **chángshòu** *(n) long life, longevity*
记下来 **jì xiàlai** *(v + CDE) to note down; to record*
太 **tài**
见 **jiàn**

Stroke order of the more difficult characters (i)

拨	扌	发 (⺈ 宀 岁 发 发)
零	雨	雪 (一 厂 宀 乕 乕 雪 雪 雪)
		令 (丿 人 入 今 令)
接	扌	妾 (丶 亠 宀 立 产 妾 妾)
旅	方	(丶 亠 方 方) 仾 (丿 ⺁ ⺈ 仾 仾 仾)
社	礻	(丶 丷 礻 礻) 土
程	禾	(一 二 千 禾 禾) 呈 (丨 冂 口 旦 旱 呈)
取	耳	(一 厂 耳 耵 耳 耳) 又 (刁 又)
送	关	(丶 丷 䒑 丷 关) 辶* (丶 辶 辶) ^{*this component is always written last}
点	占	(丨 ⼘ ⼘ 占 占) 灬 (丶 ⺍ ⺗ 灬)
定	宀	(丶 丷 宀) 疋 (一 丁 下 疋 定)
因	丨 冂 冂 因 因 因	

为	丶 丿 为 为
卖	十 (一 十) 买
留	丣 (丿 𠃌 𠃌 丣 丣) 田
放	方 (丶 宀 方 方) 攵 (丿 𠂉 攵 攵)
贵	虫 (丨 冂 曰 虫 虫) 贝
横	木	黄 (一 十 卄 艹 共 艹 艹 莆 苗 黄 黄)
竖	㐄 (丨 ‖ 𠤎 㐄) 立
永	丶 ㇇ 永 永 永
远	元 辶*
寿	丰 (一 二 三 丰) 寸
记	讠 己 (𠃍 𠃌 己)
太	大 太

* Remember this component is always written last no matter what its position is in the character.

Grammar

1 Telephone numbers

Telephone numbers in Beijing are usually made up of eight digits, beginning with an 8 and written in two blocks of four digits. Each digit is usually said separately:

8551 0978 bā wǔ wǔ **yāo** líng jiǔ qī bā
8673 8830 bā liù qī sān bā bā sān ling

Yāo is used instead of **yī** when telephone numbers or large numbers for rooms, buses, trains and so on, are broken down into single digits. This avoids any confusion with **qī** (seven).

2 Describing your 'character'

Mr King says he is 'the three horizontals and one vertical' King, that the *yǒng* in his name is the *yǒng* in *yǒngyuǎn* 'eternal' and the *shòu* is as the *shòu* in *chángshòu* 'longevity'! That leaves the box office clerk in no doubt as to how to write his name. Because Chinese is so full of homophones, it is common practice to describe one's name in this way so that there can be no misunderstanding as to what characters are used. Thus *Shǐ Àilǐ*'s name, literally 'history loves principle', could be described as *Shǐ shì lìshǐ de shǐ, ài shì ài guó de ài, lǐ shì dàolǐ de lǐ* 'the *shǐ* as in history, the *ài* as in patriotic and the *lǐ* as in principle (or truth)'.

3 (Kuài) yào V . . . le

To indicate imminent action or that the action of the verb is going to take place within a relatively short space of time we can put *yào* in front of the verb and the modal particle *le* at the end of the sentence. *Kuài* or *jiù* can be put before *yào* to make the imminence of the action even clearer:

Tā yào dǎ diànhuà le. *'She's going to phone.'*
«Rìchū» kuài yào yǎn le. *'Sunrise is coming on soon.'*
Wǒ xiàwǔ jiù yào zǒu le. *'I'm leaving this afternoon.'*

Note that an adverb or adverbial phrase of time may come before *jiù yào* V . . . *le* but not before *kuài yào* V . . . *le*.

As you can see, the concept of 'imminent' is a relatively elastic one but the juxtaposition of *míngtiān* and *kuài* as in Wǒ *péngyou míngtiān kuài yào chū guó le* does seem to be taking this too far (hence the rule) whereas Wǒ *péngyou **míngtiān jiù yào** chū guó le* 'My friend is going abroad tomorrow' is perfectly acceptable.

This construction can also appear as *kuài* V . . . *le*:

Piào kuài mài wán le. *'The tickets are almost sold out.'*

but not *jiù* V . . . *le*, which would be far too ambiguous as *jiù* can be used in so many different ways.

The question form is made by adding *ma* to the statement and *méi you* is used for an answer in the negative: *Huǒchē kuài yào kāi le ma?* 'Is the train about to leave?' **Méi you** 'No.'

Moving on!

In a big country like China, a long-distance phone call could indeed link two people a thousand miles apart. Some 20 years ago, people would usually have to go to a post office to call someone outside their own city. In many parts of China, especially in many rural regions, people have never used normal dialling phones. They have moved from no telephone, when there were no telephone lines, directly onto mobiles. In mid-2009, there were already 155 million people in China using mobiles to access the internet! (Of course, by the time you read this, this figure will be totally out of date.)

Exercise 17.1
Learn the following radicals, their romanization and their meaning:

1	艹 (草)	*cǎo*	'grass'
2	氵(水)	*shuǐ*	'water'
3	忄(心)	*xīn*	'heart'
4	女	*nǚ*	'woman'
5	耳	*ěr*	'ear'
6	宀	–	'roof'
7	贝	*bèi*	'shell, object of value'
8	八 丷 (八)	*bā*	'eight'
9	饣(食)	*shí*	'food'

Some characters appear to be made up of more than one recognizable radical. Which one do you choose to look up the character under? You will slowly learn that certain radicals seem to take precedence over others. The 'five elements' (wood, fire, earth, metal and water), for instance, but these are all defeated by 'heart'. If you are totally at sea, look at the left-hand side of the character first and see if you can spot a radical. The 'head' is another place to look (grass, bamboo, various kinds of roofs). In absolute dire straits try the horizontal or vertical lines or the dot!

Exercise 17.2
Write out each of the following characters in *pinyin* and say what its radical is; e.g. 喂 *wèi* 'mouth':

1 演 **2** 行 **3** 记 **4** 打 **5** 取
6 过 **7** 英 **8** 接 **9** 卖 **10** 天

Exercise 17.3
For each of the following characters take out the radical and then count up the number of strokes remaining. Indicate what the radical is: e.g. 行 → 3 (彳); 了 → 1 (乛):

1 话 **2** 剧 **3** 专 **4** 叫 **5** 今
6 满 **7** 星 **8** 贵 **9** 客 **10** 姓

Exercise 17.4
Fill in the square in the centre with a component or character which when combined with each of the components in the other squares forms a separate character:

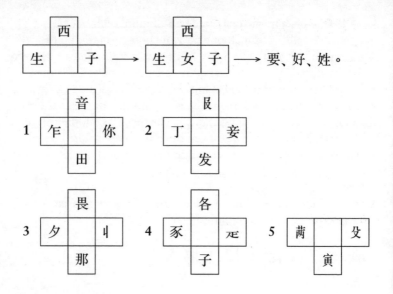

生　子 → 生 女 子 → 要、好、姓。

1 乍　你　田 2 丁　妾　发 3 夕　丬　那 4 豕　疋　子 5 兩　殳　寅

Exercise 17.5

Write the following *pinyin* sentences in Chinese characters and then translate them into English:

1 *Jīntiān méi yǒu rén gěi wǒ dǎ diànhuà.*
2 *Tiān'ān lǚxíngshè zài nǎr?*
3 *Tā míngtiān xiàwǔ jiù yào qù Běijīng* (北京) *le.*
4 *Nǐ hòutiān* (day after tomorrow) *néng bu neng lái jiē wǒ?*
5 *Xīngqīwǔ xíng bu xíng? Bù xíng, jiù xīngqīliù ba.*

TESTING YOURSELF

Translate into Chinese characters:

1 *I went to the Tian'an Travel Agency today.* (了)

2 *What is your (expensive) name? My name is Shi, Shi Aili.*

3 *He says he'll save two tickets for us.*

4 *They want to see that film this afternoon but it's sold out.*

5 *Would it be all right if I come and pick up the tickets next Friday?*

Why don't you practise writing out the Chinese characters on the sign? Can you spot the radicals?

18

问路、坐车 wèn lù、zuò chē
Directions and transport

In this unit you will learn
- *about famous places of interest in and around Tiananmen Square*
- *how to ask for and understand directions*
- *the points of the compass*
- *how to express the distance between two points*
- *about place words*
- *more about the stroke order of difficult characters*

◀ **CD 2, tr 19–20**

Pattern one: to taxi-driver, bus-conductor, etc.

我要去PW *Wǒ yào qù PW.*
我要去天坛 *Wǒ yào qù Tiāntán.*

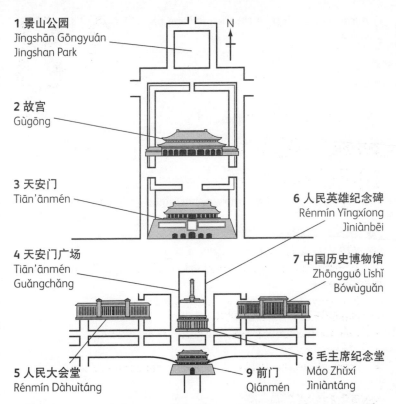

1 景山公园
Jǐngshān Gōngyuán
Jingshan Park

2 故宫
Gùgōng

3 天安门
Tiān'ānmén

6 人民英雄纪念碑
Rénmín Yīngxíong Jìniànbēi

4 天安门广场
Tiān'ānmén Guǎngchǎng

7 中国历史博物馆
Zhōngguó Lìshǐ Bówùguǎn

5 人民大会堂
Rénmín Dàhuìtáng

8 毛主席纪念堂
Máo Zhǔxí Jìniàntáng

9 前门
Qiánmén

Famous places of interest in and around Tiananmen Square

Can you make out two points of the compass on the street sign? (The street is Xīdān Běidàjiē.)

Pattern two: you are in the vicinity of a place (PW) and ask a passer-by

PW在哪儿？怎么走？
PW zài nǎr? Zěnme zǒu?

Standing in Tiananmen Square

故宫在哪儿？怎么走？
Gùgōng zài nǎr? Zěnme zǒu?

Pattern three: as for Pattern two, but slightly more formal

a 请问PW在哪儿？怎么走？
   Qǐng wèn, PW zài nǎr? Zěnme zǒu?

In the North

b 劳驾PW在哪儿？怎么走？
   Láojià, PW zài nǎr? Zěnme zǒu?

or

c 请问/劳驾PW怎么走？
   Qǐng wèn/láojià PW zěnme zǒu?
   请问，人民大会堂在哪儿？怎么走？
   Qǐng wèn, Rénmín Dàhuìtáng zài nǎr? Zěnme zǒu?

Pattern four: reply to a question asking for directions

往 direction 走　*Wàng Direction zǒu.*
往东走　　　　　*Wàng dōng zǒu.*

Linking question and answer

> 1 甲 请问，前门在哪儿？怎么走？
> Jiǎ Qǐng wèn, Qiánmén zài nǎr? Zěnme zǒu?
> 乙 前门离这儿不远。往南走就到了。
> Yǐ Qiánmén lí zhèr bù yuǎn. Wàng nán zǒu jiù dào le.
> 2 甲 劳驾，故宫在哪儿？怎么走？
> Jiǎ Láojià, Gùgōng zài nǎr? Zěnme zǒu?
> 乙 (pointing) 离这儿很近，你看，就在那儿，你往北走就到了。
> Yǐ Lí zhèr hěn jìn, nǐ kàn, jiù zài nàr, nǐ wàng běi zǒu jiù
>   dào le.
> 甲 谢谢你。
> Jiǎ Xièxie nǐ.

问路 wèn lù *(v-o)* ask the way
坐车 zuò chē
天坛 Tiāntán *(N)* Temple of Heaven
怎么 zěnme
走 zǒu
故宫 Gùgōng *(N)* the Forbidden City (the Imperial Palace)
劳驾 láojià excuse me
人民大会堂 Rénmín Dàhuìtáng *(N)* Great Hall of the People
往 wàng *(prep)* towards, to
东 dōng east
甲 jiǎ A (the first of the Ten Heavenly Stems)
乙 yǐ B (the second of the Ten Heavenly Stems) (see Unit 22)
前门 Qiánmén *(N)* Qianmen
离 lí *(prep)* (distance) from
这儿 (这里) zhèr (zhèlǐ)
不 bù
远 yuǎn *(adj)* far
南 nán south
到 dào *(v)* arrive, go to
近 jìn *(adj)* near
你 nǐ
那儿 (那里) nàr (nàlǐ) *(PW)* there
北 běi north

QUICK VOCAB

Stroke order of the more difficult characters (ii)

路	𧾷 (⸍ 口 口 咯 咯 咯 呈) 各
坐	从 (⸍ 人 从 从) 土
车	一 七 乍 车
劳	艹　 ⺍ (⸌ ⺍) 力 (𠃌 力)
驾	加　马
民	𠃌 (𠃌 𠃌 𠃌) 七 (一 七)
堂	𫩏 (⸍ ⸍ 𫩏)
	室 (⸍ ⸜ 宀 宀 宀 空 空 室)
往	彳　主 (⸍ 亠 二 主 主)
甲	丨 冂 日 日 甲
乙	乙
前	䒑　月　刂
离	⸌ 亠 亠 文 亩 亩 亩 离 离
这	文 (⸍ 亠 亠 文) 辶
里	丨 冂 日 日 旦 甲 里
南	十　南 (丨 冂 冂 冎 冎 冎 南)

242

Mr King comes out of the Imperial Palace (Forbidden City) (*Gùgōng*) and asks the way to the Great Hall of the People (*Rénmín Dàhuìtáng*):

王	人民大会堂离故宫远吗?
	Rénmín Dàhuìtáng lí Gùgōng yuǎn ma?
路人	不远，离故宫很近，就在天安门广场西边儿。
Lùrén	Bù yuǎn, lí Gùgōng hěn jìn, jiù zài Tiān'ānmén Guǎngchǎng xībianr.
王	中国历史博物馆也在西边儿吗?
	Zhōngguó Lìshǐ Bówùguǎn yě zài xībianr ma?
路人	不，中国历史博物馆和中国革命博物馆就在天安门东边儿，人民大会堂对面。
	Bù, Zhōngguó Lìshǐ Bówùguǎn hé Zhōngguó Gémìng Bówùguǎn jiù zài Tiān'ānmén dōngbianr, Rénmín Dàhuìtáng duìmiàn.
王	人民英雄纪念碑呢?
	Rénmín Yīngxióng Jìniànbēi ne?
路人	在天安门广场中间，在毛主席纪念堂前边儿。
	Zài Tiān'ānmén Guǎngchǎng zhōngjiān, zài Máo Zhǔxí Jìniàntáng qiánbianr.
王	那么，前门在毛主席纪念堂后边儿对不对?
	Nàme, Qiánmén zài Máo Zhǔxí Jìniàntáng hòubianr duì bu duì?
路人	对，这几个地方都很有意思，值得看一看。
	Duì, zhè jǐ ge dìfang dōu hěn yǒu yìsi, zhíde kànyikàn.

路人 lùrén *(n) passer-by; stranger*
天安门广场 Tiān'ānmén Guǎngchǎng *(N) Tiananmen Square*
西边儿 xībianr *(n) west (side)*
中国历史博物馆 Zhōngguó Lìshǐ Bówùguǎn *(N) Museum of National History (Lit. China history museum)*
也 yě
中国革命博物馆 Zhōngguó Gémìng Bówùguǎn *(N) Museum of Revolution (Lit. China revolution museum)*
东边儿 dōng(bianr) *(PW) east (side)*

QUICK VOCAB

对面 duìmiàn *(PW) opposite*
人民英雄纪念碑 Rénmín Yīngxióng Jìniànbēi *(N) Monument to the People's Heroes (Lit. people's hero monument)*
呢 ne
中间 zhōngjiān *(PW) middle; between*
毛主席纪念堂 Máo Zhǔxí Jìniàntáng *(N) Mao Zedong (Chairman Mao) Mausoleum*
前边儿 qiánbianr *(PW) front, in front of*
那么 nàme
后边儿 hòubianr *(PW) back, behind*
对 duì
几 jǐ *(num) several*
地方 dìfang
值得 zhíde *(v) to be worth, deserve*

Stroke order of the more difficult characters (iii)

广	丶	亠	广						
边	フ	力	辶						
历	厂	力							
史	口	史	史						
博	十	甫 (一	厂	冂	月	盲	甫	甫) 寸	
物	牛 (丿	𠂉	牛) 勿 (丿	勹	勾	勿)			
馆	饣 (丿	𠃌	饣) 官 (丶	丶	宀	宀	宀	官	官)
革	一	艹	艹	廿	苫	芑	荳	莒	革
命	人	一	叩						

面	一 丆 厂 沔 而 而 面 面 面		
雄	太 (一 ナ 太 太) 隹		
碑	石 (一 ア イ 石 石) 卑 (′ 白 田 申 卑)		
席	广	芇 (一 十 廾 廾 芦 芦 芇)	
值	亻	直 (一 十 广 市 甫 甫 直 直)	
得	彳	日	寸 (一 二 寻 寸)

Grammar

1 *Points of the compass*

◄) CD 2, tr 24

Perhaps as China is situated in the east, the important
cardinal points for her are east and west (in that order!)
rather than north and south. Whereas when listing the
cardinal points we say north, south, east, west, the Chinese
say *dōng, nán, xī, běi* (E, S, W, N).

Instead of southeast they say 'eastsouth' (*dōngnán*), instead of
northwest, 'westnorth' (*xīběi*) and so on. NB The diagram below
shows the western representation of the compass. The Chinese
version always shows south at the top.

The Chinese are more likely to give you directions in terms of
north, south, etc. than left and right. This stems from the fact that
old Chinese cities (Beijing is a good example) are laid out on a
north–south, east–west axis, so in these cases, this is the most
helpful way for someone to orientate him/herself.

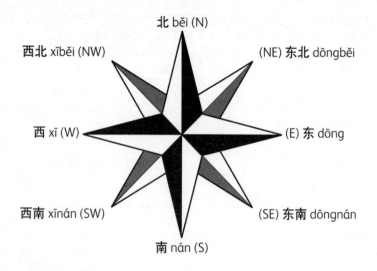

2 Place words

🔊 **CD 2, tr 25**

QUICK VOCAB

*qiánbiān *front, in front of, before*
*hòubiān *back, at the back of, behind*
*shàngbiān *top, on, over, above*
*xiàbiān *bottom, below, under*
zuǒbiān *left*
yòubiān *right*
*lǐbiān *inside*
*wàibiān *outside*
zhōngjiān *middle, between*
duìmiàn *opposite*
pángbiān *side*

All these words are often followed by *-ér* which renders the *biān* toneless: *qiánbianr*, *hòubianr*, etc. and I have generally glossed them as such.

*-biān may be replaced by -miàn or -tóu in these examples. Which one is used seems to depend on the speaker, with southerners tending to use -tóu more, and -biān and -miàn being interchangeable.

Place words such as those listed on the preceding page function as *nouns* in Chinese. When such a place word is used to tell us more about another noun it is usually followed by *de*: *qiánbiān de rén* 'the person/people in front'.

Conversely, when it is itself preceded by another noun or pronoun the *de* is normally omitted: *zhuōzi pángbiān* 'beside the table'. The same rule applies to *dōngbiān*, *xībiān*, etc. and as students often put these place words in the wrong position it may be helpful to memorize the following 'pair' of examples:

dōngbiān de xuéxiào *'the school to the east'*
xuéxiào dōngbiān *'to the east of the school'*

In the first example, we are talking about the *school*, in the second example we are talking about what exists to the *east* of it. This is exactly the same rule as in 5.4 but the frequent omission of *de* before the place word when used in this way tends to obscure this fact. Think of the *de* as being there when working out where the place word should come in such cases.

When the place word *lǐbiān* or *shàngbiān* is attached to a noun, *biān* is very often omitted:

zài jiā lǐ *'at home'*
zài chéng lǐ *'in town'*
zài yǐzi shàng *'on the chair'*

This also works with *xià* in such expressions as:

yǐzi xià *'beneath the chair'*
zhuōzi xià *'beneath the table'*

The *biān* in other place words is seldom omitted, however, and where it is, the phrase should be learnt separately: *guówài* 'overseas, abroad'.

If these phrases occur at the beginning of the sentence, the use of *zài* is optional:

Jiālǐ yǒu rén. *'There's somebody at home.'*

but it is compulsory *after* the verb:

Wǒ yào fàng zài yǐzi shàng. *'I want to put (it) on the chair.'*

Some adverbial phrases do not take *zài* wherever they occur in the sentence. Examples include:

chūntiān lǐ *'in the spring'*
jiàqī zhōng *'in the holidays'*
sānyuè zhōng *'mid-March'*

Note that *lǐ* is used in the first example and *zhōng* in the second, although both are translated into English as 'in'.

Conversely, other adverbial phrases may take an optional *zài* but no other place word:

(zài) zhōumò *'at the weekend'*
(zài) yìjiǔjiǔlíng nián *'in 1990'*

Some take neither *zài* or any other place word: *èryuè fèn(r)* 'in February' although *èryuè* by itself is also possible.

All these examples should be noted and added to as your studies progress. Listen carefully to Chinese speakers and imitate them as far as possible. The recording will help you do this.

The verbs *shì* 'to be' and *yǒu* 'to have' are both used to denote existence and are often to be found with the place words just described. The basic difference is that the object of a sentence with *yǒu* is usually indefinite whereas the object of a sentence with *shì* may be either definite or indefinite and usually implies a judgement that something is so (and not something else):

Gùgōng qiánbianr yǒu yì tiáo dà jiē. *'There's a big street in front of the Forbidden City'* (indicating existence, position).
Gùgōng qiánbianr shì Tiān'ānmén Guǎngchǎng. *'In front of the Forbidden City is Tiananmen Square'* (not the Temple of Heaven, for instance).

Exercise 18.1
Look at the map at the beginning of this unit and answer the following questions using the points of the compass. (Use the point of reference given in brackets after the question.)

Gùgōng zài nǎr? (Jǐngshān Gōngyuán) →
Gùgōng zài Jǐngshān Gōngyuán nánbianr.

1 *Jǐngshān Gōngyuán zài nǎr? (Gùgōng.)*
2 *Qiánmén zài nǎr? (Máo Zhǔxí Jìniàntáng.)*
3 *Rénmín Dàhuìtáng zài nǎr? (Rénmín Yīngxióng Jìniànbēi.)*
4 *Zhōngguó Lìshǐ Bówùguǎn zài nǎr? (Rénmín Yīngxióng Jìniànbēi.)*
5 *Máo Zhǔxí Jìniàntáng zài nǎr? (Rénmín Dàhuìtáng.)*

3 Jiǎ *and* yǐ

Jiǎ and *yǐ* are the first and second of the Ten Heavenly Stems just like alpha, beta in Greek. They are also often used in the same way as we use 'A' and 'B' in English.

4 A lí B

When we wish to express how far A is from B where the positions of A and B are fixed, the construction is as follows: A *lí* B distance in time or space:

Gōngyuán lí shāngdiàn hěn yuǎn. *'The park is a long way from the shops.'*
Hòutiān lí jīntiān hái yǒu liǎng tiān. *'The day after tomorrow is still two days away (from today).'*
Niújīn lí Lúndūn yǒu jiǔshíyī gōnglǐ. *'Oxford is 91 kilometres (public lǐ) from London.'*

Exercise 18.2

Using the map again, answer the following questions.

Gùgōng lí Qiánmén yuǎn ma? → **Gùgōng lí Qiánmén yuǎn.**

1 *Jǐngshān Gōngyuán lí Qiánmén yuǎn ma?*
2 *Rénmín Dàhuìtáng lí Rénmín Yīngxióng Jìniànbēi jìn bu jin? Zěnme zǒu?*
3 *Máo Zhǔxí Jìniàntáng lí Tiān'ānmén yuǎn bu yuan? Zěnme zǒu?*
4 *Rénmín Yīngxióng Jìniànbēi lí Zhōngguó Lìshǐ Bówùguǎn hěn jìn, shì bu shi?*
5 *Niújīn lí Lúndūn yǒu duō yuǎn?*
6 *Sānshí hào lí èrshíqī hào hái yǒu jǐ tiān?*
7 *Yuándàn* (New Year's Day) *lí Shèngdànjié* (Christmas Day) *yǒu jǐ ge xīngqī?*

Exercise 18.3

Write out the characters you have met with the following radicals or character components. (Go through Units 15–18 to find the answers.)

e.g. ⺾ → 莘

1 宀	5 阝 (RHS)	9 心/忄	13 丨	17 彡
2 刂	6 氵	10 ⺮	14 木	18 ⼈ or 亻
3 禾	7 纟	11 土	15 月	19 辶
4 门	8 目	12 女	16 口	20 火

Exercise 18.4

Write out your answers to Exercises 18.1 and 18.2 (1–4 only) in characters.

Regional differences

Given China's vastness, it is not surprising that there are a number of major dialects in China and countless minor ones. These do not include the languages of the minority peoples such as Tibetan (*Zàngwén*), Thai (*Tàiwén*), Vietnamese (*Yuènánwén*), Uighur (*Wéiwú'ěrwén*), etc. Some expressions that you will hear frequently in the north such as *láojià* are hardly heard in the south. Although *pǔtōnghuà* has standardized much of the vocabulary, you will still find regional differences. Examples include:

	North	South*
'potato'	tǔdòu	mǎlíngshǔ
'tomato'	xīhóngshì	fānqié
'pineapple'	bōluó	fènglí
'taxi'	chūzūqìchē	jìchéngchē
'bicycle'	zìxíngchē	jiǎotàchē

* Plus Taiwan and overseas Chinese communities.

TESTING YOURSELF

Translate into Chinese characters:

1 *Excuse me, where is the Temple of Heaven? How do I get there?*

2 *Is the Great Hall of the People a long way from here? No, it's just opposite.*

3 *The Monument to the People's Heroes is to the east of the Great Hall of the People but to the west of the Museum of National History.*

19

在鸟巢国家体育场
zài Niǎocháo Guójiā Tǐyùchǎng
At the Bird's Nest National Stadium

In this unit you will learn
- *how to buy tickets at a tourist attraction*
- *how to ask for a catalogue, audio guide or washrooms*
- *how to buy stamps*
- *how to move the direct object in front of the verb using* bǎ
- *more about the stroke order of difficult characters*
- *about Chinese festivals*

◀》 CD 1, tr 28–31

It's Sunday and Wang Yongshou and Shi Aili are being taken by their two Chinese friends Zhang Daming and Chen Ying to the famous Bird's Nest National Stadium. They arrive at the ticket kiosk.

今天是星期天，王永寿和史爱理被他们的两位中国朋友张大明和陈英请去参观著名的鸟巢国家体育场。他们来到售票处。
Jīntiān shì xīngqītiān. Wáng Yǒngshòu hé Shǐ Àilǐ bèi tāmen de liǎng wèi Zhōngguó péngyou Zhāng Dàmíng hé Chén Yīng qǐng qù cānguān zhùmíng de Niǎocháo Guójiā Tǐyùchǎng. Tāmen lái dào shòupiàochù.

陈英:	四张票。
Chén Yīng:	Sì zhāng piào.
售票员:	四百块。请把票收好。这是体育场的导游图。我给你们两张吧。要是你们想租语音导游机，请到那边的窗口。
Shòupiàoyuán:	Sì bǎi kuài. Qǐng bǎ piào shōu hǎo. Zhè shì tǐyùchǎng de dǎoyóutú. Wǒ gěi nǐmen liǎng zhāng ba. Yàoshi nǐmen xiǎng zū yǔyīn dǎoyóujī, qǐng dào nèibiān de chuāngkǒu.

[他们都走到那个窗口去。]
[Tāmen dōu zǒu dào nà ge chuāngkǒu qù.]

张大明:	你们要不要语音导游机？(对服务员说)一台/个语音导游机多少钱？
Zhāng Dàmíng:	Nǐmen yào bu yào yǔyīn dǎoyóujī? (Duì fúwùyuán shuō) Yì tái/ge yǔyīn dǎoyóujī duōshao qián?
服务员:	一台十五块钱。您可以听中文的、英文的或者日文的。
Fúwùyuán:	Yì tái shíwǔ kuài qián, Nín kěyǐ tīng Zhōngwénde, Yīngwénde huòzhě Rìwénde.
史爱理:	我们要一台吧。这样我们也可以练练我们的听力。
Shi Aili:	Wǒmen yào yì tái ba. Zhèyàng wǒmen yě kěyǐ liànliàn wǒmende tīnglì.

[她给了服务员60块，服务员给他们每个人一个语音导游机。]
[Tā gěi le fúwùyuán liùshí kuài, fúwùyuán gěi tāmen měi ge rén yí ge yǔyīn dǎoyóujī.]

服务员:	按这个键开始，按这个键暂停，按这个键停止。在鸟巢周围的不同地方，你们可以看到耳机的标志，标志下面有一个大的数字。把数字输进语音导游机里，按开始键就可以了。听懂了吗？不难。
Fúwùyuán:	Àn zhèi ge jiàn kāishǐ. Àn zhèi ge jiàn zàntíng. Àn zhèi ge jiàn tíngzhǐ. Zài

Niǎocháo zhōuwéi de bù tóng dìfang,
nǐmen kěyi kàn dào ěrjī de biāozhì. Biāozhì
xiàmian yǒu yí ge dà de shùzì. Bǎ shùzì
shū-jìn yǔyīn dǎoyóujī lǐ, àn kāishǐ jiàn jiù
kěyi le. Tīng-dǒng le ma? Bù nán.

[他们花了差不多一个半小时参观了体育场、跑道、更衣室、
跳远沙坑，等等，不时地停下来听听语音导游机的解说，
张大明说：]

[Tāmen huā le chàbuduō yí ge bàn xiǎoshí cānguān le
tǐyùchǎng, pǎodào (*running track*), gēngyīshì (*changing
rooms*), tiàoyuǎn shākēng (*long jump pit*), děngděng, bùshí de
(*from time to time*) tíng xiàlái tīngting yǔyīn dǎoyóujī de
jiěshuō. Zhāng Dàmíng shuō:]

张大明：	我饿死了，我们去吃点儿东西吧。
(他把体育场的导游图仔细看了一下。)	
	有很多选择。你们俩想吃快餐，还是自助餐，还是去有服务员的餐厅？
Zhāng Dàmíng:	Wǒ è sǐ le. Wǒmen qù chī diǎnr dōngxi ba.
(Tā bǎ tǐyùchǎng de dǎoyóutú zǐxì kàn le yíxia.)	
	Yǒu hěn duō xuǎnzé. Nǐmen liǎ xiǎng chī kuàicān, háishi zìzhùcān, háishi qù yǒu fúwùyuán de cāntīng?
史爱理：	我们去吃自助餐吧，比有服务员的餐厅快而且便宜。 不过我得先买几张明信片。看，那边有个礼品店。去那儿看看吧。
Shǐ Àilǐ:	Wǒmen qù chī zìzhùcān ba. Bǐ yǒu fúwùyuán de cāntīng kuài érqiě piányi. Búguò wǒ děi xiān mǎi jǐ zhāng míngxìnpiàn. Kàn, nàbiān yǒu ge lǐpǐndiàn. Qù nàr kànkan ba.
王永寿：	你们俩也去吗？我也要买几张明信片。我弟弟非常羡慕我们能来鸟巢看看。他很喜欢运动，二零零八年北京奥运会的时候他整天看电视。
Wáng Yǒngshòu:	Nǐmen liǎ yě qù ma? Wǒ yě yào mǎi jǐ zhāng míngxìnpiàn. Wǒ dìdi fēicháng xiànmu wǒmen néng lái Niǎocháo kànkan.

Tā hěn xǐhuan yùndòng. Èr-líng-líng-bā
nián Běijīng Àoyùnhuì de shíhou, tā
zhěngtiān kàn diànshì.

(在礼品店里)
(Zài lǐpǐndiàn lǐ)

史爱理:　　　　　(把四张明信片交给售货员)你们也卖
　　　　　　　　邮票吗?

Shǐ Ailǐ:　　　　(Bǎ sì zhāng míngxìnpiàn jiāo gěi
　　　　　　　　shòuhuòyuán) Nǐmen yě mài yóupiào ma?

售货员:　　　　卖。 是寄国内的还是寄到国外?

Shòuhuòyuán:　Mài. Shì jì guónèi de háishi jì dào guówài?

史爱理:　　　　一张国内的，两张寄到欧洲，另(外)一张
　　　　　　　　寄到美国。

Shǐ Ailǐ:　　　　Yì zhāng guónèi de, liǎng zhāng jì dào
　　　　　　　　Ōuzhōu, lìng(wài) yì zhāng jì dào Měiguó.

售货员:　　　　(一共) 二十五块。

Shòuhuòyuán:　(yígòng) èrshíwǔ kuài.

史爱理把她的语音导游机给王永寿，从钱包里拿出三十块钱
给售货员。

Shǐ Ailǐ bǎ tāde yǔyīn dǎoyóujī gěi Wáng Yǒngshòu, cóng
qiánbāo lǐ ná chū sānshí kuài qián gěi shòuhuòyuán.

售货员:　　　　找您五块。

Shòuhuòyuán:　Zhǎo nín wǔ kuài.

史爱理:　　　　谢谢您。(她把邮票贴在明信片上。)
　　　　　　　　邮票贴好了，这样就不会丢了。

Shǐ Ailǐ:　　　　Xièxie nín. (Tā bǎ yóupiào tiē zài
　　　　　　　　míngxìnpiàn shàng.) Yóupiào tiē hǎo le.
　　　　　　　　Zhèyàng jiù bú huì diū le.

陈英:　　　　　我们去吃饭吧。

Chén Yīng:　　Wǒmen qù chī fàn ba.

(在自助餐厅里)
(Zài zìzhù cāntīng lǐ)

张大明:　　　　真幸运，这里有空调，要不然热死了。
　　　　　　　　…你们吃饱了吗?

Zhāng Dàmíng:	Zhēn xìngyùn. Zhè lǐ yǒu kōngtiáo. Yàoburán, rè sǐ le. . . . Nǐmen chī bǎo le ma?
陈英:	吃饱了。饺子真好吃。你们俩呢?
Chén Yīng:	Chī bǎo le. Jiǎozi zhēn hǎo chī. Nǐmen liǎ ne?
王永寿:	吃饱了。
Wáng Yǒngshòu:	Chī bǎo le.
史爱理:	对不起,我要去一下洗手间。等我几分钟好吗? 厕所在哪儿?
Shǐ Ailǐ:	Duìbuqǐ. Wǒ yào qù yíxià xǐshǒujiān. Děng wǒ jǐ fēnzhōng hǎo ma? Cèsuǒ zài nǎr?
陈英:	在那儿。看得见那个标志吗? 我跟你一起去。
Chén Yīng:	Zài nàr. Kàn de jiàn nà ge biāozhì ma? Wǒ gēn nǐ yìqǐ qù.

(过了一会儿,他们两个人回来了。)
(Guò le yìhuìr, tāmen liǎng ge rén huílai le.)

史爱理:	真干净。鸟巢的设备都很好,很现代化。可惜奥运会的时候我没有亲自来这儿看。
Shǐ Ailǐ:	Zhēn gānjing. Niǎocháo de shèbèi dōu hěn hǎo, hěn xiàndàihuà. Kěxī, Àoyùnhuì de shíhou wǒ méi you qīnzì lái zhèr kàn.
张大明:	我们走吧。今天晚上电视里有一部好电影。你们要不要一起来看? 你们可以来看看我们的孩子,我们做点儿面条和麻婆豆腐。我知道你们俩都特爱吃辣的。
Zhāng Dàmíng:	Wǒmen zǒu ba. Jīntiān wǎnshang diànshì lǐ yǒu yí bù hǎo diànyǐng. Nǐmen yào bu yào yìqǐ lái kàn? Nǐmen kěyǐ lái kànkan wǒmen de háizi. Wǒmen zuò diǎnr miàntiáo hé mápó dòufu. Wǒ zhīdao nǐmen liǎ dōu tè ài chī là de.
史爱理、王永寿:	好极了! 谢谢你们。
Shǐ and Wáng:	Hǎojíle! Xièxie nǐmen.

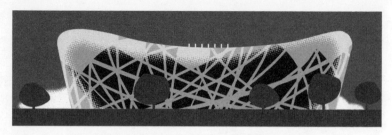

Bird's Nest National Stadium
Niǎocháo Guójiā Tǐyùchǎng

鸟巢国家体育场 Niǎocháo Guójiā Tǐyùchǎng *(N) Bird's Nest National Stadium*

参观 cānguān *(v) to visit (places, exhibition etc.)*

著名 zhùmíng *(adj) remarkable, well known*

售票处 shòupiàochù *(n) ticket office*

把 bǎ *(prep) a preposition showing disposal*

收(好) shōu (hǎo) *(v) to put away; to receive*

导游图 dǎoyóutú *(n) tourist map*

租 zū *(v) to rent, hire*

语音导游机 [台] dǎoyóujī [tái] *(n) audioguide*

窗口 chuāngkǒu *(n) window (for tickets etc.)*

可以 kěyǐ

听 tīng *(v) to listen*

中文(的) Zhōngwén (de) *(n) Chinese language (usually written form)*

英文(的) Yīngwén (de) *(n) English language*

或者 huò(zhě) *(conj; adv)*

日文(的) Rìwén (de) *(n) Japanese language*

练习 liànxí *(v; n) to practise; practice, exercise*

听力 tīnglì *(n) listening comprehension*

按 àn *(v) to press*

键 jiàn *(n) key (as on piano or keypad)*

开始 kāishǐ

暂停 zàntíng *(v) to pause*

停止 tíngzhǐ

周围 zhōuwéi *(n) around, circumference*

不同 bù tong *(adj) different*

耳机 ěrjī *(n) headphone(s)*
标志 biāozhì *(n) sign, mark, symbol*
下面 xiàmian *(PW) below, bottom, under*
数字 shùzì *(n) number, digit, numeral*
输进 shū-jìn *(RV) to input into*
听懂 tīng-dǒng *(RV) to listen with understanding, to understand*
难 nán *(adj)*
–死 -sǐ *(RVE) to be extremely the action of the verb*
一点儿 (yì) diǎnr
仔细 zǐxì *(adj/adv) careful(ly), attentive(ly)*
选择 xuǎnzé *(n; v) choice; to choose, select*
俩 liǎ
快餐 kuàicān
还是 háishi
自助餐 zìzhùcān *(n) self-service (food)*
餐厅 cāntīng *(n) restaurant*
而且 érqiě *(conj) moreover*
便宜 piányi
不过 búguò *(conj) but, moreover, only*
得 děi
先 xiān *(adv) first*
明信片[张] míngxìnpiàn *(n)* [zhāng] *postcard*
礼品店 lǐpǐndiàn *(n) souvenir shop*
弟弟 dìdi *(n) younger brother*
羡慕 xiànmu *(v) to envy, admire*
能 néng
运动 yùndòng *(n) sports, exercise; (political) movement, campaign*
北京 Běijīng
奥运会 Àoyùnhuì
时候 de shíhou
整天 zhěngtiān *(TW) the whole day*
看电视 kàn diànshì *(v-o) to watch television*
交给 jiāo gěi *(v) to hand to*
寄 jì *(v) to post, mail*
国内 guónèi *(adj) internal, domestic*
国外 guówài *(adj) abroad, overseas*
另(外) lìng(wài) *(adj; adv)*

QUICK VOCAB

欧洲 Ōuzhōu *(N)*

美国 Měiguó *(PW)*

从 cóng

钱包 qiánbāo *(n) purse, wallet*

拿出 ná chū *(RV) to take out*

贴(上) tiē (shang) *(v) to stick (on)*

丢 diū *(v) to lose*

真 zhēn

幸运 xìngyùn *(adj) lucky, fortunate*

空调 kōngtiáo *(n)*

要不然 yàoburán

热 rè

吃饱 chī-bǎo

饺子 jiǎozi *(n) dumplings (filled with meat or vegetables)*

洗手间/厕所 xǐshǒujiān/cèsuǒ *(n) toilet, WC, washroom*

等 děng *(v) to wait, etc.*

分钟 fēnzhōng *(n) minute*

看得见 kàn de jiàn *(RV) to be able to see*

跟(X)一起 gēn (X) yìqǐ *together (with X)*

回来 huí lai

干净 gānjing *(adj) clean*

设备 shèbèi *(n) facilities, equipment*

现代化 xiàndàihuà *(adj) modern, modernized*

可惜 kěxī

亲自 qīnzì *(adv) in person, personally*

这儿 zhèr

今天晚上 jīntiān wǎnshang *(TW) this evening*

孩子 háizi

做 zuò

面条 miàntiáo *(n) noodles*

麻婆豆腐 mápó dòufu *(n) spicy beancurd/tofu*

知道 zhīdao

特爱 tè ài *(v) to especially like/love*

吃辣的 chī là de *(v-o) to eat spicy/hot food*

好极了 hǎojíle *excellent*

Stroke order of the more difficult characters (iv)

被	衤（` �ﾅ ｿ 衤 衤 衤）皮（⼀ 厂 ⽪ 皮 皮）
参	㇐ ㇕ 仝 叁 𠂹 叅 参 参
鸟	⼂ 勹 鸟 鸟 鸟
巢	⼜（⼂ ⼜ ⼜）果（⼁ 冂 曱 ⽇ 旦 甲 早 果 果）
窗	宀（` ｀ 宀 宀 宀）囱（⼂ ⼁ 冂 冈 肉 肉 囱）
或	⼀ 厂 戸 ⼽ ⼽ 或 或 或
练	纟（⼂ ⼰ 纟）东（⼀ 亡 车 东 东）
每	⼃ 母（⼃ 乊 母 母 母）
键	钅 建（ｺ ⼽ ⼽ 疌 疌 建 建 建）
数	⽶（` ｀ ｀ ⼆ 半 半 米）女（⼃ 女 ⼺ 女）
懂	忄（⼁ 忄 忄）卝（⼀ 艹 艹）
	重（⼀ 亠 ｒ 亩 盲 盲 直 重 重）
解	角（⼃ ⺈ 仒 仒 角 角 角）⼑（⼁ 刀）牛（⼃ 亠 匕 牛）
餐	歺 又 食（⼃ ⼊ 仒 仑 仒 仓 食 食 食）
羡	羊（` ｀ ｀ 兰 兰 羊 羊）⼎（` ⼎）欠（⼃ 仒 ⼺ 欠）
慕	卝 ⽇ 恭（⼀ 亠 六 ⽊ 亦 亦 恭）
整	束（⼀ 万 ⼽ 币 束 束 束）夂 正（⼀ 丁 下 正 正）
拿	合 手（⼀ 二 三 手）
净	冫 争（⼃ 仒 乊 乌 乌 争）
腐	广 付 肉（⼁ 冂 冈 肉 肉 肉）
辣	辛（` 亠 亠 亠 立 ⽴ 辛）束

Grammar

1 The bǎ construction

By using *bǎ*, the direct object is brought forward to a position in front of the verb instead of after it so the sentence order becomes:

subject	bǎ	object	verb	other element(s)
Wǒ	bǎ	bāoguǒ (*parcel*)	fàng	zài zhuōzi shang.
'I		put	the parcel	on the table.'

And from the text:

Tā bǎ tǐyùchǎng de dǎoyóutú zǐxì kàn le yíxia.
'He looked carefully at the plan of the stadium.'

It is important to note that:

1 The verb cannot stand on its own after *bǎ* and that something else has to come after it even if it is only *le* or the verb is simply reduplicated:

Tā bǎ zìxíngchē mài le. 'He sold the bicycle.'
Qǐng nǐ bǎ chuānghu kāikai. 'Please open the window.'

2 The object of a *bǎ* sentence is normally a *specific* person or thing(s) even when no specification is overtly expressed in the Chinese; it cannot refer to people or things in general:

Tā bǎ shū jì zǒu le. 'She posted the books.'

3 Negatives, auxiliary verbs, adverbial phrases of 'time when' and 'time within which' go before *bǎ*. When *dōu* refers to the subject it comes directly after the subject and before *bǎ*, but when it refers to the object it comes directly after the object and before the verb.

Wǒ jīntiān méi bǎ diànhuà hàomǎ jì xiàlai. *'I didn't note down the telephone number(s) today.'*

Yíngyèyuán yào bǎ shōujù (receipt) **gěi wǒ.** *'The clerk wants/ wanted to give me the receipt.'*

Nǐ zhè liǎng ge xīngqī zěnme méi bǎ zhè běn shū kàn wán ne? *'How come you haven't finished this book during the last two weeks?'*

Wǒmen dōu bǎ yīfu chuān shang le (**chuān**: to wear). *'We **all** put the clothes on.'*

Wǒmen bǎ yīfu dōu chuān shang le. *'We put **all** the clothes on.'*

4 Although *bǎ* cannot be translated into English it does contain a sense of disposal, i.e. to hold or take an object and do something with it (hence the hand radical), which is why it cannot be used with verbs which contain no such idea of disposal such as *shì, yǒu, zhīdao, juéde, xǐhuan, zài, lái, qù* and *huí*. These points are summarized in the following table.

◀️) **CD 2, tr 32**

Subj (N or pr)	Adv time	Neg	Aux v	Prep	Obj	Verb	Other elements
Wǒ				bǎ	shìqing	zuò	wán
Wǒ			néng	bǎ	shìqing	zuò	wán
Wǒ		bù	néng	bǎ	shìqing	zuò	wán
Wǒ	jīntiān	bù	néng	bǎ	shìqing	zuò	wán
Tā				bǎ	xìn	xiě	wán le
Tā		méi		bǎ	xìn	xiě	wán
Tā	hái	méi		bǎ	xìn	xiě	wán ne

Some uses of the *bǎ* construction

1 When the main verb is followed by the resultative ending *zài* or *dào* plus a place word:

Qǐng nǐ bǎ dìtú fàng zài zhuōzi shàng. *'Please put the map on the table.'*

Wǒ yǐjīng bǎ tā sòng dào (**sòng** to see somebody off) **fēijīchǎng** ('airport') **le.** *'I've already seen her off to the airport.'*

2 When the verb is reduplicated:

Qǐng nǐ bǎ zhè jiàn shìqing hǎohǎor xiǎngyixiǎng. *'Please think over this matter carefully.'*

3 When the main verb is followed by the resultative ending *gěi* and takes both a direct and an indirect object (note that *gàosu* 'to tell' also comes into this category although it does not take *gěi*):

Wǒmen bǎ qián huán gěi (**huán** 'to give or pay back') **lǎobǎn** ('the boss') **le.** *'We've paid back the money to the boss.'*
Tā zǎo jiù bǎ nà jiàn shìqing gàosu (to tell) **wǒ le.** *'He told me about that matter ages ago.'*

4 When verbs of movement take the directional endings *lái* or *qù, huí, zǒu*, etc.:

Tāmen zuótiān bǎ zhàopiàn ('photograph') **dài huílai le.**
'They brought the photos back yesterday.'
Xuésheng bǎ guāngpán bōfàngjī jiè zǒu (**jiè** 'to borrow; lend') **le.** *'The student borrowed the CD player (and went off with it).'*

5 When there is a quantified expression in the sentence such as *yí cì*:

Wǒ bǎ kèwén kàn le yí cì. *'I('ve) read the text once.'*
(If *bǎ* were not used then the sentence would read *Wǒ kàn le yí cì kèwén.* Note that if the object were a pronoun, the word order would be reversed, i.e. *Wǒ kàn le tā yí cì.*)

6 When the main verb is followed by the resultative ending *chéng* (*Lit.* 'to become') or *zuò* (*Lit.* 'to regard as'):

Wàiguórén jīngcháng bǎ 'shǒudū' ('capital') **liǎng ge zì niàn chéng 'shóudōu'.** *'Foreigners often read 'shǒudū' as 'shóudōu'.'*
(See 19.3.)
Nǐ wèi shénme bǎ wǒ dāng zuò (*dāng* 'to be, work as') **nǐ de dírén** ('enemy') **ne?** *'Why do you regard me as your enemy?'*

Exercise 19.1

Turn the following sentences into *bǎ* sentences:

Tā mài le tā de chē. → **Tā bǎ tā de chē mài le.**

1 *Qǐng nǐ shōu hǎo shōujù* (receipt).
2 *Xìnfēng* (envelope) *shàng yào xiě qīngchu jìjiànrén* (sender) *de dìzhǐ* (address) *hé xìngmíng* (surname).
3 *Wǒ méi yǒu xiě xià nǐ de míngzi lai.*
4 *Tā yào zài zuò yí cì zhè ge liànxí.*
5 *Yóukè* (tourist) *méi (yǒu) zǐxì kànyikàn shōujù.*

Turn the following *bǎ* sentences into sentences without *bǎ*:

Wǒ jīntiān yào bǎ zhè fēng xìn jì zǒu → **Wǒ jīntiān yào jì zǒu zhè fēng xìn.**

6 *Shòupiàoyuán bǎ liǎng zhāng hǎo piào liú gěi Wáng xiānsheng le.*
7 *Wàiguó yóukè yīnggāi bǎ dàshǐguǎn* (embassy) *de diànhuà hàomǎ* (number) *jì xiàlai.*
8 *Shòuhuòyuán bú yuànyì bǎ sīchóu chènshān mài gěi tā.*
9 *Dàifu* (doctor) *yào bǎ bìngrén* (patient) *sòng* (send) *dào yīyuàn* (hospital).
10 *Wǒ yí ge Zhōngguó péngyou yì tiān néng bǎ liǎng bāo yān xī wán* (xī 'to inhale, smoke').

2 -shang

As a resultative verb ending, *-shang* is often used to indicate:

a that the object has become attached to something else as a result of the action of the verb:

Qǐng xiān bǎ yóupiào tiē shang. *'Please stick the stamps on first'* (i.e. to the envelope/wrapping paper).
Tiānqì lěng le, yīnggāi chuān shang máoyī. *'It's turned cold, you ought to put a sweater on.'*

b Or that the completion of the action of the verb has resulted in something being closed or brought together:

Qǐng nǐ bǎ mén guān shang. *'Please close the door.'*

3 Same character, different pronunciation

Several characters have two or more different readings depending on context. 都 *dōu* is read as *dū* in 首都; 大夫 'doctor' is read as *dàifu* not *dàfu*; 还 is read *huán* as a verb meaning 'to give or pay back' but as *hái* when it is an adverb meaning 'still'; 和 is read as *huo* in *nuǎnhuo* 'warm'; 行 is read as *háng* in *yínháng* 'bank' and so on. Some characters have the same pronunciation but different tones but they do not lie within the scope of this book! 得 is read as *dé* when it is a verb meaning 'to get (as in an illness)': *Tā dé le bìng* 'He got sick', but as *děi* when it is an auxiliary verb meaning 'must'.

On festivals and mooncakes

Prior to 1949 the Chinese followed the lunar calendar, which is said to have been in existence for almost 4000 years and is still used to calculate China's traditional festivals. The most important ones are: 春节 *Chūnjié* the 'Spring Festival' or 'Lunar New Year' which falls on the first day of the first lunar month. The Lunar New Year itself may occur as early as 21 January and as late as 21 February. It is the major festival in China when most Chinese have at least 3–4 days' holiday and everybody tries to get back home to celebrate. (Avoid travelling in China at this time if possible.) Couplets wishing the household happiness, prosperity and longevity are written in the old way, i.e. vertically not horizontally, on red paper and pasted on either side of the door. The children normally get new clothes, everybody consumes vast quantities of food (noodles at midnight on New Year's Eve ensure long life). Firecrackers which make a deafening sound are set off, mainly on New Year's Eve and on New Year's Day supposedly to warn off evil spirits, hence the need for a big noise.

元宵节 *Yuánxiāojié*, the 'Lantern Festival' or the 'Feast of the First Full Moon', falls on the 15th day of the first lunar month. People (or more usually work units in the cities) make lanterns (灯 *dēng*), which are then exhibited at colourful lantern fairs, usually held in a park. The lanterns were apparently used as torches to help people see the good spirits that were flying in the sky by the light of the first full moon. Dragon dances and lion dances are performed to the noisy accompaniment of gongs and drums. *Yuánxiāo* are the special food associated with the Lantern Festival. They are small round dumplings made of glutinous rice, usually with a sweet filling. Their roundness symbolizes the full moon.

清明节 *Qīngmíngjié*, the 'Pure Brightness Festival', falls during the first few days of the third lunar month. This is the day on which the Chinese traditionally 'sweep' the graves of their dead and pay them their respects. This used to involve making offerings of food and wine, burning incense, candles and paper money. This may still happen in the countryside but people in the towns generally confine themselves to tidying up the graves and laying flowers (white is for mourning in China, so don't ever give people white flowers).

端午节 *Duānwǔjié*, the 'Dragon Boat Festival', falls on the fifth day of the fifth lunar month and commemorates 屈原 *Qū Yuán* a great poet and patriot of the state of Chu during the Warring States period (475–221 BC). Qu Yuan's story is too long to be told here. Why not find it out for yourself? Why *do* the Chinese hold dragon boat races and eat 粽子 *zòngzi* (pyramid shaped dumplings made of glutinous rice wrapped in bamboo or reed leaves) on *Duānwǔjié*?

中秋节 *Zhōngqiūjié*, the 'Mid-Autumn Festival', falls on the 15th day of the eighth lunar month. People traditionally admire the full moon, said to be at its brightest and clearest on this day of the year, and eat mooncakes 月饼 *yuèbǐng*, special pastries with savoury or sweet fillings of various kinds.

Find out who or what lives on the moon in Chinese mythology. Who was *Cháng'é* (嫦娥) and why did she fly to the moon?

After the founding of the People's Republic in 1949, the solar calendar was adopted in China. The main holidays according to the solar calendar are:

元旦	*Yuándàn* 'New Year's Day'
国际劳动妇女节	*Guójì Láodòng Fùnǚjié* 'International Women's Day' (8 March)
国际劳动节	*Guójì Láodòngjié* 'International Labour Day' (1 May)*
青年节	*Qīngniánjié* 'Youth Day' (4 May)
国际儿童节	*Guójì Értóngjié* 'International Children's Day' (1 June)
	(1 July is the Anniversary of the Founding of the Communist Party of China but there is no set phrase for it with *-jié*)
建军节	*Jiànjūnjié* 'Anniversary of the Founding of the People's Liberation Army' (1 August)
国庆节	*Guóqìngjié* 'National Day' (1 October)*

* Used to be a one-week holiday, now only two days.

'Comrade' and others

Although the term 同志 *tóngzhì* is still used, it is less common than it was and will presumably eventually become even less so. Terms of address which were regarded as 'feudal' before the Great Proletarian Cultural Revolution (now written in Chinese with inverted commas to express political disapproval) are coming back into fashion. It is quite common to address youngish women as *xiǎojie*. The once universal *àiren* 'love person' for husband or wife is also slowly being replaced with the more conventional and less intimate *xiānsheng* or *zhàngfu* for 'husband' and *tàitai* or *qīzi* for 'wife'. These 'new/old' terms are particularly in favour with some people who live in the coastal provinces or come into contact with foreigners.

Exercise 19.2
Write out each of the following characters in *pinyin* and put their common component or radical in brackets afterwards.
e.g. 把、挂、打 → *bǎ, guà, dǎ* (扌):

1 想、您、怎、意、思、志。
2 请、说、谢、话。
3 喂、售、员、吗、问、号。
4 近、还、过、这、远、边。
5 部、那、邮、都。

Repeat this exercise for yourself in subsequent units.

Exercise 19.3
Write a character for each of the following phonetic transcriptions so as to make a word with the character given. e.g. 北 *biān*, 北 *jīng* → 北边，北京:

1 东 *xi*，东 *biān*.
2 *wài* 国，*Zhōng* 国.
3 售 *huò* 员，售 *piào* 员.
4 *máo* 衣，衣 *fu*.
5 电 *yǐng*，电 *huà*，电 *bào*.
6 星期 *èr*，星期 *sì*.
7 地 *tú*，地 *fang*.
8 *nà* 边，*zhèi* 边.

Exercise 19.4

◆) CD 2, tr 33

Translate this passage into colloquial English and then into Chinese characters:

Wáng xiānsheng rén hěn hǎo dànshi tā yǒu yí ge xiǎo máobìng (毛病 'defect') tā hěn xǐhuan huā (花 'spend') qián. Qù mǎi yí jiàn chènshān, tā jiù mǎi sān jiàn, nǐ yào tā mǎi yì běn zázhì jiù gěi nǐ mǎi shí běn. Tā shuō dōu hěn yǒu yìsi suǒyǐ dōu mǎi le. Ràng tā qù mǎi dōngxi, nǐ zěnme néng fàng xīn ne?

Exercise 19.5
Translate the dialogue at the beginning of the unit into colloquial English.

TESTING YOURSELF

Translate the following into *pinyin* and then into Chinese characters:

1 *This is your receipt, please put (it) away carefully.*

2 *Have you stuck the stamps on? Not yet.*

3 *Posting books is a hassle but worth it.*

4 *This is the guide (map) for the Bird's Nest National Stadium.*

5 *Press this button to start, this one to pause and this one to stop.*

收费公厕
W.C.

What does this sign mean? Two letters give a clue. It's a paying (shōu fèi) *public* (gōng) *toilet* (cè).

20

在咖啡馆 zài kāfēiguǎn
At the coffee shop

In this unit you will learn
- *about guanxi in China*
- *more about the comparative*
- *the vocabulary for opening an account, obtaining a credit card/ debit card*
- *how to use question words in a non-question way*
- *about percentages and fractions*

◄)) **CD 2, tr 34–35**

Shi Aili is sitting in a branch of Starbucks (星巴克) when a young Chinese couple (Lù Fēng 陆风 and Bái Lán 白兰) strike up a conversation with her.

史爱理坐在一家星巴克咖啡店里和一对中国夫妇 (陆风和白兰) 谈了起来。
Shǐ Àilǐ zuò zai yì jiā Xīngbākè kāfēidiàn lǐ hé yí duì Zhōngguó fūfù (Lù Fēng hé Bái Lán) tán le qǐlái.

陆风:	您好！我叫陆风，她叫白兰。您来北京多长时间了？您喜欢北京吗？	Nín hǎo! Wǒ jiào Lù Fēng, tā jiào Bái Lán. Nín lái Běijīng duō cháng shíjiān le? Nín xǐhuan Běijīng ma?
史:	你们好！我叫史爱理。认识你们真高兴。我来北京已经两个月了。我很喜欢北京，不过这儿跟美国和英国很不一样，所以有时候我很想家。今天我想先买点儿东西，再到星巴克来喝杯咖啡，就像我在家的时候一样。	Nǐmen hǎo! Wǒ jiào Shǐ Àilǐ. Rènshi nǐmen zhēn gāoxìng. Wǒ lái Běijīng yǐjing liǎng ge yuè le. Wǒ hěn xǐhuan Běijīng. Búguo zhèr gēn Měiguó hé Yīngguó hěn bù yíyàng, suǒyi yǒu shíhou wǒ hěn xiǎng-jiā. Jīntiān wǒ xiǎng xiān mǎi diǎnr dōngxi, zài dào Xīngbākè lái hē bēi kāfēi, jiù xiàng wǒ zài jiā de shíhou yíyang.
白兰:	你觉得这儿的商店怎么样？	Nǐ juéde zhèr de shāngdiàn zěnmeyang?
史:	很多服装店和鞋店跟美国差不多，可惜常常没有大号(儿)的。	Hěn duo fúzhuāng diàn hé xié diàn gēn Měiguó chàbuduō, kěxī chángcháng méi yǒu dà hào(r) de.
白兰:	可是你(并)不胖。	Kěshi nǐ (bìng) bú pàng.
史:	我不胖，可是脚很大。	Wǒ bú pàng, kěshi jiǎo hěn dà.
(很快地换了一个话题)		
(Hěn kuài de huàn le yí ge huàtí)		
陆风:	您在北京工作还是学习？	Nín zài Běijīng gōngzuò háishi xuéxí?
史:	我在北京大学学中文，可是我男朋友在一家合资企业工作。你们都工作吗？	Wǒ zài Běijīng Dàxué xué Zhōngwén, kěshi wǒ nán péngyou zài yì jiā hézī qǐyè gōngzuò. Nǐmen dōu gōngzuò ma?

陆风：	我在一家外国银行，汇丰银行工作。白兰在星巴克上班(儿)，不过今天她休息。	Wǒ zài yì jiā wàiguó yínháng, Huìfēng Yínháng gōngzuò. Bái Lán zài Xīngbākè shàng bān(r), bú guò jīntiān tā xiūxi.
史：	哦，汇丰银行。这几个星期我在想我应该在这儿开个账户，这样我可以把钱从英国转到这儿来。我在这儿的钱不多了。	Oh, Huìfēng Yínháng. Zhèi jǐ ge xīngqī wǒ zài xiǎng wǒ yīnggai zài zhèr kāi ge zhànghù, zhè yang wǒ kěyi bǎ qián cóng Yīngguó zhuǎn dào zhèr lái. Wǒ zài zhèr de qián bù duō le.
陆风：	您可以在汇丰银行开个账户，这样转钱会容易一些。	Nín kěyi zài Huìfēng Yínháng kāi ge zhànghù, zhè yàng zhuǎn qián huì róngyi yì xiē.
史：	这是个好主意。我能不能有一张信用卡和一张借记卡？	Zhè shì ge hǎo zhǔyì. Wǒ néng bu néng yǒu yì zhāng xìnyòngkǎ hé yì zhāng jièjìkǎ?
陆风：	只要您的账户里有足够的钱，我想就不会有问题。您为什么要一张信用卡还要一张借记卡呢？	Zhǐyào nínde zhànghù lǐ yǒu zúgòu de qián, wǒ xiǎng jiù bú huì yǒu wèntí. Nín wèishénme yào yì zhāng xìnyòngkǎ hái yào yì zhāng jièjìkǎ ne?
史：	我不喜欢身上带着许多现金。我愿意在需要的时候在取款机取钱。我能开一个活期存款账户跟一个定期存款账户吗？这样我的定期存款可以多得一些利息。	Wǒ bù xǐhuan shēnshang dài zhe xǔduō xiànjīn. Wǒ yuànyi zài xūyào de shíhou zài qǔkuǎnjī qǔ qián. Wǒ néng kāi yí ge huóqī cúnkuǎn zhànghù gēn yí ge dìngqī cúnkuǎn zhànghù ma? Zhè yàng wǒ de dìngqī cúnkuǎn kěyi duō dé yìxiē lìxi.

白兰：	你可以明天去陆风的银行跟他谈谈。我相信他会给你很多建议。我知道汇丰银行的利息有时候比中国银行高一点儿。	Nǐ kěyi míngtiān qù Lù Fēng de yínháng gēn tā tántan. Wǒ xiāngxìn tā huì gěi nǐ hěn duō jiànyì. Wǒ zhīdào Huìfēng Yínháng de lìxi yǒu shíhou bǐ Zhōngguó Yínháng gāo yìdiǎnr.
陆风：	对，您明天去吧。这是我的名片，上面有我们分行的地址，离这儿不远。您能不能十点钟去？谈完了以后，我们可以来这儿喝一杯浓缩咖啡，吃块儿蛋糕。白兰会在这儿上班，要是您时间不多，她会保证我们不用等。	Duì, nín míngtiān qù ba. Zhè shì wǒ de míngpiàn, shàngmian yǒu wǒmen fēnháng de dìzhǐ, lí zhèr bù yuǎn. Nín néng bu néng shí diǎn zhōng qù? Tán wán le yǐhou, wǒmen kěyi lái zhèr hē yì bēi nóngsuō kāfēi, chī kuài'r dàngāo. Bái Lán huì zài zhèr shàng bān, yàoshi nín shíjiān bù duō, tā huì bǎozhèng wǒmen bú yòng děng.
白兰：	(笑着说) 要是你不小心，天天早上喝咖啡、吃蛋糕，你就会长胖，我父母就会说你配不上我。	(Xiàozhe shuō) Yàoshi nǐ bù xiǎo xīn, tiāntiān zǎoshàng hē kāfēi, chī dàngāo, nǐ jiù huì zhǎng pàng, wǒ fùmǔ jiù huì shuō nǐ pèi bu shàng wǒ.
史：	(有点儿不好意思) 你们真是天生的一对儿。真高兴认识你们。谢谢你们的帮助。对不起，我得走了。(对陆风) 明天十点在汇丰银行见。再见！	(Yǒudiǎn[r] bù hǎo yìsi) Nǐmen zhēn shì tiānshēng de yí duìr. Zhēn gāoxìng rènshi nǐmen. Xièxie nǐmen de bāngzhù. Duìbuqǐ, wǒ děi zǒu le. (Duì Lù Fēng) míngtiān shí diǎn zài Huìfēng Yínháng jiàn. Zàijiàn!
陆风 & 白兰：	再见！	Zàijiàn!

咖啡馆 kāfēiguǎn (n) coffee shop
夫妇 fūfù (n) husband and wife
跟 . . . 一样 gēn . . . yíyàng to be the same as (see 20.1)
想家 xiǎng jiā (v-o) to be homesick, to miss home
先 . . . 再 . . . xiān . . . zài . . . first . . . then (see 20.2)
星巴克 Xīngbākè (N) Starbucks
服装店 fúzhuāng diàn (n) clothes shop
鞋店 xié diàn (n) shoe shop
差不多 chàbuduō
号 hào (n) size (number; date in Unit 16)
脚 [只] jiǎo [zhi] (n) foot
换 huàn (v) to change
话题 huàtí (n) topic of conversation
合资企业 [家] hézī qǐyè (n) [jiā] joint venture
银行 yínháng (n)
汇丰银行 Huìfēng Yínháng (N) HSBC (Bank)
开个账户 kāi ge zhànghù (v-o) to open a (bank) account
转 zhuǎn (v) to transfer; to turn
信用卡[张] xìnyòngkǎ (n) [zhāng] credit card
借记卡 [张] jièjìkǎ (n) [zhāng] debit/switch card
只要 zhǐyào (conj) so long as, provided
足够 zúgòu (adj; v) enough; to be sufficient
身上 shēnshang (adv) on one's person (Lit. body)
带 dài (v) to bring, take
许多 xǔduō (adj)
现金 xiànjīn (n) cash
愿意 yuànyi (aux v) to be willing; to want
需要 xūyào (v; n) to need, require; needs
取款机 qǔkuǎnjī (n) ATM (automatic teller machine)
活期存款账户 huóqī cúnkuǎn zhànghù (n) current account
定期存款账户 dìngqī cúnkuǎn zhànghù (n) deposit account
得 dé (v) to get (e.g. interest, sick)
利息 lìxi (n) interest (on a (bank) account)
相信 xiāngxìn (v) to be convinced/sure, to believe, have faith in
建议 jiànyì (n; v) suggestion, recommendation; to propose, suggest
名片 míngpiàn (n) visiting card, calling card
分行 fēnháng (n) branch (bank)

QUICK VOCAB

地址 dìzhǐ *(n)* address
浓缩咖啡 nóngsuō kāfēi *(n)* espresso (coffee)
蛋糕 [块儿] dàngāo *(n)* [kuài'r] cake
要是...就 yàoshi...jiù *(conj)* if ... then (see 11.14)
保证 bǎozhèng *(v; n)* to guarantee, ensure; guarantee, pledge
笑 xiào *(v; n)* to smile, laugh; smile. laugh
当心/小心 dāng xīn/xiǎo xīn *(v-o)* to take care, be careful
天天 tiāntiān *(TW)* every day (see 20.6)
早上 zǎoshàng *(TW)* morning (early)
长胖 zhǎng pàng *(v)* to get fat
配不上 pèi bu shàng *(RV)* not to be worthy of
不好意思 bù hǎoyìsi *(v)* to be embarrassed, feel ill at ease
天生的 tiānshēng *(adj)* born, innate
一对儿 yí duìr *(n)* a pair, a couple
对不起 duìbuqǐ sorry, excuse me

Note that Lù Fēng, as a young Chinese man, carefully uses *nín* throughout his conversation with Shǐ Àilǐ, whereas Bái Lán, who is probably about the same age as Shǐ Àilǐ and of the same gender, feels quite comfortable using *nǐ*.

Grammar

1 *More on the comparative*

we have already met the comparative in 9.9 and 9.10. To express that 'A is the same as B' we say *A gēn B yíyàng*: *Wǒ gēn tā yíyàng* 'I am the same as her/him.' This can be taken a step further using the formula: 'A is as adjective as B', *A gēn B yíyàng adjective*:

A gēn B yíyàng guì. *'A is as expensive as B.'*
Niúròu (beef) gēn yú (fish) yíyàng guì. *'Beef is as expensive as fish.'*

And from the text: *Búguo zhèr gēn Měiguó hé Yīngguó hěn bù yíyàng.*

Exercise 20.1

Write out the following sentences in characters and then translate them into English. Look up any characters you don't know in the index:

1 *Měiguó gēn Yīngguó yíyàng ma?*
Bù yíyàng, Yīngguó bǐ Měiguó guì duōle.

2 *Zuò huǒchē gēn zuò fēijī yǒu shénme bù yíyàng?*
Zuò huǒchē bǐ zuò fēijī piányi de duō.

3 *Nǐ gēn tā yíyàng bù xǐhuan tīng yīnyuè* (music) *ma?*
Bù, wǒ hěn xǐhuan tīng gǔdiǎn (classical) *yīnyuè.*

4 *Wǒ gēn wǒ de wèihūnqī* (未婚妻 fiancée) *yíyàng làngmàn* (romantic), *dōu xǐhuan xiě shī* (poetry).

5 *Zài Zhōngguó Rìběn diànshì gēn zài Ōuzhōu yíyàng róngyi mǎi ma?*

2 Xiān V₁ zài V₂

The construction *xiān* V_1 *zài* V_2 shows a sequence of actions, first V_1 has to be done, then V_2. This means that you can only carry out the action of the second verb when you have carried out the action of the first:

Wǒ xiǎng xiān mǎi diǎnr/xiē dōngxi, zài dào Xīngbākè lái hē bēi kāfēi. *'I thought I'd do a bit of shopping and then go to Starbucks for a coffee.'*

(Note that the *xiān* is sometimes omitted in this construction, leaving only the *zài* before the second verb. This *zài* is written 再 as in 再见 *zàijiàn* not as in 在 'at, in'.)

3 Dào . . . qù/lái

As a verb, *dào* means 'to go, to arrive (in), to reach': *Tā dào le* 'He's arrived.' If there is a place word after *dào*, the simple directional ending *lái* or *qù* is used at the end of the clause to indicate direction towards or away from the speaker (see 8.1.ii). There is a simple example of this in the text:

. . . dào Xīngbākè lái hē bēi kāfēi *'come to Starbucks and drink a cup of coffee'*

As a compound directional ending with *qù* or *lái*, *dào* can translate simply as 'to' when used with such verbs as *pǎo* 'to run', *zǒu* 'to walk' and *bān* 'to remove': *Wǒmen xiǎng míngnián* (next year) *bān dào Jiānádà qu*. (*Lit*. We/fancy/next year/move to/Canada/go) 'We plan to move to Canada next year.'

Another example from the text is:

Zhè yang wǒ kěyi bǎ qián cóng Yīngguó zhuǎn dào zhèr lái.
'In this way I can transfer money from the UK to here.'

The guānxi network

Who knows whom in China is very important when the wheels of bureaucracy need a certain amount of oiling and certain goods and services are in short supply. Your personal relations network is known as your *guānxihù* 关系户 (*Lit.* relationship household) and some people seem to have very extensive ones. Your *guānxihù* will be made up of many of those *tóng* relationships explained in Unit 21, as well as your relatives and other people you have met along life's path. Many educated young people from urban areas who were sent to the countryside during the Cultural Revolution established quite sizeable *guānxihù* during that time and these still stand them in good stead. If, for instance, a friend, colleague or *lǎo tóngxué* (old classmate) gives you an introduction (whether personally or by phone or letter) to one of his/her *guānxi* it is quite usual to present your new '*guānxi*' with a suitable present of some sort, a carton of foreign cigarettes *yì tiáo wàiguó yān* used to be quite acceptable. It would, of course, be wonderful not to have to use the *guānxihù* system to buy air or rail tickets or other goods and services (this is a small part of what the students were protesting about in 1989) but in a country so densely populated as China, it is well nigh impossible *not* to use the *guānxihù* system on occasions.

4 Question words used in a non-question way

i Question words such as *shéi (shuí)*, *shénme*, *nǎ* and *nǎr* can be used in a non-question way to mean 'anybody', 'anything', 'any' and 'anywhere':

Wǒ bú qù nǎr. *'I'm not going anywhere'.* (In response to *Nǐ qù nǎr?*, it seems, in addition, to convey a slight feeling of unwillingness to communicate with the questioner!)

ii Only *jǐ* and *duōshao* can be used in the affirmative, to indicate 'several' and 'an indefinite number' respectively:

Tāmen yǒu jǐ běn Zhōngwén shū. *'They have several Chinese books.'*

In this case, intonation and context tell the listener whether they are being used as question words or not.

iii Question words can also be used to indicate inclusiveness in the affirmative, but exclusiveness in the negative. *Dōu* or *yě* must be added before the verb to reinforce this sense of inclusiveness or exclusiveness:

Shéi dōu bú suàn. (*Lit.* Who/all/not/count) *'Nobody counts.'*

In this construction, the direct object is moved to a position before the verb (but after the subject):

Wǒ shénme yě bú zuò. (*Lit.* I/what/also/not/do) *'I'm not doing anything.'*
Tā nǎr dōu qù. (*Lit.* He/where/all/go) *'He goes everywhere.'*

(Note that *jǐ* and *duōshao* cannot be used in this way.)

iv Such concepts as 'whatever (one likes)', 'whoever (one likes)', 'wherever (one likes)' are expressed by repeating the question word and the verb in a second clause and putting *jiù* before the repeated verb in the second clause:

Nǐ yào qǐng shéi, nǐ jiù qǐng shéi. (*Lit.* You/want/invite/who/ you/then/invite/who) *'Invite whoever you like.'*
Wǒmen yào mǎi shénme, wǒmen jiù mǎi shénme. (*Lit.* We/want/buy/what/we/then/buy/what) *'We buy whatever we like.'*

v *Zěnme*, 'how?' put before the verb roughly translates as 'no matter how' or 'to what degree'. *Dōu* or *yě* must be put before the verb in the following clause. *Bù zěnme* adjective translates as 'not particularly' adjective:

Nà ge xuésheng hěn rènzhēn ('conscientious'). **Tiānqì zěnme lěng, tā dōu lái shàng kè.** (v-o attend class) *'That student is very conscientious. He comes to class no matter how cold it is.'*
Tā bù zěnme niánqīng le. *'She's no longer particularly young.'*

Exercise 20.2
Translate this passage into *pinyin* and then into Chinese characters:

1 If you have a lot of money, then you can eat whatever you like.
2 I possess many dictionaries but each one has several shortcomings (*quēdiǎn*).
3 Today's Sunday and I have had a very busy week. I am not going anywhere this afternoon.
4 However hot it is, she insists on sunbathing (*shài tàiyáng*).
5 Your (sing) health is not particularly good, so you shouldn't smoke.

5 *Adjective/noun* + shang

A neat and easy way of forming adverbs from adjectives such as *jīběn* (基本) 'basic' and nouns such as *shíjì* (实际) 'reality' is simply to add *-shang* (上) so that *jīběnshang* becomes 'basically' and *shíjìshang* becomes 'in reality'. Other examples are:

shēnshang (身上) 'on your person, on you'
yìshùshang (艺术上) 'artistically'
zhèngzhìshang (政治上) 'politically'
jīngjìshang (经济上) 'economically'
lǐlùnshang (理论上) 'theoretically'
shìshíshang (事实上) 'in actual fact' (an alternative to shíjìshang)
shēnghuóshang (生活上) 'in life'
lìshǐshang (历史上) 'historically'

6 Tiāntiān *and* niánnián

Both *tiān* and *nián* can be repeated to give the meaning 'every day' and 'every year' respectively. *Rén* 'person' can also be repeated to mean 'every person/everybody'. (Another way of doing this is by putting '*měi*' in front as we have already explained in 9.4.)

7 *The use of 'r'*

In the north of China, especially in the area around Beijing, certain words attract an additional 'r' at the end. This is something that marks out speakers from the north from those in the south, who find both the Beijing 'r' and all the other retroflexes (zh, ch, sh) very difficult to pronounce.

Some of the most common words to attract this 'r' are:

kuài(r) MW *a piece*
yìdiǎn(r) *a little bit*
liáo *or* tán tiān(r) *to chat*
shǒutào(r) *glove*
wán(r) *to enjoy oneself, to play*
yí duì(r) *a pair, a couple*

See if you can find examples of the Beijing 'r' in the text. There are six in total, although some of them are 'repeats'.

Insight: percentages and fractions

This is not exactly a learning tip – more an opportunity to explain the basic principles behind percentages and fractions should you ever need to know them.

As stated in 16.1, the Chinese move from the general to the particular, so, in line with this principle, instead of saying 75%, the Chinese say 100 parts classical possessive marker *zhī* 75, i.e. *bǎifēn zhī qīshíwǔ*. Sixty per cent would be *bǎifēn zhī liùshí*, 50% would be *bǎifēn zhī wǔshí* and so on.

To say something is 10% more expensive than something else the adjective for 'expensive' *guì* is placed in front of the percentage: *guì bǎifēn zhī shí* so 'this digital TV is 20% more expensive than that one' would be:

Zhè tái shùmǎ diànshì(jī) bǐ nà tái (shùmǎ diànshì(jī)) guì bǎifēn zhī èrshí.

'How many per cent' is expressed as *bǎifēn zhī duōshao?*

Fractions work in exactly the same way. Three quarters (3/4) is expressed as four parts *zhī* three, i.e. *sìfēn zhī sān*; 7/8 *bāfēn zhī qī*, etc. 'How many eighths' would therefore be *bāfēn zhī jǐ* (not *duōshao* as the answer has to be less than ten).

If you want to say something is 'twice as expensive as something else' the formula is *A bǐ B guì yí bèi*, where *bèi* 倍 means 'times or -fold'.

Exercise 20.3

Write out each sentence in characters including translating the percentage, fraction or -fold contained in the brackets:
Wàiguórén de fángzi bǐ Zhōngguórén guì (75%). → 外国人的房子比中国人贵百分之七十五。

1 *Zuò huǒchē bǐ zuò fēijī piányi* (50%).
2 *Shuǐdiànfèi* (water and electricity costs) *bǐ qùnián guì* (10%).
3 *Rìběn yīfu bǐ Zhōngguó yīfu guì* (300%).
4 *Píngguǒ bù hǎo chī, wǒ zhǐ chī le* (1/4).
5 *Yīnyuèhuì de piào zuótiān mài le* (1/2).
6 *Wàiguó yān hǎo chōu* (抽 to smoke), *zhè bāo yǐjīng chōu le* (2/3).
7 *Zài Zhōngguó Měiguó zhuānjiā* (expert) *bǐ Yīngguó zhuānjiā duō* (ten-fold).

中国工商银行
北京市分行 东城支行东四分理处
营 业 时 间
上午: 9:00—12:00 下午: 1:30—5:00 星期六、日休息

Opening hours of a branch of the China Industry and Commerce Bank. On which days is the bank closed?

TESTING YOURSELF

Translate the dialogue at the beginning of this unit into colloquial English.

旅途见闻 lǚtú jiànwén
Traveller's notes

In this unit you will learn
- *how to express two actions going on simultaneously*
- *about Chinese proverbs*
- *more about abbreviations in Chinese*
- *about similarities and dissimilarities*
- *more about the passive*
- *when to use* **chuān** *and when to use* **dài** *for 'to wear'*
- *about yīn and yáng*

◀) CD 2, tr 36

在中国旅行可以了解中国人生活的各个方面，比如说中国人放假、出差等情况。王永寿和史爱理正在杭州玩儿，坐在世界闻名的西湖旁边儿，一边吃着三明治，一边聊天儿。

史	来杭州旅行的可真多呀！
王	可不是吗！没想到中国旅游事业发展得那么快。
史	你知道吗？中国有一句俗话：'上有天堂，下有苏、杭'，所以来杭州找人间乐园的人总是很多！
王	那倒是，你注意了没有？中国人喜欢照相。
史	是的。听说照相机也是可以租的，各种各样的数码相机都有。
王	对了，但是凡是有游客的地方都有职业照相的。
史	中国人还有一点不太像我们，他们很喜欢合伙儿出去玩儿，或者是同学或者是同事或者是同乡。

	(说着就有一个戴着太阳镜的年轻小伙子走过来)。
张锡群	(坐下就问)你们是哪国人？是来杭州玩儿的吗？
史	是的，我们是英国人。你是本地人吗？
张锡群	不是，我是苏州人，来杭州办一点事。
王	苏州地方不错，有人叫它中国的威尼斯。也有人说'苏州出美人'。
	(他正在说话的时候有一个小孩儿拉他妈妈的手指着王永寿和史爱理大声喊着'老外老外'！)
史	(笑着说)'老外'听起来还是有一种亲密的感觉，但是听到什么'洋鬼子'、'大鼻子'，心里就有一点不自在。
张锡群	这些称呼平常并没有什么坏的意思，主要是因为一些中国人没有跟外国人接触过，所以第一次碰到觉得十分新鲜。他们不懂这样的称呼很不礼貌。你们听过这句话吗？'天不怕，地不怕，就怕洋鬼子说中国话'！
王	没听说过，真好玩儿！我想问你一个问题，可以吗？
张锡群	当然可以。什么问题？
王	你觉得中国人有种族偏见吗？
张锡群	这怎么说呢？我们受过教育的人，中国人也好，外国人也好，一般来说，都不认为自己有什么偏见，但是坦率地说，下意识肯定还是会有一点的。
王	一点也不错。咱们应该承认是有偏见的，要不很容易'自欺欺人'。承认错误等于改了一半儿了。
张锡群	太对了，我完全同意。

Zài Zhōngguó lǚxíng kěyǐ liǎojiě Zhōngguórén shēnghuó de gègè fāngmiàn, bǐrú shuō Zhōngguórén fàng jià, chū chāi děng qíngkuàng. Wáng Yǒngshòu hé Shǐ Àilǐ zhèngzài Hángzhōu wánr, zuò zài shìjiè wénmíng de Xīhú pángbiānr, yìbiān chīzhe sānmíngzhì, yìbiān liáo tiānr.

Shǐ	Lái Hángzhōu lǚyóu de kě zhēn duō ya!
Wáng	Kěbúshì ma! Méi xiǎng dào Zhōngguó lǚyóu shìyè fāzhǎn de nàme kuài.
Shǐ	Nǐ zhīdao ma? Zhōngguó yǒu yí jù súhuà: 'Shàng yǒu tiāntáng, xià yǒu Sū、Háng',

	suǒyǐ lái Hángzhōu zhǎo rénjiān lèyuán de rén zǒngshi hěn duō!
Wáng	Nà dàoshì. Nǐ zhùyì le méi you: Zhōngguórén xǐhuan zhào xiàng.
Shǐ	Shì de. Tīngshuō zhàoxiàngjī yě shi kěyǐ zū de, gèzhǒnggèyàng de shùmǎ xiàngjī dōu yǒu.
Wáng	Duìle, dànshi fánshì yǒu yóukè de dìfang dōu yǒu zhíyè zhàoxiàng de.
Shǐ	Zhōngguórén hái yǒu yìdiǎn bú tài xiàng wǒmen, tāmen hěn xǐhuan héhuǒr chū qu wánr huòzhě shì tóngxué huòzhě shì tóngshì huòzhě shì tóngxiāng!
	(Shuōzhe jiù yǒu yí ge dàizhe tàiyángjìng de niánqīng xiǎohuǒzi zǒu guòlai)
Zhāng Xīqún	(zuò xià jiù wèn) Nǐmen shì nǎ guó rén? Shì lái Hángzhōu wánr de ma?
Shǐ	Shì de. Wǒmen shì Yīngguórén. Nǐ shì běndìrén ma?
Zhāng Xīqún	Bú shì, wǒ shì Sūzhōurén, lái Hángzhōu bàn yìdiǎn shì.
Wáng	Sūzhōu dìfang búcuò, yǒu rén jiào tā Zhōngguó de Wēinísī. Yě yǒu rén shuō 'Sūzhōu chū měirén'. . . . (Tā zhèngzài shuō huà de shíhou yǒu yí ge xiǎoháir lāzhe tā māma de shǒu zhǐzhe Wáng Yǒngshòu hé Shǐ Àilì dà shēng hǎnzhe 'Lǎowài, lǎowài'!)
Shǐ	(xiàozhe shuō) 'Lǎowài' tīng qǐlai háishi yǒu yì zhǒng qīnmì de gǎnjué, dànshi tīng dào shénme 'yángguǐzi', 'dà bízi', xīnlǐ jiù yǒu yìdiǎn bú zìzài.
Zhāng Xīqún	Zhè xiē chēnghū jīngcháng bìng méi yǒu shénme huài de yìsi, zhǔyào shì yīnwei yìxiē Zhōngguórén méi yǒu gēn wàiguórén jiēchùguo suǒyǐ dì yí cì pèng dào juéde shífēn xīnxiān. Tāmen bù dǒng zhèyàng de chēnghū hěn bù lǐmào. Nǐmen tīngguo zhè jù huà ma?

	'Tiān bú pà, dì bú pà, jiù pà yángguǐzi shuō Zhōngguóhuà'!
Wáng	Méi tīngshuōguo, zhēn hǎo wánr! Wǒ xiǎng wèn nǐ yì ge wèntí, kěyǐ ma?
Zhāng Xīqún	Dāngrán kěyǐ. Shénme wèntí?
Wáng	Nǐ juéde Zhōngguórén yǒu zhǒngzú piānjiàn ma?
Zhāng Xīqún	Zhè zěnme shuō ne? Wǒmen shòuguo jiàoyù de rén, Zhōngguórén yě hǎo, wàiguórén yě hǎo, yìbān lái shuō, dōu bú rènwéi zìjǐ yǒu shénme piānjiàn, dànshi tǎnshuài de shuō, xiàyìshí kěndìng háishi huì yǒu yìdiǎn de.
Wáng	Yìdiǎn yě bú cuò. Zánmen yīnggāi chéngrèn shì yǒu piānjiàn de, yàobù hěn róngyì 'zì qī qī rén'. Chéngrèn cuòwù děngyú gǎi le yíbàn(r) le.
Zhāng Xīqún	Tài duìle, wǒ wánquán tóngyì.

旅途 **lǚtú** (n) journey, trip
见闻 **jiànwén** (n) what one sees and hears
旅行 **lǚxíng** (v; n) to travel; travel
了解 **liǎojiě** (v) to find out, understand, know
各个 **gègè** (adj) each, every
方面 **fāngmiàn**
比如说 **bǐrú shuō** for example (more formal)
放假 **fàng jià** (v-o) to have a holiday or vacation
出差 **chū chāi** (v-o) to be on a business trip
等 **děng**
情况 **qíngkuàng** (n) situation, state of affairs
杭州 **Hángzhōu** (N) Hangzhou
玩儿 **wán(r)**
闻名 **wénmíng** (adj) well known, famous
西湖 **Xīhú** (N) West Lake
旁边儿 **pángbianr** (n) side
一边...一边... **yìbiān ... yìbiān** see 21.1

三明治 sānmíngzhì *(n) sandwich*
旅游 lǚyóu *(n; v) tourism; to tour*
可 kě *(adv) emphasizes tone of speaker*
呀 yā *(interj) indicating surprise*
可不是吗 kěbúshì ma? *exactly; that's just the way it is*
事业 shìyè *(n) undertaking, cause*
发展 fāzhǎn *(v) to develop*
俗话 [句] súhuà *(n)* [jù] *common saying, proverb*
天堂 tiāntáng *(n) heaven, paradise*
苏杭 Sū、Háng *(N) Suzhou and Hangzhou*
人间乐园 rénjiān lèyuán *(n) paradise on earth*
注意 zhùyì *(v) to pay attention to*
照相 zhào xiàng *(v-o)*
听说 tīngshuō *(v) to be told, hear of*
照相机 zhàoxiàngjī *(n)* [tái] *camera*
各种各样的 gèzhǒnggèyang de *(p) all kinds of*
数码相机 shùmǎxiàngjī *(n) digital camera*
游客 yóukè *(n) tourist*
职业 zhíyè *(n) occupation, profession*
合伙 (儿) héhuǒ(r) *(v-o) form a company or partnership*
同学 tóngxué *(n) fellow student*
同乡 tóngxiāng *(n) person who was born in the same place as you*
戴 dài *(v) to wear (see 21.8)*
太阳镜 [副] tàiyángjìng *(n)* [fù] *sunglasses*
小伙子 xiǎohuǒzi *(n) young fellow*
本地 běndì *(n) this locality*
办事 bàn shì *(v-o) to arrange for something to be done*
它 tā *(ps) it*
威尼斯 Wēinísī *(N) Venice*
美人 měirén *(n) beautiful woman*
拉 lā *(v) to pull; to play (of stringed instruments)*
手 shǒu *(n) hand*
大声 (地) dàshēng(de)
喊 hǎn *(v) to shout, cry out*
老外 lǎowài *(n) 'old foreigner'*
听起来 tīng qǐlai *(v) to sound, ring*
亲密 qīnmì *(adj) close, intimate*

感觉 **gǎnjué** *(n) feeling, sense*
洋鬼子 **yángguǐzi** *(n) foreign devil*
大鼻子 **dà bízi** *(adj + n) big nose*
心里 **xīnlǐ** *in the heart or mind*
自在 **zìzài** *(adj) at ease, comfortable*
称呼 **chēnghū** *(n; v) form of address; to address*
坏 **huài** *(adj) bad; broken*
主要 **zhǔyào** *(adj; adv) principal(ly)*
觉得 **juéde** *(v)*
十分 **shífēn** *(adv) extremely, very*
新鲜 **xīnxiān** *(adj) fresh*
礼貌 **lǐmào** *(adj; n) courteous; manners*
话 [句] **huà** *(n)* [jù] *remark, word(s)*
怕 **pà** *(v) to fear, be afraid of*
种族 **zhǒngzú** *(n) race*
偏见 **piānjiàn** *(n) prejudice, bias*
受 **shòu** *(v) to receive, be subjected to (see 21.10)*
教育 **jiàoyù** *(n; v) education; to educate*
A 也好 B 也好 **A yě hǎo B yě hǎo** *(see 21.11)*
一般来说 **yìbān lái shuō** *generally speaking*
认为 **rènwéi** *(v) to think, consider*
坦率(地) **tǎnshuài(de)** *(adj; adv) frank(ly)*
下意识 **xiàyìshí** *(n) subconsciousness*
肯定 **kěndìng** *(adj; adv; v) definite(ly); affirm*
咱们 **zánmen** *(pp) we (including listener; see 21.13)*
自欺欺人 **zì qī qī rén** *deceive yourself as well as others*
错误 **cuòwù** *(n) mistake, error*
改 **gǎi** *(v) to alter, change, correct*
完全 **wánquán** *(adj; adv) complete(ly)*
同意 **tóngyì** *(v) to agree with*

Grammar

1 Yìbiān V_1 ... yìbiān V_2

When we want to indicate that two actions are going on
simultaneously we can use the construction *yìbiān* V_1, *yìbiān* V_2:

Tāmen yìbiān kàn fēngjǐng, yìbiān liáo tiānr. *'They chatted while looking at the scenery.'*

Yǒude rén yìbiān kàn diànshì, yìbiān chī fàn. *'Some people have their meals watching the TV.'*

Tāmen yìbiān chīzhe sānmíngzhì, yìbiān liáo tiānr. *'They chatted while eating (their) sandwiches.'*

When expressing the continuous past or present, one of the two verbs may be followed by *zhe* to emphasize the continuity of that verb (see the preceding example).

2 Chinese proverbs

Chinese proverbs or idioms are known as *chéngyǔ* (成语) (*Lit.* become language), which are usually set phrases made up of four characters, although they are not necessarily limited to four, or *súhuà* (*Lit.* custom talk, i.e. 'old saying'), which can be of any length. Both are an integral part of the Chinese language. All Chinese of whatever educational level seem to know and use some *chéngyǔ* or *súhuà* and the higher their level the more they are likely to use them. *Chéngyǔ* have their origins in classical poetry, traditionally regarded in China as the highest medium of artistic expression (as opposed to the novel, which is translated as *xiǎoshuō* 'small talk'). Many Chinese are now unaware of which poem a particular *chéngyǔ* comes from and who it was written by, but this cultural inheritance gives weight and beauty to the modern language and a pithiness that it would otherwise lack. The text has some good examples of different proverbs:

Shàng yǒu tiāntáng, xià yǒu Sū、 Háng.
'Above there is heaven, below there is Suzhou and Hangzhou'
(i.e. these two places are regarded as being very beautiful).

Sūzhōu chū měirén.
'Beautiful women come from Suzhou.'

Tiān bú pà, dì bú pà, jiù pà yángguǐzi shuō Zhōngguóhuà.
'I'm not afraid of heaven or earth, only of foreign devils speaking Chinese.'

Zì qī qī rén.
'Deceive oneself as well as others' (*Lit.* self cheat cheat people).

Four-character phrases are particularly concise and contain a wealth of meaning.

3 More on abbreviations

We looked briefly at abbreviations in 5.8 and can now take things a step further. As you can see in the proverb *Shàng yǒu tiāntáng, xià yǒu Sū、Háng*, the *zhōu* of *Sūzhōu* and *Hángzhōu* has been dropped, so that the famous balance that the Chinese love so much can be retained, giving four characters in each phrase. Try saying it with the two *zhōu*s back in place and you'll see what I mean. Not the same effect at all, is it? The same thing is done when referring to two countries one after another.

Zhōng、Yīng liǎng guó *'the two countries China and the UK'*
(note the reversed word order in Chinese)
Sū、Ōu (Sūlián Ōuzhōu) *'the Soviet Union and Europe'*

This practice gives a much smoother rhythm to the sentence. How unpleasing to the ear it would be to say *Zhōngguó, Yīngguó liǎng guó*!

4 Fánshì . . . dōu

One way of expressing that everyone of a certain category of person, creature or inanimate object possesses the same kind of characteristic is to use the construction: *Fánshì* identification of group *dōu* ('all') characteristic:

Fánshì xiǎoháir dōu xǐhuan chī táng. *'All children like eating sweets.'*
Fánshì Yìdàlì júzi dōu hěn tián. *'All Italian tangerines are very sweet.'*

5 *To resemble or not? (xiàng and hǎoxiàng)*

Students often confuse *xiàng* (像) and *hǎoxiàng* (好像) and, of course, they do seem to be very similar. Memorize a model sentence for each to avoid confusion. *Xiàng* means 'to resemble' in the sense of 'to look like somebody or something' whereas *hǎoxiàng* means 'to seem' or 'to look like something has happened or is going to happen':

Nǐ xiàng nǐ māma. *'You look like your mum.'*
Tā bú xiàng wǒ. *'She's not like me.'*
Nà ge xuésheng hǎoxiàng bìng le. *'It seems that student is ill.'*
Hǎoxiàng yào xià yǔ. *'It looks like rain.'*
Zhōngguórén hái yǒu yìdiǎn bú tài xiàng wǒmen. *'The Chinese have another way in which they are very different from us'* (*Lit.* Chinese people still have one point not to resemble us).

Exercise 21.1
Choose *xiàng* or *hǎoxiàng* to fill the blank space in each sentence. You can rewrite the exercise in characters for extra practice. Check your answers using the vocabularies at the back of the book. Please take this instruction as read for subsequent exercises:

1 *Xiǎohuǒzi ____ lái Hángzhōu bàn shì.*
2 *Wǒ jiějie hěn ____ wǒ bàba, wǒ bǐjiào ____ wǒ māma.*
3 *Fǎguórén* (the French) *____ bu ____ Yìdàlìrén* (Italians)?
4 *Zhōngguó lǚyóu shìyè ____ fāzhǎn de hěn kuài.*
5 *Tā tài ____ nǐ, jīntiān ____ yòu bǎ zhàoxiàngjī wàng le!*

6 *Balance with opposites*

Balance in Chinese is very important. This sometimes makes for what looks at first sight to be a slightly wordy sentence as the verb is often repeated, but with further study you will appreciate this feeling of balance and harmony within the sentence. Compare the difference in feeling between *Lǎoshī jiāo Zhōngwén hé Yīngwén* and *Lǎoshī jiāo Zhōngwén yě jiāo Yīngwén*. Both are grammatically correct and mean 'The teacher teaches (both)

Chinese and English', but the second somehow feels better. This can be taken one step further in the use of opposites or contrasting ideas within the same sentence:

Wǒ yǒu cháng de, yě yǒu duǎn de. *'I have both long ones and short ones.'*
Tāmen de zhàoxiàngjī yǒu lǎoshì de, yě yǒu xīnshì de. *'They have both modern and old-fashioned cameras'* (*Lit.* as for their cameras have old-fashioned ones, also have new style ones).

7 Tóng *with everyone?*

Tóng is an adjective with the meaning 'same', 'alike', 'similar' and has given rise to a whole series of useful expressions of which some of the more common are listed here:

tóngbāo (n) 同胞 (same parents)	'compatriot'
tónghàng (n) 同行 (same profession)	'person in the same profession'
tóngjū (v) 同居 (same live)	'cohabit'
tóngnián (n) 同年 (same year)	'of the same age'
tóngqíng (v) 同情 (same emotion)	'to sympathize with'
tóngshí (adv) 同时 (same time)	'at the same time, in the meantime'
tóngshì (n) 同事 (same job)	'colleague'
tóngxiāng (n) 同乡 (same native place)	'person who comes from the same birth place'
tóngxìng (adj; n) 同姓 (same surname)	'of the same surname'
tóngxìngliàn (adj; n) 同性恋 (same sex love)	'homosexual'
tóngxué (n) 同学 (same study)	'fellow student'
tóngyì (v) 同意 (same meaning)	'to agree with'
tóngzhì (n) 同志 (same aspiration)	'comrade'

8 Dài or chuān?

Both these verbs mean 'to wear'. *Chuān* is the more widely used whereas *dài* is confined to items worn on extremities (but *not* shoes on feet!):

dài màozi 戴帽子	*'wear a hat'* (also *'to be labelled'*, e.g. *counterrevolutionary*)
dài yǎnjìng 戴眼镜	*'wear glasses'*
dài lǐngdài 戴领带	*'wear a tie'*
dài shǒutào 戴手套	*'wear gloves'*
dài shǒubiǎo 戴手表	*'wear a watch'*
dài ěrhuán 戴耳环	*'wear earrings'*
dài jièzhǐ 戴戒指	*'wear a ring'*
dài shǒuzhuó 戴手镯	*'wear a bracelet'*

The only exceptions to this 'rule' appear to be 'shoes' and 'socks', which are both *chuān*-ed rather than *dài*-ed. **NB** This *dài* 戴 is not the same *dài* as the verb meaning 'to take' or 'to bring', which is written 带.

Exercise 21.2
Choose *dài* or *chuān* to fill the blank space in each sentence:

1 *Yǐqián zài jiàotángli* (in church) *fùnǚ yào* _____ *màozi* (hat), *xiànzài bù yídìng dài le.*

2 *Dōngtiān, tiānqì lěng* _____ *hěn hòu* (thick) *de shǒutào* (gloves) *hěn yǒu yòng.*

3 *Chū qu de shíhou, fēi* _____ *shang xié* (shoes) *bùkě yīnwei jiē* (street) *shàng tài zāng* (dirty) *le.*

4 *Yǒu yìxiē jùlèbù* (social club), *chúfēi nánrén* _____ *lǐngdài* (tie) *cái néng jìn qu.*

5 *Nǐ jīntiān* _____ *de máoyī hěn hǎo kàn. Shì zìjǐ zhī* (knit, weave) *de ma?*

9 Yīn *and* yáng *please!*

Any of you who have dabbled in Chinese philosophy or traditional Chinese medicine will have some idea of the concept of *yīn* and *yáng*. It all comes back to balance in the end! *Yīn* 阴, written with the moon radical, is the feminine or negative principle in nature, whereas *yáng* 阳, written with the sun radical, is the masculine or positive principle. To the Chinese way of thinking, each individual (and on a much larger scale the universe) is made up of *yīn* and *yáng* and only when the right balance is achieved between the two will s/he be in good mental and physical health. *Yīn* characteristics include sensitivity, softness, feelings centred around home, family and friends; *yáng* characteristics centre around work, competitiveness, assertion, hence the traditional division into male and female. This is a fascinating subject to explore and you could end up with a whole different outlook on life – go for it!

Part of the Summer Palace in Beijing
(Běijīng de Yuánmíngyuán)

Vocabulary items associated with *yīn* and *yáng*:

QUICK VOCAB

阴历 yīnlì *'lunar calendar' (the Chinese New Year or Spring Festival is based on the lunar calendar)*
阳历 yánglì *'solar calendar'*
阴天 yīntiān *'cloudy, overcast'*
太阳 tàiyáng *(excessive **yáng**) 'the sun'*
太阳镜 tàiyángjìng *(excessive **yáng** mirror) 'sunglasses'*
阳电 yángdiàn *'positive electricity' (+)*
阴电 yīndiàn *'negative electricity' (−)*

In traditional Chinese medicine a deficiency of *yáng* (*yáng xū* 阳虚) is associated with a lack of vital energy; a deficiency of *yīn* (*yīn xū* 阴虚) with an insufficiency of body fluid, irritability, thirst and constipation being its symptoms.

These are but a few examples; for a much fuller list consult any medium – sized Chinese–English dictionary.

10 Shòu *and the passive*

As we said in Unit 10, verbs in Chinese are neither active nor passive in themselves – it is the context that makes them one or the other. In Unit 10, we explored the use of *rang*, *jiào* or *bèi* to express the passive. Here we explore the use of *shòu*.

'Receiving' etc.
To express the idea of 'receiving' or 'accepting', 'suffering' or 'being subjected to something' we use *shòu* (受) + verbal noun. For example:

shòu fá 受罚   *'be punished' (suffer punishment)*
shòu hài 受害   *'be injured or killed' (suffer harm)*
shòu huānyíng 受欢迎   *'be welcomed' (receive welcome)*
shòu jiàoyù 受教育   *'be educated' (receive education)*
shòu jīng 受惊   *'be frightened' (suffer fright)*

shòu piàn 受骗	'be fooled or taken in' (suffer cheat)
shòu shāng 受伤	'be wounded' or ' to get hurt' (suffer wound)
shòu tuō 受托	'be commissioned' (accept entrust)
shòu yǐngxiǎng 受影响	'be influenced' (accept influence)

This group should be memorized before use and new ones added to your mental list only when you have read or heard them. Do not make up your own!

Exercise 21.3
Try and write the appropriate Chinese characters to fill the blank spaces in the following sentences. The correct *pinyin* version is given first:

1 *Shòu jiàoyù de rén piānjiàn yīnggāi shǎo yìxiē.* ＿＿ 教育的人偏见 ＿＿ 该少一些。

2 *Kěxī, xiǎoháir dōu hěn róngyì shòu piàn.* 可惜，小 ＿＿ 儿都很 ＿＿ 易受骗。

3 *Wǒ tèbié shòu wǒ māmā de yǐngxiǎng.* 我特 ＿＿ 受我 ＿＿ 妈的影响。

4 *Xīngbākè zài Zhōngguó shòu bu shòu huānyíng?* 星巴克在中 ＿＿ 受不受 ＿＿ 迎?

5 *Yǒu de rén hěn róngyì shòu shāng (to get injured/hurt), -bù zhīdao wèi shénme?* 有的人很容易 ＿＿ 伤，不知 ＿＿ 为什么?

11 *A yě hǎo, B yě hǎo*

This is a useful expression, meaning 'no matter whether A or B, something is still the case':

Xuéxí Hànyǔ yě hǎo, xuéxí Ālābóyǔ (Arabic) **yě hǎo**, tā dōu hěn gǎn xìngqù (*gǎn xìngqù* 'be interested in something'). '*He's very interested in studying both Chinese and Arabic.*'
Zhōngguórén yě hǎo, wàiguórén **yě hǎo**, yìbān lái shuō, dōu bú rènwéi zìjǐ yǒu shénme piānjiàn. '*Generally speaking, neither Chinese nor foreigners think they have any prejudices.*'

12 (Lián) yìdiǎn yě/dōu bù

This construction shares some similarities with 20.4. iii, question words used to indicate inclusiveness or exclusiveness. The pattern here is: (*lián*) *yìdiǎn yě/dōu bù* + adjective/verb (*Lit.* even little bit also not adj/v), (*lián*) *yìdiǎn yě bú cuò* 'absolutely right', *Wǒ* (*lián*) *yìdiǎn yě bù tóngyì* 'I don't agree at all', 'I disagree entirely.'

If the action took place in the past then *méi* is used instead of *bù*: *Zhè běn xiǎoshuō tā* (*lián*) *yìdiǎn yě méi kàn* 'He hasn't read a word of this novel.' The *yìdiǎn* may be replaced by such expressions as *yì fēn zhōng* ('one minute'), *yì fēn qián* ('one cent/penny'), any expression indeed consisting of *yī* ('one') MW noun:

Jiějie yì fēn qián yě méi huā. *My (elder) sister didn't spend any money at all.*
Kāi huì de shíhou, wǒ de tóngshì yí jù huà yě bù shuō. *My colleague never says a word at meetings (kāi huì v-o hold a meeting).*

In such cases the construction can also be used in the affirmative, i.e. without *bù* in which case *lián* is normally retained:

Tā lián xìn dōu kàn le. *'She even read the letter.'*
Wèile dádào (达到 'achieve, reach') **tāmen de mùbiāo** (aim), **lǐngdǎo** (lender[s]) **lián zìjǐ de rénmín dōu huì xīshēng** (sacrifice). *'In order to achieve their objective, leaders will even sacrifice their own people.'*

13 Zánmen *and* wǒmen

Both these personal pronouns mean 'we' but *zánmen* specifically includes both the speaker and the person or persons spoken to, so if you want to make this point use *zánmen*. You will find an example of *zánmen* in the text of this unit and in Unit 22.

14 False friends?

As I have already tried to indicate in 21.7, *tóngqíng* 'to sympathize with' and *tóngyì* 'to agree with' already contain the idea of 'with' in the verb and so there is no need to add anything else. This means that the direct object follows on directly after the verb:

Wǒ tóngyì nǐ de yìjiàn. *'I agree with your opinion.'*
Tóngqíng ta méi yǒu yòng. *'There's no point in sympathizing with him.'*

By the way, 'wear one's hair long' does not use *chuān* or *dài* as the verb but *liú* 留 'let grow'.

Doing your own thing?

In Chinese society, particularly since Liberation, the emphasis has been on the collective, not on the individual, although the advent of the responsibility system *zérènzhì* (責任制) the open-door policy and the economic reforms of the 1980s have led to more people thinking for themselves and making their own decisions about their future. The democratic movement *mínzhǔ yùndòng* (民主运动) of 1989 has also to be seen in this light. Nevertheless, the general trend is still for everyone to know everyone else's business. The ever resourceful Chinese have devised various methods of coping with this social phenomenon, one of which is the use of the term *bàn shì* (办事) 'to go and get something done'. When asked why you are late for work or why you are leaving early or why you happen to be in a particular place, the answers might be, respectively:

Duìbuqǐ, lái wǎn le, wǒ bàn le yìdiǎn shì.
Wǒ yào qù bàn yìdiǎn shì.
Wǒ lái bàn yìdiǎn shì.

Curiously enough, people rarely ask what the *shì* is. I suspect everybody needs to use this let-out clause from time to time and therefore respects other people's right to use it too.

Foreign devils and 'old' foreigners

Non-Chinese used to be classified as 'devils' *guǐ(zi)* 鬼(子),
which is generally regarded as a term of abuse in China, *guǐ*
traditionally being regarded as unhappy spirits who have to
be placated in some way by those still on earth. In Imperial
times westerners were called *yángguǐzi* 'devils from across
the sea' or 'foreign devils', while the Japanese were called
Rìběn guǐ(zi). Mr Qian's eldest son in Lu Xun's famous
novel *The True Story of Ah Q* is called Imitation Foreign
Devil *Jiǎ yángguǐzi* because he came back from Japan with
straight legs, i.e. he walked differently and had had his
pigtail cut off. I have not heard the term *yángguǐzi* for
many years but I can't say the same for the term involving
the Japanese, who have a more recent unhappy history
with China. Another expression still in use to refer to
Caucasian non-Chinese is *dà bízi* 'big noses'. Some
Chinese might cite their noses not being sufficiently 'big',
bízi bú gòu dà as a reason for not being able to enjoy
certain privileges accorded to foreigners – funny, but not
without irony, you might say. We have discussed the use of
lǎo 'old' and *xiǎo* 'young' in 8.7 and it is in this light that
I have never found the term *lǎowài* offensive. Children
and adolescents use it most, but it has always seemed to
me to express active curiosity rather than any animosity.
Wài is, of course, an abbreviation for *wàiguórén*
'foreigner'.

Exercise 21.4

◀) **CD 2, tr 37**

Answer the following questions based on the text: Work in *pinyin*
or characters:

1 *Zài Zhōngguó lǚxíng kěyǐ liǎojiě shénme ne?*
2 *Wáng Yǒngshòu hé Shǐ Àilǐ zài shénme dìfang?*

3 *Tāmen yìbiān chīzhe sānmíngzhì, yìbiān zuò shénme?*

4 *Zhōngguórén xǐhuan bu xǐhuan zhào xiàng? Tāmen yǒu shénme yàng de zhàoxiàngjī?*

5 *Zhíyè zhàoxiàng de duō bu duō?*

6 *Zhōngguórén xǐhuan yí ge rén chū qu wánr ma?*

7 *Zhāng Xīqún shì shénme dìfang rén?*

8 *Shǐ Àilǐ tīng dào yángguǐzi, dà bízi zhè yàng de chēnghū tā xīnlǐ gāoxing bu gāoxing?*

9 *Wǒmen shòuguo jiàoyù de rén yě yǒu zhǒngzú piānjiàn ma?*

10 *Wáng Yǒngshòu tóngyì bu tóngyì Zhāng Xīqún de shuōfǎ* (way of saying things)?

11 *Wǒmen wèi shénme yào chéngrèn cuòwù ne?*

Exercise 21.5

Translate the following passages into colloquial English:

1 *Zài yǒuxiē fāngmiàn Zhōngguórén hé wàiguórén chàbuduō* (to be almost the same), *dōu xǐhuan chū qu wánr, zhǎo rénjiān lèyuán! Shéi bú yuànyì zhù de hǎo, chuān de hǎo, chī de hǎo ne? Zhōngguórén yě bú lìwài* (exception). *Yǐqián zài Zhōngguó lǚyóu de Zhōngguórén hěn shǎo, xiànzài yì nián bǐ yì nián duō le.*

在有些方面中国人和外国人差不多，都喜欢出去玩儿，找人间乐园！谁不愿意住得好，穿得好，吃得好呢？中国人也不例外。以前在中国旅游的中国人很少，现在一年比一年多了。

2 *Liǎojiě lìngwài yí ge mínzú* (nation) *hěn bù róngyì, lián liǎojiě zìjǐ de mínzú yě bù róngyì. Zhōnghuá mínzú shì ge gǔlǎo* (ancient) *de mínzú. Tā de lìshǐ、wénhuà* (culture) *gēn wǒmen de hěn bù yíyàng, gèng bú bì shuō tā de wénzì* (script) *ne! Xué qǐ Zhōngwén lai búdàn* (not only) *hěn yǒu yìsi érqiě* (but also) *duì wǒmen gèrén* (individual) *hěn yǒu yòng.*

了解另外一个民族很不容易，连了解自己的民族也不容易。中华民族是个古老的民族。它的历史、文化跟我们的很不一样，更不必说它的文字呢！学起中文来不但很有意思而且对我们个人很有用。

TESTING YOURSELF

Translate the following sentences into *pinyin* and then into Chinese characters:

1 *Let's (use zánmen) talk about education while watching the sunset.*

2 *'Deceiving oneself as well as others' is a proverb well worth paying attention to.*

3 *Because of the Taiwan (台湾 Táiwān) question, relations between China and the USA have become very complex (复杂 fùzá).*

4 *He is my colleague so, of course, that influences my opinion (意见 yìjiàn). (use the passive)*

5 *You haven't had a single day's holiday this year, so no wonder you're so tired.*

6 *She hasn't even eaten a sandwich today, so how come she's not starving?*

22

Farewell to all that!

In this unit you will learn
- *how to make a toast*
- *how to give a present and make an appropriate remark on receiving one*
- *about exclamations*
- *about the Chinese zodiac*
- *more about Chinese proverbs*
- *about classical Chinese poetry*

◆》 **CD 2, tr 38–41**

Ms Shaw is preparing to return to the UK, after completing her compulsory year of study abroad. The Lis have invited her and her boyfriend for a farewell dinner.

史爱理打算回英国了，她在中国学了一年必修课程。李先生和夫人为她和她男朋友饯行。

李	欢迎，欢迎。请进。
李太太	外面冷吗？
史	有一点。风很大，我们是顶着风骑车来的，真费劲儿。
李太太	别老站在外面厅里，请屋里坐，暖和暖和。
李	喝茶还是喝咖啡？

王	还是喝茶吧。
李太太	唉，爱理，你要回国了，今天可算是‘最后的晚餐’了，多遗憾哪！
史	啊 — 一年过得真快，‘光阴似箭，日月如梭’！
李	爱理，你舍不得走，是不是？
史	是的。今年收获很大，可惜不能多留。
李	你可算是‘满载而归’了！
史	也可以这么说。
李太太	来吃饭吧。饺子包好了，正在煮。先喝酒吧，这儿有冷盘。文华，把酒打开吧。
李	这瓶酒不错，是白葡萄酒，合资企业的产品。中国酒一般是甜的，但是我们知道你们不太喜欢喝甜的。好，干杯！祝爱理一路平安，早日回来！
史	祝你们身体健康，万事如意！
李	咱们来照几张相吧。不过，等饺子来了再照，更有中国味道。啊，饺子来了！
王	你有闪光灯吗？
李	有。准备好了吗？笑一笑！
王	我也来照几张，回去后给你们发过来。
史	李太太，你的饺子真好吃，下一次一定要教我怎么包。
李太太	好吧，欢迎你尽早回来…酱油和醋都在这儿。
史	谢谢你。我放一点酱油。我这个人是绝对不会吃醋的，哈哈！
李	来，再喝一杯。祝咱们之间的友谊万古长存！干杯！
王	李老师，下个星期五是你的生日，可惜那个时候爱理已经离开中国了，所以我们现在要再敬你一杯，提前祝你‘寿比南山，福如东海’！我们还给你准备了一点小礼物。
李	你们实在太客气了。
李太太	爱理，别难过，‘后会有期’，毕业以后再来吧。
史	跟朋友告别的时候，我总会想起‘相见时难别亦难’这句话来。
李太太	你们‘不远万里而来’，确实不容易。但是你来中国的机会还是会很多的。

李	等爱理再来，我们开一个联欢会，怎么样？为了明、后年我们再相会，来，再干一杯！
李太太	这次不能不回去，爱理，你还要读一年书。但是以后机会多得很。
李	飞机几点钟起飞？
王	下午四点四十。应该三点钟到。
李	我们去送送你吧。
史	不用了，机场太远了，太不方便了。今天晚上就算告别了吧。要不，我受不了，还要告一次别！
李	看情况吧。如果能早一点下课，我们一定去。好，不谈这个了。再干最后一杯吧。
李太太	我不行了，再喝，我就要醉了！你们看，脸都红了！
李	没关系，你不是开车来的！来，为了大家幸福、快乐，干杯！
李太太史、王	干杯！

Shǐ Àilǐ dǎsuàn huí Yīngguó le, tā zài Zhōngguó xué le yì nián bìxiūkèchéng. Lǐ xiānsheng hé fūrén wèi tā hé tā nán péngyou jiànxíng.

Lǐ	Huānyíng, huānyíng. Qǐng jìn.
Lǐ (t)	Wàimiàn lěng ma?
Shǐ	Yǒu yìdiǎn. Fēng hěn dà, wǒmen shì dǐngzhe fēng qí chē lái de, zhēn fèijìnr.
Lǐ (t)	Bié lǎo zhàn zài wàimian tīng lǐ, qǐng wūlǐ zuò, nuǎnhuo nuǎnhuo.
Lǐ	Hē chá háishi hē kāfēi?
Wáng	Háishi hē chá ba.
Lǐ (t)	Ài, Àilǐ, nǐ yào huí guó le, jīntiān kě suàn shì 'zuìhòu de wǎncān' le, duō yíhàn na!
Shǐ	Ā—yì nián guò de zhēn kuài, 'guāngyīn sì jiàn, rìyuè rú suō'.
Lǐ	Àilǐ, nǐ shèbude zǒu, shì bu shì?

Shǐ	Shì de. Jīnnián shōuhuò hěn dà, kěxī bù néng duō liú.
Lǐ	Nǐ kě suàn shì 'mǎn zài ér guī' le!
Shǐ	Yě kěyǐ zhème shuō.
Lǐ (t)	Lái chī fàn ba. Jiǎozi bāo hǎo le, zhèngzài zhǔ. Xiān hē jiǔ ba. Zhèr yǒu lěngpán. Wénhuá, bǎ jiǔ dǎkāi ba.
Lǐ	Zhè píng jiǔ búcuò, shì bái pútáojiǔ, hézǐ qǐyè de chǎnpǐn. Zhōngguó jiǔ yìbān shì tián de, dànshi wǒmen zhīdao nǐmen bú tài xǐhuan hē tián de. Hǎo, gān bēi! Zhù Àilǐ yílù píng'ān, zǎorì huí lai!
Shǐ	Zhù nǐmen shēntǐ jiànkāng, wànshì rú yì!
Lǐ	Zánmen lái zhào jǐ zhāng xiàng ba. Búguò děng jiǎozi lái le zài zhào, gèng yǒu Zhōngguó wèidao. Ā, jiǎozi lái le!
Wáng	Nǐ yǒu shǎnguāngdēng ma?
Lǐ	Yǒu. Zhǔnbèi hǎo le ma? Xiàoyixiào!
Wáng	Wǒ yě lái zhào jǐ zhāng. Huí qù hòu gěi nǐmen fā guò lai.
Shǐ	Lǐ tàitai, nǐ de jiǎozi zhēn hǎo chī, xià yí cì yídìng yào jiāo wǒ zěnme bāo.
Lǐ (t)	Hǎo ba, huānyíng nǐ jīnzǎo huí lai . . . jiàngyóu hé cù dōu zài zhèr.
Shǐ	Xièxie nǐ. Wǒ fàng yìdiǎn jiàngyóu. Wǒ zhè ge rén shì juéduì bú huì chī cù de, hāhā!
Lǐ	Lái, zài hē yì bēi. Zhù zánmen zhī jiān de yǒuyì wàngǔ chángcún! Gān bēi!
Wáng	Lǐ lǎoshī, xià ge xīngqīwǔ shì nǐ de shēngrì, kěxī nà ge shíhou Àilǐ yǐjīng líkāi Zhōngguó le, suǒyǐ wǒmen xiànzài yào zài jìng nǐ yì bēi, tíqián zhù nǐ 'Shòu bǐ Nánshān, fú rú Dōnghǎi'! Wǒmen hái gěi nǐ zhǔnbèi le yìdiǎn xiǎo lǐwù.
Lǐ	Nǐmen shízài tài kèqi le.
Lǐ (t)	Àilǐ, bié nánguò, 'hòu huì yǒu qī', bìyè yǐhòu zài lái ba.
Shǐ	Gēn péngyou gàobié de shíhou, wǒ zǒng huì xiǎng qǐ 'Xiāng jiàn shí nán, bié yì nán' zhè jù huà lai.

Lǐ (t)	Nǐmen 'bù yuǎn wàn lǐ ér lái', quèshí bù róngyì. Dànshi nǐ lái Zhōngguó de jīhuì háishi huì hěn duō de.
Lǐ	Děng Àilǐ zài lái, wǒmen kāi yí ge liánhuānhuì, zěnmeyàng? Wèile míng、hòunián wǒmen zài xiānghuì, lái, zài gān yì bēi!
Lǐ (t)	Zhè cì bù néng bù huí qu, Àilǐ, nǐ hái yào dú yì nián shū. Dànshi yǐhòu jīhuì duō dehěn.
Lǐ	Fēijī jǐ diǎn zhōng qǐfēi?
Shǐ	Xiàwǔ sì diǎn sìshí . . . Yīnggāi sān diǎn zhōng dào.
Lǐ	Wǒmen qù sòngsong nǐ ba.
Shǐ	Bú yòng le, jīchǎng tài yuǎn le, tài bù fāngbiàn le. Jīntiān wǎnshang jiù suàn gàobié le ba. Yàobù wǒ shòu bù liǎo, hái yào gào yí cì bié!
Lǐ	Kàn qíngkuàng ba. Rúguǒ néng zǎo yìdiǎnr xià kè, wǒmen yídìng qù. Hǎo, bù tán zhè ge le. Zài gān zuìhòu yì bēi ba.
Lǐ (t)	Wǒ bù xíng le, zài hē, wǒ jiù yào zuì le! Nǐmen kàn, liǎn dōu hóng le!
Lǐ	Méi guānxi, nǐ bú shi kāi chē de! Lái, wèile dàjiā xìngfú, kuàilè, gān bēi!
Lǐ (t) Shǐ, Wáng	Gān bēi!

打算 dǎsuàn (v) to intend, plan
必修课(程) bìxiūkè(chéng) (n) obligatory or required course
夫人 fūrén (n) Mrs; Madame (formal)
为 wèi (prep) for, for the sake of (formal)
饯行 jiànxíng (n) give a farewell dinner
风 fēng (n) wind
顶 dǐng (v) to go against
骑 qí
费劲(儿) fèijìn(r) (adj) strenuous, energy consuming
老 lǎo

站 zhàn *(v; n) to stand; station, stop (bus etc.)*
外面 wàimian *(PW) outside*
厅 tīng *(n) hall*
屋里 wūlǐ *(PW) in the room*
暖和 nuǎnhuo *(adj) warm*
算 suàn *(v) to regard as, count as*
最后 zuìhòu *(adj, adv) the last, finally*
晚餐 wǎncān *(n) supper, dinner*
多 duō *how*
遗憾 yíhàn *(v; n) to regret, be a pity; regret*
哪 na *particle showing mood*
光阴似箭，日月如梭 guāngyīn sì jiàn, rìyuè rú suō *time flies (see 22.4)*
舍不得 shěbude *(v) be unwilling to part with, grudge*
收获 shōuhuò *(n) gains, results, harvest*
满载而归 mǎn zài ér guī *return with fruitful results*
包 bāo *(v) to make (jiǎozi); to wrap; to include*
煮 zhǔ *(v) to boil, cook*
冷盘 lěngpán *(n) cold dish; hors d'oeuvre*
打开 dǎkāi *(v) to open (up); switch on*
瓶 píng *(MW) for bottles*
白 bái *(adj) white; blank*
葡萄酒 pútáojiǔ *(n) wine*
产品 chǎnpǐn *(n) product*
甜 tián *(adj) sweet*
干杯 gān bēi *(v-o) drink a toast*
一路平安 yílù píng'ān *bon voyage, have a pleasant journey*
早日 zǎorì *(TW) at an early date; soon*
健康 jiànkāng *(adj) healthy, sound*
万事如意 wànshì rúyì *your heart's desire*
味道 wèidao *(n) flavour, taste*
闪光灯 shǎnguāngdēng *(n) flash (light)*
发 fā *(v) to send (email, fax etc.)*
尽早 jǐnzǎo *(adv) as soon as possible, at the earliest possible date*
醋 cù *(n) vinegar; jealousy (as in love affairs)*
绝对 juéduì *(adj; adv) absolute(ly)*
吃醋 chī cù *(v-o) to feel jealous*

哈哈 **hāhā** *(onom) ha ha*

之间 **zhī jiān** *between, among*

友谊 **yǒuyì** *(n) friendship*

万古长存 **wàngǔ chángcún** *last forever, be everlasting*

生日 **shēngrì** *(n) birthday*

离开 **líkāi** *(v) to leave*

敬 **jìng** *(v) to propose (a toast), toast*

提前 **tíqián** *(v) bring forward a date*

寿比南山，福如东海 **shòu bǐ Nánshān, fú rú Dōnghǎi** *May you live as long as the Southern Mountain and be as blessed as the Eastern Sea*

礼物[件] **lǐwù** *(n)* [**jiàn**] *present, gift*

难过 **nánguò** *(v) to be upset, to be sad*

后会有期 **hòu huì yǒu qī** *we'll meet again some day*

毕业 **bìyè** *(v) to graduate*

告别 **gàobié** *(v-o) to take leave of*

想起来 **xiǎng qǐlai** *(v) to remember, call to mind*

相见时难，别亦难 **xiāng jiàn shí nán, bié yì nán** *meeting and parting are both difficult (see this unit 'On Chinese poetry')*

不远万里而来 **bù yuǎn wàn lǐ ér lái** *not considering 10 000 li too far to come*

确实 **quèshí** *(adv; adj) really, indeed; true, certain*

机会 **jīhuì** *(n) opportunity, chance*

联欢会 **liánhuānhuì** *(n) get-together, party*

明年 **míngnián** *(TW) next year*

后年 **hòunián** *(TW) the year after next*

相会 **xiānghuì** *(v) meet one another*

多得很 **duō dehěn** *(adj) very many*

起飞 **qǐfēi** *(v) to take off (of aircraft)*

飞机场 **fēijīchǎng** *(n) airport*

受不了 **shòu bù liǎo** *(v) be unable to bear or endure*

醉 **zuì** *(adj) drunk*

脸 **liǎn** *(n) face*

红 **hóng** *(adj) red*

开车的 **kāi chē de** *(n) a person who drives, driver*

为了 **wèile** *(prep) for the sake of, in order to*

幸福 **xìngfú** *(adj; n) enjoy good fortune, happy; well-being*

Grammar

1 Exclamations

The Chinese language has an infinite variety of its own particular version of ahs, oohs and ohs, but it is perhaps the modal particles which occur at the end of the sentence which are of particular interest. Some of these have been scattered throughout the various texts in this book. In this Unit, we have 哪 *na*, 呢 *ne* and the all-time favourite 吧 *ba*. Apart from the few guidelines you have been given, for instance that 呢 *ne* tends to appear with the question words *shénme*, *zěnme*, *wèi shénme*, etc. and set phrases such as *Nǐ zěnme le?* you should rely on your 'feel' of the language as to whether a *ya*, a *na*, or a *ne*, etc. is needed. Chinese has a lot to do with feeling rather than specific rules so start with your exclamations and expressions of surprise. If you have the opportunity, listen to Chinese speakers and imitate them as far as possible. Failing that, just remember that such things are the icing on the cake rather than the cake itself.

2 Eating bitterness?

I have always teased Chinese friends about the emphasis that Chinese culture puts on food. Chinese people can talk for hours (and I *mean* hours) about the merits of various dishes, how to make them and how difficult (or expensive) it is to find such and such an ingredient. We can speculate endlessly on the reasons for this, which could vary from peasant poverty to magnificent Imperial banquets. Whatever the reason, it has left the Chinese language with a rich heritage based on eating. Note the following phrases which are just some of the ones in common usage:

吃醋	**chī cù** *'be jealous'* (*Lit.* eat vinegar)
吃惊	**chī jīng** *'be shocked, amazed'* (*Lit.* eat alarm)
吃苦	**chī kǔ** *'bear hardship'* (*Lit.* eat bitterness)
吃亏	**chī kuī** *'stand to lose'*, *'come to grief'*, *'get the worst of it'* (*Lit.* eat loss)
吃力	**chī lì** *'strenuous, difficult'* (*Lit.* eat strength)

吃软不吃硬	**chī ruǎn bù chī yìng** 'be open to persuasion but not to coercion' (*Lit.* eat soft not eat hard)
吃闲饭	**chī xiánfàn** 'lead an idle life, be a sponger' (*Lit.* eat idle rice)
吃香	**chī xiāng** 'be popular' (coll) (*Lit.* eat spice)
吃药	**chī yào** 'take medicine' (*Lit.* eat medicine).

The Chinese zodiac

The existence of the **Ten Heavenly Stems** was mentioned in the vocabulary of Unit 17, but not elaborated upon further. They are 甲 *jiǎ*, 乙 *yǐ*, 丙 *bǐng*, 丁 *dīng*, 戊 *wù*, 己 *jǐ*, 庚 *gēng*, 辛 *xīn*, 壬 *rén* and 癸 *guǐ* in that order, 甲 *jiǎ* being the first. The Ten Heavenly Stems also combine in pairs, each pair corresponding to each of the five elements used in traditional Chinese medicine, viz. wood, fire, earth, metal and water. Thus *jiǎ* and *yǐ* are associated with 木 *mù* 'wood', *bǐng* and *dīng* with 火 *huǒ* 'fire' and so on.

In addition to the Ten Heavenly Stems, there are also the **Twelve Earthly Branches**, each of which is associated with a different animal which occurs in 12 year cycles. Each of us is born in the lunar year of a particular animal. 1950 was the Year of the Tiger, therefore everyone born in 1962, 1974, 1986 and 1998 is a tiger. 1951 was the Year of the Rabbit so all those born in 1963, 1975, 1987 and 1999 are rabbits. Of course each Animal Year is said to possess certain characteristics and in the old days this played a role in deciding whether or not you were a suitable bride or bridegroom for somebody. Tiger women were thought of as being particularly difficult to handle! The order is as follows:

Earthly branches   **Symbolical animals**

1	子	*zǐ*	鼠	*shǔ*	rat
2	丑	*chǒu*	牛	*niú*	ox
3	寅	*yín*	虎	*hǔ*	tiger
4	卯	*mǎo*	兔	*tù*	rabbit/hare
5	辰	*chén*	龙	*lóng*	dragon
6	巳	*sì*	蛇	*shé*	snake

7	午	*wǔ*	马	*mǎ*	horse
8	未	*wèi*	羊	*yáng*	ram
9	申	*shēn*	猴	*hóu*	monkey
10	酉	*yǒu*	鸡	*jī*	cockerel
11	戌	*xū*	犬	*quǎn*	dog
12	亥	*hài*	猪	*zhū*	pig

Astrology books are now being produced combining the Chinese zodiac with our own western one. A Tiger who is also a Scorpio probably presents quite a challenge, wouldn't you say? What are you? (NB The Chinese have traditionally used the Ten Heavenly Stems and the Twelve Earthly Branches in a sequential order of two-character combinations to denote different years, months and days.)

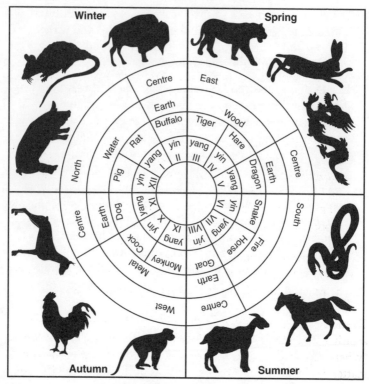

Chinese zodiac

3 Adjective + dehěn

This is a simple construction meaning 'very much' of the adjective:

duō dehěn *'very many'*
hǎo dehěn *'very good'*
yǒu yìsi dehěn *'very interesting'.*

It is different from *hěn duō* and *hěn hǎo* insofar as the *hěn* in the latter phrases does not really carry the force of 'very' (see 6.2.4) or is put there merely for balance.

4 More on proverbs

To put proverbs in their historical context we are going to trace the origins of two of the proverbs that occur in this text.

i *Guāngyīn sì jiàn, rìyuè rú suō*. A similar phrase *guāng liú sì jiàn* (time flows like (an) arrow) first appeared in a Tang poem by Wei Zhuang but it was the famous Song dynasty (960–1279) poet Su Shi (also known as Su Dongpo) who used *guāngyīn sì jiàn* in one of his poems. The complete proverb *guāngyīn sì jiàn, rìyuè rú suō* occurred in Chapter 9 of the Ming dynasty novel *Xīyóujì* 西游记 translated variously as *Journey to the West* or *Monkey*, written by one Wu Cheng'en.

ii *Bù yuǎn wàn lǐ ér lái*. An alternative version *bù yuǎn qiān lǐ ér lái* may sometimes be found but *wàn* (10 000) makes it sound more of a big thing than *qiān* (1000) so I have used the former rather than the latter. (NB *lǐ* 'half a kilometre'.) This phrase first appeared in one of the books of Mencius, the famous Chinese Confucian philosopher of the fourth century BC who believed in the intrinsic goodness of human nature.

To end on a really positive note, particularly appropriate for aspiring students of Chinese, there is *Yǒu zhìzhě shì jìng chéng* 'Where there's a will there's a way' (*Lit*. have aspiration person, matter finally achieve). This occurred in a chapter of the *Hànshū* 'A History of the Han dynasty' (in 120 volumes) written by

班固 Ban Gu who died in AD 92. As you can see, Chinese history is still alive and well today if we know where to go and look for it.

Exercise 22.1
Answer the following questions based on the text.

1 *Wáng xiānsheng hé Shǐ xiǎojie lái de shíhou guā bu guā fēng?*
2 *Shǐ Àilǐ zài Zhōngguó xué de zěnmeyàng? Nǐ zěnme zhīdao ne?*
3 *Tāmen hē de jiǔ shì guóchǎn de ma?*
4 *Chī jiǎozi de shíhou kěyǐ fàng shénme?*
5 *Shǐ xiǎojie huì bu huì chī cù ne?*
6 *Lǐ xiānsheng shénme shíhou guò shēngrì? Nà ge shíhou Shǐ Àilǐ dàgài ('probably') zài nǎr?*
7 *Shǐ Àilǐ wèi shénme hěn nánguò ne?*
8 *Lǐ xiānsheng dǎsuàn shénme shíhou kāi yí ge liánhuānhuì?*
9 *Shǐ Àilǐ de fēijī shénme shíhou qǐfēi? Tā yīnggāi jǐ diǎn zhōng dào jīchǎng?*
10 *Shǐ Àilǐ wèi shénme bú ràng Lǐ xiānsheng hé Lǐ tàitai qù sòng tā ne?*
11 *Lǐ tàitai zěnme zhèngmíng (证明 'prove') tā kuài yào zuì le?*
12 *Lǐ xiānsheng wèi shénme shuō Lǐ tàitai duō hē yìdiǎn jiǔ méi yǒu guānxi?*

1 王先生和史小姐来的时候刮不刮风？
2 史爱理在中国学得怎么样？你怎么知道呢？
3 他们喝的酒是国产的吗？
4 吃饺子的时候可以放什么？
5 史小姐会不会吃醋呢？
6 李先生什么时候过生日？那个时候史爱理大概在哪儿？
7 史爱理为什么很难过呢？
8 李先生打算什么时候开一个联欢会？
9 史爱理的飞机什么时候起飞？她应该几点钟到机场？
10 史爱理为什么不让李先生和李太太去送她呢？
11 李太太怎么证明她快要醉了？
12 李先生为什么说李太太多喝一点酒没有关系？

Exercise 22.2
Translate the dialogue at the beginning of this unit into colloquial English.

Let's finish with this beautiful poem by Li Yu (937–978 AD), the last emperor of the Southern Tang.

◀) CD 2, tr 42

....

On Chinese poetry

To understand the Chinese, you also have to understand their poetry. People who regularly use poetry in their language also have poetry in their hearts.

Xiāng jiàn shí nán, bié yì nán quoted in the text comes from an untitled poem by Li Shangyin (812?–868). This line has come to symbolize, in seven brief characters, the difficulties often involved in meeting someone and the pain involved in parting. (*Nán* means *kùnnan* 'difficult' in the first case, *nánkān* 'unbearable' in the second.)

Perhaps if I quote a poem written by Li Yu (937–978), the last emperor of the Southern Tang, you will get a taste of the beauty I am referring to. Li Yu was captured by the Song army and taken north to Kaifeng. This poem was written during his captivity, shortly before his death and laments his grievous loss and heavy heart.

> 无言独上西楼，
> 月如钩。
> 寂寞梧桐深院锁清秋。
> 剪不断，
> 理还乱，
> 是离愁，
> 别是一般滋味在心头。

> *Wú yán dú shàng Xīlóu*
> No word(s) alone climb West Tower
> *Yuè rú gōu.*
> moon like sickle
> *Jìmò wútóng shēn yuàn suǒ qīng qiū.*
> Lonely wútóng dark (deep?) courtyard lock clear autumn
> *Jiǎn bú duàn,*
> cut not sever

> *Lǐ hái luàn,*
> reason still disorderly
> *Shì lí chóu*
> Is separation melancholy
> *Bié shì yìbān zīwèi zài xīntóu.*
> Parting is just like (bitter) taste in heart.

Even after more than 1000 years, the lines still rhyme, an incredible comment on the nature of the Chinese language. The visual impact of the characters is very important in poetry. *Chóu*, the character for 'sorrow' or 'melancholy' is made up of an autumn over a heart (愁), with all the symbolism which that conjures up.

The fact that classical Chinese poetry does not have a grammatical subject makes it seem so much more universal and heightens its effect. Let us look at the content of the poem more closely. Whoever it is, climbs the Western Tower, (the west – the setting sun, the end of one's life?) alone and in silence, the moon like a sickle overhead. (A new moon to heighten his grief, or the last sliver of a waning one?) The *wútóng* (it has a straight trunk of a beautiful shade of green and is said to be the only tree on which the phoenix will rest) is 'lonely' and the clear autumn is as though locked into the dark, deep courtyard. There is a great deal to be got from this line if you only think about it carefully.

The next four lines are truly famous and speak of the pain of parting and separation. Had you ever thought of this pain as being like a skein of wool which refuses to be disentangled and cannot be cut off cleanly? Or of the word 'parting' as leaving 'a taste in the heart'? These four lines are known to millions of Chinese and written as they were, by an emperor, prisoner in a foreign land, who had lost everything and was soon to die (forced to take poison by his captors), they take on a particular poignancy. May they say something to you as they have done to me over a period of many years.

TESTING YOURSELF

Correct the following *bìngjù* ('sick sentences'). Give the correct version (This exercise is based on the grammar of Units 17–22.)

Běijīng cóng Tiānjīn hěn jìn → Běijīng lí Tiānjīn hěn jìn.

1 *Zhǔnbèi hǎo le ma? Wǒ liǎng diǎn zhōng kuài yào zǒu le.*

....

2 *Yúnnán zài Zhōngguó de nánxī bù.*

....

3 *Bǎ zhàoxiàngjī bù kěyǐ jiè* ('lend; borrow') *gěi tā.*

....

4 *Wǒ yǒu sìshí zhī bǎi fēn de bǎwò* (把握 'certainty').

....

5 *Yīngguó de shēnghuófèi* (cost of living) *bǐ Zhōngguó hěn guì.*

....

6 *Gǔdiǎn yīnyuè gēn xiàndài* (现代 'modern') *yīnyuè hǎo tīng yíyàng.*

....

7 *Fánshì lǎoshī cái xǐhuan jiāo shū.*

....

8 *Shàngjí* (上级 'superiors') *xiàng bù xǐhuan tā, bù zhīdao shénme yuányīn* (原因 'reason, cause').

---

9 *Nǐ chuān shang tàiyángjìng qù cānjiā* (参加 'take part in') *liánhuānhuì tài bù héshì* (合适 'suitable') *le.*

---

10 *Tā jiào dǎ le yídùn.*

---

11 *Wǒmen yīnggāi dōu tóngqíng gēn qióng rén* (穷人 'poor person').

---

12 *Wǒ gēn nǐ de kànfǎ bú tóngyì – tā bìng bú shi ge huài rén.*

---

13 *Qǐng nǐ èrshí'èr kè de kèwén zài kàn yícì.*

Congratulations

You have now finished *Complete Mandarin Chinese*! If you have stuck at it right to the end that is quite some achievement. You may now like to think how you are going to take your Chinese further.

For those of you who have battled with Chinese characters in this book, my hearty congratulations. They are fiendishly difficult in one sense but so much fun in another. All the character texts for Units 1–12 are to be found in the back of the book. Why not read through each dialogue in *pinyin* first and then turn to the corresponding character text and try recognizing as many characters as you can? Do this as many times as it takes for you to become familiar with all of them. (This should work for Units 1–8, but you probably need to be content with recognizing most but not all of the characters in Units 9–12.) Then try reading out the character text aloud and see how you get on.

Another tip is to follow the character text as you are listening to the recording of each Unit – that way you are associating sounds with characters and imprinting them in your brain – believe me, it does work! Do this a few times for each Unit and you will find that your recognition of characters will have greatly improved.

Chinese language and culture are rich treasure-troves for us to explore. My hope is that, through this book, as well as learning some useful Chinese, you have been able to catch glimpses of them and are eager for more.

I hope that you have enjoyed *Complete Mandarin Chinese*!

Key to the exercises

Exercise 1.1
1 *Wǒ bú zuò.*
2 *Nǐ bù hǎo.*
3 *Wǒ bù hē chá.*
4 *Nǐ bù xǐhuan Zhōngguó.*
5 *Lǐ xiānsheng bú xièxie wǒ.*
6 *Wáng xiānsheng bù qǐng nǐ hē Zhōngguó chá.*

Exercise 1.2
1 *Wǒ xǐhuan bu xǐhuan hē kāfēi? Wǒ xǐhuan hē kāfēi. Wǒ bù xǐhuan hē kāfēi.*
2 *Nǐ xièxie bu xièxie wǒ? Nǐ xièxie wǒ. Nǐ bú xièxie wǒ.*
3 *Wáng xiānsheng qǐng bu qǐng wǒ zuò? Wáng xiānsheng qǐng wǒ zuò. Wáng xiānsheng bù qǐng wǒ zuò.*
4 *Lǐ xiānsheng xǐhuan bu xǐhuan hē shuǐ? Lǐ xiānsheng xǐhuan hē shuǐ. Lǐ xiānsheng bù xǐhuan hē shuǐ.*
5 *Tā xǐhuan bu xǐhuan hē Zhōngguó chá? Tā xǐhuan hē Zhōngguó chá. Tā bù xǐhuan hē Zhōngguó chá.*

Exercise 1.3
1 Mr King invites me to drink Chinese tea.
2 Mr Li greatly dislikes Mr King. (Mr Li can't stand Mr King.)
3 Mr King doesn't like Mr Li much either.
4 You don't thank me so I don't thank you either.
5 He asked me to sit down. He also offered me coffee.

Testing yourself
1 *Lǐ xiānsheng, nǐ hǎo.*
2 *Qǐng zuò.*
3 *Nǐ hē kāfēi ma?*
4 *Wǒ bù hē kāfēi.*
5 *Nàme, (hē) chá xíng ma? (Nàme, (hē) chá xíng bu xíng?)*

6 *Wǒ bù hē chá.*
7 *Wǒ xǐhuan hē Zhōngguó chá.*
8 *Xièxie nǐ.*
9 *Wǒ xǐhuan nǐ.*
10 *Wǒ hěn xǐhuan nǐ.*

Exercise 2.1
Mr King invites Mr Li for a drink. Mr Li is very pleased. He's a great drinker. What about his wife, Zhou Dejin? His wife doesn't drink. She drinks orange juice. She is also very much against Mr Li drinking.

Exercise 2.2
1 *Lǐ tàitai, rènshi nín wǒ zhēn gāoxìng.*
2 *Nàme, júzizhī hǎo ba?*
3 *Wǒ hěn xǐhuan hē jiǔ.*
4 *Nín bú huì hē sì bēi pútáojiǔ.*
5 *Wáng xiānsheng, zhè shì wǒ tàitai.*

Testing yourself
1 *Nǐ hē jiǔ ma?*
2 *Wǒ bú huì hē jiǔ. Nín ne?*
3 *Zhōu xiānsheng, zhè shì wǒ tàitai/àiren.*
4 *Tā rènshi tā ma? (Tā rènshi bu rènshi tā?)*
5 *Wǒ àiren xī yān, wǒ hěn bù gāoxìng.*
6 *Kāfēi hǎo ba?*
7 *Zhāng xiānsheng bú huì Yīngyǔ.*
8 *Nǐ bú huì hē qī bēi jiǔ.*

Exercise 3.1
1 *Wǒmen hē shénme?*
2 *Lǐ xiānsheng hé Lǐ tàitai yǒu jǐ ge xiǎoháir?*
3 *Pútáojiǔ zěnmeyàng?*
4 *Wáng xiānsheng zài nǎr?*
5 *Tā nǚ péngyou míngtiān xiàwǔ jǐ diǎn (zhōng) lái Zhōngguó?*
6 *Nǚháir jǐ suì?*

Exercise 3.2

1 *Wǒ yǒu liǎng ge xiǎoháir.*
2 *Tā méi yǒu nǚháir.*
3 *Nǐmen yǒu liù ge péngyou.*
4 *Zhōngguó zài nǎr?*
5 *Tāmen jǐ suì?*
6 *Wǒ hěn xǐhuan hē Zhōngguó chá.*
7 *Lǐ tàitai rènshi nín zhēn gāoxìng.*
8 *Tā yě zài Zhōngguó ma?*
9 *Wǒ méi yǒu nǚ péngyou.*
10 *Wáng xiānsheng míngtiān lái Zhōngguó.*

Testing yourself

1 *Nǐ yǒu háizi ma?* or *Nǐ yǒu mei yǒu háizi?*
2 *Nǐ yǒu nǚ'er ma?* or *Nǐ yǒu mei yǒu nǚ'er?*
3 *Nǐ yǒu érzi ma?* or *Nǐ yǒu mei yǒu érzi?*
4 *Nǐde háizi jǐ suì le?* or *Nǐde háizi duō dà le?*
5 *Nǐ jié hūn le ma?*
6 *Nǐ yǒu nǚ péngyou ma?* or *Nǐ yǒu mei yǒu nǚ péngyou?*
7 *Nǐ yǒu nán pengyou ma?* or *Nǐ yǒu mei yǒu nán péngyou?*
8 *Nǐde nán péngyou zài nǎr?*
9 *Nǐde nǚ péngyou zài nǎr?*
10 *Nǐ míngtiān lái ma?* or *Nǐ míngtiān lái bu lái?*
11 *Nǐ zài Zhōngguó xuéxí ma?* or *Nǐ zài bu zài Zhōngguó xuéxí?*
12 *Wǒ (hái) méi jié hūn.*

Exercise 4.1

1 *Jiǔ diǎn (zhōng)*
2 *Shíyī diǎn bàn*
3 *Liǎng diǎn èrshíwǔ (fēn)*
4 *Sān diǎn wǔshí (fēn); chà shí fēn sì diǎn; sì diǎn chà shí fēn*
5 *Yī diǎn yí kè, yī diǎn shíwǔ fēn*
6 *Bā diǎn líng wǔ fēn*
7 *Wǔ diǎn sìshíwǔ (fēn); chà yí kè liù diǎn; liù diǎn chà yí kè*
8 *Shí'èr diǎn shí fēn*

Exercise 4.2

1 *Wǒmen shí diǎn zhōng qù.*
2 *Hē lǜchá zěnmeyàng?*

3 *Zhōu Déjīn méi yǒu jié hūn.*
4 *Wáng tàitai wǎnshang bù chī fàn.*
5 *Zhāng xiānsheng xiǎng qǐng wǒmen, wǒmen jiù bù qǐng tā.*

Exercise 4.3
We have four children, three girls and a boy. I have many friends. I have invited two friends to come to our house tomorrow evening for a meal. My wife is very put out because she doesn't know them.

Testing yourself
1 *Nǚháir sān suì, nánháir liǎng suì.*
2 *Tā jié hūn le ma?/Tā jié hūn le méi you?/Tā jié hūn méi jié hūn./ Méi yǒu.*
3 *Nǐmen míngtiān wǎnshang qù tā jiā chī fàn ma?*
4 *Tā xiànzài zài nǎr? Tā zài Lúndūn.*
5 *Nǐ yǒu nán péngyou ma?/Nǐ yǒu mei yǒu nán péngyou? Méi yǒu, wǒ cái shíwǔ suì.*
6 *Wǒmen liǎ hěn xǐhuan hē kāfēi.*
7 *Nǐ jǐ diǎn zhōng zài jiā?/Qī diǎn zěnmeyàng?/Hǎo, jiù qī diǎn ba.*
8 *Wǒ tàitai/àiren hěn hǎo dànshi tā bú tài xǐhuan shuō huà.*
9 *Nǐ de péngyou zài nǎr? Wǒ xiǎng qǐng tā chī fàn.*

Mini revision

I
a) *Wáng tàitai rènshi bu rènshi Lǐ xiānsheng?*
b) *Tā míngtiān wǎnshang lái chī fàn.*
c) *Wǒ yǒu liǎng ge xiǎoháir.*
d) *Nǐmen méi yǒu jié hūn.*
e) *Lǐ xiānsheng hé (and) Lǐ tàitai shíyī diǎn zhōng qù hē kāfēi.*

II
Zhāng xiānsheng hái (still) méi yǒu jié hūn. Tā yǒu hěn duō péngyou dànshi (but) tā méi yǒu nǚ péngyou. Tā hěn xǐhuan chī fàn、 hē jiǔ bù chángcháng (often) zài jiā. Yǒu yī tiān (day) tā qù hē kāfēi rènshi yí ge Liú xiǎojie (Miss/Ms). Xiànzài (now) Zhāng xiānsheng yǒu nǚ péngyou, tā zhēn gāoxìng.

III A

a) qī **b)** jiǔ **c)** èrshí'èr **d)** sìshíwǔ **e)** liùshíbā **f)** bāshíyī
g) jiǔshísān **h)** qīshísì

III B

a) bā diǎn èrshí **b)** shí'èr diǎn líng wù fēn **c)** liǎng diǎn bàn **d)** wǔdiǎn
sìshí, chà èrshí fēn liù diǎn, liù diǎn chà èrshí fēn (the last two are not
as common as the first) **e)** jiǔ diǎn sìshíwǔ, jiǔ diǎn sān kè, chà yí kè shí
diǎn, shí diǎn chà yí kè **f)** shíyī diǎn shí fēn **g)** liù diǎn shíwǔ, liù diǎn yí
kè **h)** sì diǎn wǔshíwǔ, chà wǔ fēn wǔ diǎn, wǔ diǎn chà wǔ fēn (the last
two are not so common as the first)

Exercise 5.1
 1 Zhè **wèi** xiǎojie zài Běijīng Dàxué xuéxí Hànyǔ.
 2 Nǎ **wèi** xiānsheng shì nǐ lǎogōng/àiren?
 3 Wáng tàitai yǒu jǐ **ge** xiǎoháir?
 4 Nà wǔ **ge** rén dōu shì nǐ péngyou ma?
 5 Tāmen jǐ **diǎn** zhōng lái wǒmen jiā chī fàn?

Exercise 5.2
 1 Shǐ Àilǐ (xiǎojie).
 2 Shì.
 3 Měiguó.
 4 Duì. Tā yǐqián zài Měiguó gōngzuò.
 5 Tā māma shì Měiguórén.
 6 Měiguó.
 7 Duì. Tā zài Běijīng Dàxué xuéxí.
 8 (Tā shuō) hěn hǎo.

Testing yourself
 1 Nǐ shì zài nǎr chūshēng de?
 2 Nǐ shì Fǎguórén ma? Wǒmen liǎ yě (dōu) shì Fǎguórén.
 3 Nǐ shì zài nǎr zhǎngdà de?
 4 Nà wèi xiānsheng shì liǎng diǎn bàn lái de ma? Bù, tā shì sān diǎn
 lái de.
 5 Nǐ zài nǎr xuéxí Hànyǔ? Xuéxí de zěnmeyàng?
 6 Tā shì cóng Měiguó lái de. Tā zài zhèr gōngzuò.
 7 Xiànzài jǐ diǎn? Nǐ(men) yídìng hěn è le!

8 *Wǒ jīntiān méi yǒu kòng dànshi (wǒ) míngtiān bù gōngzuò. Shí diǎn (zhōng) xíng ma?*

Exercise 6.1
1 *Tāmen jīntiān wǎnshang chī Zhōngguó cài.*
2 *Wáng xiānsheng hé Shǐ xiǎojie kuàizi yòng de búcuò (hǎo).*
3 *Lǐ tàitai zuò cài zuò de hěn hǎo.*
4 *Shǐ xiǎojie huì zuò Yīngguó cài.*
5 *Tā Zhōngguó cài zuò de bù zěnmeyàng.*

Exercise 6.2
1 *Wǒmen xuéxí de hěn shǎo.*
2 *Nǐmen shuō Hànyǔ, shuō de búcuò. Nǐmen Hànyǔ shuō de búcuò. Hànyǔ nǐmen shuō de búcuò.*
3 *Tā shēnghuó de bù zěnmeyàng.*
4 *Nà ge rén zuò Zhōngguó cài zuò de hěn hǎo. Nà ge rén Zhōngguó cài zuò de hěn hǎo. Zhōngguó cài nà ge rén zuò de hěn hǎo.*
5 *Zhè ge péngyou shuō huà shuō de bù duō. Zhè ge péngyou huà shuō de bù duō. Huà zhè ge péngyou shuō de bù duō.*

Exercise 6.3
1 *Tā shuō Hànyǔ shuō de hǎo ma? Tā shuō Hànyǔ shuō de hǎo bu hǎo? Tā shuō Hànyǔ shuō de zěnmeyàng? Tā shuō Hànyǔ shuō de bù hǎo.*
2 *Wǒ yí ge péngyou hē jiǔ hē de duō ma? Wǒ yí ge péngyou hē jiǔ hē de duō bu duō? Wǒ yí ge péngyou hē jiǔ hē de zěnmeyàng? Wǒ yí ge péngyou hē jiǔ hē de bù duō.*
3 *Shǐ xiǎojie xuéxí de màn ma? Shǐ xiǎojie xuéxí de màn bu màn? Shǐ xiǎojie xuéxí de zěnmeyàng? Shǐ xiǎojie xuéxí de bú màn.*
4 *Gōngrén jīntiān lái de shǎo ma? Gōngrén jīntiān lái de shǎo bu shǎo? Gōngrén jīntiān lái de zěnmeyàng? Gōngrén jīntiān lái de bù shǎo.*
5 *Yīngguórén zuò Yīngguó cài, zuò de hǎo ma? Yīngguórén zuò Yīngguó cài, zuò de hǎo bu hǎo? Yīngguórén zuò Yīngguó cài, zuò de zěnmeyàng? Yīngguórén zuò Yīngguó cài, zuò de bù hǎo.*
6 *Měiguórén zuò Fǎguó cài, zuò de bù hǎo ma? Měiguórén zuò Fǎguó cài, zuò de hǎo bu hǎo? Měiguórén zuò Fǎguó cài, zuò de zěnmeyàng? Měiguórén zuò Fǎguó cài, zuò de bù hǎo.*

Exercise 6.4

1 I can cook but not very well. My girlfriend says I'm a very plain cook. We have many Chinese friends, they cook Chinese food very well. They use chopsticks very well too. What about you?

2 A friend of mine went to France to work. French food is delicious – he ate a lot of it. Now he's very fat. His wife says 'How about your eating less and working more?' My friend says 'Eating less is OK but not working more!'

Testing yourself

1 *Wǒ zìjǐ bú huì zuò cài dànshi wǒ lǎogōng/àiren zuò cài zuò de fēicháng hǎo.*

2 *Wǒ māma shuō Hànyǔ shuō de hěn hǎo.*

3 *Wǒ shì zài Měiguó chūshēng de, kěshì (shì) zài Fǎguó zhǎngdà de.*

4 *Wǒ de yí ge péngyou chōu yān chōu de tài duō.*

5 *Wǒ zuò Zhōngguó cài zuò de bù zěnmeyàng.*

6 *Jīntiān wǎnshang wǒmen chī Fǎguó cài zěnmeyàng?*

7 *Tā yòng kuàizi yòng de bú tài hǎo dànshi (tā) zuò Zhōngguó cài zuò de hǎo jíle (hěn hǎo/fēicháng hǎo).*

8 *Qǐng yuánliàng.*

Testing yourself (Unit 7)

1	**chuáng**	**zhāng**	**wòshì**
2	**dìtǎn**	**zhāng, kuài**	**chúfáng, kètīng, xǐzǎojiān, wòshì**
3	**wēibōlú**	**tái**	**chúfáng**
4	**diànnǎo**	**tái**	**kètīng, shūfáng**
5	**cèsuǒ**	**jiān**	**xǐzǎojiān**
6	**shāfā**	**tào**	**kètīng, shūfáng**
7	**bīngxiāng**	**tái**	**chúfáng**
8	**línyù**	**ge**	**xǐzǎojiān**
9	**chájī**	**ge**	**kètīng**
10	**jìngzi**	**miàn**	**kètīng, shūfáng, xǐzǎojiān, wòshì**
11	**guāngpán bōfàngjī**	**ge**	**kètīng, shūfáng, wòshì**
12	**wèishēngzhǐ**	**juǎn**	**xǐzǎojiān**
13	**bǐjìběn diànnǎo**	**tái**	**kètīng, wòshì**

14	zhěntou	ge	wòshì
15	xǐyījī	tái	chúfáng
16	yùjīn	tiáo	xǐzǎojiān
17	shùmǎ diànshì(jī)	tái	kètīng, shūfáng, wòshì
18	yīguì	ge	wòshì
19	chuānglián	fù	chúfáng, kètīng, shūfáng, wòshì
20	yáshuā	bǎ	xǐzǎojiān
21	guōjià	ge	chúfáng
22	nàozhōng	ge	chúfáng, wòshì
23	shǒujī	ge	chúfáng, kètīng, shūfáng, wòshì
24	bèizi	ge	wòshì
25	bīngguì	tái	chúfáng
26	nuǎnqìpiàn	kuài	chúfáng, kètīng, shūfáng, xǐzǎojiān, wòshì
27	kōngtiáo	tái	kètīng, shūfáng, wòshì
28	shūjià	ge	kètīng, shūfáng
29	chuānghu	ge, shàn	chúfáng, kètīng, shūfáng, xǐzǎojiān, wòshì
30	bǎiyèchuāng	ge	chúfáng, kètīng, shūfáng, xǐzǎojiān, wòshì

Exercise 8.1

1 *Dèng xiǎojie yào huí Zhōngguó* **qù***.*
2 *Érzi jìn kètīng* **lái** *le.*
3 *Tā jìn wòshì* **qù** *le.*
4 *Nǐmen yīnggāi huí jiā* **lái***.*
5 *Wǒ xiǎng huí Yīngguó* **qù***.*

Exercise 8.2

1 *Tāmen xǐhuan chī fàn háishi xǐhuan shuō huà?*
2 *Dèng tàitai yào mǎi bīngxiāng háishi yào mǎi xǐyījī?*
3 *Zhōu xiānsheng qù Fǎguó háishi Lǐ xiānsheng qù (Fǎguó)?*
4 *Zhāng xiānsheng huí Měiguó háishi Shǐ xiǎojie huí (Měiguó)?*
5 *Shíjiān guò de kuài háishi guò de màn?*
6 *Wǒ péngyou de fángzi méi yǒu chúfáng háishi méi yǒu yùshì?*

7 *Nǐ xuéxí Hànyǔ háishi xuéxí dìlǐ?*

8 *Tāmen jiā yǒu sì ge wòshì háishi yǒu sān ge (wòshì)?*

Exercise 8.3

1 *Shǐ xiǎojie yǒu liǎng ge gēge hé yí ge mèimei.*

2 *Wǒ dìdi èrshíqī suì.*

3 *Lǎo xiānsheng bāshí suì, shēntǐ hěn hǎo.*

4 *Jiǔshíjiǔ ge péngyou zài Zhōngguó gōngzuò.*

5 *Nà ge yīshēng hē liù bēi jiǔ hé liǎng bēi kāfēi.*

Exercise 8.4

1 *Dìfang xiǎo, bīngxiāng、 xǐyījī yě dōu bù dà.*

2 *Xiǎoháir xiànzài zài chúfáng hē niúnǎi.*

3 *Tā yǒu zìjǐ de fángjiān, dú shū hěn ānjìng.*

4 *Wǒ gěi nǐmen tiān le hěn duō máfan.*

5 *Lǐ lǎoshī huí dàxué qu le.*

6 *Kètīng lǐ de rén dōu shì nánde.*

Exercise 8.5

The kids are going to my mum's place this evening. She's got a lot of space and has both a washing machine and a fridge. The children like to enjoy themselves, my mum also likes to take them to the cinema but she has neither the time nor the money so she has to let them play in the big garden. When they stop playing they can sit in the kitchen and chat and have something to eat. After the meal they can watch the TV.

Testing yourself

1 *Wǒ hé wǒ péngyou xiǎng qù Měiguó.*

2 *Tā zài nǎr kàn diànshì? Zài wòshì háishi zài kètīng?*

3 *Fùqīn shuō tā bú rènshi nǐ le.*

4 *Lǎo le, tā jiù bù hē jiǔ le.*

5 *Nǐ xiǎng hē chá háishi (hē) kāfēi?*

6 *Shíjiān guò de zhēn kuài. Wómen gāi huí qù le.*

7 *Nǐmen de kètīng bùzhì de zhēn piàoliang.*

8 *Xièxie nǐ de rèqíng zhāodài, wǒ yídìng zài lái.*

Exercise 9.1

1 *Érzi bǐ nǚ'ér dà wǔ suì.*

2 *Jiějie bǐ mèimei dà liù suì.*

3 *Shǐ Àilǐ bǐ Wáng Yǒngshòu xiǎo liǎng suì.*
   4 *Lǐ tàitai bǐ Lǐ xiānsheng xiǎo sān suì.*
   5 *Zhōngguó chá bǐ Zhōngguó jiǔ hǎo hē.*
   6 *Zhōngguó cài bǐ Yīngguó cài hǎo chī.*
   7 *Tā de shēntǐ bǐ nǐ (de shēntǐ) hǎo.*
   8 *Wǒ nán péngyou bǐ wǒ gāoxìng.*

Exercise 9.2

1	Hot dog	**2**	McDonald's
3	(Beef) hamburger	**4**	Coca-Cola
5	KFC	**6**	Starbucks
7	Yamaha	**8**	Nikon
9	Canon	**10**	Beethoven
11	Mozart	**12**	Canada
13	Cuba	**14**	Cambridge
15	Warsaw	**16**	Washington
17	President Obama		

Exercise 9.3

   1 *Méi chī-guo.*
   2 *Liǎng ge.*
   3 *Érzi bǐ nǚ'ér dà.*
   4 *Nǚ'ér bǐ érzi gāo.*
   5 *Kuàicān bǐ Zhōngguó cài guì* or *Zhōngguó cài bǐ kuàicān piányi.*
   6 *Rénmen juéde chī kuàicān shímáo.*

Exercise 9.4

1 *Duì.* **2** *Bú duì.* **3** *Duì.* **4** *Bú duì.* **5** *Duì.* **6** *Bú duì.* **7** *Bú duì.* **8** *Duì.*
9 *Duì.*

Exercise 9.5

   1 *Lúndūn de fángzū dōu hěn guì.*
   2 *Zhōngguórén hǎo, Yīngguórén yě dōu hěn hǎo.*
   3 *Tā měi nián mǎi hěn duō yīfu.*
   4 *Shuì jiào yǐqián yīnggāi shuā yá.*
   5 *Tā nà tiān xiūxi le.*
   6 *Tā měi nián qù Fǎguó.*
   7 *Wǒmen cónglái méi chī guo Rìběn fàn.*

8 *Yìxiē Rìběnrén gōngzī hěn gāo.*

9 *Sūgélán bǐ Měiguó ānjìng de duō.*

10 *Tiānqì hǎo de shíhou kěyǐ qù kàn diànyǐng.*

11 *Wǒde nǚ'ér yòu gāo yòu shòu.*

Testing yourself

1 *Fàntīng lǐ yǒu yì zhāng zhuōzi hé liù bǎ yǐzi.*

2 *Suīrán shūfáng lǐ yìbān hěn ānjìng, dànshi hěn duō rén dōu méi yǒu.*

3 *Tiānqì lěng de shíhou, dàjiā (dōu) xǐhuan shāo nuǎnqì.*

4 *Wǒ zǎo jiù xiǎng chī Běijīng kǎoyā le.*

5 *Wǒ mèimei bǐ wǒ hái cōngming.*

6 *Bú shi měi ge shāfā dōu hǎo zuò.*

7 *Wǒ nǚ'ér bǐ érzi dà sān suì bàn.*

8 *Fùmǔ zuótiān méi qu, wǒ hé jiějie jīntiān yě bú qù.*

9 *Dānrénchuáng bǐ shuāngrénchuáng hái (gèng) piányi.*

10 *Wǒ yě bù zhīdào wèishénme.*

11 *Xièxie nǐmen qǐng wǒmen lái zhèr chī fàn.*

12 *Suīrán chuānghu、mén děng dōu hěn gānjìng, dànshi zhuōzi、yǐzi dōu hěn zāng.*

Exercise 10.1

1 *Fùmǔ zǒu* **jìn** *kètīng* **lai**.

2 *Tāmen bān* **chū** *shūzhuō* **qu**.

3 *Xiōngdì bān* **jìn** *shuāngrénchuáng* **qu**.

4 *Xiǎoháir pǎo* **chū** *cèsuǒ* **lai**.

5 *Jiàoyuán ná* **xià** *liǎng běn shū* **lai** or *Jiàoyuán ná* **xiàlai** *liǎng běn shū.*

Exercise 10.2

1 *xīngqīsì*	**2** *xīngqījǐ? xīngqīyī*	**3** *qīyuè*
4 *shí'èr ge yuè*	**5** *qī tiān*	**6** *sānshí tiān*

7 *èrshíbā tiān; èrshíjiǔ tiān*

8 *sānbǎiliùshíwǔ tiān; sānbǎiliùshíliù tiān.*

Exercise 10.3

1 *bèi, jiào, ràng*

2 *bèi (rang and jiào would not normally be used in this context)*

3 *bèi, ràng, jiào*

4 *bèi, jiào, ràng*

5 *bèi, ràng, jiào*

Exercise 10.4

1 *Tā de yì kē yá diào le.*

2 *Tāmen bu zháojí.*

3 *Zhāng Dàmíng.*

4 *Tā shuì zháo le.*

5 *Tā jīntiān gēn xiǎo péngyoumen qí zìxíngchē dàochù wánr.*

6 *Mǎi de shíhou yǒu yìdiǎnr guì.*

7 *Míngtiān shì xīngqītiān.*

8 *Tāmen shì zài Màidāngláo chī de.*

9 *Tā shuō kuàicān méi yǒu yíngyǎng, hái huì ràng rén zhǎng pàng.*

10 *Xǐhuān.*

Testing yourself

1 *Zhè liàng zìxíngchē yòu jiēshi yòu hǎokàn.*

2 *Zhè ge xiǎo nánháir lèi le kěshi shuì bu zháo.*

3 *Wǒ xiàng tā jiěshì le wèishénme tā děi xǐ shǒu, xǐ liǎn hé shuā yá.*

4 *Kuàicān huì ràng wǒmen zhǎng pàng.*

5 *Nǐ zěnme le? Nǐ hěn zháojí ma?*

6 *Wǒ mèimei yìzhí zài kū. Wǒ bù zhīdāo (shì) zěnme huí shì.*

Exercise 11.1

1 *zuò, zuò* → 坐火车比坐公共汽车快多了。

2 *kāi* → 开车的人工资很高。

3 *qí* → 在中国骑自行车的人非常多。

4 *qí* → 有的人喜欢骑摩托车因为很自由。

5 *kāi* → 英国人十七岁才可以开车。

Exercise 11.2

1 *Tā xī shí fēn zhōng de yān.*

2 *Lǎoshī jiāo yí ge xiǎoshí de shū.*

3 *Gēge lù bàn ge zhōngtóu de yīn.*

4 *Wǒ tàitài huà sān kè zhōng de huàr.*

5 *Chǎngzhǎng kāi sān ge bàn xiǎoshí de chē.*

6 *Dìdi kàn shū, kàn bàn ge xiǎoshí.*

7 *Lǎorén shuì jiào, shuì yí ge bàn xiǎoshí.*

8 *Wǒ yí ge péngyou zǒu lù, zǒu qī ge zhōngtóu.*

9 *Nà wèi xiānsheng shuō huà, shuō hěn cháng shíjiān le.*

10 *Nǎ wèi xiǎojie néng dǎ zì, néng dǎ jiǔ ge xiǎoshí?*

Exercise 11.3

1 (–) **2** (+) **3** (+) **4** (–) **5** (+) **6** (+) **7** (–) **8** (–) **9** (–)
10 (+)

Exercise 11.4

Some people think (that) British weather is pretty awful but, conversely, there are some people who feel that British weather is pretty good – neither hot, nor cold; neither does it always snow in winter; but there's no getting away from one thing and that's no matter where you are, it often rains (in Britain). In China, there are normally many sunny days and few cloudy ones but Britain is just the opposite with lots of cloudy days and few sunny ones. Some say this ties in with British people's peculiar temperament but others say it is related to their lovable character. Which view is right? Over to you!

Testing yourself

1 *Xīngqītiān wǒ péngyou lái de shíhou, wǒ zhèngzài kàn diànshì ne.*

2 *Wǒ xiǎng gēn nǐ yìqǐ qù wǎngbā.*

3 *Tā yī kāishǐ dǎ hūlu wǒ jiù zǒu!*

4 *Chuānghu kāizhe dànshi mén guānzhe.*

5 *Gōngyuán lǐ rènào jíle, dǎ tàijíquán de dǎ tàijíquán, zhào xiàng de zhào xiàng, dǎ pái de dǎ pái.*

6 *Tiānqì hǎo de shíhou, wǒ zài wàimiàn zuòzhe kàn shū.*

7 *Wǒmen měi tiān wǎnshang chàng bàn ge xiǎoshí de gēr.*
   Wǒmen měi tiān wǎnshang chàng gēr chàng bàn ge xiǎoshí.

8 *Yīnwèi tā xīngqī'èr bìng méi yǒu dǎ diànhuà, suǒyǐ wǒ bù zhīdao wǒ qù bu qù.*

9 *Yàoshi zài fùmǔ jiā, wǒ chángcháng dào fùjìn de gōngyuán qù dǎ wǎngqiú.*

10 *Tā xiàozhe shuō tā yǐjīng jié hūn le.*

11 *Nǐmen zài tīng shōuyīnjī ma? Méi yǒu, wǒmen tīng lù yīn ne.*

12 *Nǐ míngtiān qù kàn xì shì bu shi? Kěxī wǒ bù néng gēn nǐ yìqǐ qù.*

Exercise 12.1

1 *Tā de fāyīn qīngchu shi qīngchu dànshi . . .*
2 *Wáng xiānsheng de Hànyǔ shuǐpíng gāo shi gāo kěshì . . .*
3 *Zhè běn xiǎoshuō yǒu yìsi shi yǒu yìsi kěshì . . .*
4 *Duì wàiguórén lái shuō, Zhōngwén de sìshēng nán shi nán dànshi . . .*
5 *Qīngdǎo píjiǔ hǎo hē shi hǎo hē kěshì . . .*

Exercise 12.2

1 *cái* **2** *jiù* **3** *jiù* **4** *cái* **5** *cái* **6** *cái* **7** *jiù* **8** *cái*

Exercise 12.3

1 *dǒng*; **2** *chūqu/chūlai or jìnqu/jìnlai*; **3** *chūlai*; **4** *wán*; **5** *bǎo*; **6** *shàng*; **7** *jiàn*; **8** *qǐlai*; **9** *xià*; **10** *dà/hǎo/qīngchu*; *dǒng/jiàn/chūlai*; **11** *dào/zháo*; **12** *xiàqu*

Exercise 12.5

Liu Honggang is a waiter. He likes his job a lot because he has the chance to meet lots of different people. They may be American or British or then again Chinese or Japanese. Some foreigners can speak very fluent Chinese (*pǔtōnghuà*) but with a strong foreign accent, their pronunciation and grammar are not very accurate but you can still understand them. It's very funny when some foreigners start speaking Chinese because they don't use tones. There are also some foreigners with a very high level of Chinese who have been living in China for ages and can read (and understand) Chinese newspapers and novels and can also write Chinese more or less. It's not at all easy for adults to learn Chinese (start learning Chinese); you have to take your hat off to them. Some people can't even speak their own language properly, let alone a foreign one!

Testing yourself

1 *Wǒ cāi tā bú shi Měiguórén jiù shi Yīngguórén.*
2 *Tā de shēngdiào fēicháng hǎo dànshi tā de fāyīn bù xíng.*
3 *Wǒ yǐjīng qù le liù cì Zhōngguó kěshì wǒ háishi tīng bu dǒng Zhōngguórén shuō shénme.*
4 *Duì wǒ zuì hǎo de péngyou lái shuō, xiě zì bǐ kàn shū gèng (hái) yǒu yìsi.*

5 Tā (de) tóufa zhēn cháng. Tā zěnme hái méi jiǎn ne?

6 Tā zhǐ yòng le liǎng nián (de shíjiān) jiù xué hǎo le pǔtōnghuà.

7 Tā xué Zhōngwén xué le sān nián le suǒyǐ tā de shuǐpíng xiāngdāng gāo.

8 Wǒ (shì) zuótiān cái zhīdao tā bú huì chá Zhōngwén cídiǎn/zìdiǎn (de).

9 Dàjiā dōu xǐhuan gēn yǒu yìsi de rén tán tiān/liǎo tiān dànshi zhè yàng de rén bù duō.

10 Yǒu zhòngyào (de) shìqing wǒ cái dǎrǎo nǐ.

11 Wǒ cái gēn tā shuō le yì、liǎng cì huà, jiù hěn xǐhuan tā le. (This one is difficult!)

12 Tā tèbié lǎn. Tā jīntiān cái kàn wán yí yè.

Halfway review

Exercise 12A

Nouns:	1c	2f	3b	4e	5d
Verbs:	1d	2a	3b	4e	5c
Adjectives:	1d	2f	3b	4e	5c

Exercise 12B

1) yìdiǎn(r) 一点儿 **2)** yìzhí 一直 **3)** yíhuì'r 一会儿 **4)** yìbān 一般
5) yídìng 一定 **6)** liǎng tiān 两天 **7)** sān nián 三年
8) sì shēng 四声 **9)** wǔ suì 五岁 **10)** liù cì 六次

Exercise 12C

1	xiǎngshòu shēnghuó	享受生活
2	gēn (rén) liáo tiānr	跟(人)聊天儿
3	shímáo de kuàicān	时髦的快餐
4	yòu hǎo chī yòu hǎokàn	又好吃又好看
5	hěn cháng de gùshi	很长的故事
6	yuè lái yuè míngxiǎn	越来越明显
7	qí zìxíngchē (qù) shàng bān	骑自行车(去)上班
8	dà bùfen Ōuzhōu guójiā	大部分欧洲国家
9	chúle zhèxiē yǐwài	除了这些以外
10	yǒu Zhōngguó tèsè de shèhuì zhǔyì	有中国特色的社会主义

Exercise 12D

1. *Bú yào děng dào nǐ tuìxiū le zài kāishǐ xiǎngshòu shēnghuó.*
   不要等到你退休了再开始享受生活。

2. *Wǒ méi yǒu shíjiān zài wǎng shàng gēn (rén) liáo tiānr.*
   我没有时间在网上跟人聊天儿。

3. *Zài zhè ge chéngshì, Màidāngláo hé Kěndéjī shì bu shì shímáo de kuàicān?*
   在这个城市，麦当劳和肯德基是不是时髦的快餐？

4. *Tā zuò de fàncài yòu hǎochī yòu hǎokàn.*
   她做的饭菜又好吃又好看。

5. *Wǒ gěi tā jiǎng le yí ge hěn cháng de gùshi, kěshì tā shuō bú gòu cháng.*
   我给他讲了一个很长的故事，可是他说不够长。

6. *'Quán qiú biàn nuǎn' shì bu shì yuè lái yuè míngxiǎn?*
   '全球变暖'是不是越来越明显？

7. *Yàoshi/rúguǒ tiānqi hǎo, wǒ jiù qí zìxíngchē (qù) shàng bān.*
   要是/如果天气好，我就骑自行车(去)上班。

8. *Dà bùfen Ōuzhōu guójiā shì fādá guójiā.*
   大部分欧洲国家是发达国家。

9. *Chúle zhèxiē (Hàn)zì yǐwài, biéde zì wǒ dōu bú huì xiě.*
   除了这些(汉)字以外，别的字我都不会写。

10. *Nǐ néng bu néng jiěshi yíxià shénme shì 'yǒu Zhōngguó tèsè de shèhuì zhǔyì'?*
    你能不能解释一下什么是'有中国特色的社会主义'？

Exercise 15.1

1 *zhāng* 张 **2** *jiàn* 件 **3** *jiàn* 件 **4** *bāo* 包 **5** *kuài* 块 **6** *jiàn* 件, *mǐ* 米

Exercise 15.2

1 八十五块 **2** 二十四块八 **3** 十三块九 **4** 二十六块七 **5** 九毛二
6 八块四

Exercise 15.4

1 *píng* 'grass' **2** *chèn* 'clothing' **3** *méi* 'water' **4** *xiè* 'speech' **5** *kuài* 'earth' **6** *běn* 'tree' **7** *shì* 'sun' **8** *yān* 'fire' **9** *zhì* 'heart' **10** *mǎi* 'big'

Exercise 15.5

1 4 (一) **2** 4 (亻) **3** 5 (口) **4** 3 (女) **5** 3 (戈)
6 4 (扌) **7** 5 (阝) **8** 7 (大) **9** 7 (心) **10** 4 (扌)

Exercise 15.6

1 售货员是中国人。 The shop assistant is Chinese.
2 地图两块四一张。 Maps are 2.40 yuan each.
3 那本杂志一块九毛五。 That magazine costs 1.95 yuan.
4 您没买东西。 You haven't bought anything. You haven't been shopping.
5 苹果三块八一斤。 Apples are 3.8 yuan a catty.

Testing yourself

1 我要买三本杂志和一份报。 (张 is used as the MW for newspaper if there are only four pages!)
2 我昨天买了两件衬衫。
3 他要买东西。
4 你(您)要几米丝绸?
5 谢谢。再见。

Exercise 16.2

1 *yì, zhì, zěn* (心) 2 *bào, tǐng, pái* (扌) 3 *hào, yuán, wèn* (口)
4 *dōu, bù, yóu* (阝) 5 *lái, shí, xià* (一)

Exercise 16.3

1 地、块、去。 2 要、好。 3 中、出。 4 杂、本、果、乐、样。
5 服、有、期。 6 图、四、国。 7 影。 8 会、个。
9 件、份、什、你。 10 这、还。

Exercise 16.4

1 看电影怎么样? How about seeing a film?
2 楼下有人吗? Is anybody downstairs? Are there people downstairs?
3 《日出》这部电影有没有意思? Is the film *Sunrise* any good? (interesting)
4 上个星期你没来。 You didn't come last week.
5 音乐会几月几号? When is the concert? (What day of what month)

Testing yourself

1 今天十一月三号(日)。
2 请问,今天几月几号?
3 楼上没有人。
4 大家说买东西很有意思。

5 你还有钱吗？你要多少？

6 我一九六八年在中国。

Exercise 17.2

1 *yǎn* 'water' **2** *xíng* 'to step with left foot' **3** *jì* 'speech'

4 *dǎ* 'hand' **5** *qǔ* 'ear' **6** *guò* 'walking' **7** *yīng* 'grass'

8 *jiē* 'hand' **9** *mài* 'ten' **10** *tiān* 'horizontal line'

Exercise 17.3

1 6 (讠) **2** 8 (刂) **3** 3 (一) **4** 2 (口) **5** 2 (人)

6 10 (氵) **7** 5 (日) **8** 5 (贝) **9** 6 (宀) **10** 5 (女)

Exercise 17.4

1 心 → 意、您、思、怎。 **2** 扌 → 报、接、拔、打。

3 口 → 喂、叫、哪、名。 **4** 宀 → 客、定、字、家。

5 氵 → 没、演、满。

Exercise 17.5

1 今天没有人给我打电话。Nobody phoned me today.

2 天安旅行社在哪儿？Where is the Tian'an travel agency?

3 他明天下午就要去北京了。He's going to Beijing tomorrow afternoon.

4 你后天能不能来接我？Can you come and meet me the day after tomorrow?

5 星期五行不行？不行，就星期六吧。Is Friday OK? If not, then how about Saturday?

Testing yourself

1 我今天去天安旅行社了。

2 您贵姓？我姓史，名字叫史爱理。

3 他说他给我们留两张票。

4 他们要今天下午看那部电影，可是票卖完了。

5 我下个星期五来取票行吧？

Exercise 18.1

1 *Jǐngshān Gōngyuán zài Gùgōng běibianr.*

2 *Qiánmén zài Máo Zhǔxí Jìniàntáng nánbianr.*

3 *Rénmín Dàhuìtáng zài Rénmín Yīngxióng Jìniànbēi xībianr.*

4 *Zhōngguó Lìshǐ Bówùguǎn zài Rénmín Yīngxióng Jìniànbēi dōngbianr.*

5 *Máo Zhǔxí Jìniàntáng zài Rénmín Dàhuìtáng dōngnánbianr.*

Exercise 18.2

1 *Jǐngshān Gōngyuán lí Qiánmén bǐjiào yuǎn.*

2 *Rénmín Dàhuìtáng lí Rénmín Yīngxióng Jìniànbēi hěn jìn. Wàng dōng zǒu jiù dào le.*

3 *Máo Zhǔxí Jìniàntáng lí Tiān'ānmén bú tài yuǎn. Wàng běi zǒu jiù dào le.*

4 *Shì, jiù zài Zhōngguó Lìshǐ Bówùguǎn duìmiàn. (jiù zài Zhōngguó Lìshǐ Bówùguǎn hé Rénmín Dàhuìtáng zhōngjiān)*

5 *Niújīn lí Lúndūn yǒu jiǔshíyī gōnglǐ.*

6 *Sānshí hào lí èrshíqī hào yǒu sān tiān.*

7 *Yuándàn lí Shèngdànjié yǒu yí ge xīngqī.*

Exercise 18.4

(Exercise 18.1 set of answers.)

1 景山公园在故宫北边儿。

2 前门在毛主席纪念堂南边儿。

3 人民大会堂在人民英雄纪念碑西边儿。

4 中国历史博物馆在人民英雄纪念碑东边儿。

(Exercise 18.2 set of answers.)

1 景山公园离前门比较远。

2 人民大会堂离人民英雄纪念碑很近，往东走就到了。

3 毛主席纪念堂离天安门不太远，往北走就到了。

4 是，就在中国历史博物馆对面。(就在中国历史博物馆和人民大会堂中间。)

Testing yourself

1 请问，天坛在哪儿? 怎么走?

2 人民大会堂离这儿远吗? 不远，就在对面。

3 人民英雄纪念碑在人民大会堂东边儿，中国历史博物馆西边儿。

Exercise 19.1

1 *Qǐng nǐ bǎ shǒujù shōu hǎo.*

2 *Xìnfēng shàng yào bǎ jìjiànrén de dìzhǐ he xìngmíng xiě qīngchu.*

3 *Wǒ méi yǒu bǎ nǐ de míngzi xiě xià lai.*

4 *Tā yào bǎ zhè ge liànxí zài zuò yí cì.*

5 *Yóukè méi bǎ shōujù zǐxì kànyikàn.*

6 *Shòupiàoyuán liú gěi le Wáng xiānsheng liǎng zhāng hǎo piào.*

7 *Wàiguó yóukè yīnggāi jì xiàlai dàshǐguǎn de diànhuà haòmǎ.*

8 *Shòuhuòyuán bú yuànyì mài gěi tā sīchóu chènshān.*

9 *Dàifu yào sòng bìngrén dào yīyuàn.*

10 *Wǒ yí ge Zhōngguó péngyou yì tiān néng xī wán liǎng bāo yān.*

Exercise 19.2

1 *xiǎng, nín, zěn, yì, sī, zhì* (心).

2 *qǐng, shuō, xiè, huà* (讠).

3 *wèi, shòu, yuán, ma, wèn, hào* (口).

4 *jìn, hái, guò, zhè, yuǎn, biān* (辶).

5 *bù, nà, yóu, dòu* (阝).

Exercise 19.3

1 东西、东边。 **2** 外国、中国。 **3** 售货员、售票员。

4 毛衣、衣服。 **5** 电影、电话、电报。 **6** 星期二、星期四。

7 地图、地方。 **8** 那边、这边。

Exercise 19.4

Mr King is a very nice person but he has one small defect: he really likes spending money. If he goes to buy a shirt, he ends up with three, if you want him to buy a magazine he buys you ten. He says they were all very interesting so he bought them all. How can you feel relaxed if you let him go and do the shopping?

王先生人很好，但是他有一个小毛病，他很喜欢花钱。去买一件衬衫，他就买三件；你要他买一本杂志，他就给你买十本。他说都很有意思，所以都买了。让他去买东西，你怎么能放心呢？

Exercise 19.5

Chen Ying	*Four tickets*
Ticket seller	*(That'll be) 400 kuai. Please keep/put away your tickets carefully. Here is the tourist map. I'll give you 2 of them. If you would like to rent audioguides then please go over there (to that counter/window).*

[They all walk over to the counter.]

Zhang Daming   *Would you like audioguides [Then to the attendant.] How much does an audioguide cost?*

Fuwuyuan   *15 kuai each. You can listen to the commentary in Chinese, English or Japanese.*

Shi Aili   *Oh yes, let's have one. That way we can also get to practise our listening comprehension.*

[She gives the fuwuyuan 60 kuai and the fuwuyuan hands each of them an audioguide.]

Fuwuyuan   *This is the start button, this is the pause button and that is the stop button. At various places around the Bird's Nest you will see a sign with headphones on it and a large number written underneath it. Put the number into your audioguide and press the start button. Do you understand? It is not difficult.*

[They spend about an hour and a half looking round the stadium, at the track, the changing rooms, the long jump pit and so on and stopping and listening to the commentary on the audioguide from time to time.]

Zhang Daming   *I'm starving. Let's go and eat something. There's a huge choice. Would you two like to go to a snack bar, a self-service restaurant or one with waiter/waitress service?*

Shi Aili   *Let's go to one of the self-service restaurants. It should be quicker and cheaper than a sit down one. But first I have to buy some postcards. Look – there's a souvenir shop over there. Do you mind?*

Wang   *Is that all right with you two? I need to buy a few postcards too. My brother was really envious that we were going to look around the Bird's Nest. He loves athletics and spent hours watching the 2008 Olympic Games here in Beijing on TV.*

[In the souvenir shop.]

Shi Aili *[hands over four postcards to the shop assistant]* Do you also sell stamps?

Shop assistant Yes, we do. Internal/domestic or for abroad?

Shi Aili One internal, two for Europe and one for the USA.

Shop assistant That'll be 25 kuai.

[Shi Aili gives her audioguide to Wang Yongshou and takes 30 kuai out of her purse and gives them to the assistant.]

Shop assistant Here's (your) 5 kuai change.

Shi Aili Thank you.

[She takes the stamps and sticks them onto her postcards.]

  I've stuck the stamps on. That way I won't lose them.

Chen Ying Let's go and eat.

[In the self-service restaurant.]

Zhang Daming Luckily there is air conditioning in here otherwise it would be much too hot ... Have you all had enough to eat?

Chen Ying I have. The steamed dumplings were delicious. What about you two?

Wang Yongshou Yes, I have.

Shi Aili Sorry, but I need to go to the ladies/washroom. Can you wait for me a couple of minutes? Now where's the ladies?

Chen Ying Over there. Can you see the sign? I'll come with you.

[After a while they both come back.]

Shi Aili They were really clean. The Bird Nest's Stadium's facilities are all excellent, very modern. What a pity I wasn't here to watch the Olympic Games in person.

Zhang Daming Let's go. There's a good movie on the TV tonight. Would you two like to come (over) and watch it with us. You can come and see the kids and we can cook up some noodles and spicy beancurd – I know how much you both like spicy food.

Shi and Wang That would be great! Thank you.

Testing yourself

1 *Zhè shì shōujù, qǐng shōu hǎo.*
2 *Yóupiào tiē hǎo le ma? Hái méi yǒu ne.*
3 *Jì shū hěn máfan, dànshi (hěn) zhíde.*
4 *Zhè shì Niǎocháo tǐyùchǎng de dǎoyóutú.*
5 *Àn zhèi ge jiàn kāishǐ. Àn zhèi ge jiàn zàntíng. Àn zhèi ge jiàn tíngzhǐ.*

1 这是收据，请收好。
2 邮票贴好了吗？还没有呢。
3 寄书很麻烦，但是(很)值得。
4 这是鸟巢体育场的导游图。
5 按这个键开始，按那个键暂停，按这个键停止。

Exercise 20.1

1 美国跟英国一样吗？不一样。英国比美国贵多了。
2 坐火车跟坐飞机有什么不一样？坐火车比坐飞机便宜得多。
3 你跟她一样不喜欢听音乐吗？不，我很喜欢听古典音乐。
4 我跟我的未婚妻一样浪漫，都喜欢写诗。
5 在中国日本电视机跟在欧洲一样容易买吗？

1 Is America the same as Britain? No. Britain is much more expensive than America.
2 In what way is travelling by train different from travelling by plane? Travelling by train is much cheaper than travelling by plane.
3 Are you and she alike in not enjoying listening to music? No, I like listening to classical music very much.
4 I am as romantic as my fiancée, we both like writing poetry.
5 Are Japanese TVs as easy to buy in China as they are in Europe?

Exercise 20.2

1 *Yàoshi/rúguǒ nǐ yǒu hěn duō qián, nǐ kěyǐ xiǎng chī shénme jiù chī shénme.*
2 *Wǒ yǒu hěn duō zìdiǎn, kěshì měi běn dōu yǒu yìxiē quēdiǎn.*
3 *Jīntiān shì xīngqītiān, wǒ máng le yí ge xīngqī, (suǒyǐ) jīntiān xiàwu wǒ nǎr dōu bú qù.*
4 *Búlùn duō rè, tā dōu yào shài tàiyang.*
5 *Nǐ de shēntǐ bú tèbié hǎo, suǒyi nǐ bù yīnggāi chōu yān.*

1 要是/如果你有很多钱，你可以想吃什么就吃什么。
2 我有很多字典，可是每本都有一些缺点。
3 今天是星期天，我忙了一个星期，(所以)今天下午我哪儿都不去。
4 不论多热，她都要晒太阳。
5 你的身体不特别好，所以你不应该抽烟。

Exercise 20.3
1 坐火车比坐飞机便宜**百分之五十**。
2 水电费比去年贵**百分之十**。
3 日本衣服比中国衣服贵**百分之三百**。
4 苹果不好吃，我只吃了**四分之一**。
5 音乐会的票昨天卖了**一半**。
6 外国烟好抽，这包已经抽了**三分之二**。
7 在中国美国专家比英国专家多**十倍**。

Testing yourself

Lu Feng	*Hello, my name is Lu Feng and this is Bai Lan. How long have you been in Beijing? Do you like Beijing?*
Shi Aili	*Oh hello, my name is Shi Aili – nice to meet you. I've been in Beijing a couple of months now. Yes, I like it very much but it's very different from America or (Lit. 'and') the UK so sometimes I get a bit homesick. That's why I thought I would first do some shopping and then have a coffee in Starbucks – just like I do at home.*
Bai Lan	*What do you think of the shops here?*
Shi	*Quite a few of the clothes and shoe shops are not much different from back home but they often don't stock large sizes.*
Bai Lan	*But you are not very fat!*
Shi Aili	*No, but I have quite big feet.*
Lu Feng	*[changing the subject quickly] Do you have a job in Beijing or are you studying?*

Shi Aili	*I'm studying Chinese at Beijing University but my boyfriend is working in a joint venture company. Do you both work?*
Lu Feng	*I work for a foreign bank, HSBC, and Bai Lan works here at Starbucks but it's her day off.*
Shi Aili	*Oh, HSBC. I've been thinking for a few weeks that I ought to open a bank account here so that I can have money transferred here from the UK. I'm getting a bit low on funds.*
Lu Feng	*You could open an account at HSBC. It would make transferring money easier.*
Shi Aili	*What a good idea. Can I also get a credit card and a debit card?*
Lu Feng	*Well, so long as you have enough money in your account I don't think that should be a problem. Why do you want a debit card as well as a credit card?*
Shi Aili	*I don't like to carry a lot of cash on me. I prefer to get money out of an ATM when I need to. Can I open a savings account as well as a current account? That way I will earn more interest on the money in the savings account.*
Bai Lan	*Why don't you go and talk to Lu Feng at the bank tomorrow? I am sure he can give you lots of advice and I know that the interest rates at HSBC are sometimes a tiny bit better than at the Bank of China, say.*
Lu Feng	*Yes, why don't you do that? Here is my card and on it is the address of our branch. It's not far from here. Can you come at around 10.00 and after we've finished we can come here for a nice espresso and a muffin (Lit. 'a little bit of cake'). Bai Lan will be working then so she'll make sure we get served quickly if you don't have much time.*
Bai Lan	*[smiling] You're addicted to your morning coffee and muffin – you'll get fat if you're not careful and then my parents will say that you don't deserve me!*

Exercise 21.1

1 *hǎoxiàng* **2** *xiàng, xiàng* **3** *xiàng, xiàng* **4** *hǎoxiàng* **5** *xiàng, hǎoxiàng*

Exercise 21.2

1 *dài* **2** *dài* **3** *chuān* **4** *dài* **5** *chuān*

Exercise 21.3

1 受教育的人偏见应该少一些。
2 可惜，小孩儿都很容易受骗。
3 我特别受我妈妈的影响。
4 星巴克在中国受不受欢迎？
5 有的人很容易受伤，不知道为什么？

Exercise 21.4

1 *Kěyǐ liǎojiě Zhōngguórén shēnghuó de gègè fāngmiàn.*
2 *Tāmen zài Hángzhōu.*
3 *Tāmen yìbiān chīzhe sānmíngzhì, yìbiān liáo tiān(r).*
4 *Zhōngguórén xǐhuan zhào xiàng. Tāmen yǒu gèzhǒnggèyang de zhàoxiàngjī.*
5 *Zhíyè zhàoxiàng de hěn duō.*
6 *Zhōngguórén bù xǐhuan yí ge rén chū qu wán(r).*
7 *Zhāng Xīqún shì Sūzhōurén. Tā lái Hángzhōu bàn shì(!).*
8 *Tā xīnlǐ bú tài gāoxìng.*
9 *Wǒmen shòuguo jiàoyù de rén yě yǒu yìdiǎn zhǒngzú piānjiàn.*
10 *Tā wánquán tóngyì tā de shuōfǎ.*
11 *Yīnwèi chéngrèn cuòwù děngyú gǎi le yíbàn(r) le.*

1 可以了解中国人生活的各个方面。
2 他们在杭州。
3 他们一边吃着三明治一边聊天(儿)。
4 中国人喜欢照相。他们有各种各样的照相机。

5 职业照相的很多。
6 中国人不喜欢一个人出去玩(儿)。
7 张锡群是苏州人。他来杭州办事。
8 她心里不太高兴。
9 我们受过教育的人也有一点种族偏见。
10 他完全同意他的说法。
11 因为承认错误等于改了一半(儿)了。

Exercise 21.5

1 In some ways Chinese and foreigners are pretty similar – they both like to go out and enjoy themselves and seek paradise on earth! Who doesn't want to live comfortably, wear nice clothes and eat well? The Chinese are no exception. In the past there were very few Chinese tourists but now they are getting more and more numerous every year.

2 It is very difficult to understand another nationality (ethnic group), it's not even easy to understand your own! The Chinese people are a very ancient people. Their history and culture are very different from our own, let alone their script! Learning Chinese is not only very interesting but also of use to us as individuals.

Testing yourself

1 *Zánmen yìbiān tán jiàoyu yìbiān kàn rìluò ba.*
2 *'Zì qī qī rén' shì yí jù hěn zhíde zhùyì de chéngyǔ.*
3 *Yīnwei Táiwān wèntí, Zhōng、Měi guānxi biàn de hěn fùzá.*
4 *Tā shì wǒ de tóngshì suǒyǐ wǒ de yìjiàn dāngrán (huì) shòu yǐngxiǎng.*
5 *Nǐ jīnnián lián yì tiān jià dōu méi yǒu (fàng), nánguài nǐ nàme (or zhème) lèi.*
6 *Tā jīntiān lián yí ge sānmíngzhì dōu méi chī, tā zěnme bú è ne?*

1 咱们一边谈教育，一边看日落吧。
2 '自欺欺人'是一句很值得注意的成语。
3 因为台湾问题，中、美关系变得很复杂。
4 他是我的同事，所以我的意见当然(会)受影响。
5 你今年连一天假都没有(放)，难怪你那么 (or 这么) 累。
6 她今天连一个三明治都不吃，她怎么不饿呢？

Exercise 22.1

1 *Tāmen lái de shíhou guā dà fēng.*

2 *Tā xué dào le hěn duō dōngxi (tā xué de hěn hǎo) yīnwei tā shuō 'jīnnián shōuhuò hěn dà'.*

3 *Shì guóchǎn de.*

4 *Hái kěyǐ fàng jiàngyóu hé cù.*

5 *Tā shuō tā bu huì chī cù.* or *Tā shuō tā shì bu huì chī cù de.*

6 *Lǐ xiānsheng xià ge xīngqīwǔ guò shēngrì. Nà ge shíhou Shǐ Àilǐ dàgài zài Yīngguó.*

7 *Yīnwei tā bù xǐhuan gēn péngyou gàobié.*

8 *Tā dǎsuàn děng Shǐ Àilǐ zài lái Zhōngguó kāi yí ge liánhuānhuì.*

9 *Tā (de) fēijī xiàwǔ sì diǎn sìshí qǐfēi. Tāmen yīnggāi sān diǎn (zhōng) dào.*

10 *Yīnwei tā bù xiǎng zài gào yí cì bié.* (**NB** *bù xiǎng* not *bú yào*)

11 *Tā ràng tāmen kàn tā de liǎn, dōu hóng le.*

12 *Yīnwei Lǐ tàitai bú (shi) kāi chē (de).*

1 他们来的时候刮大风。

2 她学到了很多东西(她学得很好)因为她说'今年收获很大'。

3 是国产的。

4 还可以放酱油和醋。

5 她说她不会吃醋。 or 她说她是不会吃醋的。

6 李先生下个星期五过生日，那个时候史爱理大概在英国。

7 因为她不喜欢跟朋友告别。

8 他打算等史爱理再来中国开一个联欢会。

9 她的飞机下午四点四十起飞。她应该三点(钟)到。

10 因为她不想再告一次别。

11 她让他们看她的脸，都红了。

12 因为李太太不(是)开车(的)。

Exercise 22.2

Li	There you are (welcome, welcome). Come in.
Mrs Li	Is it cold outside?
S	A bit. It's very windy, we were cycling against the wind, it was really strenuous.

Mrs Li	*Stop hanging about (don't keep standing) in the hall, come inside and sit down and warm up.*
Li	*Would you like tea or coffee?*
K	*Tea, I think.*
Mrs Li	*Ah, Aili, you're going back soon, so today is really your 'last supper', what a (great) shame.*
S	*Oh, a year goes by so quickly – how time flies.*
K	*Aili, you don't want to leave do you?*
S	*No, I've really got a lot out of this year. What a pity I can't stay any longer.*
Li	*You really are returning with a sack full of goodies!*
S	*I suppose you could put it like that.*
Mrs Li	*Come and eat. I've made the dumplings and they're cooking. Let's have some wine first. Here's a plate of hors d'oeuvres. Wenhua, how about opening the wine?*
Li	*This is a pretty good bottle. It's white wine from (made by) a joint venture. Most Chinese wine is sweet but we know that you're not too keen on sweet wines. Right, bottoms up! Bon voyage (safe journey) and come back soon!*
S	*Here's to your good health and your heart's desire!*
Li	*Let's take a few photos. Hang on (wait though) let's take them after the dumplings have come, there'll be more of a Chinese atmosphere (flavour!) then. Ah, here they are.*
K	*Have you got a flash?*
Li	*Yes. Is everybody ready? Smile!*
K	*I'll take a few snaps too. When I've had them developed, I'll email them to you.*
S	*Mrs Li, your dumplings are really delicious, next time you'll definitely have to teach me how to make them.*
Mrs Li	*No problem (fine), I hope you'll come back as soon as possible . . . the soya sauce and vinegar are both here.*
S	*Thanks. I'll have a little soya sauce. There's no way that a person like me can take vinegar (be jealous), ha ha!*
Li	*Come on, let's have another drink. May our friendship last for ever! Bottoms up!*

K	*Next Friday is your birthday, (Mr/Teacher) Li, what a shame that Aili will have already left China by then so we're going to propose a toast to you now and wish you 'a life as long as the Southern Mountain and as blessed as the Eastern Sea' in advance. We've also got you a little present.*
Li	*You really shouldn't have.*
Mrs Li	*What's the matter Aili? Don't cry, we'll meet again some day (!) Come back (again) after you've graduated.*
S	*Whenever I part from friends, I always think of the phrase 'meeting and parting are both difficult'.*
Mrs Li	*Your coming from so many thousands of miles away was really quite something but you'll still have plenty of opportunities to come to China in the future.*
Li	*How about our having a get-together when Aili comes back? Come on, another toast, to our meeting again next year or the year after.*
Mrs Li	*You have to (can't not) go back, this time Aili, you've still got one year of studying to do but later on there'll be masses of opportunities.*
Li	*When's the plane leaving?*
K	*At 4.40 pm. We should get there by 3.*
Li	*We'll come and see you off, eh?*
S	*There's no need. The airport's miles away, it's much too inconvenient. Let's count this evening as our goodbye, otherwise I won't be able to stand it if we have to say yet another one.*
Li	*We'll see. If I can get off class a bit earlier we'll definitely go. All right, that's enough of that (the subject's closed). Let's drink a last toast.*
Mrs Li	*No more for me (I've had it!). I'll be drunk if I drink any more. Look, my face is all red.*
Li	*Never mind, you're not driving! Come on, joy and happiness to us all! Bottoms up!*
Mrs Li, K and S	*Bottoms up!*

Testing yourself

1 *Zhǔnbèi hǎo le ma? Wǒ liǎng diǎn zhōng **jiù** yào zǒu le.*
2 *Yúnnán zài Zhōngguó de **xīnán** bù.*
3 ***Bù kěyǐ** bǎ zhàoxiàngjī jiè gěi tā.*
4 *Wǒ yǒu **bǎifēn zhī sìshí** de bǎwò.*
5 *Yīngguó de shēnghuófèi bǐ Zhōngguó **guì duō le** (or **guì de duō**).*
6 *Gǔdiǎn yīnyuè gēn xiàndài yīnyuè **yíyàng hǎo tīng**.*
7 *Fánshì lǎoshī **dōu** xǐhuan jiāo shū.*
8 *Shàngjí **hǎoxiàng** bù xǐhuan tā, bù zhīdao shénme yuányīn.*
9 *Nǐ **dài** shang tàiyángjìng qù cānjiā liánhuānhuì tài bù héshì le!*
10 *Tā **bèi** dǎ le yídùn or Tā **jiào rén** dǎ le yídùn.*
11 *Wǒmen **dōu** yīnggāi tóngqíng qióng rén.*
12 *Wǒ **bù tóngyì** nǐ de kànfǎ – tā bìng bú shi ge huài rén.*
13 *Qǐng nǐ **bǎ** èrshí'èr kè de kèwén zài kàn yícì.*

Chinese–English vocabulary

Pinyin (alphabetical order)	Characters	Unit	English
à *(interj)*	啊	5	*ah, oh*
à *(interj)*	啊	8	*ah, oh*
āiyā *(interj)*	哎呀	10	*oh dear (exclamation)*
àn *(v)*	按	19	*to press*
ānjìng *(adj)*	安静	8	*quiet*
Àolínpīkè yùndòng huì *(N)*	奥林匹克运动会	11	*Olympic Games*
Àoyùnhuì *(N)*	奥运会	19	*abbreviation for Olympic Games*
ba *(num)*	吧	2	*particle indicating suggestion*
bā *(num)*	八	15	*eight*
bǎ *(prep)*	把	19	*a preposition showing disposal*
bàba *(n)*	爸爸	5	*Dad, papa*
bái *(adj)*	白	22	*white; blank*
bǎi *(num)*	百	16	*100*
bǎiyèchuāng *(n)*	百叶窗	7	*blind*
bàn *(num)*	半	9	*half*
bàn shì *(v-o)*	办事	21	*to arrange for something to be done*
bàng *(adj)*	棒	12	*excellent (coll)*
bàngōngyǐ *(n)*	办公椅	7	*office chair*
bāo *(MW)*	包	15	*packet (of), package*
bāo *(v)*	包	22	*to make (**jiāozi**); to wrap; to include*
bào(zhǐ) *(n)* [**zhāng** *or* **fèn**]	报(纸) [张/份]	12	*newspaper*
bāokuò *(v)*	包括	9	*to include*
bǎozhèng *(v; n)*	保证	20	*to guarantee, ensure; guarantee, pledge*

Pinyin (alphabetical order)	Characters	Unit	English
bàozhǐ (n)	报纸	7	newspaper
bāozi (n)	包子	9	steamed bun
bǎwò (n)	把握		certainty
bēi (MW)	杯	2	cup(ful)
běi	北	18	north
Běijīng Dàxué (N)	北京大学	5	Beijing University
bēizi (n)	杯子	7	cup
bèizi (n) [chuáng]	被子 [床]	7	duvet, quilt
běn (MW)	本	15	MW for books, magazines
běndì (n)	本地	21	this locality
bǐ (prep)	比	9	compared with
biàn (v)	变	11	to change
biànhuà (n)	变化	11	change
biǎoyáng (v)	表扬		to praise, commend
biāozhì (n)	标志	19	sign, mark, symbol
biāozhǔn (adj; n)	标准	12	accurate; standard, criterion
bié (adv)	别	6	don't
bǐfang shuō	比方说	12	for example
bǐjiào (adv)	比较	8	relatively
bǐjìběn diànnǎo/ shǒutí diànnǎo (n)	笔记本电脑/ 手提电脑	7	laptop
bìng (adv) (bù/méi)	并(不/没)	11	see 11.1
bīngguì (n)	冰柜	7	freezer
bīngxiāng (n)	冰箱	8	refrigerator
bǐrú shuō	比如说	21	for example (more formal)
bìxiūkè(chéng) (n)	必修课(程)	22	obligatory or required course
bìyè (v)	毕业	22	to graduate
bō (v)	拨	17	to dial
bōli bēi (n)	玻璃杯	7	glass
bówùguǎn (n)	博物馆	18	museum
bù (MW)	部	16	MW for films
bù (neg)	不	1	not
bù dé bù (v)	不得不		cannot but have to
bù . . . le	不 . . . 了	8	not . . . any more

Pinyin (alphabetical order)	Characters	Unit	English
bù hǎoyìsi (v)	不好意思	20	*to be embarrassed, feel ill at ease*
bú shi A jiù shi B	不是A就是B	12	*if it's not A then it's B*
bú shi . . . ér shi . . .	不是 . . . 而是	12	*not . . . but . . .*
bù tóng (adj)	不同	19	*different*
bú yòng (v)	不用	10	*need not*
bù yuǎn wàn lǐ ér lái	不远万里而来	22	*not considering 10 000 li too far to come*
bù zěnmeyàng	不怎麼样	6	*not up to much*
búcuò (adj)	不错	5	*pretty good*
búdàn . . . érqiě (conj)	不但 . . . 而且		*not only . . . but also*
bùfen (n)	部分	11	*part, section*
bùguǎn (conj)	不管		*no matter*
búguò (conj)	不过	19	*but, moreover, only*
bùzhì (v)	布置	8	*to decorate*
cāi (v)	猜	12	*to guess*
cái (adv)	才	12	*not . . . until . . .; only*
cài (n)	菜	6	*dish; vegetable*
cǎiqǔ (v)	采取	11	*to adopt (e.g. measures)*
cānguān (v)	参观	19	*to visit (places, exhibition etc.)*
cānjiā (v)	参加		*to participate*
cāntīng (n)	餐厅	19	*restaurant*
cèsuǒ (n)	厕所	7	*toilet*
chá (n)	茶	1	*tea*
chá (v)	查	12	*to check*
chá zìdiǎn (v-o)	查字典	12	*to consult a dictionary*
chàbùduō (adv; v)	差不多	11	*almost, nearly; to be almost the same*
cháhú (n)	茶壶	7	*teapot*
chájī (n) [zhāng, ge]	茶几 [张, 个]	7	*coffee table*

Pinyin (alphabetical order)	Characters	Unit	English
chātóu (n)	插头	7	plug
chāzuò (n)	插座	7	socket
cháng (adj)	长	10	long
cháng (cháng) (adv)	常(常)	9	often
chángshòu (n)	长寿	17	long life, longevity
chǎnpǐn (n)	产品	22	product
cházhǎo xìnxī (v-o)	查找信息	11	to look up information (on the web)
chēnghū (n; v)	称呼	21	form of address; to address
chéngniánrén (n)	成年人	12	an adult
chéngrèn (v)	承认		acknowledge
chéngshì (n)	城市	11	city, town
chènshān (n)	衬衫	15	shirt, blouse
chī cù (v-o)	吃醋	22	to feel jealous
chī fàn (v-o)	吃饭	4	to eat (meal)
chī là de (v-o)	吃辣的	19	to eat spicy/hot food
chī-bǎo (RV)	吃饱	8	to eat one's fill
chū (v)	出	11	to come or to go out
chū chāi (v-o)	出差	21	be on a business trip
chuān (v)	穿		to wear
chuángdān (n)	床单	7	sheet
chuángdiàn (n)	床垫	7	mattress
chuānghu (n)	窗户	7	window
chuāngkǒu (n)	窗口	19	window (for tickets etc.)
chuānglián	窗帘	7	curtain
chúfáng (n) [jiān, ge]	厨房 [间/个]	8	kitchen
chúle (. . . yǐwài) (conj)	除了 (. . . 以外)	11	except, apart from
chūntiān (n)	春天	11	spring
chūshēng (v)	出生	5	to be born
cì (MW)	次	12	time, occasion
cóng (prep)	从	5	from
cōngming (adj)	聪明	9	clever, intelligent

Pinyin (alphabetical order)	Characters	Unit	English
cù *(n)*	醋	22	vinegar; jealousy (as in love affairs)
cuòshī *(n)*	措施	11	measure
cuòwù *(n)*	错误	21	mistake, error
dà *(adj)*	大	9	big, old (of age)
dà bízi *(adj; n)*	大鼻子	21	big nose
dǎ diànhuà *(v-o)*	打电话	17	to telephone
dǎ pái *(v-o)*	打牌	11	to play cards or mahjong
dǎ tàijíquán *(v-o)*	打太极拳	11	to do taijiquan
dàbùfen	大部分	11	most
dàgài *(adv)*	大概		probably
dāi *(v)*	呆	12	to stay
dài *(v)*	带	20	to bring, take
dài *(v)*	戴	21	to wear (see 21.8)
dàibǔ *(v)*	逮捕		to arrest
dàjiā *(pr)*	大家	11	everybody
dǎkāi *(v)*	打开	22	to open (up); switch on
dàngāo *(n)* [kuài'r]	蛋糕 [块儿]	20	cake
dāngrán *(adv)*	当然	10	of course, naturally
dāng xīn/xiǎo xīn *(v-o)*	当心/小心	20	to take care, be careful
dānrénchuáng *(n)*	单人床	7	(single) bed
dànshi *(conj)*	但是	5	but
dào *(v)*	到	18	arrive, go to
-dào *(RVE)*	–到	10	to manage to do the action of the verb, up to
dào . . . qù/lái	到...去/来	9	to go/come to; to arrive (see 20.3)
dào(shì) *(adv)*	到(是)	12	indeed, as it happens (indicates something contrary to the general train of thought)
dàochù *(PW)*	到处	10	everywhere
dǎoyóujī *(n)* [tái]	导游机[台]	19	audioguide

Pinyin (alphabetical order)	Characters	Unit	English
dǎoyóutú *(n)*	导游图	19	*tourist map*
dāozi *(n)* [**bǎ**]	刀子[把]	7	*knife*
dǎrǎo *(v)*	打扰	12	*to disturb*
dàshēng(de) *(adv)*	大声(地)	10	*loudly*
dǎsuàn *(v)*	打算	22	*to intend, plan*
dǎyìnjī *(n)* [**tái**]	打印机[台]	7	*printer*
dé *(v)*	得	20	*to get (e.g. interest, sick)*
-de	…的	6	*see 6.2*
… de shíhou *(conj)*	…的时候	10	*when …*
Déguó *(N)*	德国		*Germany*
děi *(aux. v)*	得	8	*must, need*
děng *(v)*	等	19	*to wait*
děng (děng) *(n)*	等(等)	9	*and so on, etc.*
dì	第	12	*ordinal prefix*
diǎn *(n)*	点	12	*point, aspect*
diǎn zhōng *(MW + n)*	点钟	4	*o'clock*
diàndēng *(n)*	电灯	7	*electric light*
diànhuà(jī) *(n)* [**tái**]	电话(机)[台]	7	*telephone*
diànnǎo *(n)*	电脑	7	*PC*
diànnǎoyóuxì *(n)*	电脑游戏	10	*computer game*
diànshàn *(n)*	电扇	7	*electric fan*
diànshì (jī) *(n)* [**tái**]	电视(机) [台]	8	*television*
diànxiàn *(n)* [**gēn**]	电线 [根]	7	*electric cable*
diànyǐng *(n)*	电影	16	*film*
dìdi *(n)*	弟弟	19	*younger brother*
dìfang *(n)*	地方	8	*place*
dìlǐ *(n)*	地理		*geography*
dǐng *(v)*	顶	22	*to go against*
dìng *(v)*	订	12	*to order (in advance); to book, reserve; to subscribe to*
dìngqī cúnkuǎn zhànghù *(n)*	定期存款 账户	20	*deposit account*
dìtǎn *(n)* [**kuài**]	地毯 [块]	7	*carpet*
dìtú *(n)*	地图	15	*map*

Pinyin (alphabetical order)	Characters	Unit	English
diū (v)	丢	19	to lose
dìzhǐ (n)	地址	20	address
dōng	东	18	east
-dǒng (RVE; v)	一懂	12	-ing with understanding; to understand
dōng(bianr) (PW)	东(边)儿	18	east (side)
dōngtiān (n)	冬天	11	winter
dōngxi (n)	东西	15	thing(s)
dōu (adv)	都	5	both, all
dú shū (v-o)	读书	8	to study
duǎn (adj)	短	11	short (in length)
duàn (v)	断	10	to break
duì (adj)	对	5	correct
duì X lái shuō	对X来说	12	as far as X is concerned
duìbuqǐ	对不起	20	sorry, excuse me
duìfu (v)	对付	11	to deal with
duìmiàn (PW)	对面	18	opposite
duō (adj; adv)	多	6	more; many
duō (num)	多	12	used to express an approximate number
duō	多	22	how
duō dehěn (adj)	多得很	22	very many
duōshao (QW)	多少	15	how many, how much
è (adj)	饿	5	hungry
èr (num)	二	15	two (number)
ěrjī (n)	耳机	19	headphone(s)
èrlóu	二楼	7	first floor
érqiě (conj)	而且	19	moreover
érzi (n)	儿子	8	son
fā (v)	发	22	to send (email, fax etc.)
Fǎguó (N)	法国		France
fàncài (n)	饭菜	9	food
fàndiàn (n)	饭店	9	restaurant
fǎn'ér (conj)	反而	11	on the contrary

Pinyin (alphabetical order)	Characters	Unit	English
fàng jià *(v-o)*	放假	21	*have a holiday or vacation*
fàng xīn *(v-o)*	放心	17	*to set one's mind at rest*
fángjiān *(n)*	房间	8	*room*
fāngmiàn *(n)*	方面	11	*aspect, respect*
fǎnguòlái	反过来		*conversely*
fángzi *(n)* [suǒ/ge]	房子[所/个]	8	*house*
fàntīng *(n)*	饭厅	7	*dining room*
fāxiàn *(v)*	发现	12	*to discover*
fāyīn *(n)*	发音	12	*pronunciation*
fāzhǎn *(v)*	发展	21	*to develop*
fēicháng *(adv)*	非常	6	*extremely*
fēijī *(n)* [jià]	飞机[架]	17	*aeroplane*
fēijīchǎng *(n)*	飞机场	22	*airport*
fèijìn(r) *(adj)*	费劲(儿)	22	*strenuous, energy consuming*
Fēizhōu *(N)*	非洲		*Africa*
fēn *(MW)*	分	15	*portion; MW for money; (a) minute*
fèn *(MW)*	份	15	*a copy; portion*
fēng *(n)*	风	22	*wind*
fēnháng *(n)*	分行	20	*branch (bank)*
fēnzhōng *(n)*	分钟	19	*minute*
fú rú Dōnghǎi	福如东海	22	*as blessed as the Eastern Sea*
fūfù *(n)*	夫妇	20	*husband and wife*
fùmǔ *(n)*	父母	9	*parents*
fūrén *(n)*	夫人	22	*Mrs; Madame (formal)*
fúwù *(n; v)*	服务	11	*service; to serve*
fùzá *(adj)*	复杂		*complex*
fúzhuāng/yīfū diàn *(n)*	服装/衣服店	20	*clothes shop*
gǎi *(v)*	改	21	*to alter, change, correct*
gān bēi *(v-o)*	干杯	22	*drink a toast*
gāngcái *(TW)*	刚才	12	*just now*
gānjìng *(adj)*	干净	19	*clean*
gǎnjué *(n)*	感觉	21	*feeling, sense*

Pinyin (alphabetical order)	Characters	Unit	English
gāo (adj)	高	6	tall, high
gàobié (v-o)	告别	22	to take leave of
gàosu (v)	告诉		to tell
gāoxìng (adj)	高兴	2	happy
gè (MW)	个	3	see 3.1
gēge (n)	哥哥	9	elder brother
gègè (adj)	各个	21	each, every
gěi (prep; v)	给	5	for; give
gēn (prep; conj)	跟	10	with; and
gēn X xiāngduì de	跟 X相对的	11	in contrast to/with, contrary to, relative to
gēn (X) yìqǐ	跟 (X)一起	19	together (with X)
gēn . . . yíyàng	跟...一样	20	to be the same as (see 20.1)
gèng (adv)	更	9	even more, still more
gèrén (n)	个人		individual
gèzhǒnggèyàng de (p)	各种各样的	21	all kinds of
gōnggòng (adj)	公共	11	public
gōnggòngqìchē (n)	公共汽车	11	bus (Lit. public together steam vehicle)
gōngrén (n)	工人		worker
gōngyuán (n)	公园	11	park
gōngyù(lóu) (n) [zhuàng]	公寓(楼) [幢]	7	apartment block
gōngzī (n)	工资		wages
gōngzuò (v; n)	工作	5	to work; work
gǒu (n)	狗		dog
guài (adj)	怪		strange
guàng dà jiē (v-o)	逛大街	11	to go window shopping
guǎngchǎng (n)	广场	18	square
guāngpán bōfàngjī (n)	光盘播放机	7	CD player
guàntóu (n)	罐头	7	tin/can
gǔdiǎn (adj)	古典		classical
Gǔgē (N)	谷歌	11	Google

Pinyin (alphabetical order)	Characters	Unit	English
Gùgōng *(N)*	故宫	18	the Forbidden City (the Imperial Palace)
guì *(adj)*	贵	9	expensive
guìxìng? *(Lit. expensive name)*	贵姓	17	what is (your/her . . .) name?
guò *(v)*	过	8	to pass, to cross
-guo	过	9	verbal suffix (see 9.1)
guōjià *(n)*	锅架	7	hob
guójiā *(n;v)*	国家	11	country; national
guòjiǎng	过奖	12	you flatter me
guónèi *(adj)*	国内	19	internal, domestic
guówài *(adj)*	国外	19	abroad, overseas
gùshi *(n)*	故事	10	story
hāhā *(onom)*	哈哈	22	ha ha
hái *(adv)*	还	8	still, in addition
hài *(v)*	害		to harm/persecute
háishi *(conj)*	还是	8	or (used in questions)
háishi *(adv)*	还是	12	after all, still (emphatic)
háizi *(n)*	孩子	8	child
hǎn *(v)*	喊	21	to shout, cry out
hángyè *(n)*	行业	11	trade, profession
Hángzhōu *(N)*	杭州	21	Hangzhou
Hànyǔ *(n)*	汉语	5	Chinese language
Hànzì *(n)*	汉字	12	Chinese character(s)
hǎo *(adj)*	好	1	good
-hǎo *(RVE)*	–好	12	to do the action of the verb satisfactorily
hào *(n)*	号	16	number, date
hào *(n)*	号	20	size (number; date in Unit 16)
hǎochī *(adj)*	好吃	8	tasty, delicious
hǎokàn *(adj)*	好看	10	nice looking
hē *(v)*	喝	1	to drink
hé *(conj)*	和	8	and
héhuǒ(r) *(v-o)*	合伙(儿)	21	form a company or partnership

Pinyin (alphabetical order)	Characters	Unit	English
hěn *(adv)*	很	*1*	*very*
héng *(adj)*	横	*17*	*horizontal*
héshi *(adj)*	合适		*suitable*
hézī qǐyè *(n)* [jiā]	合资企业 [家]	*20*	*joint venture*
hóng *(adj)*	红	*22*	*red*
hóngchá *(n)*	红茶	*7*	*Indian tea*
hòu huì yǒu qī	后会有期	*22*	*we'll meet again some day*
hòubianr *(PW)*	后边儿	*18*	*back, behind*
hòunián *(TW)*	后年	*22*	*the year after next*
huā *(n)* [duǒ]	花 [朵]	*7*	*flowers*
huà *(n)* [jù]	话 [句]	*21*	*remark, word(s)*
huá bīng *(v-o)*	滑冰		*to skate*
huá xuě *(v-o)*	滑雪		*to ski*
huà(r) *(n)* [zhāng, fú]	画(儿) [张，幅]	*7*	*picture*
huāchá *(n)*	花茶	*7*	*jasmine tea*
huài *(adj)*	坏	*21*	*bad; broken*
huàn *(v)*	换	*20*	*to change*
huānyíng *(v)*	欢迎	*8*	*to welcome*
huāpíng *(n)*	花瓶	*7*	*vase*
huàtí *(n)*	话题	*20*	*topic of conversation*
huāyuán *(n)*	花园	*7*	*communal garden*
huí *(v)*	回	*8*	*to return*
huì *(aux v)*	会	*2*	*to know how to; can; will*
huíchéng *(n)*	回程	*17*	*return journey*
Huìfēng Yínháng *(N)*	汇丰银行	*20*	*HSBC (Bank)*
hújiāo *(n)*	胡椒	*7*	*pepper*
huò (zhě) *(conj; adv)*	或(者)	*11*	*or; perhaps*
huóqī cúnkuǎn zhànghù *(n)*	活期存款 账户	*20*	*current account*
jǐ *(QW)*	几	*3*	*how many (less than ten)*
jǐ *(adv; v)*	挤	*11*	*crowded; to squeeze*
jǐ *(num)*	几	*18*	*several*

Pinyin (alphabetical order)	Characters	Unit	English
jì (v)	寄	19	to post, mail
jì xiàlai (v + DE)	记下来	17	to note down; to record
jiā (n) (MW)	家	4	home; family; measure word for restaurant
jiǎ	甲	18	A (the first of the Ten Heavenly Stems)
jiān (MW)	间	8	for room
jiàn (MW)	件	15	MW for piece, article, item
jiàn (n)	键	19	key (as on piano or keypad)
jiàn (v)	见	9	to see; to meet
jiǎng (v)	讲	10	to tell (a story); to speak; to explain
jiàngyóu (n)	酱油	7	soya sauce
jiànkāng (adj)	健康	22	healthy, sound
jiànwén (n)	见闻	21	what one sees and hears
jiànxíng (n)	饯行	22	give a farewell dinner
jiànyì (n; v)	建议	20	suggestion, recommendation; to propose, suggest
jiǎo (n) [zhi]	脚 [只]	20	foot
jiào (v)	叫	17	to be called; to call
jiāo gěi (v)	交给	19	to hand to
jiàotáng (n)	教堂		church
jiàoyù (n; v)	教育	21	education; to educate
jiǎozi (n)	饺子	19	dumplings (filled with meat or vegetables)
jiē (v)	接	17	take hold of, receive; to meet
jié hūn (v-o)	结婚	3	to marry, to get married
jiějie (n)	姐姐		elder sister
jièjìkǎ (n) [zhāng]	借记卡[张]	20	debit/switch card
jiěmǎqì (n)	解码器	7	decoder/digibox
jièmo (n)	芥末	7	mustard
jièshào (v)	介绍	5	to introduce
jiēshi (adj)	结实	10	strong, sturdy

Pinyin (alphabetical order)	Characters	Unit	English
jīguān (n)	机关	11	offices, organization
jīhuì (n)	机会	22	opportunity, chance
jìjié (n)	季节	11	season
jíle (adj)	...极了	6	extremely (adj)
jīn (n)	斤	15	catty
jìn (adj)	近	18	near
jìn (v)	进		to enter
jìng (v)	敬	22	to propose (a toast), toast
jǐngchá (n)	警察		police
jīngcháng (TW)	经常		regularly, frequently
jǐnggào (v)	警告		to warn
jīngshén (adj; n)	精神	11	spiritual; spirit, mind
jìngzi (n) [kuài, miàn]	镜子 [块，面]	7	mirror
jīnnián (TW)	今年	11	this year
jīntiān (TW)	今天	6	today
jīntiān wǎnshang (TW)	今天晚上	19	this evening
jǐnzǎo (adv)	尽早	22	as soon as possible, at the earliest possible date
jìshù (n)	技术	6	technique
jiǔ (num)	九	15	nine
jiǔ (n)	酒	2	alcohol
jiù (adv)	就	4	then; just, only, merely
jiǔbēi (n)	酒杯	7	wineglass
jiǔpíng (n)	酒瓶	7	wine bottle
jiùshì	就是	12	(be) precisely
juéde (v)	觉得	9	to feel
juédìng (v)	决定	9	to decide
juéduì (adj; adv)	绝对	22	absolute(ly)
jùlèbu (n)	俱乐部		social club
júzi-zhī (n)	橘子汁	2	orange juice
kāfēi (n)	咖啡	1	coffee
kāfēihú (n)	咖啡壶	7	coffee filter machine
kāi (v)	开	11	to start; to open; to drive

Pinyin (alphabetical order)	Characters	Unit	English
kāi chē (v-o)	开车	11	to drive a car
kāi chē de (n)	开车的	22	a person who drives, driver
kāi ge zhànghù (v-o)	开个账户	20	to open a (bank) account
kāiguān (n)	开关	7	switch
kāishǐ (v)	开始	12	to begin
kàn (v)	看	8	to look; to see; to watch; to read
kàn de jiàn (RV)	看得见	19	to be able to see
kàn diànshì (v-o)	看电视	19	to watch television
kān háizi (v-o)	看孩子	9	to babysit
kǎojià (n)	烤架	7	grill
kǎoxiāng (n)	烤箱	7	oven
kǎoyā (n)	烤鸭	9	roast duck
kǎoyā diàn (n)	烤鸭店	9	roast duck restaurant
kě (adv)	可	21	emphasizes tone of speaker
kěbúshì	可不是	21	exactly; that's just the way it is
Kěndéjī (N)	肯德基	9	Kentucky Fried Chicken
kěndìng (adj; adv; v)	肯定	21	definite(ly); affirm
kèqi (adj)	客气	6	polite (Lit. guest air)
kěshì (conj)	可是	9	but
kètīng (n)	客厅	8	living room, lounge
kěxī	可惜	11	it's a pity that
kěyǐ (aux v)	可以	8	can, may
kōngtiáo (n)	空调	7	air conditioning
kū (v)	哭	10	to cry, weep
kuài (adj)	快	8	quick, fast
kuài (MW)	块	15	MW for money
kuài . . . le	快…了	17	see 17.3
kuàicān (n)	快餐	9	fast food
kuàikuài de (adv)	快快地	10	hurriedly
kuàilè (adj)	快乐	10	happy, joyful
kuàizi (n)	筷子	6	chopsticks
kùnnan (adj; n)	困难	12	difficult; difficulty

Pinyin (alphabetical order)	Characters	Unit	English
lā *(v)*	拉	21	to pull; to play (of stringed instruments)
lái *(v)*	来	3	to come
làngmàn *(adj)*	浪漫		romantic
lǎo *(adj)*	老	8	old
lǎo *(adj)*	老	10	always
lǎogōng *(n)*	老公		husband (coll)
lǎohǔ *(n)*	老虎		tiger
láojià	劳驾	18	excuse me
lǎorén *(n)*	老人	11	old people
lǎoshī *(n)*	老师	11	teacher
lǎowài *(n)*	老外	21	'old foreigner'
le	了	3	modal particle
le	了	5	new situation
le	了	17	modal particle
lèi *(adj)*	累	10	tired
lěng *(adj)*	冷	11	cold
lěngpán *(n)*	冷盘	22	cold dish; hors d'oeuvre
lí *(prep)*	离	18	(distance) from
lǐ *(n+)*	里	5	inside (+ n)
liǎ *(num MW)*	俩	4	two
liǎn *(n)*	脸	22	face
liáng *(adj)*	凉	6	cool
liǎng *(num)*	两	3	two (of a kind)
liángtái *(n)*	凉台	7	balcony
liánhuānhuì *(n)*	联欢会	22	get-together, party
liànxí *(v; n)*	练习	19	to practise; practice, exercise
liáo tiān(r) *(v-o)*	聊天(儿)	11	to chat
liǎojiě *(v)*	了解	21	to find out, understand, know
líkāi *(v)*	离开	22	to leave
lǐmào *(adj; n)*	礼貌	21	courteous; manners
líng *(num)*	零	17	zero
lìng(wài) *(adj; adv)*	另(外)	11	another; separately
lǐngdài *(n)*	领带		tie

Pinyin (alphabetical order)	Characters	Unit	English
línyù (n)	淋浴	7	shower
lǐpǐndiàn (n)	礼品店	19	souvenir shop
liú (v)	留	17	to reserve for someone; remain; let grow
liù (num)	六	15	six
liúxíng (adj)	流行	11	popular, fashionable
lìwài (n)	例外		exception
lǐwù (n)	礼物	22	present, gift
lìxi (n)	利息	20	interest (on a (bank) account)
lóngtou (n)	龙头	7	tap
lóutī (n)	楼梯	7	stairs, staircase
lóuxià (PW)	楼下	16	downstairs
lù yīn (v-o)	录音		record, recording, tape
lǜ (adj)	绿		green
lǜchá (n)	绿茶	7	Chinese (green) tea
Lúndūn (N)	伦敦		London
lùrén (n)	路人	18	passer-by; stranger
lǚtú (n)	旅途	21	journey, trip
lǚxíng (v)	旅行	11	to travel
lǚxíngshè (n)	旅行社	17	travel agency
lǚyóu (n; v)	旅游	21	tourism, to tour
ma	吗	2	question particle
mǎ (n)	马		horse
mà (v)	骂		to curse, swear
máfan (n/v; adj)	麻烦	8	trouble, troublesome
mǎi (v)	买	15	buy
mǎi dōngxi (v-o)	买东西	15	go shopping
mài (v)	卖	17	to sell
Màidāngláo (N)	麦当劳	9	McDonald's
māma (n)	妈妈	5	Mum, mama
màn (adj)	慢	8	slow
mǎn zài ér guī	满载而归	22	return with fruitful results
mǎnzú (v)	满足	11	to satisfy
máo (MW)	毛	15	MW for money

Pinyin (alphabetical order)	Characters	Unit	English
Máo Zhǔxí Jìniàntáng (N)	毛主席纪念堂	18	Mao Zedong (Chairman Mao) Mausoleum
máojīnjià (n)	毛巾架	7	towel rail
máoyī (n)	毛衣	15	sweater, woolly
màozi (n) [dǐng]	帽子 [顶]		hat
mápó dòufu (n)	麻婆豆腐	19	spicy beancurd/tofu
méi (neg)	没	3	not (only used with **yǒu**)
měi (p/adj)	每	9	each, every
méi (yǒu) guānxi	没(有)关系	6	it doesn't matter
méi (yǒu) shénme	没(有)什么	8	it's nothing
Měiguó (N)	美国	5	America (USA)
mèimei (n)	妹妹	9	younger sister
měirén (n)	美人	21	beautiful woman
mén (n)	门	7	door
mǐ (MW; n)	米	15	metre; rice
miǎnfèi (v; adj)	免费	11	to be free of charge; free
miànfěn (n)	面粉	7	flour
miànjīn/máojīn (n) [kuài, tiáo]	面巾/毛巾 [块，条]	7	face flannel
miàntiáo (n)	面条	19	noodles
mìmì (adj)	秘密		secret
míngnián (TW)	明年	22	next year
míngpiàn (n)	名片	20	visiting card, calling card
míngtiān (TW)	明天	3	tomorrow
míngxiǎn (adj)	明显	11	obvious
míngxìnpiàn (n) [zhāng]	明信片 [张]	19	postcard
míngzi (n)	名字	17	(given) name
mínzú (n)	民族		nation
mótuōchē (n)	摩托车		motorbike
mǔyǔ (n)	母语	12	mother tongue
na	哪	22	particle showing mood
nǎ or **něi** (QW)	哪	5	which?

Pinyin (alphabetical order)	Characters	Unit	English
nà or **nèi** (dem p/adj)	那	4	that
ná chū (RV)	拿出	19	to take out
nà xiē or **nèi xiē** (dem pp)	那些	9	those
nàme	那么	1	in that case, so
nán (adj)	男	3	male
nán	南	18	south
nán (adj)	难	10	difficult
nánguò (v)	难过	22	to be upset, to be sad
nánkàn (adj)	难看	10	ugly
nàozhōng (n)	闹钟	7	alarm clock
nǎr (QW)	哪儿	3	where
nàr (nàlǐ) (PW)	那儿 (那里)	18	there
ne	呢	2	question particle
néng (aux v)	能	9	to be able to, can
ǹg (interj)	嗯	6	hm
nǐ (ps)	你	1	you
niánqīng (adj)	年轻		young
niánqīngrén (n)	年轻人	11	young person/people
Niǎocháo Guójiā Tǐyùchǎng (N)	鸟巢国家体育场	19	Bird's Nest National Stadium
nǐmen (pp)	你们	2	you (pl)
nín (ps)	您	2	you (polite)
niúnǎi (N)	牛奶		milk
Niǔyuē (n)	纽约		New York
nóngsuō kāfēi (n)	浓缩咖啡	20	espresso coffee
nǚ (adj)	女	3	female
nǚ'ér (n)	女儿	8	daughter
nuǎnhuo (adj)	暖和	22	warm
nuǎnqì (n)	暖气	7	central heating
nuǎnqìpiàn (n)	暖气片	7	radiator
nǔlì (v)	努力		to work hard (at)
Ōuzhōu (N)	欧洲	11	Europe

Pinyin (alphabetical order)	Characters	Unit	English
pà (v)	怕	21	to fear, be afraid of
pái (n)	排	16	row, line
pàng (adj; v)	胖	10	fat; to be fat
pángbianr (n)	旁边儿	21	side
pǎo (v)	跑		to run
péi (v)	陪	8	to accompany
pèi-shàng (v)	配上	20	to be worthy of/deserve
pèi bu shàng (RV)	配不上	20	not to be worthy of, not to deserve
péngyou (n)	朋友	3	friend
piàn (v)	骗		to deceive
piānjiàn (n)	偏见	21	prejudice, bias
piányi (adj)	便宜	9	cheap
piào (n)	票	16	ticket
piàoliang (adj)	漂亮	8	beautiful
píjiǔ (n)	啤酒	12	beer
píng (MW)	瓶	22	for bottles
píngcháng (adv; adj)	平常	11	usually; ordinary, commonplace
píngguǒ (n)	苹果	10	apple
píngmiàn (n)	平面	8	flat screen
píngzi (n)	瓶子	7	bottle
píqi (n)	脾气		temperament
pútáojiǔ (n)	葡萄酒	22	wine
pǔtōnghuà (n)	普通话	12	common spoken language (Modern Standard Chinese; Mandarin)
qī (num)	七	15	seven
qí (v)	骑	10	to ride (as of bicycle, horse)
qǐ (v)	起	10	to get up, rise
qián (n)	钱	15	money
qiánbāo (n)	钱包	19	purse, wallet
qiánbianr (PW)	前边儿	18	front, in front of
Qiánmén (N)	前门	18	Qianmen

Pinyin (alphabetical order)	Characters	Unit	English
qìchē (n)	汽车		car
qǐfēi (v)	起飞	22	to take off (of aircraft)
qíguài (adj)	奇怪	11	strange
qìhòu (n)	气候	11	climate
-qǐlai (RVE)	–起来	12	see 12.13
qíng (adj)	晴	11	(of weather) fine, clear, bright
qǐng (v)	请	1	to invite
qīngchu (adj; RVE)	清楚	8	clear; clearly
Qīngdǎo (N)	青岛	12	Qingdao
qíngkuàng (n)	情况	21	situation, state of affairs
qīnmì (adj)	亲密	21	close, intimate
qīnzì (adv)	亲自	19	in person, personally
qióng rén (n)	穷人		poor person
qítā (pr)	其他/其它	11	other
qiūtiān (n)	秋天	11	autumn
qǔ (v)	取	17	to get, fetch; withdraw (money)
qù (v)	去	4	to go
quēdiǎn (n)	缺点		shortcoming
quèshí (adv; adj)	确实	22	really, indeed; true, certain
qǔkuǎnjī (n)	取款机	20	ATM (automatic teller machine)
ràng (v)	让	10	to let, allow
rè (adj)	热	11	hot
rén (n)	人	17	person
rènào (adj)	热闹	11	bustling; exciting
rénjiān lèyuán (n)	人间乐园	21	paradise on earth
Rénmín Dàhuìtáng (N)	人民大会堂	18	Great Hall of the People
Rénmín Yīngxióng Jìniànbēi (N)	人民英雄纪念碑	18	Monument to the People's Heroes
rénmínbì (n)	人民币	17	RMB (Chinese currency)
rènshi (v)	认识	2	to know, recognize
rènwéi (v)	认为	21	to think, consider

Pinyin (alphabetical order)	Characters	Unit	English
rényuán (n)	人员	11	personnel, staff
rèqíng (adj)	热情	8	warm hearted, enthusiastic
rèshuǐpíng (n)	热水瓶	7	Thermos flask
Rìběn (N)	日本		Japan
rìchū (n)	日出	16	sunrise
rìqī (n)	日期	17	date
Rìwén(de) (n)	日文(的)	19	Japanese language
rìyuè rú suō	日月如梭	22	how time flies (see 22.4)
róngyì (adj)	容易	12	easy
rǔyá (n) [kē]	乳牙[颗]	10	milk tooth
sāizi (n)	塞子	7	plug
sān (num)	三	15	three
sàn bù (v-o)	散步	11	to take a walk, to stroll
sānlóu (n)	三楼	7	second floor (UK usage)
sānmíngzhì (n)	三明治	21	sandwich
sǎo xìng (v-o)	扫兴	10	to deflate somebody's feelings
shāfā (n)	沙发	7	sofa
shài tàiyáng (v-o)	晒太阳		to sunbathe
shàng bān (v-o)	上班	11	to go to work
shàng kè (v-o)	上课	11	to attend class
shāngdiàn (n)	商店	11	shop
shàngjí (n)	上级		superior
shǎnguāngdēng (n)	闪光灯	22	flash (light)
shǎo (adv, adj)	少	6	less; few
sháozi (n)	勺子	7	spoon
shèbèi (n)	设备	19	facilities, equipment
shěbude (v)	舍不得	22	be unwilling to part with, grudge
shéi (QW)	谁		who
shēngdiào (n)	声调	12	tone
shēnghuó (n, v)	生活	5	life; to live
shēnghuó fāngshì (n)	生活方式	11	way of life, lifestyle
shēnghuō fēi (n)	生活费		cost of living

Pinyin (alphabetical order)	Characters	Unit	English
shēngrì (n)	生日	22	birthday
shénme shíhou (QW)	什么时候		when
shēnshang (adv)	身上	20	on one's person (Lit. body)
shēntǐ (n)	身体		health, body
shī (n) [shǒu]	诗 [首]		poem
shí (num)	十	15	ten
shì (v)	是	2	to be
shì . . . de	是...的	5	see 5.7
shífēn (adv)	十分	21	extremely, very
shīgē (n)	诗歌	7	poetry
shíjiān (n)	时间	8	time (length of)
shìjiè (n)	世界	11	world
shímáo (adj)	时髦	9	fashionable
shì'r/shì(qing) (n) [jiàn]	事(儿)/事(情) [件]	10	matter, thing
shìyè (n)	事业	21	undertaking, cause
shǒu (n)	手	21	hand
shòu (adj)	瘦		slim
Shòu bǐ Nánshān	寿比南山	22	May you live as long as the Southern Mountain
shòu bù liǎo (RV)	受不了	22	be unable to bear or endure
shōu (hǎo) (v)	收 (好)	19	to put away; to receive
shōuhuò (n)	收获	22	gains, results, harvest
shòuhuòyuán (n)	售货员	15	shop assistant
shǒujī (n)	手机	7	mobile phone
shòupiàochù (n)	售票处	19	ticket office
shòupiàoyuán (n)	售票员	16	box office clerk; ticket seller
shōuyīnjī (n) [tái, ge]	收音机 [台，个]	7	radio
shū (n) [běn]	书 [本]	7	book
shù (n) [kē]	树 [棵]	7	tree
shù (adj)	竖	17	vertical
shuā yá (v-o)	刷牙	10	to brush one's teeth
shuāngrénchuáng (n) [zhāng]	双人床 [张]	7	double bed
shūfáng (n)	书房	7	study

Pinyin (alphabetical order)	Characters	Unit	English
shuǐ (n)	水		water
shuǐdiànfèi (n)	水电费		water and electricity charges
shuì(jiào) (v[-o])	睡(觉)	10	to sleep, go to bed
shuǐjiǎo (n)	水饺	9	boiled dumpling
shuǐpíng (n)	水平	12	level, standard
shuǐtǒng (n)	水桶	7	pail, bucket
shūjià (n)	书架	7	bookcase
shū-jìn (RV)	输进	19	to input into
shùmǎ (adj)	数码	8	digital
shùmǎ diànshì(jī) (n) [tái]	数码电视(机) [台]	7	digital television
shùmǎxiàngjī (n)	数码相机	21	digital camera
shuō (v)	说	6	to speak
shuō huà (v-o)	说话	6	to speak, talk
shuōfǎ (n)	说法		way of saying things
shūzhuō (n)	书桌，办公桌	7	desk
shūzi (n) [bǎ]	梳子 [把]	7	brush or comb
shùzì (n)	数字	19	number, digit, numeral
shùzìshìpán bōfàngjī (n)	数字视盘播放机	7	DVD player
-sǐ (RVE)	–死	19	to be extremely the action of the verb
sì (num)	四	15	four
sì shēng (n)	四声	12	the four tones
sīchóu (n)	丝绸	15	silk
sìlóu (n)	四楼	7	third floor (UK usage)
sīxiǎng (n)	思想	11	thinking, ideology
sòng (v)	送	17	send; give as a present; see somebody off
Sū、Háng (N)	苏、杭	21	Suzhou and Hangzhou
suàn (v)	算	22	to regard as, count as
Sūgélán (N)	苏格兰		Scotland
súhuà (n) [jù]	俗话 [句]	21	common saying, proverb
suì (n)	岁	3	year (of age)

Pinyin (alphabetical order)	Characters	Unit	English
suíbiàn *(adv; v)*	随便	5	*do as one pleases*
suīrán *(conj)*	虽然	11	*although*
suǒyǐ *(conj)*	所以	8	*therefore*
tā *(ps)*	他	2	*he, she, it*
tā *(ps)*	它	21	*it*
tài *(adv)*	太	4	*too, extremely*
táidēng *(n)*	台灯	7	*table lamp*
tàitai *(n)*	太太	2	*Mrs, wife*
Táiwān *(N)*	台湾		*Taiwan*
tàiyángjìng *(n)* [副]	太阳镜 [副]	21	*sunglasses*
tāmen *(pp)*	他们	2	*they, them*
tán huà *(v-o; n)*	谈话	8	*to chat; conversation*
tán tiān *(v-o)*	谈天		*chit chat; have a chat*
táng *(n)*	糖	7	*sugar*
tàngyījià *(n)*	烫衣架	7	*ironing board*
tǎnshuài(de) *(adj; adv)*	坦率(地)	21	*frank(ly)*
tǎnzi *(n)* [tiáo]	毯子 [条]	7	*blanket*
tào *(MW)*	套	15	*set*
tè ài *(v)*	特爱	19	*to especially like/love*
tèbié *(adv; adj)*	特别	11	*specially, special*
tèsè *(n)*	特色	9	*characteristic, special feature*
tiān *(v)*	添	8	*to add, increase*
tiān *(n)*	天		*day*
tián *(adj)*	甜	22	*sweet*
Tiān'ān *(N)*	天安	17	*Heavenly Peace*
Tiān'ānmén Guǎngchǎng *(N)*	天安门广场	18	*Tiananmen Square*
tiānqì *(n)*	天气	11	*weather*
tiānshēng *(adj)*	天生的	20	*born, innate*
Tiāntán *(N)*	天坛	18	*Temple of Heaven*
tiāntáng *(n)*	天堂	21	*heaven, paradise*
tiāntiān *(TW)*	天天	20	*every day (see 20.6)*
tiē(shang) *(v)*	贴(上)	19	*to stick (on)*
tīng *(v)*	听	19	*to listen*

Pinyin (alphabetical order)	Characters	Unit	English
tīng *(n)*	厅	22	hall
tǐng *(adj)*	挺	16	very, rather
tíng(zhǐ) *(v)*	停(止)	10	to stop
tīng-dǒng *(RV)*	听懂	19	to listen with understanding, to understand
tīng qǐlai *(v)*	听起来	21	to sound, ring
tīnglì *(n)*	听力	19	listening comprehension
tīngshuō *(v)*	听说	21	to have heard it said, be told
tíqián *(v)*	提前	22	bring forward a date
tōng huà *(v-o)*	通话	11	to chat (on the phone)
tóngxiāng *(n)*	同乡	21	person who was born in the same place as oneself
tóngxué *(n)*	同学	21	fellow student
tóngyì *(v)*	同意	21	to agree with
tuìxiū *(v)*	退休	9	to retire
wā *(interj)*	哇	9	wow (exclamation)
wàimian *(PW)*	外面	22	outside
-wán *(RVE)*	...完	8	to finish verb -ing
wán(r) *(v)*	玩(儿)	4	to have fun, to play
wǎncān *(n)*	晚餐	22	supper, dinner
wàng *(prep)*	往	18	towards, to
wǎngbā *(n)*	网吧	11	internet café
wàngǔ chángcún	万古长存	22	last forever, be everlasting
wǎngqiú *(n)*	网球		tennis
wánquán *(adj; adv)*	完全	21	complete(ly)
wǎnshang *(TW)*	晚上	4	evening
wànshì rúyì	万事如意	22	your heart's desire
wèi *(MW)*	位	5	for persons (polite)
wèi	喂	17	hello (on telephone)
wèi *(prep)*	为	22	for, for the sake of (formal)
wèi shénme *(conj)*	为什么	9	why
wěiba *(n)*	尾巴		tail
wēibōlú *(n)*	微波炉	7	microwave oven
wèidao *(n)*	味道	22	flavour, taste

Pinyin (alphabetical order)	Characters	Unit	English
wèihūnqī (n)	未婚妻		fiancée
wèile (prep)	为了	22	for the sake of, in order to
Wēinísī (N)	威尼斯	21	Venice
wèishēngzhǐ (n) [juǎn]	卫生纸 [卷]	7	toilet paper
wèn (v)	问	16	ask
wèn lù (v-o)	问路	18	ask the way
wénhuà (n)	文化		culture
wénmíng (adj)	闻名	21	well known, famous
wèntí (n)	问题	11	question, problem
wénzì (n)	文字		written language
wǒ (ps)	我	1	I, me
wǒmen (pp)	我们	2	we, us
wòshì (n)	卧室	7	bedroom
wǔ (num)	五		five
wūdǐng (n)	屋顶	7	roof
wǔdǒuchú/ wǔdǒuguì (n)	五斗橱/ 五斗柜	7	chest of drawers
wūlǐ (PW)	屋里	22	in the room
wūrǎn (n)	污染	11	pollution
xǐ liǎn (v-o)	洗脸	10	to wash one's face
xǐ shǒu (v-o)	洗手	10	to wash one's hands
xī yān、 chōu yān (v)	吸烟、抽烟		to smoke
xià (adj)	下	16	next
xià bān (v-o)	下班		to finish work
xià qí (v-o)	下棋	11	to play chess
xià xuě (v-o)	下雪	11	to snow
xià yǔ (v-o)	下雨	11	to rain
xiàmian (PW)	下面	19	below, bottom, under
xiān (adv)	先	19	first
xiān . . . zài . . . (conj)	先...再...	20	first . . . then (see 20.2)
Xī'ān (N)	西安	17	name of city in NW China

Pinyin (alphabetical order)	Characters	Unit	English
xiàndài(huà) (adj; n)	现代(化)	11	modern, modernized; modernization
xiǎng (aux v; v)	想	4	to feel like doing something; to think
xiàng (v)	像	9	to resemble; like, such as
xiǎng jiā (v-o)	想家	20	to be homesick, to miss home
xiǎng qǐlai (v)	想起来	22	to remember, call to mind
xiàng X jiěshi	向...解释	10	to explain (something) to X
xiāngdāng (adv)	相当	12	quite (a bit)
xiāngfǎn (adj)	相反		opposite
xiānghuì (v)	相会	22	meet one another
xiǎngshòu (v; n)	享受	9	to enjoy rights, etc.; treat
xiāngxìn (v)	相信	20	to be convinced/sure, to believe, have faith in
(xiāng)yān (n)	(香)烟	15	cigarette
xiāngzào (n) [kuài]	香皂 [块]	7	toilet soap
xiànjīn (n)	现金	20	cash
xiànmù (v)	羡慕	19	to envy, admire
xiānsheng (n)	先生	1	Mr, gentleman
xiànzài (TW)	现在	9	now, at present
xiǎo (adj)	小	8	small
xiào (v; n)	笑	20	to smile, laugh
xiǎohái(r) (n)	小孩(儿)	3	child (small)
xiǎohuǒzi (n)	小伙子	21	young fellow
xiǎojie (n)	小姐	5	Ms, young lady
xiǎoshí (n)	小时		hour
xiǎoshuō (n) [běn]	小说 [本]	7	novel
xiàtiān (n)	夏天	11	summer
xiàwǔ (TW)	下午	17	afternoon
xiàyìshí (n)	下意识	21	subconsciousness
xībianr (n)	西边儿	18	west (side)
xiě(zì) (v(-o))	写(字)	12	to write (characters)
xié diàn (n)	鞋店	20	shoe shop
xièxie (v)	谢谢	1	to thank

Pinyin (alphabetical order)	Characters	Unit	English
xīfāngrén *(n)*	西方人	12	westerner
Xīhú *(N)*	西湖	21	West Lake
xǐhuan *(v)*	喜欢	1	to like
xǐliǎnpén *(n)*	洗脸盆	7	washbasin
xīn *(adj)*	新	10	new
xìn *(n)*	信	12	letter
xíng *(v)*	行	1	to be all right
xìng *(v)*	姓	17	(sur)name; to have as a surname
Xīngbākè *(N)*	星巴克	20	Starbucks
xìngfú *(adj; n)*	幸福	22	enjoy good fortune, happy; well-being
xīngqī *(n)*	星期	10	week
xīngqītiān/xīngqīrì *(n)*	星期天/ 星期日	10	Sunday
xìngyùn *(adj)*	幸运	19	lucky, fortunate
xīnlǐ *(n)*	心里	21	in the heart or mind
xìnyòngkǎ *(n)* [zhāng]	信用卡 [张]	20	credit card
xīnxiān *(adj)*	新鲜	21	fresh
xǐshǒujiān *(n)*	洗手间	19	toilet, WC, washroom
xiūxi *(v)*	休息	11	to rest
xǐwǎnchí/ chízi *(n)*	洗碗池/ 池子	7	sink
xīwàng *(v; n)*	希望	9	to hope; hope
xǐwǎnjī *(n)* [tái]	洗碗机 [台]	7	dishwasher
xǐyījī *(n)* [tái]	洗衣机 [台]	8	washing machine
xǐzǎojiān *(n)*	洗澡间	7	bathroom
xǐzǎopén/ yùpén *(n)*	洗澡盆/ 浴盆	7	bath
xuǎnzé *(n; v)*	选择	19	choice; to choose, select
xǔduō *(adj)*	许多	11	many
xué(xí) *(v)*	学(习)	3	to study
xuéshēng *(n)*	学生	11	student
xuéxiào *(n)*	学校	5	school
xūyào *(v; n)*	需要	20	to need, require; needs

Pinyin (alphabetical order)	Characters	Unit	English
yā (interj)	呀	21	indicating surprise
yá(chǐ) (n) [kē]	牙(齿) [颗]	10	tooth
yágāo (n) [tǒng]	牙膏 [筒]	7	toothpaste
yán (n)	盐	7	salt
yángguǐzi (n)	洋鬼子	21	foreign devil
yángwèi(r) (n)	洋味(儿)	12	foreign flavour
yānhuīgāng (n)	烟灰缸	7	ashtray
yǎnjing (n)	眼睛		eye
yánzhòng (adj)	严重	11	serious
yāo (num)	幺	17	one (used orally only)
yào (aux v; v)	要	10	want to, must, to want
yào(shi) . . . (de huà), (jiù) . . . (conj)	要(是) . . . (的话) (就) . . .	11	if . . . then . . .
yàobù(rán) (conj)	要不(然)	6	otherwise
yāoqiú (n; v)	要求	11	demand; to demand, request
yàoshi . . . jiù (conj)	要是 . . . 就	20	if . . . then
yáshuā (n) [bǎ]	牙刷 [把]	7	toothbrush
Yàzhōu (N)	亚洲		Asia
yě (adv)	也	3	also, too
yī (num)	一	2	one
yī . . . jiù . . . (conj)	一 . . . 就 . . .	11	no sooner . . . than . . . ; as soon as
yǐ	乙	18	B (the second of the Ten Heavenly Stems) (see Unit 22)
yí duìr (n)	一对儿	20	a pair, a couple
yìbān (adv; adj)	一般	11	generally; general
yìbān lái shuō	一般来说	21	generally speaking
yìbiān . . . yìbiān (conj)	一边 . . . 一边 . . .	21	see 21.1
Yìdàlì (N)	意大利		Italy
yìdiǎn(r) (n)	一点(儿)	6	a little
yídìng (adv)	一定	5	certainly, definitely
yīfu (n)	衣服	15	clothes

Pinyin (alphabetical order)	Characters	Unit	English
yígòng	一共	15	altogether
yīguì (n)	衣柜	7	wardrobe
yíhàn (v; n)	遗憾	22	to regret, be a pity; regret
yǐhòu (conj; adv)	以后	9	after; afterwards
yíhuìr (TW)	一会儿	10	a short while, (after) a moment
yìjian (n)	意见		opinion
yǐjīng (adv)	已经	9	already
yīlóu	一楼	7	ground floor (UK usage)
yílù píng'ān	一路平安	22	bon voyage, have a pleasant journey
yīn (adj)	阴	11	cloudy, overcast
Yìndù (N)	印度		India
(yīng)gāi (aux v)	(应)该	8	ought, should
Yīngguó (N)	英国	5	Britain, England
Yīngguórén (n)	英国人	5	British (person)
yǐngjùyuàn (n)	影剧院	16	cinema and theatre (buildings)
Yīngwén(de) (n)	英文(的)	19	English language
yíngyè (v)	营业	11	to do business
Yīngyǔ (n)	英语	12	English language
yínháng (n)	银行	11	bank
yīnwèi (conj)	因为	12	because (also read **yīnwei**)
yīnyuè (n)	音乐		music
yīnyuèhuì (n)	音乐会	16	concert
yìqǐ (adv; PW)	一起	11	together
yǐqián (adv; conj)	以前	9	previously, before
yīshēng (n)	医生		doctor
yíxià	一下	5	see 5.2
(yì)xiē	(一)些	9	some, a few
yíyàng (v; adj; adv)	一样	9	alike, the same
yìzhí	一直	10	to keep on doing something
yǐzi [bǎ]	椅子 [把]	7	chair
yòng (v)	用	6	to use
yǒngyuǎn (adj)	永远	17	forever

Pinyin (alphabetical order)	Characters	Unit	English
yǒu (v)	有	3	to have
yǒu(de)shíhou (TW)	有(的)时候	11	sometimes
yǒu kòng (v-o)	有空	4	to have free time
yǒu shénme bù hǎo?	有什么不好?	10	what's wrong with that?
yǒu yíngyǎng (v-o)	有营养	9	to be nutritious
yǒu yìsi (v-o)	有意思	12	to be interesting
yóuyǒng (v)	游泳		to swim
yòu . . . yòu (conj)	又...又	9	both . . . and . . . (see 9.14)
yǒudeshì	有的是	11	to have plenty of, there's no lack of
yǒuhǎo (adj)	友好	12	friendly
yóujú (n)	邮局	11	post office
yóukè (n)	游客	21	tourist
yóupiào (n)	邮票	15	postage stamp
yǒuyì (n)	友谊	22	friendship
yuǎn (adj)	远	18	far
yuánliàng (v)	原谅	6	to forgive
yuànyi (aux v)	愿意	20	to be willing; to want
yuányīn (n)	原因		cause, reason
yuè (n)	月	11	month
yuè lái yuè	越来越...	11	more and more
yǔfǎ (n)	语法	12	grammar
yùjīn/dà máojīn (n) [kuài]	浴巾/大毛巾 [块]	7	bath towel
yùndòng (n)	运动	19	sports, exercise; (political) movement, campaign
yùndǒu (n)	熨斗	7	iron
yùshi (n)	浴室	7	bathroom
zài (v; prep)	在	3	to be at; at
zài (adv)	再	8	again
zài. . .	在	10	to be in the middle of . . .ing
zàijiàn	再见	8	goodbye
zāng (adj)	脏		dirty

Pinyin (alphabetical order)	Characters	Unit	English
zánmen *(pp)*	咱们	21	we (including listener; see 21.3)
zàntíng *(v)*	暂停	19	to pause
zǎo *(adj)*	早	8	early
zǎo jiù . . . le	早就 . . . 了	9	for a long time now
zāogāo	糟糕	10	what a mess
zǎorì *(TW)*	早日	22	at an early date; soon
zǎoshàng *(TW)*	早上	20	morning (early)
zázhì *(n)* [**běn**]	杂志 [本]	15	magazine
zěnme *(QW)*	怎么	12	how
(zhè shì)zěnme yì huí shì	(这是)怎么一回事	9	why this happens/ happened
zěnmeyàng *(QW)*	怎么样	4	what about (it)?, how?
zhàn *(v; n)*	站	22	to stand; station, stop (bus etc.)
zhāng *(MW)*	张	15	MW for flat, rectangular objects
zhǎngchū *(v)*	长出	10	to grow
zhǎngdà *(v)*	长大	5	to grow up
zhǎng pàng *(v)*	长胖	10	to get fat
zhǎng shàng diànnǎo *(n)*	掌上电脑	7	palmtop
-zháo *(RVE)*	–着	10	to succeed in doing the action of the verb
zhǎo (qián) *(v(-o))*	找(钱)	15	give back (as of change)
zhào xiàng *(v-o)*	照相	11	to take a picture; to have one's picture/photo taken
zhāodài *(n, v)*	招待	8	hospitality, to entertain
zháojí *(adj)*	着急	10	to worry, to be anxious
zhàoxiàngjī *(n)* [**tái**]	照相机 [台]	21	camera
zhè *or* **zhèi** *(dem p/adj)*	这	2	this
zhè yàng *(dem adj; n)*	这样	12	this kind of, such a

Pinyin (alphabetical order)	Characters	Unit	English
zhēn *(adv; adj)*	真	2	really; true, real
zhèngcháng *(adj)*	正常	11	normal, regular
zhèngfǔ *(n)*	政府	11	government
zhěnggè *(adj)*	整个	11	whole, entire
zhèngmíng *(v; n)*	证明		to prove; proof
zhěngtiān *(TW)*	整天	19	the whole day
zhèngzài . . . ne	正在 . . . 呢	10	in the middle of -ing (see 10.2)
zhěntào *(n)*	枕套	7	pillow case
zhěntou *(n)*	枕头	7	pillow
zhèr *or* zhèlǐ *(PW)*	这儿(这里)	5	here
zhī *(v)*	织		to knit, to weave
zhǐ *(adv)*	只	8	only
zhǐ *(v)*	指	12	to refer to; to point at/to
zhī jiān	之间	22	between, among
zhīdao *(v)*	知道	9	to know (a fact)
zhíde *(v)*	值得	18	to be worth, deserve
zhǐyào *(conj)*	只要	20	so long as, provided
zhíyè *(n)*	职业	21	occupation, profession
zhǒng *(MW)*	种	9	sort, kind
Zhōngguó *(N)*	中国	1	China
Zhōngguó Gémìng Bówùguǎn *(N)*	中国革命博物馆	18	Museum of Revolution (Lit. China Revolution Museum)
Zhōngguó Lìshǐ Bówùguǎn *(N)*	中国历史博物馆	18	Museum of National History
zhōngjiān *(PW)*	中间	18	middle; between
zhōngtóu *(n)*	钟头		hour
Zhōngwén *(n)*	中文	12	Chinese language (usually written form)
zhòngyào *(adj)*	重要	12	important
zhǒngzú *(n)*	种族	21	race
zhōumò *(n)*	周末	11	weekend
zhōuwéi *(n)*	周围	19	around, circumference
zhǔ *(v)*	煮	22	to boil, cook
zhuǎn *(v)*	转	20	to transfer; to turn

Pinyin (alphabetical order)	Characters	Unit	English
zhuānjiā *(n)*	专家		expert
zhùmíng *(adj)*	著名	19	remarkable, well known
zhuōzi *(n)* [zhāng]	桌子 [张]	7	table
zhǔyào *(adj; adv)*	主要	21	principal(ly)
zhǔyì *(n)*	主意	10	idea
zhùyì *(v)*	注意	21	to pay attention to
zì qī qī rén	自欺欺人	21	deceive yourself as well as others
zìdiǎn *(n)* [běn]	字典 [本]	12	dictionary
zìjǐ *(p)*	自己	6	oneself
zǐxì *(adj/adv)*	仔细	19	careful(ly), attentive(ly)
zìxíngchē *(n)* [liàng]	自行车 [辆]	10	bicycle (self-propelling machine)
zìyóu *(n)*	自由		freedom, liberty
zìzài *(adj)*	自在	21	at ease, comfortable
zìzhùcān *(n)*	自助餐	19	self-service (food)
zǒnglǐ *(n)*	总理		premier/prime minister
zǒng(shi) *(adv)*	总(是)	9	always
zǒngtǒng *(n)*	总统		president
zǒu *(v)*	走	8	to leave, to walk, to go
zū *(v)*	租	19	to rent, hire
zúgòu *(adj; v)*	足够	20	enough; to be sufficient
zuì *(adv)*	最	6	most
zuì *(adj)*	醉	22	drunk
zuìhǎo *(adv; adj)*	最好	6	had better; best
zuìhòu *(adj; adv)*	最后	22	the last, finally
zuò *(v)*	坐	1	to sit
zuò *(v)*	做	6	to do, to make
zuò chē *(v-o)*	坐车	11	to go by transport
zuò lǐbài *(v-o)*	做礼拜	11	to go to church
zuótiān *(TW)*	昨天		yesterday

English–Chinese vocabulary

a good many **hǎo jǐ**
a little **yìdiǎn(r)**
a short while, after a moment
  yíhuìr
able to, can **néng**
abroad, overseas **guówài**
absolute(ly) **juéduì**
accompany **péi**
accomplish, get something done
  bàn dào
account (bank) **zhànghù**
add, increase **tiān**
address **dìzhǐ**
admire **pèifú**
admit (e.g. mistake) **chéngrèn**
adopt (measures) **cǎiqǔ**
adult **chéngniánrén** or **dàrén**
aeroplane **fēijī**
after all, still **háishi**
after (conj), afterwards **yǐhòu**
afternoon **xiàwǔ**
again **zài**
age **niánjì**
agree with **tóngyì**
ah, oh **à**
air conditioning **kōngtiáo**
airmail **hángkōng**
airport **fēijīchǎng**
alarm clock **nàozhōng**
alcohol **jiǔ**
alike, the same **yíyàng**
all right **xíng**
all, both **dōu**

almost, nearly **chàbuduō**
already **yǐjīng**
also, too **yě**
alter, change, correct **gǎi**
although **suīrán . . . dànshi**
altogether **yígòng**
always **zǒng (shi), lǎo**
always (doing something) **lǎo**
America, USA **Měiguó**
American (person) **Měiguórén**
ancient **gǔlǎo**
and **hé**
and so on **shénmede**
another, separately **lìng(wài)**
appearance **yàngzi**
apple **píngguǒ**
around, circumference **zhōuwéi**
arrange for something to be done
  bàn shì
arrest **dàibǔ**
arrive, go to **dào**
as far as . . . is concerned
  duì . . . lái shuō
as soon as possible, at the earliest
  possible date **jǐnzǎo**
ash tray **yānhuīgāng**
Asia **Yàzhōu**
ask **wèn**
ask the way **wèn lù**
aspect, respect **fāngmiàn**
at, in **zài**
at an early date, soon **zǎorì**
at ease, comfortable **zìzài**

at the same time; moreover
   tóngshí
ATM **qǔkuǎnjī**
attend, take part in, join **cānjiā**
attend to, handle, do **bàn**
attend class **shàng bān**
attendant **fúwùyuán**
audioguide **dǎoyóujī**
autumn **qiūtiān**

babysit **kān háizi**
back, behind **hòubianr**
bad, broken **huài**
bank **yínháng**
bank account **zhànghu**
Bank of China **Zhōngguó**
   Yínháng
basic(ally) **jīběn (shang)**
bath (tub) **yùpén** or **xǐzǎopén**
bath towel **dà máojīn** or **yùjīn**
   (MW **tiáo**)
bathroom **xǐzǎojiān** or **yùshì**
be **shì**
beat a drum **dǎ gǔ**
beautiful, pretty **piàoliang**
beautiful woman **měirén**
because **yīnwèi (yīnwei)**
become **chéng**
bed **chuáng** (MW **zhāng**)
bedroom **wòshì**
beer **píjiǔ**
Beethoven **Bèiduōfēn**
begin **kāishǐ**
Beijing **Běijīng**
Beijing University **Běijīng Dàxué**
belch, burp, hiccough **dǎ gē(r)**
believe, be sure **xiāngxìn**
best; had better **zuìhǎo**

bicycle **zìxíngchē** (MW **liàng**)
big **dà**
Bird's Nest National Stadium
   Niǎocháo Guójiā Tǐyùchǎng
birthday **shēngrì**
black tea (Indian) **hóngchá**
blanket **tǎnzi**
boat (n) **chuán**
boil, cook **zhǔ**
bon voyage, have a pleasant
   journey **yílù píng'ān**
book **shū**
book, reserve, subscribe to **dìng**
bookcase, bookshelf **shūjià**
borrow; lend **jiè**
both, all **dōu**
both . . . and **yòu . . . yòu**
bottle **píngzi**
box office clerk **shòupiàoyuán**
branch (bank) **fēnháng**
bring forward a date **tíqián**
bring, take **dài**
Britain, England **Yīngguó**
British (person) **Yīngguórén**
brush teeth **shuā yá**
bucket, pail **shuǐtǒng**
burn **shāo**
bus **gōnggòngqìchē** (MW **liàng**)
bustling, exciting **rènao**
but **dànshi** or **kěshì**
but, however, only **búguò**
buy **mǎi**

cake **dàngāo**
call, be called **jiào**
camera **zhàoxiàngjī**
can, know how to **huì**
can, may **kěyǐ**

can (physically able) **néng**
cannot but, have to **bù dé bù**
capital **shǒudū**
car **qìchē** (MW **liàng**)
careful(ly) **zǐxì**
carpet **dìtǎn**
cash **xiànjīn**
catty (½ kilogram) **jīn**
central heating **nuǎnqì**
certainly, definitely **yídìng**
certainty **bǎwò**
certificate, to prove **zhèngmíng**
chair **yǐzi** (MW **bǎ**)
change (clothes, bus etc.) **huàn**
change (verb) **biàn**
change (noun) **biànhuà**
change money **huàn qián**
characteristic **tèsè**
chat **liáo tiān(r)**
chat, conversation **tán huà**
cheap **piányi**
check; investigate **chá**
chest of drawers **wǔdǒuchú** or
    wǔdǒuguì
child **háizi**
child (small) **xiǎohái**
China **Zhōngguó**
Chinese language **Hànyǔ**
Chinese language (older term)
    Zhōngguóhuà
Chinese character(s) **Hànzì**
Chinese language (usually written
    form) **Zhōngwén**
choose, select **xuǎn(zé)**
chopsticks **kuàizi** (MW **shuāng**)
church **jiàotáng**
cigarette **(xiāng)yān** (MW **zhī/**
    bāo)

cinema and theatre **yǐngjùyuàn**
city, town **chéngshì**
classical **gǔdiǎn**
clean **gānjìng**
clear, clearly **qīngchu**
clever, intelligent **cōngming**
climate **qìhòu**
close, intimate **qīnmì**
clothes **yīfu** (MW **jiàn**)
cloudy, overcast **yīn**
club (social) **jùlèbù**
coffee **kāfēi**
coffee table **chájī**
cold **lěng**
colleague, fellow worker **tóngshì**
comb, brush **shūzi**
come **lái**
come or go out **chū**
comfortable **shūfu**
common saying, proverb **súhuà**
common spoken language
    (Modern Standard Chinese)
    pǔtōnghuà
compared with **bǐ**
complete(ly) **wánquán**
complicated, complex **fùzá**
computer **diànnǎo**
computer game **diànnǎo yóuxì**
comrade **tóngzhì**
concert **yīnyuèhuì**
consult a dictionary **chá zìdiǎn**
conversely **fǎnguòlái**
cool **liáng**
copy **fèn**
correct **duì**
country **guójiā**
couple **yí duì(r)**
courteous, manners **lǐmào**

credit card **xìnyòngkǎ**
cry, weep **kū**
crowded, squeeze **jǐ**
culture **wénhuà**
cup **bēizi**
cup(ful) **bēi**
current account **huóqī cúnkuǎn
zhànghù**
curtain **chuānglián**

daddy, dad **bàba**
daughter **nǚ'ér**
day after the day after tomorrow
dàhòutiān
day after tomorrow **hòutiān**
day, sky, heaven **tiān**
deal with **duìfu**
debit, switch card **jièjìkǎ**
deceive yourself as well as others
zì qī qī rén
decide **juédìng**
decorate **bùzhì**
defect **máobìng**
definite(ly), affirm **kěndìng**
demand, request **yāoqiú**
deposit account **dìngqī cúnkuǎn
zhànghù**
desk **shūzhuō** (MW **zhāng**)
develop **fāzhǎn**
developed, advanced **fādá**
dial **bō**
dictionary **zìdiǎn** (MW **běn**)
die **sǐ**
different **bù tóng**
difficult **nán**
difficulty; difficult **kùnnan**
dining room **fàntīng**
dirty **zāng**

discover **fāxiàn**
dish, vegetable **cài**
disturb **dǎrǎo**
divide, distinguish **fēn**
do as one pleases **suíbiàn**
do business **yíngyè**
do taijiquan **dǎ tàijíquán**
do the action of the verb
satisfactorily **hǎo**
do, to make **zuò**
doctor **yīshēng**
domestic, internal (post) **guónèi**
don't **bié**
door, gate **mén**
double bed **shuāngrénchuáng**
(MW **zhāng**)
double room **shuāngrénfángjiān**
downstairs **lóuxià**
draw, paint **huà huàr**
draw up, subscribe to, order **dìng**
drink **hē**
drink a toast **gān bēi**
drive (a car etc.) **kāi (chē)**
driver **kāi chē de**
drunk **zuì**
dumpling, kind of ravioli **jiǎozi**
duvet, quilt **bèizi**

each, every **měi**
each and every **gègè**
east (side) **dōng(bianr)**
easy **róngyì**
eat one's fill **chī bǎo**
eat (meal) **chī fàn**
education, to educate **jiàoyù**
egg(s) **jīdàn**
eight **bā**
elder brother **gēge**

elder sister **jiějie**
electric cable **diànxiàn**
electric fan **diànshàn**
electric light **diàndēng**
embarrassed **bù hǎoyìsi**
English language **Yīngyǔ**
English language (usually written)
   Yīngwén
enjoy rights, etc., treat **xiǎngshòu**
enjoy good fortune, happy,
   well-being **xìngfú**
enough **zúgòu**
enter **jìn**
entertaining, enjoyable
   hǎowán(r)
envelope **xìnfēng**
envy, admire **xiànmu**
equipment, facilities **shèbèi**
especially, special **tèbié**
etc. **děng**
Europe **Ōuzhōu**
even (conj) **lián**
even more, still more **gèng**
evening **wǎnshang**
evening meal **wǎnfàn**
everlasting, last forever **wàngǔ**
   chángcún
every, any, all **fánshì**
every day **měitiān/tiāntiān**
everybody **dàjiā**
everywhere **dàochù**
exactly, that's just the way it is
   kěbúshì
excellent (coll) **bàng**
except, apart from **chúle . . .**
   (yǐwài)
exception **liwài**
excuse me **láojià**

exercise (n and v) **liànxí**
expensive **guì**
expert, specialist **zhuānjiā**
explain, speak at length **jiǎng**
explain (sth) to sb **xiàng (X)**
   jiěshì
expresso **nóngsuō kāfēi**
extremely **fēicháng** or **shífēn**
extremely (follows adjective) **-jíle**

face **liǎn**
face flannel **miànjīn**
factory **gōngchǎng**
family, home **jiā**
famous **yǒu míng**
far **yuǎn**
fashionable **shímáo**
fast food **kuàicān**
fat **pàng**
father **fùqīn**
fear, be afraid of **pà**
feel **juéde**
feeling, sense **gǎnjué**
feelings **gǎnqíng**
fellow student **tóngxué**
female **nǚ**
few **shǎo**
fiancé **wèihūnfū**
fiancée **wèihūnqī**
fifteen **shíwǔ**
film **diànyǐng**
find out, understand, know **liǎojiě**
finally, the last **zuìhòu**
fine, clear, bright (of weather)
   qíng
finish work **xià bān**
first (adv) **xiān**
first. . . then. . . **xiān. . . zài. . .**

flash (light) **shǎnguāngdēng**
flavour, taste **wèidao**
floor (first) **èrlóu**
floor (ground) **yìlóu**
flour **miànfěn**
flower(s) **huā**
fluent **liúlì**
food **fàncài**
foot **jiǎo**
for, for the sake of **wèi**
for; give **gěi**
for example **bǐfang shuō** or **bǐrú (shuō)**
for the sake of, in order to **wèile**
Forbidden City (Imperial Palace) **Gùgōng**
foreign country **wàiguó**
foreign currency **wàibì**
foreign devil **yángguǐzi**
foreign flavour **yángwèi(r)**
forever **yǒngyuǎn**
forget **wàng(jì)**
forget it, let it pass **suàn le**
forgive **yuánliàng**
form a company or partnership **héhuǒ**
form of address, to address **chēnghū**
fortunate, lucky **xìngyùn**
four **sì**
France **Fǎguó**
frank(ly) **tǎnshuài (de)**
free (of charge) **miǎnfèi**
free, freedom **zìyóu**
freezer **bīngguì**
French (person) **Fǎguórén**
fresh **xīnxiān**
Friday **xīngqīwǔ**

friend **péngyou**
friendly **yǒuhǎo**
friendship **yǒuyì**
from (movement involved) **cóng**
from (static) **lí**
front, in front of **qiánbian(r)**
fruit **shuǐguǒ**
fruit juice **shuǐguǒzhī**
full, to reach the limit; expire **mǎn**
funny, laughable **hǎoxiào**

gains, results, harvest **shōuhuò**
garden **huāyuán**
generally speaking **yìbān lái shuō**
generally, general **yìbān**
geography **dìlǐ**
Germany **Déguó**
get (interest, sick) **dé**
get, fetch **qǔ**
get-together, party **liánhuānhuì**
get up, rise **qǐ**
give; far **gěi**
give a farewell dinner **jiànxíng**
give/have an injection **dǎ zhēn**
give as a present; see somebody off **sòng**
give back as of change; to look for **zhǎo**
glad, happy **gāoxìng**
glass (tumbler) **bōlibēi**
glove(s) **shǒutào**
go **qù**
go, come out **chū**
go against (e.g. wind) **dǐng**
go by transport **zuò chē**

go shopping **mǎi dōngxi**
go to the toilet **shàng cèsuǒ**
go window shopping **guàng dà jiē**
go/come to, to arrive **dào . . . qù/lái**
good **hǎo**
goodbye **zàijiàn**
Google **Gǔgē**
government **zhèngfǔ**
graduate **bìyè**
grammar **yǔfǎ**
grape **pútáo**
Great Hall of the People **Rénmín Dàhuìtáng**
Great Wall **Chángchéng**
green tea (Chinese) **lǜchá**
grow (as of teeth) **zhǎng chū**
grown up, big **dà**
grudge doing something **shěbude**
guarantee **bǎozhèng**
guess **cāi**

ha ha **hāhā**
had better; best **zuìhǎo**
hair **tóufa**
half **bàn**
hall **tīng**
hand **shǒu**
hand to **jiāo gěi**
hand towel **shǒujīn** (MW **tiáo**)
handle, attend to, do **bàn**
hat **màozi**
happy, joyful, cheerful **kuàilè** or **yúkuài**
have **yǒu**
have a holiday or vacation **fàng jià**

have an injection **dǎ zhēn**
have free time **yǒu kòng**
have fun **wán(r)**
have plenty of **yǒudeshì**
have the capacity to **-xià**
have to, had better **zhǐhǎo**
he **tā**
headphones **ěrjī**
health, body **shēntǐ**
healthy, sound **jiànkāng**
hear of, be told **tīngshuō**
heart's desire **wànshì rúyì**
heaven, paradise **tiāntáng**
heavy **zhòng**
hello (on telephone) **wèi**
help **bāngzhù**
her **tā**
here **zhèr (zhèlǐ)**
him **tā**
hm **ng**
holidays, vacation **jiàqí**
home, family **jiā**
homesick, miss home **xiǎng jiā**
Hong Kong **Xiānggǎng**
hope **xīwàng**
horizontal **héng**
hors d'oeuvres **lěngpán**
horse **mǎ**
hospital **yīyuàn**
hospitality, entertain **zhāodài**
hot **rè**
hotel **lǚguǎn**
hour **xiǎoshí** or **zhōngtóu**
house **fángzi**
how (as in 'how do you know?') **zěnme**
how (as in 'how long?' or 'how lovely') **duō**

how many **duōshao**
how many (less than 10)?;
    several **jǐ**
HSBC **Huìfēng Yínháng**
hundred **(yì)bǎi**
hundred million **yì**
hungry **è**
hurriedly **kuàikuài (de)**
husband, wife **àiren**
husband and wife **fūfù**

I, me **wǒ**
idea **zhǔyì**
if **rúguǒ** or **yàoshi**
if it's not . . ., then it's . . . **bú
    shi . . . jiù shi**
if . . . then **yào(shi) . . . (de huà),
    jiù**
if . . . then **rúguǒ . . . (de huà), jiù**
immediately **mǎshàng**
important **zhòngyào**
in, at **zài**
in person, personally **qīnzì**
in the heart or mind **xīnlǐ**
in the middle of -ing
    zhèngzài . . . ne
in the room **wūlǐ**
include **bāokuò**
indeed, really, true, certain
    quèshí
individual (person) **gèrén**
innate **tiānshēngde**
inside **lǐ**
intend, to plan **dǎsuàn**
interest (e.g. bank) **lìxī**
interested in something **gǎn
    xìngqù**
interesting **yǒu yìsi**

internet café **wǎngbā**
interpret **fānyì**
introduce **jièshào**
invite **qǐng**
invite somebody for a meal
    qǐng kè
iron **yùndǒu**
ironing board **tàngyījià**
it **tā**
Italy **Yìdàlì**
Italian (person) **Yìdàlìrén**
it doesn't matter **méi (yǒu) guānxi**
it's a pity that **kěxī**
it's nothing **méi shénme**

Japan **Rìběn**
Japanese language **Rìwén**
(usually written form)
jasmine tea **huāchá**
be jealous **chī cù**
join, attend **cānjiā**
joint venture **hézī qǐyè**
journey, trip **lǚtú**
just (now) **gāng(cái)**

Kentucky Fried Chicken **Kěndéjī**
key (on piano, keyboard) **jiàn**
kilogram **gōngjīn**
kilometre **gōnglǐ**
kitchen **chúfáng**
knife **dāozi**
knit, weave **zhī**
know (a fact) **zhīdao**
know how to, can **huì**
know, recognize **rènshi**

last, up **shàng**
laugh, smile **xiào**

laughable, ridiculous **kěxiào**
lazy **lǎn**
learn, study **xué(xí)**
leave (place or person) **líkāi**
leave, walk, go **zǒu**
leave (behind or for somebody) **liú**
lend; borrow **jiè**
less, few **shǎo**
let, to allow **ràng**
letter **xìn**
level, standard **shuǐpíng**
life, to live **shēnghuó**
lifestyle **shēnghuó fāngshì**
like (v) **xǐhuan**
like especially **tè ài**
like this, in this way **zhèyàng**
listen **tīng**
listening comprehension **tīnglì**
live in, at **zhù**
living room, lounge **kètīng**
London **Lúndūn**
long **cháng**
long life **chángshòu**
look for **zhǎo**
look, see, watch, read **kàn**
look up information **chá zhǎo**
   xìnxī
lose **diū**
lot of, much **xǔduō**
loudly **dàshēng(de)**
lovable **kě'ài**
luggage, baggage **xínglǐ**
lunar calendar **yīnlì**

magazine **zázhì**
make **zuò**
make (jiaozi); to wrap; to include
   bāo

male **nán**
*manage to do action of verb, -up
   to;* **-dào**
many, more **duō**
Mao Zedong Mausoleum **Máo
   Zhǔxí Jìniàntáng**
map **dìtú**
marry, get married **jié hūn**
matter, thing **shì (qing)** *(MW
   jiàn)*
mattress **chuángdiàn**
meaning **yìsi**
measures (as in adopt) **cuòshī**
McDonald's **Màidāngláo**
meet (by appointment) **jiē**
meet one another **xiānghuì**
menu **càidān**
merely **jiù**
method **bànfǎ**
metre **mǐ**
microwave oven **wēibōlú**
middle, between **zhōngjiān**
milk **niúnǎi**
minute (time) **fēnzhōng**
mirror **jìngzi**
mistake, error **cuòwù**
modern **xiàndài**
modernized **xiàndàihuà**
money **qián**
month **yuè**
*Monument to the People's
   Heroes* **Rénmín Yīngxióng
   Jìniànbēi**
moon **yuèliàng**
more, many **duō**
more and more **yuè lái yuè**
moreover **érqiě**
morning (early) **zǎoshang**

morning **shàngwǔ**
most **zuì**
most (e.g. people) **dàbùfen**
mother tongue **mǔyǔ**
motorbike **mótuōchē** (MW
   liàng)
Mozart **Mòzhātè**
Mr, gentleman **xiānsheng**
Mrs, Madam (formal) **fūrén**
Mrs, wife **tàitai**
Ms, young lady **xiǎojie**
mummy, mum **māma**
Museum of National History
   Zhōngguó Lìshǐ Bówùguǎn
Museum of Revolution **Zhōngguó**
   Gémìng Bówùguǎn
music **yīnyuè**
must, need **děi**
mustard **jièmo**

name (full) **xìngmíng**
name (given) **míngzi**
national **guójiā**
naturally **dāngrán**
near **jìn**
nearby **fùjìn**
need not **bú yòng** or **béng**
need, require, needs (n) **xūyào**
new **xīn**
New Year's Day **Yuándàn**
newspaper **bào(zhǐ)** (MW
   zhāng)
next **xià**
nine **jiǔ**
no matter **bùguǎn**
no sooner . . . than . . ., as soon as
   yī . . . jiù
noodles **miàntiáo**

normal, regular **zhèngcháng**
north **běi**
not **bù**
not (used with **yǒu**) **méi**
not only . . . but also
   búdàn . . . érqiě
not up to much **bù zěnmeyàng**
not . . . any more **bù . . . le**
not . . . but **bú shi . . . ér shi**
not . . . until . . .; only **cái**
novel **xiǎoshuō** (MW **běn**)
now, at present **xiànzài**
number **hào**
number (telephone) **hàomǎ**
numeral, digit **shùzi**
nutritious **yǒu yíngyǎng**

o'clock **diǎn zhōng**
obligatory or required course
   bìxiūkè(chéng)
obvious **míngxiǎn**
occupation, profession **zhíyè**
odd, strange **guài**
of course, naturally **dāngrán**
offer good wishes **zhù**
offices, organization **jīguān**
often **cháng(cháng)**
oh! **ò**
oh dear **āiyā**
old **lǎo** (of people)
old **jiù** (of things)
'old foreigner' **lǎowài**
old person or people **lǎorén**
Olympic Games **Àolínpīkè**
   yùndòng huì
on business **chū chāi**
on the contrary **fǎn'ér**
one **yī**

one (used in speech instead of **yi** in telephone and train numbers) **yāo**
oneself; own **zìjǐ**
only **zhǐ**
open; switch on **kāi**
open (personality) **kāilǎng**
open (up); switch on **dǎkāi**
opinion **yìjiàn**
opposite, i.e. facing **duìmiàn**
opposite, contrary **xiāngfǎn**
opportunity, chance **jīhuì**
or (used in questions) **háishi**
or, perhaps **huò(zhě)**
orange juice **júzizhī**
order (in advance) **dìng**
other **qítā**
otherwise **yàobù(rán)**
ought, should **(yīng)gāi**
outside **wàimiàn**
overcoat **dàyī** (MW **jiàn**)
overseas, abroad **guówài**
Oxford **Niújīn**

pail, bucket **shuǐtǒng**
painting **huàr**
parents **fùmǔ**
park **gōngyuán**
part, section **bùfen**
pass, cross **guò**
passer-by, stranger **lùrén**
passport **hùzhào**
patient, sick person **bìngrén**
pause (v) **zàntíng**
pay **fù**
pay attention to, take note of **zhùyì**
pepper **hújiāo**

per cent **bǎifēn zhī . . .**
person **rén**
personally, in person **qīnzì**
personnel, staff **rényuán**
photograph (n) **zhàopiàn**
pillow **zhěntou**
pillowcase **zhěntào**
pitiable, pitiful **kělián**
place **dìfang**
play (n) **xì**
play ball **dǎ qiú**
play cards or mahjong **dǎ pái**
play (stringed instrument) **lā**
play chess **xià qí**
plenty of **yǒudeshì**
plug **sāizi**
plug (electric) **chātóu**
poem **shī** (MW **shǒu**)
poetry **shīgē**
point at **zhǐ**
point, aspect **diǎn**
police, policeman **jǐngchá**
polite **kèqi**
political **zhèngzhì**
pollution **wūrǎn**
poor (person) **qióng(rén)**
popular, fashionable **liúxíng**
portion; MW for money; minutes **fēn**
post and telecommunications office **yóudiànjú**
post, mail (verb) **jì**
postage **yóufèi**
postcard **míngxìnpiàn**
pound sterling **Yīngbàng**
practise; practice **liànxí**
precisely **jiùshì**
prejudice, bias **piānjiàn**

prepare **zhǔnbèi**
premier **zǒnglǐ**
present, gift **lǐwù**
press (v) **àn**
pretty, beautiful **piàoliang**
president **zǒngtǒng**
pretty good **búcuò**
previously; before (conj) **yǐqián**
price **jiàqián**
principal(ly) **zhǔyào**
printer **dǎyìnjī**
probably **dàgài**
product **chǎnpǐn**
profession, trade **hángyè**
pronunciation **fāyīn**
propose (a toast), toast **jìng**
prove **zhèngmíng**
provided that **zhǐyào**
public **gōnggòng**
pull, to play (of stringed
    instrument) **lā**
put away, receive **shōu(hǎo)**

question, problem **wèntí**
quick, fast **kuài**
quiet **ānjìng**
quite (+ adj) **xiāngdāng**
quite a bit, quite a few **bù shǎo**

RMB (Chinese currency) **rénmínbì**
race (as in racism) **zhǒngzú**
radiator **nuǎnqìpiàn**
radio **shōuyīnjī**
railway station **huǒchēzhàn**
rain (v-o) **xià yǔ**
read **kàn**
read aloud **niàn**
really, true **zhēn**

reason, cause **yuányīn**
recall, call to mind **xiǎng qǐlai**
receipt **shōujù**
receive, accept **shōu**
record (v); recording (tape) **lù yīn**
red **hóng**
refer to **zhǐ**
refrigerator **bīngxiāng**
regard as, count as **suàn**
regret; to regret, be a pity **yíhàn**
regularly, frequently **jīngcháng**
relation(ship) **guānxi**
relatively **bǐjiào**
reliable **kěkào**
remark, word **huà**
remarkable, well known **zhùmíng**
remember **jìde**
remove, move **bān**
rent (n) for house **fángzū**
rent, hire (v) **zū**
resemble **xiàng**
reserve for someone; remain;
    let grow; leave **liú**
rest **xiūxi**
restaurant **fàndiàn** or **fànguǎn**
    or **cāntīng**
retire **tuìxiū**
return **huí**
return to your own country
    huí guó
ride (as of horse, bicycle) **qí**
road **lù**
roast duck **kǎoyā**
romantic **làngmàn**
roof **wūdǐng** or **fángdǐng**
room **fángjiān**
row, line **pái**
run **pǎo**

salt **yán**

same **yíyàng**

sandwich **sānmíngzhì**

satisfy **mǎnzú**

school **xuéxiào**

Scotland **Sūgélán**

script (writing system) **wénzì**

season (of year) **jìjié**

secret (adj; n) **mìmì**

see, meet **jiàn**

see, watch **kàn**

seem **hǎoxiàng**

self-service (food) **zìzhùcān**

sell **mài**

send **sòng**

send by post or mail **yóujì**

sense of humour **yōumògǎn**

serious **yánzhòng**

service, to serve **fúwù**

set (n) **tào**

set one's mind at rest **fàng xīn**

seven **qī**

several **jǐ**

she **tā**

sheet **chuángdān**

shirt, blouse **chènshān**

shoe(s) **xié**

shoe shop **xiédiàn**

shop **shāngdiàn**

shop assistant **shòuhuòyuán**

short (in length) **duǎn**

shout, cry out **hǎn**

shower **línyù**

sick person **bìngrén**

side **pángbianr**

sign, signature **qiān zì**

silk **sīchóu**

single bed **dānrénchuáng**

single room **dānrénfángjiān**

sink **chízi** or **xǐwǎnchí**

sit **zuò**

situation **qíngkuàng**

six **liù**

size, number (street) **hào**

skate (v) **huá bīng**

ski (v) **huá xuě**

sleep, go to bed **shuì (jiào)**

sleeper (in train) hard **yìngwò**

sleeper (in train) soft **ruǎnwò**

slow **màn**

small **xiǎo**

smile, laugh **xiào**

smoke (v-o) **chōu yān** or **xī yān**

snore (v-o) **dǎ hān**

snore (colloq) (v-o) **dǎ hū(lu)**

snow (v-o) **xià xuě**

so, in that case **nàme** or **zhème**

soap **féizào** (MW **kuài**)

soap (toilet) **xiāngzào**

socket **chāzuò**

sofa, settee **shāfā**

some **(yì)xiē**

sometimes **yǒu(de) shíhou**

son **érzi**

soon **zǎorì**

sorry, excuse me **duìbuqǐ**

sort, kind **zhǒng**

sound (v) **tīng qǐlai**

south **nán**

souvenir shop **lǐpǐndiàn**

soya sauce **jiàngyóu**

Spanish language **Xībānyáwén**

spank (v-o) **dǎ pìgu**

speak **shuō**

speak, talk (v-o) **shuō huà**

special(ly) **tèbié**

spend **huā**
spicy or hot (food) **là(de)**
spirit, mind, spiritual **jīngshén**
spoon **sháozi**
sport, exercise **yùndòng**
spring (season) **chūntiān**
stairs, staircase **lóutī**
stamp (postage) **yóupiào**
stand **zhàn**
standard, criterion **biāozhǔn**
Starbucks **Xīngbākè**
start, to open; to drive **kāi**
start work **shàng bān**
stay **dāi**
stick (on) **tiē(shang)**
still, in addition **hái**
stop (v) **tíngzhǐ**
stop (bus etc.) **zhàn**
story **gùshi**
street **jiē**
strange **qíguài**
strenuous, energy consuming
   fèijìn(r)
strong, sturdy **jiēshi**
student **xuésheng**
study (v), learn **dú shū** or **xuéxí**
study (n) **shūfáng**
stupid **bèn**
subconsciousness **xiàyìshí**
subject to; receive **shòu**
sugar, sweets, candy **táng**
suitable **héshì**
suite (settee and two easy chairs)
   shāfā (MW **tào**)
summer **xiàtiān**
suggestion, recommendation
   jiànyì
sunbathe **shài tàiyáng**

Sunday **xīngqītiān** or **xīngqīrì**
sunglasses **tàiyángjìng**
sunrise **rìchū**
sunset **rìluò**
superior(s) **shàngjí**
supper, dinner **wǎncān**
suspect **huáiyí**
swear at, curse **mà**
sweater, woolly **máoyī**
sweet **tián**
sweets, sugar **táng**
swim (v-o) **yóuyǒng**
switch (n) **kāiguān**
Switzerland **Ruìshì**
sympathize with **tóngqíng**

table **zhuōzi** (MW **zhāng**)
table lamp **táidēng**
Taiwan **Táiwān**
take a photo **zhào xiàng**
take a stroll, walk **sàn bù**
take care **dāngxīn** or **xiǎoxīn**
take hold of, receive, to meet **jiē**
take leave of **gàobié**
take off (of aircraft) **qǐfēi**
take out **ná chū**
tall, high **gāo**
tap **lóngtou**
tape recorder **lùyīnjī**
tasty, delicious **hǎo chī**
tea **chá**
tea (Chinese) **lǜchá**
tea (Indian) **hóngchá**
tea (jasmine) **huāchá**
tea (leaves) **cháyè**
teach **jiāo**
teacher **lǎoshī** or **jiàoyuán**
   (more formal)

teacup **chábēi**
technique **jìshù**
telephone (n) **diànhuà(jī)**
telephone (v-o) **dǎ diànhuà**
telephone number **diànhuà**
  hàomǎ
television **diànshì(jī)** (MW **tái**)
tell, let know **gàosu**
temperament **píqi**
Temple of Heaven **Tiāntán**
ten thousand **(yí) wàn**
tennis **wǎngqiú**
text **kèwén** (MW **kè**)
thank, thank you **xièxie**
that **nà** (or **nèi**)
that is, viz. **jí**
the same as . . . **gēn . . . yíyàng**
theatre and cinema
  yǐngjùyuàn
then **jiù**
there **nàr** or **nàlǐ**
there is/there are **yǒu**
therefore **suǒyǐ**
Thermos flask **rèshuǐpíng**
they **tāmen**
thick **hòu**
thing(s) **dōngxi**
think; feel like doing something
  xiǎng
think, consider **rènwéi**
thinking, ideology **sìxiǎng**
this **zhè** (or **zhèi**)
this kind of **zhè yàng**
this locality **běndì**
this year **jīnnián**
those **nà xiē** or **nèi xiē**
thousand **(yì) qiān**
three **sān**

Tiananmen Square **Tiān'ānmén**
  Guǎngchǎng
ticket **piào**
ticket office **shòupiàochù**
ticket price **piàojià**
ticket seller **shòupiàoyuán**
tie **lǐngdài**
time (length of) **shíjiān**
time, occasion **cì**
tin, can **guàntóu**
tired **lèi**
to **dào**
tobacco, cigarette **yān**
today **jīntiān**
together **yìqǐ**
toilet **cèsuǒ**
toilet paper **wèishēngzhǐ**
toilet soap **xiāngzào**
tomorrow **míngtiān**
tone **shēngdiào**
too, extremely **tài**
tooth **yáchǐ**
toothbrush **yáshuā** (MW **bǎ**)
toothpaste **yágāo**
  (MW **tǒng**)
topic **huàtí**
tourism; to tour **lǚyóu**
tourist, sightseer **yóukè**
tourist map **dǎoyóutú**
towards, to, in the direction of
  wàng
towel **máojīn** (MW **tiáo**)
towel rail **máojīnjià**
town, city **chéngshì**
train **huǒchē**
transfer (money) **zhuǎn**
translate **fānyì**
travel **lǚxíng**

travel agency **lǚxíngshè**
tree **shù** (MW **kē**)
trouble, troublesome **máfan**
turn, transfer **zhuǎn**
two **liǎ**
two (number) **èr**
two (of a kind) **liǎng**
type (v-o) **dǎ zì**
type, kind **yàng**

US dollar **Měiyuán**
ugly **nánkàn**
uh-huh **m̀**
unbearable **shòu bù liǎo**
under(neath), below
   xiàbianr
understand **dǒng**
understand, clear **míngbai**
undertaking, cause **shìyè**
up, last **shàng**
upstairs **lóushàng**
us **wǒmen**
use **yòng**
useful **yǒu yòng**
usually, ordinary **píngcháng**

vase **huāpíng**
vegetables **shūcài**
Venice **Wēinísī**
vertical **shù**
very **hěn**
very many **duō dehěn**
very, rather **tǐng**
video recorder **lùxiàngjī**
vinegar; jealousy (as in love
   affairs) **cù**
visit (places etc.) **cānguān**
visiting card **míngpiàn**

wages **gōngzī**
wait **děng**
walk **zǒu**
wallet, purse **qiánbāo**
want to, must **yào**
wardrobe **yīguì**
warm **nuǎnhuo**
warm hearted, enthusiastic
   rèqíng
wash face **xǐ liǎn**
wash hands **xǐ shǒu**
washbasin **xǐliǎnpén**
washing machine **xǐyījī**
washroom **xǐshǒujiān**
watch, see **kàn**
water **shuǐ**
water and electricity charges
   shuǐdiànfèi
way of saying something **shuōfǎ**
way of doing something **zuòfǎ**
we **wǒmen**
we (including listener) **zánmen**
we'll meet again some day
   hòuhuì yǒu qī
wear (clothes) **chuān**
wear (hat, gloves, glasses, etc.)
   dài
weather **tiānqì**
week **xīngqī**
weekend **zhōumò**
weep, cry **kū**
welcome **huānyíng**
well-being, happy **xìngfú**
well known, famous **wénmíng**
well matched, well suited
   pèishàng
west, the west **Xīfāng**
West Lake **Xīhú**

west (side) **xī(bianr)**
western food **Xīcān**
westerner **Xīfāngrén**
what/what? **shénme**
what about (it)?; how?
  zěnmeyàng
what one sees and hears **jiànwén**
what's the matter? **zěnme le**
what's to be done? **zěnme bàn**
when **de shíhou**
when? **shénme shíhou**
where? **nǎr**
which? **nǎ** (or **něi**)
white **bái**
who? **shéi** (or **shuí**)
whole, entire **zhěnggè**
whole day **zhěngtiān**
why? **wèi shénme**
will (showing possibility) **huì**
willing **yuànyì**
wind **fēng**
window **chuānghu**
window (for tickets etc.)
  chuāngkǒu
wine **pútáojiǔ**
wine bottle **jiǔpíng**
winter **dōngtiān**
with, and **gēn**

withdraw money **qǔ qián**
woman **fùnǚ**
work out bill, make bill **suàn zhàng**
work, to work **gōngzuò**
worker **gōngrén**
world **shìjiè**
worried, anxious **zháojí**
worry about **cāo xīn**
worth, deserve **zhíde**
write (characters) **xiě (zì)**

year **nián**
year (of age) **suì**
year after next **hòunián**
yen **Rìyuán**
yesterday **zuótiān**
you **nǐ**
you (pl) **nǐmen**
you (polite form) **nín**
you flatter me **guòjiǎng**
young **niánqīng**
young fellow **xiǎohuǒzi**
young person **niánqīngrén**
younger brother **dìdi**
younger sister **mèimei**

zero **líng**

Character texts

1 *Making friends (I)*
第一课　交朋友（1）

李　王先生，你好!
王　李先生，你好!
李　请坐。
王　谢谢。
李　请喝咖啡。
王　谢谢，我不喝咖啡。
李　那么，中国茶行不行?
王　行，谢谢你! 我很喜欢喝中国茶。

2 *Making friends (II)*
第二课　交朋友（2）

李　　　王先生，这是我太太，周德津。
王　　　李太太，您好!
李太太　王先生，您好! 认识您，我真高兴。
王　　　请坐，请坐。喝一杯酒吧。
李　　　谢谢，我喝一杯。
王　　　李太太呢?
李太太　谢谢，我不会喝酒。
王　　　那么，桔子汁好吗?
李太太　好，谢谢您。

3 *Making friends (III)*
第三课　交朋友（3）

王　李先生，你们有小孩儿吗?
李　有，我们有两个，一个男孩儿，一个女孩儿。
王　男孩儿几岁? 女孩儿几岁?
李　男孩儿十四岁，女孩儿九岁。

李太太	王先生结婚了吗？
王	没有。
李太太	有女朋友吗？
王	有。
李太太	她在哪儿？她也在中国吗？
王	她明天来中国学习。

4 Two days later
第四课 两天以后

李太太	王先生，你好。我想请你们去我们家玩儿好吗？
王	那太好了！
李太太	你们明天晚上有空吗？
王	有空。
李太太	那么，请你们俩明天晚上去我们家吃饭吧。
王	那太谢谢你们了。几点钟去呢？
李太太	六点怎么样？
王	行，就六点吧。

5 At the Lis' (I)
第五课 在李先生家（1）

王	我给你们介绍一下，这位是我的女朋友，史爱理。 这位是李先生，这位是李太太。
李太太	史小姐，您好！
史	李先生、李太太，你们好！
李	请随便坐吧。
李太太	史小姐，您也是从英国来的吗？
史	是，我也是从英国来的，但是在美国出生长大的。
李	你爸爸以前在美国工作吗？
史	对，我爸爸以前在美国工作。 我妈妈是美国人。
李太太	史小姐，您来这儿学习什么？
史	我来这儿学习汉语。
李	您在哪个学校学习汉语？
史	我在北京大学学习汉语。

李	学校里生活怎么样?
史	很不错。
李太太	你们一定很饿了。我们吃饭吧。

6 At the Lis' (II)
第六课 在李先生家（2）

李太太	今天晚上吃中国菜行吗?
王	好极了!
李	别客气，自己来吧。你们会用筷子吗?
王	会用，但是用得不好。
李	没关系......嗯，你们都用得不错啊!
李太太	我做菜做得不好。请原谅。
史	您菜做得真好。
李太太	史小姐会做菜吗?
史	会一点儿，但是技术不高。
王	她英国菜做得非常好。
李	中国菜做得怎么样?
史	我中国菜做得不怎么样。
李太太	你们最好少说话，多吃饭吧，要不然菜都凉了!

8 At the Lis' (III)
第八课 在李先生家（3）

李	别客气，再多吃一点儿。
王	吃饱了，菜都很好吃。
李太太	你们想喝咖啡还是喝茶?
王	我随便。
史	喝茶吧。
	(喝完了茶)
李太太	史小姐，看一看我们的小房子吧?
史	好，谢谢您。永寿，你陪李先生谈话吧。
李太太	这是厨房，地方很小，所以冰箱、洗衣机也都不大。我们只有四个房间，我和老李一间，儿子一间，女儿一间。还有客厅。

史	孩子们有自己的房间不错，读书很安静。
	你们的客厅布置得很漂亮。平面电视也很好看。
	是数码的吗?
李太太	对，是数码的。数码的比较清楚。
史	啊，时间不早了，我们(应)该回去了。
王	时间过得真快。李先生、李太太，我们得走了，
	谢谢你们的热情招待。我们玩儿得非常高兴，
	给你们添了不少麻烦。
李	没什么，欢迎你们再来玩儿。
王/史	一定来，谢谢你们。再见。
李	慢走，慢走。

9 Eating out
第九课 在饭馆

一对中国夫妇，张大明和陈英，都是独生子女。他们坐在
一家著名的北京烤鸭店等着他们请来吃饭的两个外国人，
王永寿和他的女朋友史爱理。今天晚上，张大明的父母在家
看着他们的孙子和孙女。这时，王先生和史小姐走进饭店
找他们来。

王	你们已经来了。我以前没吃过烤鸭，我早就想吃了。
史	我也一样。
张	北京有不少烤鸭店，每个都有他们的特色。这家
	有点儿贵，可是，每个人都说这儿的烤鸭最好吃。
陈	是啊。我来这家(烤鸭)店以前，常去在王府井的那家，
	现在我总来这家。
张	我父母也都喜欢来这家吃烤鸭。他们退休以后，
	决定要好好享受享受生活。
陈	这是不是也包括给我们看孩子?
史	你们的孩子多大了? 王永寿说你们有两个孩子。
张	是啊。(我们的)儿子比他妹妹大两岁半，可是女儿
	比她哥哥高多了。我们也不知道这是怎么一回事。
	他们都很聪明，可是我觉得女儿比儿子更聪明。

史 希望(有一天)能见见他们。(烤鸭来了。)哇，
我最喜欢吃有中国特色的饭菜，像烤鸭、水饺和包子
等等，非常好吃，也比麦当劳、肯德基便宜多了，
为什么要吃那种快餐呢？

陈 人们觉得吃麦当劳、肯德基那种快餐时髦，可是那些
快餐又贵又没有什么营养。

王 嗯，这烤鸭真好吃。谢谢你们请我们来这儿吃饭。以后
我们请你们吃有英国特色的饭菜。

史 希望你们会喜欢。

10 *Teething troubles*
第十课　牙的问题

**张大明和陈英跟王永寿和他的女朋友吃完饭回到家。张的父
母松了一口气，笑着迎上去。**

张母 哎呀，你们快过来吧。真糟糕，珍珍睡不了觉。
我给了她一个苹果，不知道怎么(一)回事，她的一颗
牙掉了，她一直在哭，我想现在她还没有停呢。她说
牙齿掉了她会很难看。

陈 别着急。珍珍的牙只是乳牙，她会长出新牙的。
她在哪儿？

张父 她在她的房间里。我们跟她说她可以玩儿电脑
游戏，就不会老想着牙的事儿了。

张 好主意。我去跟她谈谈，向她解释一下牙的事情。

陈 儿子呢？他睡了吗？

张母 早就睡着了。他今天跟小朋友们骑自行车到处
玩儿，所以回来的时候又累又饿。他说他明天还要
骑。他很喜欢他的新车。

陈 那太好了。那辆自行车有一点儿贵，但是又结实
又好看。
(过了一会儿，张大明走进客厅来。)

张母 珍珍怎么样了？

张 她睡着了。我给她讲了一个很长的故事，还没讲完
她就睡着了。

陈	明天(是)星期天，他们不用早起。(对张母)睡觉前他们洗手、洗脸、刷牙了吗？
张母	这些当然都做了。你觉得……
张	(快快地) 他们晚饭吃的是什么？
张母	哦，我们去吃了麦当劳。你们知道他们多喜欢吃麦当劳。
陈	(大声地)可是快餐没有营养，还会让他们长胖！
张父	噢，陈英，你真(让人)扫兴。让孩子们快乐快乐有什么不好？！

11 *Weather, dates and seasons*
第十一课 气候、日期和四季

王永寿谈了他对北京的气候的看法，他还谈了首都的娱乐消遣生活的情况。

今年北京的天气很不正常。冬天不冷，夏天也不热。应该下雪的时候并没有下，应该下雨的时候也没有下，真奇怪！是不是整个世界的气候正在变呢？

气候变化越来越明显。欧洲平常没有北京那么冷，但是今年反而有的时候比北京还冷。春天、秋天是北京最好的季节，可惜太短了。

要是在中国旅行的话，五月和九月天气最好，晴天多，阴天少。天气一好，公园里的人就很多。老人下棋的下棋，打牌的打牌，聊天儿的聊天儿，早上打太极拳的有的是。

虽然十年以前大部分人骑自行车上班，现在人们或者坐公共汽车或者开车，所以在大城市自行车越来越少。另一方面，汽车越来越多，污染也越来越严重。在开奥林匹克运动会的时候，政府采取了许多措施对付污染问题。

中国人一般一个星期工作五天，像大部分欧洲国家星期六、星期天也休息。周末一般机关的工作人员不上班，学校的老师和学生不上课。可是，银行、邮局、商店和其他服务行业一个星期七天都营业。

星期天，天气特别好的时候，大家都出去玩儿。公园里散步的散步，照相的照相。很多人喜欢逛大街，所以商店里总是很挤，整个北京热闹极了。

除了这些活动以外，网吧里总是有很多人，差不多都是年轻人。他们大部分人在玩儿电脑游戏，用谷歌跟百度查找信息，用Skype跟朋友们聊天儿，都跟欧洲国家一样。Skype很流行，因为用Skype通话是免费的。

跟这些现代化的生活方式相对的是做礼拜的人也越来越多。是不是因为现代化生活方式和思想没有满足一些中国人的精神要求呢？你说呢？

12 *In the restaurant*
第十二课 在饭馆里

一天，王先生和史小姐在吃午饭，他们遇到了一位很友好的服务员(刘洪刚)。

刘 你们菜订好了没有？

史 订好了，谢谢你。啤酒来了。啊！不是北京啤酒而是青岛啤酒。

刘 没关系，青岛啤酒更好喝。您普通话说得真好。

史 过奖，过奖，说得不好。

刘 说得很好。您是哪国人？

史 你猜猜吧。

刘 不是美国人就是英国人。

史 我是英国人，但是我妈妈是美国人。你怎么知道呢？

刘 因为刚才您是跟您朋友说英语！您朋友也会说汉语吗？

史 也会说。

王 说得没她好。

刘 啊！你们俩的汉语真棒，学了几年了？

史 学了两年了。

刘 您呢？(指的是王永寿)

王 学了四年了。

刘 你们在中国待了很长时间了吧？

王　不长，来了三个多月了。

刘　这是你们第一次来中国吗？

王　不，她是第一次，我是第二次。

刘　你们真行，发音很清楚，没什么洋味儿，很标准的
　　普通话。中文不是很难学吗？

王　难是难，可是也有它容易的地方，比方说中文发音、
　　语法都并不难，难的是声调。对我们西方人来说，
　　中文的四声还是相当困难的。

刘　写汉字呢？

史　写汉字很不容易，因为我们外国人一般是成年人才开始
　　学中文，不像你们六、七岁就开始了。当然还有一点，
　　中文就是你们的母语。

刘　那倒是。像你们这样的水平，报纸看得懂吗？

史　看得懂。

刘　小说呢？

史　也行，但是不认识的字还要查字典。啊！菜来了，
　　真漂亮啊！看起来一定很好吃。

刘　那么，你们慢慢儿吃吧，不再打扰你们了。有什么事，
　　随时可以叫我。

王　好的，谢谢你，有什么事一定找你。跟你聊天儿
　　很有意思。

Index

The first number in each entry refers to the unit, the second to the section within the grammar of the unit.